The Postal Service Guide to U.S. Stamps

W9-DJC-870

United States Postal Service
Washington, D.C. 20260-2435
Item No. 8895

Library of Congress catalog Card Number 87-656545
ISBN: 1-877707-05-8

Printed in the United States of America

Table of Contents

Now Showing: Reel History

Stamp collecting

Lights, camera, action: it's time for the great stamp collecting show! Real history and "reel" history come to life in the world of stamp collecting. With a stamp collection of both old and new stamps, you'll meet hundreds of influential people, such as movie star Marilyn Monroe, Native American heroine Pocahontas and jazz legend Louis Armstrong. You'll also visit some of this world's most exciting "sets," such as the awesome Alaska Highway, planets far and near, and the very lands once roamed by prehistoric animals.

Best of all, stamp collecting is a very affordable hobby. And unlike the movies, your stamp collection never needs to come to an end. Read on to see how to start your own stamp collection.

What is philately?

The word philately (fi-latt´-eh-lee) means the study and collecting of stamps and other postal materials. Stamp collectors are called philatelists.

How do I start collecting stamps? It's easy. You can start by simply saving stamps from letters, packages and postcards. Ask your friends and family to save stamps from their mail. Neighborhood businesses that get a lot of mail—banks, stores, travel agencies—might save their envelopes for you, too.

Or, start your collection by choosing one or two favorite subjects. Then, collect only stamps that fit your theme—art, history, sports, transportation, science—whatever you choose! This is called topical collecting. See the boxes on pages 7 and 12 and the stamps pictured in this article for ideas to get you started on a movie theme.

Definitive

Commemorative

Special

Airmail

Booklet

Coil

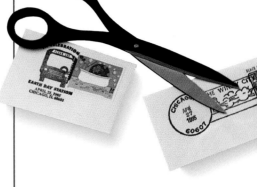

to start a collection?
No! Start with used stamps and a few inexpensive accessories (such as a small album and a package of hinges), and you can have a great time on a limited budget. Remember to put stamps, albums and hinges on your birthday and holiday wish lists, too!

What kinds of stamps are there?
-Definitive
-Commemorative
-Special
-Airmail
-Booklet format
-Coil format

Definitive stamps are found on most mail. They feature former presidents, statesmen, prominent persons and national shrines. Their denominations range from 1 cent to 14 dollars. Definitives are usually available for several years, since large quantities for specific postal rates.

Commemorative stamps are usually larger and more colorful than definitives. They honor important people, events or subjects. Only a limited number of each commemorative is printed, and most post offices only have them for a few months. The U.S. Postal Service's Philatelic Fulfillment Service Center also offers commemorative stamps by mail order for about one year after they are issued.

Special stamps supplement each year's regular stamp issues. They include the Christmas and Love stamps.

Airmail stamps are mainly used for sending mail overseas.

Booklet stamps come in small folders that contain panes of 3 to 20 stamps each.

Each booklet stamp has at least one straight edge.

Coil stamps are issued in rolls. Each coil stamp has two straight edges and two edges with either slit-like cuts or little holes, called perforations.

How do I remove stamps from envelopes?

If you wish, you can save whole envelopes with stamps on them and store them anywhere—from shoe boxes to special albums. But if you want to remove stamps from envelopes, it pays to be careful. The best way to remove stamps from envelopes is to soak them. Here's how:

1. Tear or cut off the upper right-hand corner of the envelope.

2. Place it, stamp side down, in a small pan of warm water. After a few minutes, the stamp will sink to the bottom.

3. Wait a few more minutes for any remaining gum to dislodge from the stamp.

4. Lift the stamp out with tongs (a metal tool, like tweezers)

if you have a pair. It's better to handle stamps with tongs because oil from your skin can damage stamps.

5. Place the stamp between two paper towels and put a heavy object, such as a book, on top. This will keep the stamp from curling as it dries. Leave the stamp there overnight.

6. If the stamp is a newer one with "invisible" gum, dry it face down with nothing touching the back, and flatten it later if necessary. Otherwise, it may stick to the paper towel when drying.

How should I organize my stamps?

However you want to, of course—it's your collection. But be sure to protect them so they don't get damaged or lost. You can attach your stamps to loose-leaf paper and put them in a three-ring binder.

Making Movies, Making Music

Many notable musicians who appear on stamps also had connections to the movies they played in, acted in or composed for the big screen; among them are George Gershwin, Duke Ellington, George M. Cohan, Cole Porter, Elvis Presley, Hank Williams, Bill Haley, and the list goes on. Keep your eyes open as you read The Postal Service Guide to U.S. Stamps to recognize the musicians you've seen or heard in the movies.

How do I collect First Day Covers?

The fastest way to get a First Day Cover is to buy the stamp yourself (it will usually go on sale the day after the first day of issue), attach it to your own envelope (or cover), and send it to the first day post office for cancellation. You can submit up to 50 envelopes, up to 30 days after the stamp's issue date. Here's how:

1. Write your address in the lower right-hand corner of each first day envelope, at least 5/8" from the bottom. Leave plenty of room for the stamp(s) and cancellation. Use a peel-off label if you prefer.

2. Insert a piece of cardboard (about as thick as a postcard) into each envelope. You can tuck the flap in or seal the envelope.

3. Affix your stamp(s) to your first day envelope(s).

4. Put your first day envelope(s) inside another, larger envelope and mail it to "Customer-Affixed Envelopes" in care of the postmaster of the first day city.
Your envelopes will be canceled and returned.

Or, you can purchase a plain envelope with the stamp(s) already affixed and canceled. These are now sold directly by mail order through the U.S. Postal Service.

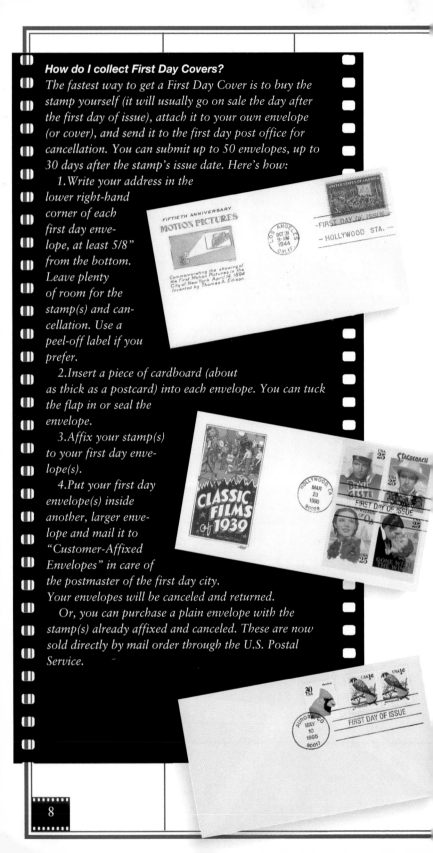

Or, arrange them in a more formal album, which you can buy in stores.

What kinds of stamp albums can I buy?

Some stamp albums feature specific categories with pictures of the stamps that should appear on each page. You may want to select one with loose-leaf pages so you can add pages as your collection grows. A stock book is an album with plastic or paper pockets on each page. There are no pictures of stamps, so you can organize the album your way.

How do I put a stamp in the album?

It's best to use a hinge—a small strip of thin plastic with gum on one side. Unlike tape or glue, hinges let you peel the stamp off the page without damaging it. Hinges come either folded or unfolded. Here's how to use a folded hinge:

1. Moisten the short end of the hinge lightly. Press it to the back of the stamp, placing the fold about 1/8 inch from the top of the stamp.

2. Place the stamp in the album and press down to secure it.

3. Using your tongs, gently lift the corners of the stamp to make sure it's not stuck to the page.

Instead of a hinge, you can insert the entire stamp into a mount—a small, clear plastic sleeve. Mounts are more expensive than hinges, but they protect stamps from air, dirt and moisture.

Is there anything else I need?

Here's a list of other equipment you may find helpful:

Glassine envelopes are made of a special thin, see-through paper that protects stamps from grease and air. You can use them to keep stamps until you put them in your album.

A **stamp catalog** is a reference book with illustrations to help you identify stamps. It also lists the values of used and unused stamps.

A **magnifying glass** helps you examine stamps by making them appear larger.

A **perforation gauge** measures perforations along the edges of stamps. Sometimes the size and number of perforations (perfs) are needed to identify stamps.

A **watermark tray** and **watermark fluid** help make watermarks on stamps more visible. A watermark is a design or pattern that is pressed into some stamp paper during manufacturing.

How can I tell what a stamp is worth?

Ask yourself two questions: "How rare is it?" and "What condition is it in?" The price listed in a stamp catalog gives you some idea of how rare it is. However, the stamp may sell at more or less than the catalog price, depending on its condition.

Always try to find stamps in the best possible condition.

Superb

Light Cancel–Very Fine

Very Fine

Medium Cancel–Fine

Fine

Heavy Cancel

Good

How should I judge the condition of a stamp?

Stamp dealers put stamps into categories according to their condition. Look at the pictured examples to see the differences among categories. A stamp in mint condition is the same as when purchased from the post office. An unused stamp has no cancel but may not have any gum on the back. Mint stamps are usually worth more than unused stamps.

You can begin to judge the condition of a stamp by examining the front of it. Are the colors bright or faded? Is the stamp clean, dirty or stained? Is the stamp torn? Torn stamps are not considered "collectible." Is the stamp design centered on the paper, crooked, or off to one side? Are all the perforations intact? Has the stamp been canceled? A stamp with a light cancellation is in better condition than one with heavy marks across it.

Now look at the back of the stamp. Is there a thin spot in the paper? If so, it may have been caused by careless removal from an envelope or hinge.

The values listed in this book are for used and unused stamps in Fine-Very Fine condition that have been hinged.

Where else can I find stamps?
Check the classified ads in philatelic newspapers and magazines at your local library. Also, there is a listing of philatelic publishers on page 51 of this book. These publishers will send you one free copy of their publications. Then you can decide if you'd like to subscribe.

What other stamp materials can I collect?
Postal stationery products are popular among some collectors. These have the stamp designs printed or embossed (printed with a raised design) directly on them.

Stamped Envelopes were first issued in 1853. More

Armstrong: Playing at the Movies

(Daniel) Louis "Satchmo" Armstrong (1901-71) is one of the most influential figures in the history of jazz music. A trumpet virtuoso, Armstrong was an improvisational genius who strongly affected the development of jazz melody, and is largely responsible for the rise of the jazz soloist.

Trumpeter, singer, arranger, bandleader– Armstrong was all of these and more – including, would you believe, movie performer. After leaving his native New Orleans for a budding career in Chicago, his brand of foot-tapping swing caught the ears of America, and Hollywood was listening. Most of his appearances were "cameos," but they did carry a message. This was a time when African-Americans in movies were usually relegated to menial roles, but Armstrong's spirited-yet-dignified presence as a world-renowned African-American artist presented a positive role model in a strictly segregated industry. Armstrong's appearances on the silver screen include New Orleans *(1947),* High Society *(1956) and* Hello Dolly *(1969).*

The Louis Armstrong stamp is part of a 10-stamp 1995 commemorative set saluting many respected jazz musicians, including saxophonists Coleman Hawkins, Charlie Parker and John Coltrane, bassist Charles Mingus; and pianists Eubie Blake, Thelonious Monk, Jelly Roll Morton, James P. Johnson and Errol Garner.

11

Let's Go to the Movies!

The Marilyn Monroe stamp is the latest in a series of stamps saluting movie industry figures both behind and in front of the camera. There are many other film-related stamps featured throughout The Postal Service Guide including producers, composers, screenwriters and actors. Be sure to check out these "silver-screen" editions:

Motion Pictures	926
Walt Disney	1355
George Gershwin	1484
D.W. Griffith	1555
Talking Pictures	1727
Will Rogers	975, 1801
W.C. Fields	1803
The Barrymores	2012
Douglas Fairbanks	2088
William Faulkner	2350
Classic Films (4)	2445-2448

    Wizard of Oz (*Judy Garland*)
    Gone with the Wind (*Clark Gable*)
    Beau Geste (*Gary Cooper*)
    Stagecoach (*John Wayne*)

Cole Porter	2550
Comedians	2562-2565

    Laurel & Hardy
    Bergen & McCarthy
    Jack Benny
    Fanny Brice
    Abbot & Costello

Dorothy Parker	2698
Elvis Presley	2721, 2724, 2731
Oklahoma!	2722, 2769
My Fair Lady	2770
Silent Screen	2819-2828
Al Jolson	2849
Bing Crosby	2850
Ethel Merman	2853

than 600 million of them are now printed each year.

Postal Cards were first issued in 1873. The first U.S. multicolored commemorative postal cards came out in 1956. Several different postal cards are issued each year.

Aerogrammes (air letters) are designed to be letters and envelopes all in one. They are specially stamped, marked for folding and already gummed.

Other philatelic collectibles include:

Plate Blocks usually consist of four stamps from the corner of a pane, with the printing plate number in the margin (or selvage) of the pane.

Copyright Blocks feature the copyright symbol © followed by "United States Postal Service" or "USPS" in the margin of the pane. The USPS began copyrighting new stamp designs in 1978.

Booklet Panes are panes of three or more of the same stamp issue. Panes are affixed inside a thin folder to form a booklet. Usually, collectors of booklet panes save the entire pane.

First Day Covers are envelopes bearing new stamps that are postmarked on the first day of sale. For each new postal issue, the USPS selects one location, usually related to the stamp subject, as the place for the first day dedication ceremony and the first day postmark. There is even an annual First Day Cover Collecting Week. See the article on page 8 for information on how to collect these covers.

Souvenir Programs are given to persons who attend first day ceremonies. They contain a list of participants, information on the stamp subject and the actual stamp attached and postmarked.

Are there any stamp groups I can join?
Yes! Stamp clubs can be a great source for new stamps and for stamp collecting advice. These clubs often meet at schools, YMCAs and community centers. Write to:

LINN'S CLUB CENTER
P.O. BOX 29
SIDNEY, OH
        45365-0029

for the locations of clubs near you.

13

REMEMBERING A LEGEND

Marilyn comes alive in 1995 stamp release

Combining breathtaking beauty with an enchanting naiveté, Marilyn Monroe's unique screen persona captivated movie audiences worldwide and made her one of the top box-office draws of the 1950s.

Sixty-nine years after her birth, the United States Postal Service salutes Marilyn Monroe's potent brew of innocence and allure.

She continues to maintain an almost magical hold on moviegoers' imaginations, fueling her status as a major icon in American popular culture.

Born Norma Jeane Mortenson in Los Angeles on June 1, 1926, she grew up in a series of orphanages and foster homes. She married at age 16, but the marriage soon failed. A chance photograph taken of her while she worked at an aircraft factory became an extremely popular "pin-up" poster for American soldiers who fought during World War II. The photograph led to modeling work, which she then parlayed into a movie career.

Signed to a $125-per-week contract by 20th Century Fox in 1946, and given the screen name Marilyn Monroe, her early roles were small parts in largely forgettable movies. But her dazzling and glamorous screen presence was undeniable. In 1950, Marilyn broke into

the public eye with noteworthy supporting roles in *The Asphalt Jungle* and *All About Eve*. Her leading role as a scheming murderess in *Niagara* (1953), made her a star.

But it was with two movies released in 1953–the classic musical *Gentlemen Prefer Blondes* and *How to Marry a Millionaire*–that Marilyn's unique appeal and her natural comedic gifts reached maturity, transforming her into a worldwide sensation. Her sultry performance in *The Seven-Year Itch* (1955) further cemented her reputation as the era's leading sex

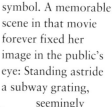

symbol. A memorable scene in that movie forever fixed her image in the public's eye: Standing astride a subway grating, seemingly oblivious to passersby, she luxuriates in

Marilyn Monroe, Producer

Considered the last of the great movie studio queens, Marilyn Monroe's career between 1947 through 1961 spans an important period in Hollywood history. Faced by competition from the new-fangled invention called "television" and hobbled by anti-trust lawsuits, the all-powerful movie studios (including 20th Century Fox, Warner Brothers, MGM and RKO) began to give way to a new power structure in which independent movie stars and talented directors drove the creative process. Marilyn, in fact, was one of the first modern stars to use her massive popularity to form a production company to produce her own movie, The Prince and the Showgirl (1957), which also starred British actor Laurence Olivier.

the cool breeze from below, as her skirt revealingly billows upwards.

Marilyn's acting abilities ranged beyond light comedy. Her dramatic performance as the troubled nightclub singer Cherie in *Bus Stop* (1956), based on the Pulitzer Prize-winning play by William Inge, is considered to be her best performance. Critics also acclaimed her brilliant parody of her own "sex symbol" image in the classic comedy *Some Like It Hot* (1959).

Off-screen, Marilyn was an intelligent, complex woman. Practical and unassuming, she often dressed plainly and preferred reading at home to the glamorous Hollywood nightlife. Although stereotyped for much of her career as the beautiful "dumb blonde," Marilyn was an accomplished actress who studied at the Actor's Lab in Los Angeles and with Lee Strasberg at the fabled Actor's Studio in New York—the source of such talents as Marlon Brando and Paul

A Marilyn Monroe Filmography

As were many film stars of the day, Marilyn was under studio contract and usually had little choice in the roles she played. (Exceptions include The Prince and the Showgirl, *which Marilyn produced, and* The Misfits, *which was written for her by husband Arthur Miller.) Many of the movies she appeared in can best be described as "forgettable"–although Marilyn herself tended to dazzle, whatever the role. Among the 29 films in which Marilyn appeared, there were undeniable classics, including* The Asphalt Jungle, All About Eve, Gentlemen Prefer Blondes, Bus Stop *and* Some Like It Hot.

Scudda-Hoo! Scudda-Hay!	*(1948)**
Dangerous Years	*(1947)*
Ladies of the Chorus	*(1948)*
Love Happy	*(1950)*
A Ticket to Tomahawk	*(1950)*
The Asphalt Jungle	*(1950)*
All About Eve	*(1950)*
The Fireball	*(1950)*
Right Cross	*(1950)*
Home Town Story	*(1951)*
As Young as You Feel	*(1951)*
Love Nest	*(1951)*
Let's Make It Legal	*(1951)*
Clash by Night	*(1952)*
We're Not Married	*(1952)*
Don't Bother to Knock	*(1952)*
Monkey Business	*(1952)*
O. Henry's Full House	*(1952)*
Niagara	*(1953)*
Gentlemen Prefer Blondes	*(1953)*
How to Marry a Millionaire	*(1953)*
River of No Return	*(1954)*
There's No Business Like Show Business	*(1954)*
The Seven-Year Itch	*(1955)*
Bus Stop	*(1956)*
The Prince and the Showgirl	*(1957)*
Some Like It Hot	*(1959)*
Let's Make Love	*(1960)*
The Misfits	*(1961)*
Something's Got to Give	*(unfinished)*

*Filmed first, but released after Dangerous Years

Newman. Dissatisfied with "formula" roles, she constantly fought studio bosses for parts that could expand her acting range.

Though her professional career bloomed, her personal life was troubled. She married and divorced three times. Her second marriage, to baseball star Joe DiMaggio, ended in 1954. In 1956 she married playwright Arthur Miller. He wrote the screenplay for what would be her final film, the highly regarded *The Misfits*

(1961), which also starred Clark Gable.

By this time, mounting personal and career problems were taking their toll. Divorced from Miller, suffering ill health and frustrated by what she saw as her failure to

be accepted as a serious actress, Marilyn was found dead from an overdose of sleeping pills in her Brentwood, California home on August 5, 1962. She was 36 years old.

1995 Issues—New U.S. Postage Stamps

Sheet version   Self-adhesive

Love (Cherubs)
Date of Issue: February 1, 1995
Place of Issue: Valentines, VA

Florida Statehood
Date of Issue: March 3, 1995
Place of Issue: Tallahassee, FL

Butte
Date of Issue: March 10, 1995
Place of Issue: State College, PA

Automobile
Date of Issue: March 10, 1995
Place of Issue: State College, PA

Flag Over Field
Date of Issue: March 17, 1995
Place of Issue: New York, NY

Bureau Printing   Private Printing

Bureau Printing   Private Printing

Juke Box
Date of Issue: March 17, 1995
Place of Issue: New York, NY

Auto Tail Fin
Date of Issue: March 17, 1995
Place of Issue: New York, NY

Love (Cherubs) (#2948 sheet, #2949 self-adhesive)

The popular series of Love stamps continues with this design, released in both sheet version with conventional adhesive and in self-adhesive booklet form (booklet contains 20 stamps). The stamps were issued without denomination immediately following a rate change; the "face value" is 32¢ (see denominated versions under May 12).

Designer: Terry McCaffrey

Printing: Offset/intaglio

Florida Statehood (#2950)

The Postal Service commemorates the 150th anniversary of Florida's admission to the union with this colorful stamp. The "Gator," Florida's most commonly used statewide symbol, represents the state's history, strength, adaptability, ecological system and ability to survive.

Designer: Laura Smith

Printing: Offset

Butte (#2902)

This coil stamp was issued without denomination for use by nonprofit mailers at various presort rates. The "face value" is 5¢.

Designer: Tom Engeman

Printing: Gravure

Automobile (#2905)

This coil stamp was issued without denomination for use by bulk mailers for various presort rates. The "face value" is 10¢.

Designer: Robert Brangwynne

Printing: Gravure

Flag Over Field (#2919)

Self-adhesive booklet of 18, for Automatic Teller Machines (ATMs).

Designer: Sabra Field

Printing: Gravure

Juke Box (#2911 Bureau, #2912 Private)

These coils were issued for various presorted First-Class rates. The "face value" is 25¢. Two different printers were used in the production.

Designer: Bill Nelson

Printing: Gravure

Auto Tail Fin (#2908 Bureau, #2909 Private)

These coils were issued for various presorted First-Class postcard rates. The "face value" is 15¢. Two different printers were used.

Designer: Bill Nelson

Printing: Gravure

Circus Wagon (#2452D)

A new version of this design was issued to begin restoring the "¢" sign to low-value stamps. See #2452 for the original version.

Designer: Susan Sanford

Printing: Gravure

Flag Over Porch (#2920)

The popularity of self-adhesive stamps continues to grow. Customer demand led to the earlier release of this design in self-adhesive booklets, each containing 20 stamps.

Designer: Dave LaFleur

Printing: Gravure

Kids Care! (#2951-2954)

These four stamp designs commemorate Earth Day as well as the youth involved with the protection of the environment. The Postal Service, in partnership with McDonald's, sponsored a nationwide stamp design contest. Two winning entries from each state and two from the District of Columbia formed the pool from which these four winning designs were chosen.

Designer: Christy Millard (age 12), Bathtub
          Jennifer Michalove (age 10), Solar Energy
          Brian Hailes (age 13), Tree Planting
          Melody Kiper (age 8), Litter Clean-up

Printing: Offset

Richard Nixon (#2955)

This portrait of Richard Nixon, 37th president of the United States, is a memorial stamp issued by the Postal Service. The Postal Service's long-standing tradition is to issue a memorial stamp in the year following the death of a president, often on the birth anniversary.

Designer: Daniel Schwartz

Printing: Offset/intaglio

Bessie Coleman (#2956)

This stamp in the "Black Heritage" series commemorates the first woman to earn an international aviation license and the world's first licensed Black aviator. An illiterate who taught herself to read, Bessie was denied flying lessons for being both Black and a woman. Forced to pursue her dream in Europe, she eventually returned to the United States where she lectured, educated and traveled with her barnstorming show.

Designer: Chris Calle

Printing: Intaglio

Circus Wagon
Date of Issue: March 20, 1995
Place of Issue: Kansas City, MO

Flag Over Porch
Date of Issue: April 18, 1995
Place of Issue: Washington, DC

Kids Care!
Date of Issue: April 20, 1995
Place of Issue: Washington, DC

Richard Nixon
Date of Issue: April 26, 1995
Place of Issue: Yorba Linda, CA

Bessie Coleman
Date of Issue: April 27, 1995
Place of Issue: Chicago, IL

Official Mail
Date of Issue: May 9, 1995
Place of Issue: Washington, DC

American Kestrel

Date of Issue: May 10, 1995

Place of Issue: Aurora, CO

Sheet

Self-adhesive

Sheet

Booklet

Love (Cherubs)

Date of Issue: May 12, 1995

Place of Issue: Lakeville, PA

Bureau coil

Private coil

Sheet version

Booklet version

Flag Over Porch

Date of Issue: May 19, 1995

Place of Issue: Denver, CO

POW and MIA

Date of Issue: May 29, 1995

Place of Issue: Washington, DC

Recreational Sports

Date of Issue: May 20, 1995

Place of Issue: Jupiter, FL

American Kestrel (#2481A)

A new printing of this design was required, and a "¢" sign was added. See #2481 for the original version. The design features the American Kestrel, the smallest and most common North American falcon.

Designer: Michael Matherly

Printing: Offset

Love (Cherubs)
  32¢: (#2957 sheet, #2959 booklet)
  55¢: (#2958 sheet, #2960 peel and stick)

Another coordinated pair in the postal Love series, these contemplative angels are ideal for Valentine's Day cards, wedding invitations or any heavenly correspondence. The 32¢ stamp was printed in both sheet and booklet forms, while the 55¢ stamp was printed in sheet and peel and stick formats.

Designer: Terry McCaffrey

Printing: Offset/Intaglio

Flag Over Porch (#2897 sheet, #2916 booklet, #2913-2914 coils)

Following the advance release of the self-adhesive version due to popular demand (see April 18), the sheet, booklet and coil versions were released nearly a month later. Flag designs are among the most popular and widely demanded stamps produced. The coil version was produced by two printers.

Designer: Dave LaFleur

Printing: Gravure

Recreational Sports (five designs) (#2961-2965)

Five "moments" have been captured in this series of recreational sports. In addition to the popular sports of softball and tennis, these stamps specifically commemorate the 100th anniversaries of the invention of volleyball, the development of golf's national championships and the establishment of the American Bowling Congress.

Designer: Don Weller

Printing: Offset

POW and MIA (#2966)

This stamp is a tribute to those Americans who served their country and were captured or missing in action. An earlier tribute to these brave Americans was issued in 1970 (see #1422). The new stamp, combining the creative efforts of a number of veterans and other individuals close to the POW and MIA issue, was coordinated by art director Carl Herrman.

Designer: Carl Herrman

Printing: Offset

Marilyn Monroe (#2967)

This commemorative honors a legend who epitomized the glamour of Hollywood's golden age. Born Norma Jeane Mortenson on June 1, 1926, Marilyn starred in nearly 30 films, captivating a nation of moviegoers. Today, Marilyn is considered to be a one-in-a-million Hollywood legend who continues to enrapture moviegoers everywhere. This stamp begins a new "Legends of Hollywood" series. The full pane of 20 stamps features special text and an enlarged image of Marilyn Monroe along the side. The perforations forming the corners of each stamp are shaped like stars.

Designer: Michael Deas

Printing: Gravure

Ferryboat (#2466)

This 32¢ coil continues the popular "Transportation" series. The design features a composite image of a typical ferryboat from the early 1900s.

Designer: Richard Schlecht

Printing: Intaglio

Pink Rose

This peel and stick stamp was issued in both booklets of 20 and coils. The original design featured a red rose and was used in 1993 to create a peel and stick booklet of 29¢ stamps (#2479). It soon became one of the most popular and widely used self-adhesive stamps ever issued up to that time. With a simple color change from red to pink, the design continues to appeal to mailers at 32¢.

Designer: Gyo Fujikawa

Printing: Gravure

Cog Railway Car (#2463)

This 20¢ coil was released to meet the postcard rate. The image features a cog railway car designed to climb steep inclines. It is the last new design planned for the long-running "Transportation" series, which began in 1981 and featured more than 50 different vehicles or transportation devices.

Designer: Robert Brangwynne

Printing: Intaglio

Blue Jay

This beautiful bird was chosen for new booklets of postcard-rate stamps.

Designer: Bob Giusti

Printing: Gravure

Marilyn Monroe
Date of Issue: June 1, 1995
Place of Issue: Universal City, CA

Ferryboat
Date of Issue: June 2, 1995
Place of Issue: McLean, VA

Pink Rose
Date of Issue: June 2, 1995
Place of Issue: McLean, VA

Cog Railway Car
Date of Issue: June 9, 1995
Place of Issue: Dallas, TX

Blue Jay
Date of Issue: June 15, 1995
Place of Issue: Kansas City, MO

Texas Statehood
Date of Issue: June 16, 1995
Place of Issue: Austin, TX

Great Lakes Lighthouses
Date of Issue: June 17, 1995
Place of Issue: Cheboygan, MI

***Challenger* Shuttle**
Date of Issue: June 22, 1995
Place of Issue: Anaheim, CA

United Nations
Date of Issue: June 26, 1995
Place of Issue: San Francisco

Texas Statehood (#2968)

This distinctive stamp honors the 150th anniversary of statehood for Texas, which was an independent republic before becoming a state.

Designer: Laura Smith

Printing: Offset

Great Lakes Lighthouses (five designs) (#2969-2973)

This booklet of 20 stamps contains five historic lighthouses commemorating the great towers that made coastal and Great Lakes navigation possible. Lighthouses depicted are Split Rock, Lake Superior; St. Joseph, Lake Michigan; Spectacle Reef, Lake Huron; Marblehead, Lake Erie; and Thirty-mile Point, Lake Ontario.

Designer: Howard Koslow

Printing: Gravure

Booklet cover

Challenger Shuttle (#2544)

This stamp, based on a NASA photograph of the space shuttle *Challenger* above the earth on one of its missions, meets the $3.00 Priority Mail rate.

Designer: Phil Jordan

Printing: Offset/Intaglio

United Nations (#2974)

This stamp honors the 50th anniversary of the founding of the United Nations. The design features the distinctive U.N. emblem and blue color.

Designer: Howard Paine

Printing: Intaglio

Shiloh	**Union Lt. General Ulysses S. Grant**	**Union Nurse Clara Harlowe Barton**	**Confederate General Robert Edward Lee**	***Monitor & Virginia (Merrimack)***
April 6-7, 1862	1822-1885	1821-1912	1807-1870	March 9, 1862
Confederates surprised Grant at Pittsburg Landing, TN, but lost General A.S. Johnston. Union counterattack at Shiloh Church forced Southerners to withdraw. Casualties: 13,050 Union, 10,700 Confederate.	Gained national fame with "unconditional surrender" victory at Fort Donelson. Crafted brilliant wins at Vicksburg, Chattanooga. Forced Lee's surrender. U.S. President 1869-77.	"Angel of the Battlefield" nursed the wounded at Antietam and at Virginia battlefields. Helped identify and mark graves at Andersonville prison. Founded American Red Cross.	Army of Northern Virginia Commander, 1862-65. Won Seven Days' Campaign, 2nd Manassas, Chancellorsville. Repelled at Gettysburg. Surrendered April 9, 1865. Became college president.	In the first clash of the iron-clads, U.S.S. *Monitor* and C.S.S. *Virginia* battled to a stalemate, preserving U.S. blockade at Hampton Roads, VA. *Virginia* burned in May. Hatteras gale sank *Monitor*.

16th U.S. President Abraham Lincoln	**Confederate Rear Admiral Raphael Semmes**	**Journalist-Orator Frederick Douglass**	**Union Vice Admiral David Glasgow Farragut**	**President of the Confederacy Jefferson Finis Davis**
1809-1865	1809-1877	c1818-1895	1801-1870	1808-1889
Illinois "Rail-Splitter" pursued war vigorously to restore the Union. "of . . . by . . . for the people." Urged "malice toward none." Assassinated five days after Lee's surrender.	Audacious commander of C.S.S. *Sumter* and *Alabama* plagued Union shipping, capturing or destroying more than 90 vessels. Professor, editor, lawyer. Wrote books of exploits.	"Wielding . . . pen . . . voice." ex-slave campaigned for rights for Blacks, women. Assisted runaways to Canada. Helped recruit Blacks for 54th Massachusetts Regiment. U.S. Minister to Haiti.	A midshipman at age 9. Electrified the North with daring naval assault to capture New Orleans. Yelled "Damn the torpedoes! Full speed ahead!" during the attack at Mobile Bay.	Ex-U.S. Senator from Mississippi, named provisional CSA head Feb. 1861. Quarreled with military about war tactics and strategy but supported Lee. Captured May 1865 in GA, imprisoned two years.

Confederate Diarist Mary Boykin Miller Chesnut	**Union Major General Winfield Scott Hancock**	**Confederate General Joseph Eggleston Johnston**	**Confederate Brig. General Stand Watie (De-ga-do-ga)**	**Abolitionist Harriet Ross Tubman**
1823-1886	1824-1886	1807-1891	1806-1871	c1821-1913
Astute, articulate hostess. Wife of aide to Jefferson Davis. Wrote of daily life, events, amid South's officialdom. Her plain-spoken journal, published posthumously, sparkles with wit and irony.	Brigade, Division, Corps Commander at Fredericksburg, Chancellorsville. Played major role in Union victory at Gettysburg, but was severely wounded. Presidential candidate 1880.	Commander CSA forces Northern Virginia 1861-62. Wounded at Seven Pines. Master defensive strategist bickered often with Davis. Led Army of Tennessee. Dalton to Atlanta.	Known for guerrilla tactics tying down Union troops. Sole CSA Indian General raised Cherokee regiment, fought at Pea Ridge, captured federal steamboat. Last CSA General to surrender.	Fugitive slave who fled to freedom. As "Moses of her people," led over 200 Blacks north via Underground Railroad. Served Union Army as cook, spy and scout.

Gettysburg	**Confederate Lt. General Thomas Jonathan Jackson**	**Confederate Nurse Phoebe Yates Levy Pember**	**Union Major General William Tecumseh Sherman**	**Chancellorsville**
July 1-3, 1863	1824-1863	1823-1913	1820-1891	May 1-6, 1863
Lee invaded North 2nd time. Encounter led to carnage as Union Gen. George Meade elected "to stay and fight," repelling Pickett's Charge. Casualties: 23,050 Union, 28,075 Confederate.	Nicknamed "Stonewall" at First Manassas. Brilliant tactician in Shenandoah Valley Campaign. Fatally wounded by own men after routing Union right flank at Chancellorsville.	Directed care and dietary needs of over 10,000 soldiers at Richmond's Chimborazo, one of CSA's largest hospitals. Specialty: chicken soup. Criticized poor care in her *A Southern Woman's Story*.	Blunt, grizzled strategist distinguished himself at Shiloh and Vicksburg. Captured Atlanta. Introduced total warfare in his March across GA and through the Carolinas. Negotiated lenient peace.	Greatly outnumbered, Lee boldly split forces, routed Hooker's Union army. Mortal wounding of Stonewall Jackson overshadowed Rebel victory. Casualties: 17,300 Union, 12,800 Confederate.

Civil War (#2975)

This Civil War pane is the second issue in the U.S. Postal Service's Classic Collection format. This new sheet will let you relive a tiny part of history from the battles of Shiloh and Gettysburg to the legendary Stonewall Jackson. These twenty images of the War Between the States have been researched by experts for accuracy. Descriptive text appears on the gummed side (illustrated above).

Designer: Mark Hess

Printing: Gravure

Peaches and Pears

These stamps were produced in conventional booklets, peel and stick booklets and peel and stick coils.

Designer: Ned Seidler

Printing: Gravure

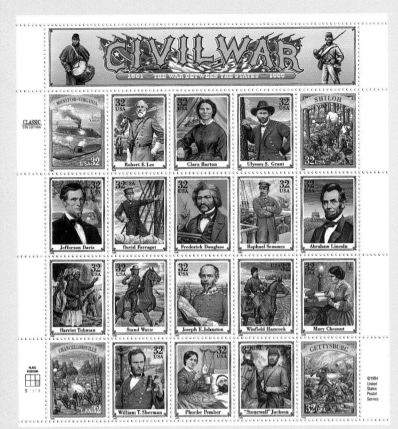

Civil War

Date of Issue: June 29, 1995
Place of Issue: Gettysburg, PA

Booklet (pair)

Peaches and Pears

Date of Issue: July 8, 1995
Place of Issue: Reno, NV

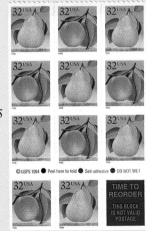

Self-adhesive

Alice Hamilton, MD
Date of Issue: July 11, 1995
Place of Issue: Boston, MA

Carousel Horses
Date of Issue: July 21, 1995
Place of Issue: Lahaska, PA

***Endeavour* Shuttle**
Date of Issue: August 4, 1995
Place of Issue: Irvine, CA

Alice Paul
Date of Issue: August 18, 1995
Place of Issue: Mount Laurel, NJ

Women's Suffrage
Date of Issue: August 26, 1995
Place of Issue: Washington, DC

Louis Armstrong
Date of Issue: September 1, 1995
Place of Issue: New Orleans, LA

Alice Hamilton, MD

This stamp features the first woman faculty member of Harvard University, who was a pioneer in the study and advancement of industrial medicine.

Designer: Chris Calle

Printing: Intaglio

Carousel Horses

A tribute to the unique beauty of the American Carousel, these four carousel horses represent three carving styles that developed during the Golden Age of the Carousel. These carved horses recall the music, motion and magic of the carousels etched in our childhood memories.

Designer: Paul Calle

Printing: Offset

Endeavour Shuttle

This stamp, based on a NASA photograph of the space shuttle *Endeavour* lifting off, meets the new Express Mail rate.

Designer: Phil Jordan

Printing: Offset/intaglio

Alice Paul

Sometimes referred to as the mother of the Equal Rights Amendment, Alice Paul formed the National Woman's Party in 1913. In 1923, she submitted to Congress the first version of the Equal Rights Amendment and later formed the World Woman's Party.

Designer: Chris Calle

Printing: Intaglio

Women's Suffrage

This stamp represents the long struggle of the movement for women's voting rights. In 1878, an amendment giving women the right to vote was first introduced in Congress, and reintroduced in every session of Congress until 1920, when the 19th Amendment was passed guaranteeing women the right to vote.

Designer: April Greiman

Printing: Offset/intaglio

Louis Armstrong

Louis "Satchmo" Armstrong, the famous and beloved trumpeter, singer and band leader, is singled out from this year's installment in the "Legends of American Music" series. This "Jazz Ambassador" not only introduced jazz to America, but also to the world. His signature white handkerchief is included in the stamp illustration.

Designer: Dean Mitchell

Printing: Offset

World War II—Victory at Last

The Postal Service commemorates the 50th anniversary of the final year of World War II with the issuance of a miniature sheet of 32¢ stamps. The stamps highlight the following 1945 events and subjects: Marines raise flag on Iwo Jima; fierce fighting frees Manila; Okinawa, the last big battle; U.S. and Soviets link up at Elbe River; Allies liberate holocaust survivors; Germany surrenders at Reims; World War II has uprooted millions; Truman announces Japan's surrender; news of victory hits home; and hometowns honor their returning veterans. With the end of the war in 1945, the 50th anniversary tributes also come to a close. This pane of stamps represents the fifth and final installment in the annual series that began in 1991.

Designer: Bill Bond

Printing: Offset/intaglio

Milton S. Hershey

Milton Hershey (1857-1945), an American manufacturer and philanthropist who founded the Hershey Chocolate Company, is the latest addition to the "Great Americans" series. After perfecting a formula for chocolate bars, he began building a factory at the site of what would become Hershey, Pennsylvania, and the world's largest chocolate manufacturing plant. The town that grew up around the business became a model American community, due in large part to the efforts of Hershey himself. He donated much of his fortune to support various community services and to establish educational institutions such as the Hershey Industrial School (for orphan boys) and Hershey Junior College (for boys and girls).

Designer: Dennis Lyall

Printing: Intaglio

Jazz Musicians

The newest in the "Legends of American Music" series, the jazz artists were issued at the Monterey Jazz Festival. The stamps feature pianists Eubie Blake, Jelly Roll Morton, James P. Johnson and Thelonious Monk by designer Thomas Blackshear; pianist Erroll Garner, saxophonists Coleman Hawkins, Charlie Parker and John Coltrane; trumpeter Louis Armstrong and bassist Charles Mingus are featured by designer Dean Mitchell. All 10 of these jazz greats were composers as well, and they represent some of the true legends in American jazz.

Designer: Thomas Blackshear and Dean Mitchell

Printing: Offset

World War II - Victory at Last
Date of Issue: September 2, 1995
Place of Issue: Honolulu, HI

Milton S. Hershey
Date of Issue: September 13, 1995
Place of Issue: Hershey, PA

Jazz Musicians
Date of Issue: September 16, 1995
Place of Issue: Monterey, CA

Fall Garden Flowers
Date of Issue: September 19, 1995
Place of Issue: Encinitas, CA

Eddie Rickenbacker
Date of Issue: September 25, 1995
Place of Issue: Columbus, OH

Republic of Palau
Date of Issue: September 29, 1995
Place of Issue: Agana, GU

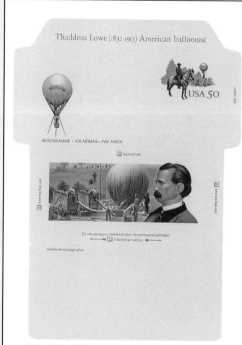

Thaddeus Lowe aerogramme
Date of Issue: September 23, 1995
Place of Issue: Tampa, FL

For a listing of other 1995 postal stationery items, see page 42.

Fall Garden Flowers

Some of the most beautiful fall garden flowers are issued in a 20-stamp booklet of 32¢ stamps. The stamps feature five colorful fall garden flowers: aster, chrysanthemum, dahlia, hydrangea and rudbeckia. This is the third in an annual series of flower booklet stamps. Each booklet of 20 stamps includes four panes of five stamps each.

Designer: Ned Seidler

Printing: Offset/intaglio

Eddie Rickenbacker

Born in Columbus, Ohio, Eddie Vernon Rickenbacker first showed his talents for machines by his success as an automobile mechanic and a racing driver. Enlisting in the Army in 1917, Rickenbacker went on to become the leading U.S. air ace of World War I. In 1938, he became the president of Eastern Airlines and owned the Indianapolis Speedway for 18 years. With the issuance of this stamp in the Aviation Pioneers series, the series reflects a major change in U.S. postage: since all basic overseas letters and postcards now travel by air, the "airmail" designation no longer is necessary. Just as domestic airmail disappeared many years earlier, a similar change in designations is beginning in international mail. Thus, the word "airmail" does not appear on this new 60¢ stamp.

Designer: Davis Meltzer

Printing: Gravure

Garden Flowers booklet cover

Republic of Palau

The Palau islands (also spelled Belau) are a group of islands in the Western Pacific Ocean; part of the area known as Micronesia, the islands, which are surrounded by coral reef, are only 100 miles long and 20 miles wide. Administered for many years by the U.S. as part of the U.N. Trust Territories in the Pacific, the islands became a republic in 1994.

Designer: Herb Kane

Printing: Offset

To receive your own souvenir edition of the hardcover *American Comic Strip Classics* tabletop book featuring exciting stories, colorful illustrations, and two full sheets of these stamps, please call 1-800-STAMP 24 or send $29.95 plus $4.20 for shipping and handling to:

Comic Strips Book Offer
US Postal Service
Post Office Box 419219
Kansas City MO 64141-6219

Dagwood:
©1995 King Features
Syndicate, Inc.

Please allow six weeks for delivery. Offer expires October 1, 1996, while supplies last.
Offer valid only for orders delivered in the United States.

BRINGING UP FATHER
George McManus (1884-1954)
Also known as *Maggie & Jiggs*, this was the story of a *nouveau riche* Irish immigrant and his social-climbing wife. Jiggs' habit of escaping from Maggie's fancy parties to eat corned beef and cabbage popularized this dish.
The strip began in 1913.
©1995 King Features Syndicate, Inc.

LITTLE NEMO IN SLUMBERLAND
Winsor McCay (c.1867-1934)
Little Nemo was the first strip to be drawn realistically and to utilize quality color printing. Nemo's daydreams were filled with nightmares were fantasies with dragons and monsters, travels to Mars, and slums that turned into gardens.
The strip ran 1905-11; 1924-27

THE KATZENJAMMER KIDS
Rudolph Dirks (1877-1968)
The oldest comic strip still being produced, this comic stars the mischievous antics of Hans and Fritz. *The Katzenjammer Kids* was one of the first comics to use regular characters, sequential drawings, and cartoon symbols.
The strip started in 1897.
©1995 King Features Syndicate, Inc.

THE YELLOW KID
R.F. Outcault (1863-1928)
The first popular newspaper color cartoon was *Hogan's Alley* starring the Yellow Kid. The tenement exploits of the Irish immigrant kid ignited public affection; when two New York papers fought over rival versions, "Yellow Journalism" was born.
The cartoon ran 1895-1898.

GASOLINE ALLEY*
Frank King (1883-1969)
It began as a panel about men's interest in autos, but *Gasoline Alley* evolved to become a strip about the life and growth of average Americans. It was the first major strip where characters grew up in real time.
The strip began in 1919.
© Tribune Media Services, Inc.

TOONERVILLE FOLKS
Fontaine Fox (1884-1964)
"The Toonerville Trolley That Meets All Trains" began its run as a part of the colorful landscape of Toonerville in Fox's panel cartoons around 1910. The Skipper and his out-of-control car inspired toys, games, and movies.
The panel ran 1910-1955.

RUBE GOLDBERG "INVENTIONS"
Rube Goldberg (1883-1970)
Rube Goldberg was a cartoonist with an engineering degree. This combination led him to create a series of crazy inventions – in this case an automatic napkin – that amused readers for decades.
The panel ran 1914-1964.
© Rube Goldberg, Inc.

KRAZY KAT
George Herriman (1880-1944)
Krazy Kat was a surrealistic comic strip with changing backgrounds, poetic dialog, and strange props. While not widely popular in its own day, it's now generally considered to be a high mark of the art form.
The strip ran 1913-1944.
©1995 King Features Syndicate, Inc.

BLONDIE
Chic Young (1901-1973)
Young once said that he found the magic formula for creating a comic strip with which simply restricted his premises to eating, sleeping, going to work, and raising a family.
The strip began in 1930.
©1995 King Features Syndicate, Inc.

POPEYE
E.C. Segar (1894-1938)
Popeye was an overnight success when he made his debut on the stage of the *Thimble Theatre* comic strip in 1929. His adventures mixed thrills, satire, parody, and nonsense; his sayings ("I yam what I yam...") are part of our language.
The strip began in 1919.
©1995 King Features Syndicate, Inc.

LITTLE ORPHAN ANNIE*
Harold Gray (1894-1968)
During the Great Depression, Annie was as responsible as anyone for keeping up the nation's spirits. Gray's morality tales of perseverance, independence, and courage helped make newspaper comics indispensable.
The strip began in 1924.
© Tribune Media Services, Inc.

BARNEY GOOGLE
Billy DeBeck (1890-1942)
The schemer Barney Google (with the goo-goo-googly eyes, as the popular song went) was the most prominent player in a marvelous parade of character types. Later the strip became a hillbilly saga starring Snuffy Smith.
The strip began in 1919.
©1995 King Features Syndicate, Inc.

FLASH GORDON
Alex Raymond (1909-1956)
Cartoonist Alex Raymond steered the Sunday funnies toward Romanticism with exotic locales, memorable villains, and breathless action in this science-fiction classic.
The strip began in 1934.
©1995 King Features Syndicate, Inc.

NANCY
Ernie Bushmiller (1905-1982)
Many of his fellow cartoonists admired Bushmiller for his ability to reduce gags and art to their simplest levels. In so doing, Nancy and her friend Sluggo became favorites of millions.
The strip began in 1938.
© United Feature Syndicate, Inc.

ALLEY OOP
V.T. Hamlin (1899-1993)
Hamlin's love of history and legend inspired him to create an epic strip filled with the strange and mysterious, leaving a legacy of impressive art and stories of time-travel, stone-age adventure, humor and romance.
The strip began in 1933.
© Newspaper Enterprise Association, Inc.

DICK TRACY*
Chester Gould (1900-1985)
Although his Sunday pages utilized flat colors, Tracy's world was black-and-white: good vs. evil, right vs. wrong. The villains especially – Flattop, the Brow, Mumbles, Pruneface – were as ugly as their natures.
The strip began in 1931.
© Tribune Media Services, Inc.

BRENDA STARR*
Dale Messick (1906-   )
This classic soap-opera strip was a pioneer – a comic featuring a strong female lead character created by a female cartoonist. Brenda's big-city newsroom assignments usually led to adventure and romance.
The strip began in 1940.
© Tribune Media Services, Inc.

PRINCE VALIANT
Harold R. Foster (1892-1982)
Prince Valiant was the last major strip to be created as a full-page, full-color picture-story. Foster's meticulous research for his Arthurian legend lent authenticity to battle scenes and domestic scenes alike.
The strip began in 1937.
©1995 King Features Syndicate, Inc.

TERRY AND THE PIRATES*
Milton Caniff (1907-1988)
Caniff's artwork looked photographic; his characters spoke realistic dialogue; and readers identified with their personalities. Mood, evocation, atmosphere were Caniff's trademarks.
The strip ran 1934-1973.
© Tribune Media Services, Inc.

LI'L ABNER
Al Capp (1909-1979)
Abner's corner of Dogpatch was Capp's crossroads of the best and worst of the humanity he lampooned. His creations included the Shmoo, the Bald Eagle, Fearless Fosdick, and Sadie Hawkins' Day.
The strip ran 1934-1977.
© Capp Enterprises, Inc.

Gum side (back) of Comic Strip sheet

Comic Strip Classics

From The Yellow Kid to Brenda Starr, a century of comics is celebrated with the third issue of the Postal Service's Classic Collection series.

Designer: Carl Herrman

Printing: Gravure

U.S. Naval Academy

This stamp celebrates the 150th anniversary of the U.S. Naval Academy.

Designer: Dean Ellis

Printing: Offset

Tennessee Williams

This award-winning playwright, best known for *A Streetcar Named Desire*, is commemorated with 1995's addition to the Literary Arts Series.

Designer: Michael Deas

Printing: Offset

Comic Strip Classics

Date of Issue: October 1, 1995
Place of Issue: Boca Raton, FL

U.S. Naval Academy
Date of Issue: October 10, 1995
Place of Issue: Annapolis, MD

Tennessee Williams
Date of Issue: October 13, 1995
Place of Issue: Clarksdale, MS

Block of 4

Holiday Contemporary

Self-adhesive sheet

Date of Issue: September 30, 1995
Place of Issue: North Pole, NY

Children Sledding
Date of Issue: October 19, 1995
Place of Issue: Christmas, FL

Midnight Angel
Date of Issue: October 19, 1995
Place of Issue: Christmas, FL

Holiday Traditional
Date of Issue: October 19, 1995
Place of Issue: Washington, DC

Holiday Contemporary (four designs)

The holiday stamp design choices for 1995 include four images reminiscent of the Victorian era. Taken from greeting cards, writing tablet covers, postcards and other similar printed materials from the decades surrounding the turn of the 20th century, these images depict Santa going down a chimney; Santa making a sled; a child holding a tree; and a child holding a toy puppet known as a jumping jack. These stamps are issued in panes of 50, booklets of 20, peel and stick booklets of 20, and peel and stick coils.

Designer: John Grossman and Laura Alders

Printing: Offset

Children Sledding

This stamp, available in Automated Teller Machine (ATM) booklets of 18 stamps each, celebrates those cold winter afternoons American children have spent happily sledding down snow-covered hills. The image is taken from a postcard dating back to the early 1900s.

Designer: John Grossman and Laura Alders

Printing: Gravure

Midnight Angel

This angelic image from a greeting card from the early 1900s features a heavenly messenger floating in a midnight sky, holding a garland of flowering holly and ringing a trio of bells. The original illustration is attributed to Ellen H. Clapsaddle (1865-1934), an American greeting card illustrator of the era. This stamp is issued in peel and stick booklets of 20.

Designer: John Grossman and Laura Alders

Printing: Offset

Holiday Traditional

The traditional holiday stamp features a Madonna and Child by Florentine artist Giotto (c.1266-1337). The artist, Giotto di Bondone, is called by some "the father of Italian painting," and he is credited with adding more realism and three-dimensional quality to paintings. This stamp is produced in panes of 50 and booklets of 20 stamps.

Designer: Richard D. Sheaff

Printing: Offset/intaglio

Most stamps remain on sale from the U.S. Postal Service at least one year from date of issue, especially by mail order. Ask for them at your local post office, or request a free copy of the Stamps etc. *mail-order catalog. Send for the catalog using the postage-paid card in this book, or call toll-free: **1-800-STAMP24**.*

Ruth Benedict

This stamp features Ruth Fulton Benedict, who made major contributions to the field of anthropology. It continues the Great Americans series of sheet-format regular-issue stamps.

Designer: Roy Andersen

Printing: Intaglio

James K. Polk

This stamp features an engraved portrait of James K. Polk surrounded by an ornate oval frame replicating a nineteenth-century style typical of our earliest postage stamps. The first man younger than age fifty to become president of the United States, Polk was the eleventh chief executive of the United States. During his presidency the Naval Academy opened, the Smithsonian Institution was established, the first known baseball game was played and the first U.S. postage stamp was issued.

Designer: John Thompson

Printing: Intaglio

Antique Automobiles

The five images in this series are representative of turn-of-the-century automobiles. Charles E. and J. Frank Duryea successfully tested and ran in Springfield, Massachusetts, the first American gasoline-powered automobile. Contemporary inventors included Elwood Haynes, Alexander Winton, Henry Ford and others.

Designer: Ken Dallison

Printing: Gravure

1995 Issues—Stamped Envelopes

32¢ Liberty Bell (#U632)	January 3, 1995
(5¢) Nonprofit Sheep (#U635)	March 10, 1995
(10¢) Bulk Rate Eagle (#U636)	March 10, 1995
32¢ Spiral Heart (#U637)	May 12, 1995
32¢ Security Liberty Bell (#U638)	May 16, 1995
32¢ Space Station Hologram	September 22, 1995

1995 Issues—Postal Cards

20¢ Red Barn (#UX198)	January 3, 1995
20¢ Civil War (set of 20)	June 29, 1995
50¢ Soaring Eagle	August 24, 1995
20¢ Clipper Ship	September 3, 1995
20¢ Comic Strip Classics (set of 20)	October 1, 1995

Ruth Benedict
Date of Issue: October 20, 1995
Place of Issue: Virginia Beach, VA

James K. Polk
Date of Issue: November 2, 1995
Place of Issue: Columbia, TN

Antique Automobiles
Date of Issue: November 3, 1995
Place of Issue: New York, NY

1995 Issues—Duck Stamp

Migratory Bird Hunting and Conservation Stamps ("Duck Stamps") are issued by the U.S. Department of the Interior and are sold as bird hunting permits. They are sold at numerous locations, including many post offices, but they are not usable for postage. The 1995 issue features a pair of Mallards in flight. **(#RW62)**

Mallards
Date of Issue: June 30, 1995
Place of Issue: Washington, D.C.

Space Station Hologram
*For illustrations of other new 1995
stamped envelopes, see pages 404-405.*

Share the Excitement of New Stamp Issues

- Provides a great way to collect new U.S. postal issues
- Includes postmark with date and place of official issuance for a complete historical record

First day covers are a great way to enjoy the best elements of stamp collecting, and the U.S. Postal Service now offers first day covers for all new issues.

First Day Benefits

In addition to providing the new stamps, each envelope includes blank covers (no cachets) with stamps affixed. Stamps are postmarked with the official United States Postal Service "first day of issue" cancellation, to complete the historical record of the stamps' date and place of issuance.

Different Sizes

Depending on the size or number of stamps in a particular issue, covers come in one of three sizes: *Personal* (#6³/₄) for single stamps and many blocks, *Monarch* (@ 7¹/₂" x 4") for larger blocks and booklet panes, or *Legal* (#10) for larger items and panes. Customers may have self-addressed envelopes canceled through the office of the Postmaster of any official First Day city.

For More Information

Send the postage-paid request card in this book or call toll-free:

1-800-STAMP24

Stamp Collecting Words and Phrases

Accessories
The tools used by stamp collectors, such as tongs, hinges, etc.

Adhesive
A gummed stamp made to be attached to mail.

Aerophilately
Stamp collecting that focuses on stamps or postage relating to airmail.

Album
A book designed to hold stamps and covers.

Approvals
Stamps sent by a dealer to a collector for examination. Approvals must either be bought or returned to the dealer within a specified time.

Auction
A sale at which philatelic material is sold to the highest bidder.

Black Jack
The nickname for the very popular U.S. two-cent black Andrew Jackson stamp, which was issued in various forms between 1863 and 1875.

Block
An unseparated group of stamps, at least two stamps high and two stamps wide.

Bluish Paper
Used to print portions of several issues in 1909; the paper was made with 35 percent rag stock instead of all wood pulp. The color goes through the paper, showing clearly on back and face.

Bogus
A completely fictitious, worthless "stamp," created only for sale to collectors. Bogus stamps include labels for nonexistent values added to regularly issued sets, issues for nations without postal systems, etc.

Booklet Pane
A small sheet of stamps specially cut to be sold in booklets.

Bourse
A marketplace, such as stamp exhibition, where stamps are bought, sold or exchanged.

Cachet (ka-shay')
A design on an envelope describing an event. Cachets appear on first day of issue, first flight and stamp exhibition covers, etc.

Cancellation
A mark placed on a stamp by a postal authority to show that it has been used.

Centering
The position of the design on a postage stamp. On perfectly centered stamps the design is exactly in the middle.

Classic
An early stamp issue. Most people consider these to be rare stamps, but classic stamps aren't necessarily rare.

Coils
Stamps issued in rolls (one stamp wide)

for use in dispensers or vending machines.

Commemoratives
Stamps that honor anniversaries, important people or special events.

Compound Perforations
Different gauge perforations on different (normally adjacent) sides of a single stamp.

Condition

Condition is the most important characteristic in determining a stamp's value. It refers to the state of a stamp regarding such details as centering, color and gum.

Cover

An envelope that has been sent through the mail.

Cracked Plate

A term used to describe stamps which show evidence that the plate from which they were printed was cracked.

Definitives

Regular issues of postage stamps, usually sold over long periods of time.

Denomination

The postage value appearing on a stamp, such as 5 cents.

Directory Markings

Postal markings that indicate a failed delivery attempt, stating reasons such as "No Such Number" or "Address Unknown."

Double Transfer

The condition on a printing plate that shows evidence of a duplication of all or part of the design.

Dry Printing

Begun as an experiment in 1953, this type of printing results in a whiter paper, a higher sheen on the surface, a thicker and stiffer feel and designs that stand out more clearly than on more standard "wet" printings.

Duplicates

Extra copies of stamps that can be sold or traded. Duplicates should be examined carefully for color and perforation variations.

Entire

An intact piece of postal stationery, in contrast to a cut-out of the printed design.

Error

A stamp with something incorrect in its design or manufacture.

Exploded

A stamp booklet is said to be "exploded" when it has been separated into its various components for show.

Face Value

The monetary value or denomination of a stamp.

Fake

A genuine stamp that has been altered in some way to make it more attractive to collectors. It may be repaired, reperfed or regummed to resemble a more valuable variety.

First Day Cover (FDC)

An envelope with a new stamp and cancellation showing the date the stamp was issued.

Franks

Marking on the face of a cover, indicating it is to be carried free of postage. Franks may be written, handstamped, imprinted or represented by special adhesives. Such free franking is usually limited to official correspondence, such as the President's mail.

Freak

An abnormal variety of stamps occurring because of paper fold, over-inking, perforation shift, etc., as opposed to a continually appearing variety or a major error.

Grill

A pattern of small, square pyramids in parallel rows impressed or embossed on the stamp to break paper fibers, allowing cancellation ink to soak in and preventing washing and reuse.

Gum

The coating of glue on the back of an unused stamp.

Hinges

Small strips of gummed material used by collectors to affix stamps to album pages.

Imperforate

Indicates stamps without perforations or separating holes. They usually are separated by scissors and collected in pairs.

Label
Any stamp-like adhesive that is not a postage stamp.

Laid Paper
When held to the light, the paper shows alternate light and dark crossed lines.

Line Pairs (LP)
Most coil stamp rolls prior to #1891 feature a line of ink printed between two stamps at varying intervals.

Miniature Sheet
A single stamp or block of stamps with a margin on all sides bearing some special wording or design.

On Paper
Stamps "on paper" are those that still have portions of the original envelope or wrapper stuck to them.

Overprint
Additional printing on a stamp that was not part of the original design.

Packet
A presorted unit of all different stamps. One of the most common and economical ways to begin a collection.

Pane
A full "sheet" of stamps as sold by a Post Office. Four panes typically make up the original sheet of stamps as printed.

Par Avion
French for mail transported "by air."

Perforations
Lines of small holes or cuts between rows of stamps that make them easy to separate.

Philately
The collection and study of postage stamps and other postal materials.

Pictorials
Stamps with a picture of some sort, other than portraits or static designs such as coats of arms.

Plate Block (PB) (or Plate Number Block)
A block of stamps with the margin attached that bears the plate number used in printing that sheet.

Plate Number Coils (PNC)
For most coil stamp rolls beginning with #1891, a small plate number appears at varying intervals in the roll in the design of the stamp.

Postage Due
A stamp issued to collect unpaid postage.

Postal Stationery
Envelopes, postal cards and aerogrammes with stamp designs printed or embossed on them.

Postmark
A mark put on envelopes or other mailing pieces showing the date and location of the post office where it was mailed.

Precancels
Cancellations applied to stamps before the stamps were affixed to mail.

Registered Mail
First class mail with a numbered receipt, including a valuation of the registered item. This guarantees customers will get their money back if an item is lost in the mail.

Reissue
An official reprinting of a stamp that was no longer being printed.

Replicas
Reproductions of stamps sold during the early days of collecting. Usually printed in one color on a sheet containing a number of different designs. Replicas were never intended to deceive either the post office or the collector.

Reprint
A stamp printed from the original plate after the issue is no longer valid for postage. Official reprints are sometimes made for presentation purposes, official collections, etc., and are often distinguished in some way from the "real" ones.

Revenue Stamps
Stamps not valid for postal use but issued for collecting taxes.

Ribbed Paper
Paper which shows fine parallel ridges on one or both sides of a stamp.

Se-tenant
An attached pair, strip or block of stamps that differ in design, value or surcharge.

Secret Marks
Many stamps have included tiny reference points in their designs to foil attempts at counterfeiting and to differentiate issues.

Selvage
The unprinted paper around panes of stamps, sometimes called the margin.

Series
All the variations of design and value of a particular issue.

Set
A unit of stamps with a common design or theme issued at one time for a common purpose or over an extended period.

Souvenir Sheet
A small sheet of stamps with a commemorative inscription of some sort.

Speculative
A stamp or issue released primarily for sale to collectors, rather than to meet any legitimate postal need.

Strip
Three or more unseparated stamps in a row.

Surcharge
An overprint that changes the denomination of a stamp from its original face value.

Sweatbox
A closed box with a grill over which stuck-together unused stamps are placed. A wet, sponge-like material under the grill creates humidity so the stamps can be separated without removing the gum.

Thematic
A stamp collection that relates to a specific theme and is arranged to present a logical story and progression.

Tied On
Indicates a stamp whose postmark touches the envelope.

Tongs
A tool, used to handle stamps, that resembles a tweezers with rounded or flattened tips.

Topicals
Indicates a group of stamps with the same theme—space travel, for example.

Unhinged
A stamp without hinge marks, but not necessarily with original gum.

Unused
The condition of a stamp that has no cancellation or other sign of use.

Used
The condition of a stamp that has been canceled.

Want List
A list of philatelic material needed by a collector.

Watermark
A design pressed into stamp paper during its manufacture.

Wet Printing
Has a moisture content of 15-35 percent, compared to 5-10 percent for "dry" printings; also, has a duller look than "dry" printings.

Wove Paper
A uniform paper which, when held to the light, shows no light or dark figures.

Organizations, Publications and Resources

For Your Information ...

Here's a list of philatelic resources that can increase your knowledge of stamps as well as your collecting enjoyment.

Organizations

Please enclose a stamped, self-addressed envelope when writing to these organizations.

American Air Mail Society
Stephen Reinhard
PO Box 110
Mineola, NY 11501-0110

Specializes in all phases of aerophilately. Membership services include Advance Bulletin Service, Auction Service, free want ads, Sales Department, monthly journal, discounts on Society publications, translation service.

American First Day Cover Society
Founder-Member
2 Vreeland Road
Florham Park, NJ 07932

A full-service, not-for-profit, noncommercial society devoted exclusively to First Day Covers and First Day Cover collecting. Offers information on 300 current cachet producers, expertizing, foreign covers, translation service, color slide programs and archives covering First Day Covers.

American Philatelic Society
Robert E. Lamb
Executive Director
PO Box 8000
Dept. PG
State College, PA
16803-8000

A full complement of services and resources for stamp collectors. Annual membership offers: library services, educational seminars and correspondence courses, expertizing service, estate advisory service, translation service, a stamp theft committee that functions as a clearinghouse for philatelic crime information, intramember sales service and a monthly journal, The American Philatelist, sent to all members. Membership 57,000 worldwide.

American Society for Philatelic Pages and Panels
Gerald Blankenship
PO Box 475
Crosby, TX 77532-0475

American Stamp Dealers' Association
Joseph B. Savarese
3 School St.
Glen Cove, NY 11542-2517

Association of dealers engaged in every facet of philately, with 11 regional chapters nationwide. Sponsors national and local shows. Will send you a complete listing of dealers in your area or collecting specialty. A #10 self-addressed, stamped envelope must accompany your request.

American Topical Association
Donald W. Smith
PO Box 630
Johnstown, PA 15907-0630

A service organization concentrating on the specialty of topical stamp collecting. Offers handbooks and checklists on specific topics; exhibition awards; Topical Time, a bimonthly publication dealing with topical interest areas; a slide loan service; and information, translation and sales services.

Booklet Collectors Club
Jim Natele
PO Box 2461-U
Cinnaminson, NJ
08077-2461

Devoted to the study of worldwide booklets and booklet collecting, with special emphasis on U.S. booklets. Publishes The Interleaf, a quarterly journal.

Bureau Issues Association
PO Box 23707
Belleville, IL 62223-0707

Devoted to the study of all U.S. stamps, principally those produced by the Bureau of Engraving and Printing.

**Junior Philatelists
of America**
Central Office
PO Box 850
Boalsburg, PA 16827-0850

*Publishes a bimonthly
newsletter,* The Philatelic
Observer, *and offers auction,
exchange, pen pal and other
services to young stamp
collectors. Adult supporting
membership and gift
memberships are available.
The Society also publishes
various brochures on stamp
collecting.*

Linn's Stamp Club Center
PO Box 29
Sidney, OH 45365-0029

*Write for the address of a
stamp club near your ZIP
Code. Will also provide
information on specialized
national societies.*

**Mailer's Postmark
Permit Club**
Florence M. Sugarberg
PO Box 5793
Akron, OH 44372-5793

*Publishes bimonthly
newsletter,* Permit Patter,
*which covers all aspects
of mailer's precancel
postmarks, as well as a
catalog and two checklists.*

**Modern Postal
History Society**
Bill DiPaolo
404 Dorado Ct.
High Point, NC 27265-9650

*Emphasizes the collection
and study of postal history,
procedures and rates
beginning with the early
20th century and including
rates as shown by use of
definitive stamps on
commercial covers, modern
markings such as bar codes
and ink-jet postmarks, and
auxiliary markings such as
"Return to Sender," etc.
Publishes the quarterly*
Modern Postal History
Journal.

Philatelic Foundation
501 Fifth Ave. Rm. 1901
New York, NY 10017-6103

*A nonprofit organization
known for its excellent
expertization service.
The Foundation's broad
resources, including
extensive reference
collections, 5,000-volume
library and Expert
Committee, provide collectors
with comprehensive
consumer protection. Slide
and cassette programs are
available on such subjects as
the Pony Express, classic
U.S. stamps, Confederate
Postal History and collecting
basics for beginners. Book
series include expertizing
case histories in* Opinions, *
Foundation seminar
subjects in "textbooks" and
specialized U.S. subjects in
monographs.*

Postal History Society
Kalman V. Illyefalvi
8207 Daren Ct.
Pikesville, MD 21208-2211

*Devoted to the study of
various aspects of the
development of the mails
and local, national and
international postal systems;
Universal Postal Union
treaties; and means of
transporting mail.*

**Souvenir Card
Collectors Society**
Dana M. Marr
PO Box 4155
Tulsa, OK 74159-4155

*Provides member auctions,
a quarterly journal and
access to limited-edition
souvenir cards.*

**United Postal
Stationery Society**
Mrs. Joann Thomas
PO Box 48
Redlands, CA 92373-0601

**Universal Ship
Cancellation Society**
David Kent
PO Box 127
New Britain, CT
06050-0127

*Specializes in naval ship
postmarks.*

Free Periodicals

*The following publications
will send you a free copy of
their magazine or newspaper
upon request:*

Linn's Stamp News
PO Box 29
Sidney, OH 45365-0029

*The largest weekly stamp
newspaper.*

**Mekeel's Weekly Stamp
News and Market Report**
PO Box 5050-fa
White Plains, NY 10602

*World's oldest stamp
weekly, for intermediate and
advanced collectors.*

Stamp Collector
PO Box 10
Albany, OR 97321-0006

*For beginning and advanced
collectors of all ages.*

Stamps Auction News
85 Canisteo St.
Hornell, NY 14843-1544

*The monthly financial
journal of the stamp market.*

Stamps etc.
Philatelic Fulfillment
Service Center
United States Postal Service
Kansas City, MO
64144-9997

*Published quarterly; includes
every philatelic item offered
by the USPS.*

Stamps Magazine
85 Canisteo St.
Hornell, NY 14843-1544

*The weekly magazine of
philately.*

U.S. Stamp News
PO Box 5050-fb
White Plains, NY 10602

*Monthy magazine for all
collectors of U.S. stamps,
covers and postal history.*

Museums, Libraries and Displays

There is no charge to visit any of the following institutions. Please contact them before visiting because their hours may vary.

American Philatelic Research Library
PO Box 8338
State College, PA
                16803-8338

Founded in 1968; now the largest philatelic library in the U.S. Currently receives more than 400 worldwide periodical titles and houses extensive collections of bound journals, books, auction catalogs and dealer pricelists. Directly serves members of the APS and APRL (library members also receive the quarterly Philatelic Literature Review). *The public may purchase photocopies directly or borrow materials through the national interlibrary loan system.*

Cardinal Spellman Philatelic Museum
235 Wellesley St.
Weston, MA 02193-1538

America's first fully accredited museum devoted to the display, collection and preservation of stamps and postal history. It has three galleries of rare stamps, a philatelic library and a post office/philatelic counter. Telephone: (617) 894-6735.

The Collectors Club
22 E. 35th St.
New York, NY 10016-3806

Bimonthly journal, publication of various reference works, one of the most extensive reference libraries in the world, reading and study rooms. Regular meetings on the first and third Wednesdays of each month at 6:30 p.m., except July, August. Telephone: (212) 683-0559.

Friends of the Western Philatelic Library
P.O. Box 2219
Sunnyvale, CA 94087-2219

Hall of Stamps
United States Postal Service
475 L'Enfant Plaza
Washington, DC
                20260-0001

Located at USPS headquarters, this exhibit features more than $500,000 worth of rare U.S. stamps, a moon rock and letter canceled on the moon, original stamp design art, etc.

National Postal Museum
Smithsonian Institution
2 Massachusetts Ave. NE
Washington, DC
                20560-0001

Houses more than 16 million items for exhibition and study purposes. Research may be conducted by appointment only on materials in the collection and library. This new museum, which is housed in the old Washington, D.C. Post Office next to Union Station, opened to the public in mid-1993. Telephone: (202) 633-9360.

The Postal History Foundation
PO Box 40725
Tucson, AZ 85717-0725

Regular services include a library, USPS contract post office, philatelic sales, archives, artifacts and collections and a Youth Department. Membership includes subscription to a quarterly journal, The Heliograph. *Telephone: (602) 623-6652.*

San Diego County Philatelic Library
4133 Poplar St.
San Diego, CA 92105-4541

Western Philatelic Library
Sunnyvale Public Library
665 W. Olive Ave.
Sunnyvale, CA 94086-7622

Wineburgh Philatelic Research Library
University of Texas at Dallas
PO Box 830643
Richardson, TX 75083-0643

Open Monday-Thursday, 9 a.m.– 6 p.m.; Friday, 9 a.m. – 5 p.m.; first Saturday each month (except May and June), 1 p.m. – 5 p.m.

Exchange Service

Stamp Master
PO Box 17
Putnam Hall, FL 32685

An "electronic connection" for philatelists via modem and computer to display/review members' stamp inventories for trading purposes, etc.

Literature

Basic Philately
Stamp Collector
PO Box 10
Albany, OR 97321-0006

Brookman Disney, Baseball & Entertainment Topical Price Guide
Arlene Dunn
Brookman Stamp Company
10 Chestnut Dr.
Bedford, NH 03110-5566

Illustrated, 128-page, perfect-bound book.

1995 Brookman Price Guide of U.S., U.N. and Canada Stamps and Postal Collectibles
Arlene Dunn
Brookman Stamp Company
10 Chestnut Dr.
Bedford, NH 03110-5566

Illustrated, 304-page, perfect-bound catalog.

Catalogue of U.S. Souvenir Cards
Washington Press
2 Vreeland Rd.
Florham Park, NJ
07932-1587

Commemorative Cancellation Catalog
General Image, Inc.
PO Box 335
Maplewood, NJ 07040-0335

Catalog covering all pictorial cancellations used in the U.S. during 1988 to 1990 is available. Please send self-addressed, stamped envelope for prices and description.

Compilation of U.S. Souvenir Cards
PO Box 4155
Tulsa, OK 74159-4155

Durland Plate Number Catalog
c/o: Bureau Issues Association
P.O. Box 23707
Belleville, Il 62223-0707

First Day Cover Catalogue (U.S.-U.N.)
Washington Press
2 Vreeland Rd.
Florham Park, NJ
07932-1587

Includes Presidential Inaugural covers.

Fleetwood's Standard First Day Cover Catalog
Fleetwood
Cheyenne, WY 82008-0001

The Fun of Stamp Collecting
Arlene Dunn
Brookman Stamp Company
10 Chestnut Dr.
Bedford, NH 03110-5566

Illustrated, 96-page, perfect-bound book.

The Hammarskjold Invert
Washington Press
2 Vreeland Rd.
Florham Park, NJ
07932-1587

Tells the story of the Dag Hammarskjold error/invert. FREE for #10 SASE.

Linn's U.S. Stamp Yearbook
PO Box 29
Sidney, OH 45365-0029

A series of annual books providing facts and figures on every collectible variety of U.S. stamps, postal stationery and souvenir cards issued since 1983.

Linn's World Stamp Almanac
P.O. Box 29
Sidney, OH 45365-0029

The most useful single reference source for stamp collectors. Contains detailed information on U.S. stamps.

19th Century Envelopes Catalog
PO Box 48
Redlands, CA 92373-0601

Postage Stamp Identifier and Dictionary of Philatelic Terms
Washington Press
2 Vreeland Rd.
Florham Park, NJ
07932-1587

1992 edition, with new country listings.

Precancel Stamp Society Catalog of U.S. Bureau Precancels
108 Ashwamp Rd.
Scarborough, ME 04074

Precancel Stamp Society Catalog of U.S. Local Precancels
108 Ashwamp Rd.
Scarborough, ME 04074

Scott Specialized Catalogue of U.S. Stamps
PO Box 828
Sidney, OH 45365-8959

Scott Stamp Monthly
PO Box 828
Sidney, OH 45365-8959

Scott Standard Postage Stamp Catalogue
PO Box 828
Sidney, OH 45365-8959

Stamp Collecting Made Easy
PO Box 29
Sidney, OH 45365-0029

An illustrated, easy-to-read, 96-page booklet for beginning collectors.

The 24c 1918 Air Mail Invert
Washington Press
2 Vreeland Rd.
Florham Park, NJ
07932-1587

Tells all there is to know about this famous stamp. FREE for #10 SASE.

20th Century Envelopes Catalog
PO Box 48
Redlands, CA 92373-0601

U.S. Postal Card Catalog
PO Box 48
Redlands, CA 92373-0601

The U.S. Transportation Coils
Washington Press
2 Vreeland Rd.
Florham Park, NJ
07932-1587

FREE for #10 SASE.

Philatelic Centers

In addition to the more than 20,000 postal facilities authorized to sell philatelic products, the U.S. Postal Service also maintains hundreds of Philatelic Centers located in major population centers.

These Philatelic Centers have been established to serve stamp collectors and make it convenient for them to acquire an extensive range of current postage stamps, postal stationery and philatelic products issued by the Postal Service.

Hours of operation vary by location. Centers are located at Main Post Offices unless otherwise indicated. This listing is subject to change.

Note: ZIP + 4 is "XXXXX-9998" unless otherwise indicated.

Alabama
351 N. 24th St.
Birmingham AL 35203-

2000 Riverchase
Galleria
Space 102
Birmingham AL 35244-

307 N. Oates St.
Dothan AL 36302-

615 Clinton Street
Huntsville AL 35801-

250 St. Joseph
Mobile AL 36601-

Downtown Station
135 Catoma St.
Montgomery AL 36104-

Alaska
Downtown Station
3rd & C Streets
Anchorage AK 99510-

Arizona
2400 N. Postal Blvd.
Flagstaff AZ 86004-

Osborn Station -
Philatelic Unit
3905 N. 7th Ave.
Phoenix AZ
85013-9995

General Mail Facility
4949 E. Van Buren
Phoenix AZ 85026-

1501 S. Cherrybell
Tucson AZ 85726-

Arkansas
1020 Garrison Ave.
Fort Smith AR 72901-

Main Office
600 E. Capitol Ave.
Little Rock AR 72202-

California
Holiday Station
1180 W. Ball Road
Anaheim CA 92802-

2730 W. Tregallas Road
Antioch CA 94509-

General Mail Facility
3400 Pegasus Drive
Bakersfield CA 93380-

2000 Allston Way
Berkeley CA 94704-

135 East Olive St.
Burbank CA
91502-1820

Cerritos Branch
18122 Carmencita
Cerritos CA 90703-

6330 Fountains
Square Drive
Citrus Heights CA
95621-

2121 Meridian
Park Blvd.
Concord CA 94520-

2020 Fifth Street
Davis CA 95616-

8111 East Firestone
Downey CA 90241-

401 W. Lexington Ave.
El Cajon CA 92020-

Cutten Station
3901 Walnut Dr.
Eureka CA 95501-

600 Kentucky St.
Fairfield CA 94533-

1900 E St.
Fresno CA 93706-

313 E. Broadway
Glendale CA 91209-

Hillcrest Station
303 E. Hillcrest
Inglewood CA 90311-

5200 Clark Ave
Lakewood CA 90712-

300 Long Beach Blvd
Long Beach CA 90801-

Terminal Annex
900 N. Alameda
Los Angeles CA 90052-

407 C St.
Marysville CA 95901-

18th & K Street
Merced CA 95341-

715 Kearney Ave
Modesto CA 95350-

Civic Center Annex
201 13th St
Oakland CA 94612-

211 Brooks
Oceanside CA 92054-

281 E. Colorado Blvd.
Pasadena CA 91109-

4300 Black Ave.
Pleasanton CA 94566-

2323 Churn Creek Rd.
Redding CA 96049-

1201 N. Catalina
Redondo Beach CA
90277-

Downtown Station
3890 Orange St.
Riverside CA 92501-

330 Vernon St.
Roseville CA 95678-

2000 Royal Oaks Dr.
Sacramento CA
95813-9996

2535 Midway Dr.
San Diego CA 92199-

1750 Meridian Ave.
Retail Specialists
San Jose CA
95101-7027

180 Stewart St.
San Francisco CA
94119-3737

1750 Lundy Ave.
Philatelic Clerk/Main
Office Windows
San Jose CA
95101-9713

1750 Meridian Ave.
San Jose CA 95125-

St. Matthews Station
210 S. Ellsworth
San Mateo CA
94401-9991

Main Station
40 Bellum Blvd.
San Rafael CA 94901-

54

Spurgeon Station
615 North Bush
Santa Ana CA 92701-

836 Anacapa St.
Santa Barbara CA
93102-

201 E. Battles Rd
Santa Maria CA 93454-

730 Second St.
Santa Rosa CA 95404-

3131 Arch Road
Stockton CA 95213-

Hammer Ranch Station
7554 Pacific Ave.
Stockton CA 95213-

200 Prairie Ct.
Vacaville CA 95687-

15701 Sherman Way
Van Nuys CA 91409-

396 S. California Ave.
West Covina CA
91793-

Area Mail Processing
Center
3775 Industrial Blvd.
West Sacramento CA
95647-

Colorado
16890 E. Alameda
Pkwy.
Aurora CO 80017-

1905 15th St.
Boulder CO 80302-

201 E. Pikes Peak
Colorado Springs CO
80901-

Downtown Station
951 20th St.
Denver CO 80202-

222 W. Eighth St.
Durango CO 81301-

241 N. 4th St.
Grand Junction CO
81501-

5733 S. Prince St.
Littleton CO 80120-

421 N. Main St.
Pueblo CO 81003-

Connecticut
Bayview Station
115 Boston Ave.
Bridgeport CT 06610-

141 Weston St.
Hartford CT 06101-

11 Silver St.
Middletown CT 06457-

50 Brewery St.
New Haven CT 06511-

27 Masonic St.
New London CT 06320-

469 Main St.
Ridgefield CT 06877-

421 Atlantic St.
Stamford CT 06904-

135 Grand St.
Waterbury CT 06701-

Delaware
55 The Plaza
Dover DE 19801-

General Mail Facility
147 Quigley Blvd.
New Castle DE 19720-

Federal Station
110 E. Main St.
Newark DE 19711-

Rodney Square Station
1101 N. King St.
Wilmington DE 19850-

District of Columbia
Headquarters Center
475 L'Enfant Plaza SW
Washington DC 20260-

National Capitol Station
North Capitol St. &
Massachusetts Ave.
Washington DC 20002-

Old Post Office Bldg.
1100 Pennsylvania NW.
Washington DC 20004-

Florida
100 South Belcher Road
Clearwater FL 34625-

Daytona Beach GMF
500 Bill France Blvd.
Daytona Beach FL
32114-

1900 W. Oakland Pk.
Fort Lauderdale FL
33310-

2655 N. Airport Rd.
Fort Myers FL 33906-

5000 W. Midway Road
Fort Pierce FL 34981-

4600 SW. 34th St.
Gainesville FL 32608-

1801 Polk St.
Hollywood FL 33022-

1100 Kings Rd.
Jacksonville FL 32203-

Southpoint Station
4150 Belfort Rd.
Jacksonville FL 32255-

210 N. Missouri Ave.
Lakeland FL 33802-

50 8th Ave. SW.
Largo FL 34640-

2200 NW. 72nd Ave.
Miami FL 33152-

1200 Goodlette
Naples FL 33940-

U.S. Postal Service
6550 Nebraska Ave.,
Attn: Philatelic Clerk
New Port Richey FL
34653-

400 SW. 1st Ave.
Ocala FL 34478-

1335 Kingsley Ave.
Orange Park FL 32073-

46 E. Robinson St.
Orlando FL 32801-

421 Jenks Ave.
Panama City FL 32401-

1400 West Jordan St.
Pensacola FL 32501-

1661 Ringling Blvd.
Sarasota FL 34230-

99 King St.
St. Augustine FL 32084-

Open Air Postique
76 Fourth St. N.
St. Petersburg FL 33701-

3135 First Avenue N.
St. Petersburg FL 33730-

2800 S. Adams St.
Tallahassee FL 32301-

5201 W. Spruce St.
Tampa FL 33630-

850 E. Lime St.
Tarpon Springs FL
34689-

3200 Summit Blvd.
West Palm Beach FL
33401-

Georgia
575 Olympic Dr.
P.O. Box 80308
Athens GA 30608-

Downtown Station
101 Marietta St. NW.
Atlanta GA 30301-

Perimeter Mall Shopping
Center
I-285 & Ashford
Dunwoody Rd.
Atlanta GA 30346-

Columbus GMF
3916 Milgen Road
Columbus GA 31901-

3470 McClure Bridge
Rd.
Duluth GA 30136-

364 Green St.
Gainesville GA 30501-

451 College St.
Macon GA 31213-

257 Lawrence St.
Marietta GA 30060-

5600 Spaulding Dr.
Norcross GA 30092-

2 N. Fahm St.
Savannah GA 31402-

904 Russell Pky.
Warner Robins GA
31088-

Hawaii
3600 Aolele St.
Honolulu HI 96819-

Idaho
770 S. 13th St.
Boise ID 83708-

220 E. 5th St.
Moscow ID 83843-

730 E. Clark St.
Pocatello ID 83201-

Illinois
909 W. Euclid Ave.
Arlington Heights IL
60004-

525 N. Broadway
Aurora IL 60507-

Moraine Valley Station
7401 100th Place
Bridgeview IL
60455-2405

1301 E. Main St.
Carbondale IL 62901-

Loop Station
211 S. Clark St.
Chicago IL 60604-

433 W. Van Buren St.
Chicago IL 60607-

1000 E. Oakton
Des Plaines IL 60018-

1101 Davis St.
Evanston IL 60204-

2350 Madison Ave.
Granite City IL 62040-

2000 McDonough St.
Joliet IL 60436-

1750 W. Ogden Ave.
Naperville IL 60566-

123 Indianwood
Park Forest IL 60466-

N. University Station
6310 N. University
Peoria IL 61614-3454

*In addition to these Philatelic Centers, some larger Post Offices have
dedicated "Philatelic" Windows with many current stamps and products.*

401 William
River Forest IL
60305-1900

211 19th St.
Rock Island IL 61201-

5225 Harrison Ave.
Rockford IL 61125-

Schaumburg Station
450 W. Schaumburg Rd.
Schaumburg IL 60194-

2105 E. Cook St.
Springfield IL 62703-

Edison Square Station
1520 Washington
Waukegan IL
60085-5370

1241 Central Ave.
Wilmette IL 60099-

Indiana
3450 State Rd. 26
East Lafayette IN
47901-

North Park Branch
44928 1st Ave.
Evansville IN 47710-

Fort Wayne Postal
Facility
1501 S. Clinton St.
Fort Wayne IN
46802-3509

5530 Sohl St.
Hammond IN 46320-

125 W. South Street
Indianapolis IN 46206-

2719 S. Webster
Kokomo IN 46902-

424 S. Michigan
South Bend IN 46624-

Cross Roads Station
70 Rose Ave.
Terre Haute IN 47803-

Iowa
615 6th Ave. SE.
Cedar Rapids IA
52401-1923

1165 Second Ave.
Des Moines IA 50318-

214 Jackson St.
Sioux City IA
51101-9706

Kansas
6029 Broadmoor
Shawnee Mission KS
66202-

Santa Fe Room
424 S. Kansas Ave.
Topeka KS 66603-

Downtown Station
330 W. 2nd Street
Wichita KS 67202-

Kentucky
100 Nandino Blvd.
Lexington KY
40511-9703

St. Matthews Stamp
Shoppe
4600 Shelbyville Rd.
Louisville KY 40207-

Okolona Branch
7400 Jefferson Blvd.
Louisville KY 40219-

Louisiana
1715 Odom St.
Alexandria LA 71301-

8101 Bluebonnet
Baton Rouge LA 70826-

3301 17th St.
Metairie LA 70009-

501 Sterlington Rd.
Monroe LA 71201-

701 Loyola Ave.
New Orleans LA 70113-

Vieux Carre Station
1022 Iberville St.
New Orleans LA
70112-3145

2400 Texas Ave.
Shreveport LA 71102-

Maine
40 Western Ave.
Augusta ME 04330-

202 Harlow St.
Bangor ME 04401-

125 Forest Ave.
Portland ME 04101-

Maryland
1 Church Cir.
Annapolis MD 21401-

900 E. Fayette St.
Baltimore MD 21233-

Chevy Chase Finance
Unit
5910 Connecticut Ave.
Bethesda MD 20815-

215 Park St.
Cumberland MD 21502-

201 E. Patrick St.
Frederick MD 21701-

44 W. Franklin St.
Hagerstown MD 21740-

500 N. Washington St.
Rockville MD 20850-

816 E. Salisbury Pkwy.
Salisbury MD 21801-

Silver Spring Centre
Finance Station
8455 Colesville Rd.
Silver Spring MD
20911-

Massachusetts
120 Commercial St.
Brockton MA 02402-

2 Government Center
Fall River MA 02722-

881 Main St.
Fitchburg MA 01420-

330 Cochituate Rd.
Framingham MA
01701-

431 Common St.
Lawrence MA 01842-

Main Post Office
Post Office Square
Lowell MA 01853-

695 Pleasant St.
New Bedford MA
02741-

212 Fenn St.
Pittsfield MA 01201-

2 Margin St.
Salem MA 01970-

Main St. Station
1883 Main St.
Springfield MA 01101-

Turner Falls Post Office
178 Ave. A
Turner Falls MA
01376-

462 Washington St.
Woburn MA 01888-

4 E. Central St.
Worcester MA 01613-

Michigan
2075 W. Stadium Blvd.
Ann Arbor MI 48106-

90 S. McCamly
Battle Creek MI 49016-

26200 Ford Rd.
Dearborn Hgts. MI
48127-

1401 W. Fort St.
Detroit MI 48233-

250 E. Boulevard Dr.
Flint MI 48502-

225 Michigan Ave.
Room 101
Grand Rapids MI
49501-9818

200 S.Otsego
Jackson MI 49201-

1121 Miller Rd.
Kalamazoo MI 49001-

General Mail Facility
4800 Collins Rd.
Lansing MI 48924-

735 W. Huron St.
Pontiac MI 48343-

1300 Military St.
Port Huron MI 48060-

30550 Gratiot St.
Roseville MI 48066-

200 W. 2nd St.
Royal Oak MI 48068-

Log Mark Post -
Philatelic Center
1233 S. Washington
Saginaw MI 48605-

6300 N. Wayne Rd.
Westland MI 48185-

Minnesota
Burnsville Branch
12212 12th Avenue S.
Burnsville MN 55337-

2800 W. Michigan
Duluth MN 55806-

Stamp Shoppe
100 S. First St.
Minneapolis MN
55401-9635

Downtown Station
102 S. Broadway
Rochester MN 55904-

Mississippi
2421 13th St.
Gulfport MS 39501-

P.O. Box 332
Jackson MS 39205-9714

500 W. Miln St.
Tupelo MS 38801-

Missouri
401 S. Washington St.
Chillicothe MO 64601-

Columbia Mail Branch
2300 Bernadette Dr.
Columbia MO 65203-

315 Pershing Rd.
Kansas City MO
64108-

500 W. Chestnut Expwy.
Springfield MO 65801-

Northwest Plaza Station
44 Northwest Plaza
St. Ann MO 63074-

Pony Express Station
8th & Edmond
St. Joseph MO 64503-

Trading Post
1720 Market St.
St. Louis MO 63155-

Clayton Branch
7750 Maryland
St. Louis MO 63105-

Montana
841 S. 26th
Billings MT 59101-9614

215 First Ave. N.
Great Falls MT 59401-

1100 W. Kent
Missoula MT 59801-

Nebraska
204 W. South Front St.
Grand Island NE
68801-

700 R St.
Lincoln NE 68501-9804

1124 Pacific
Omaha NE 68108-

300 E. Third St.
North Platte NE 69101-

Nevada
1001 Sunset Rd.
Las Vegas NV 89199-

2000 Vassar St.
Reno NV 89510-

New Hampshire
50 S. Main St.
Hanover NH 03755-

955 Goffs Falls Rd.
Manchester NH 03103-

80 Daniel St.
Portsmouth NH 03801-

New Jersey
1701 Pacific Ave.
Atlantic City NJ 08401-

421 Benigno Blvd.
Bellmawr NJ
08099-9706

25 Veterans Plaza
Bergenfield NJ 07621-

3 Miln St.
Cranford NJ 07016-

229 Main St.
Fort Lee NJ 07024-

Route 35 & Hazlet Ave.
Hazlet NJ 07730-

Borough Complex
East End & Van Sant
Ave.
Island Heights NJ
08732-
69 Montgomery St.
Jersey City NJ 07305-

160 Maplewood Ave.
Maplewood NJ 07040-

150 Ridgedale
Morristown NJ 07960-

86 Bayard St.
New Brunswick NJ
08906-
Federal Square
Newark NJ 07102-

Nutley Branch
372 Franklin Ave.
Nutley NJ 07110-

194 Ward St.
Paterson NJ 07510-

171 Broad St.
Red Bank NJ 07701-

680 Highway 130
Trenton NJ 08650-

Sheffield Station
150 Pompton Plains
Crossroads
Wayne NJ 07470-9994

411 Greenwood Ave.
Wyckoff NJ 07481-

New Mexico
1135 Broadway NE.
Albuquerque NM
87101-

201 E. Las Cruces Ave.
Las Cruces NM 88001-

415 N. Pennsylvania
Ave.
Roswell NM 88201-

New York
Superintendent USPS
Albany NY 12220-

General Mail Facility
30 Old Karner Rd.
Albany NY 12288-

115 Henry St.
Binghamton NY 13902-

Bronx General P.O.
149th St. & Grand
Concourse
Bronx NY 10451-

Parkchester Station
1449 West Ave
Bronx NY 10462-

Riverdale Station
5951 Riverdale Ave.
Bronx NY 10471-

Throggs Neck Station
3630 East Tremont Ave.
Bronx NY 10465-

Wakefield Station
4165 White Plains Rd.
Bronx NY 10466-

Bayridge Station
5501 7th Ave.
Brooklyn NY 11220-

Brooklyn General P.O.
271 Cadman Plaza E.
Brooklyn NY 11201-

Greenpoint Station
66 Meserole Ave.
Brooklyn NY 11222-

Homecrest Station
2002 Ave. U
Brooklyn NY 11229-

1200 William St.
Buffalo NY 14240-

60 Barron DeHirsch Rd.
Crompond NY 10517-

Downtown Station
255 Clemens Center
Pkwy.
Elmira NY 14901-

4165 Main St.
Flushing NY 11351-

77 Old Glenham Rd.
Glenham NY 12527-

185 W. John St.
Hicksville NY 11802-

8840 164th St.
Jamaica NY 11431-

300 E. 3rd St.
Jamestown NY 14701-

324 Broadway
Monticello NY 12701-

Ansonia Station
1980 Broadway
New York NY 10023-

Bowling Green Station
25 Broadway
New York NY 10036-

Church St. Station
90 Church St.
New York NY
10007-9998

Empire State Station
350 Fifth Ave.
New York NY 10001-

F.D.R. Station
909 Third Ave.
New York NY 10022-

Grand Central Station
45th St. & Lexington
Ave.
New York NY 10017-

Madison Square Station
149 E. 23rd St.
New York NY 10010-

New York General P.O.
33rd St. and 8th Ave.
New York NY 10001-

Rockefeller Center
610 Fifth Ave.
New York NY
10020-9991

Times Square Station
340 West 42nd St.
New York NY 10036-

Main St. & Hunt St.
Oneonta NY 13820-

35 S. Main St.
Pearl River NY 10965-

10 Miller St.
Plattsburgh NY 12901-

Branch Office
407 East Main St.
Port Jefferson NY
11777-

55 Mansion St.
Poughkeepsie NY
12601-

250 Merrick Rd.
Rockville Ctr. NY
11570-

1335 Jefferson Rd.
Rochester NY 14692-

29 Jay St.
Schenectady NY 12305-

25 Route 11
Smithtown NY 11787-

New Springville Station.
2843 Richmond Ave.
Staten Island NY
10314-

10 Broad St.
Utica NY 13503-

108 Main St.
Warwick NY 10990-

100 Fisher Ave.
White Plains NY 10602-

7881 Main St.
Yonkers NY 10701-

North Carolina
West Asheville Station
1300 Patton Ave.
Asheville NC
28806-2604

Starmount Station
6241 South Blvd.
Charlotte NC 28210-

1764 Rte. 9
Clifton Park NC
28806-2604
301 Green St.
Fayetteville NC 28302-

Four Seasons Town Ctr.
Ste. 303
Greensboro NC 27427-

311 New Bern Ave.
Raleigh NC 27611-

*In addition to these Philatelic Centers, some larger Post Offices have
dedicated "Philatelic" Windows with many current stamps and products.*

57

North Dakota
220 East Rosser Ave.
Bismarck ND 58501-

675 2nd Ave. N.
Fargo ND 58102-

Ohio
675 Wolf Ledges Pky.
Akron OH 44309-

4420 Dressler Rd.
Canton OH 44718-

Queen City Station
525 Vine St.
Cincinnati OH 45202-

2400 Orange Ave.
Cleveland OH 44101-

6316 Nicholas Drive
Columbus OH 43235-

1111 E. 5th St.
Dayton OH 45401-

345 E. Bridge St.
Elyria OH 44035-

105 Court St.
Hamilton OH 45011-

200 N. Diamond St.
Mansfield OH 44901-

435 S. St. Clair St.
Toledo OH 43601-

200 N. 4th St.
Steubenville OH
43952-2104

99 S. Walnut St.
Youngstown OH
44503-

Oklahoma
208 First Street SW.
Ardmore OK 73401-

101 E. First
Edmond OK 73034-

115 W. Broadway
Enid OK 73701-

501 S.W. 5th St.
Lawton OK 73501-

525 W. Okmulgee
Muskogee OK 74401-

129 W. Gray
Norman OK 73069-

320 SW. 5th St.
Oklahoma City OK
73125-

333 W. 4th, 1st Flr.
Tulsa OK 74103-9612

12 S. 5th
Yukon OK 73099-

Oregon
311 SW 2nd St.
Corvallis OR 97333-

520 Willamette St.
Eugene OR 97401-2627

715 N.W. Hoyt
Portland OR 97208-

1050 25th St. S.E.
Salem OR 97301-

Pennsylvania
442 W. Hamilton St.
Allentown PA
18101-1611

535 Wood St.
Bethlehem PA 18016-

115 Boylston St.
Bradford PA 16701-

Philatelic Center
44 N. Brady St.
Du Bois PA 15801-

Downtown Station
1314 Griswold Plaza
Erie PA 16501-

115 Buford Ave.
Gettysburg PA 17325-

238 S. Pennsylvania
Greensburg PA 15601-

10th and Market St.
Harrisburg PA 17105-

Johnstown Main Post
Office
111 Franklin St.
Johnstown PA 15901-

Downtown Station
48-50 W. Chestnut St.
Lancaster PA 17603-

Langhorne Post Office
980 Wheeler Way
Langhorne PA 19047-

980 Wheeler Way
Langhorne PA 19047-

Lehigh Valley Branch
17 S. Commerce Way
Lehigh Valley PA
18002-9610

Monroeville Mall
Branch
348 Mall Circle Dr.
Monroeville PA 15146-

435 S. Cascade St.
New Castle PA 16101-

501 11th St.
New Kensington PA
15068-

28 East Airy St.
Norristown PA 19401-

B. Free Franklin
316 Market St.
Philadelphia PA
19106-9996

William Penn Annex
900 Market St.
Philadelphia PA 19107-

Main Office
Philadelphia
2970 Market St.
Philadelphia PA 19104-

Franklin Station
316 Market St.
Philadelphia PA 19106-

William Penn Annex
Station
9th & Chestnut St.
Philadelphia PA 19107-

Main Post Office
Pittsburgh PA 15219-

General Mail Facility -
Finance Station
1001 California Ave.,
Rm 1002
Pittsburgh PA 15233-

59 N. 5th St.
Reading PA 19603-

Steamtown Station -
Postal Retail Store
100 The Mall at
Steamtown
Scranton PA 18502-

237 S. Frazer St.
State College PA 16801-

701 Ann St.
Stroudsburg PA 18360-

300 S. Main St.
Wilkes Barre PA 18701-

Center City Finance
Station 240 West
Third St.
Williamsport PA
17703-

200 S. George St.
York PA 17405-

Puerto Rico
General Post Office
Roosevelt Ave.
San Juan PR 00936-

Plaza Las Americas
Station
San Juan PR 00938-

Rhode Island
320 Thames St.
Newport RI 02840-

40 Montgomery St.
Pawtucket RI 02860-

24 Corliss St.
Providence RI 02904-

South Carolina
Cross County Branch
7075 Cross County Rd.
Charleston SC
29423-9615

1601 Assembly St.
Columbia SC 29201-

600 W. Washington
Greenville SC 29602-

South Dakota
500 E. Boulevard
Rapid City SD 57701-

320 S. 2nd Ave.
Sioux Falls SD 57101-

Tennessee
5424 Bell Forge Lane E.
Antioch TN 37013-

111 Sixth St.
Bristol TN 37620-

General Facility
6050 Shallowford Rd.
Chattanooga TN 37421-

200 Martin Luther King
Jr. Blvd.
Jackson TN 38301-

530 E. Main St.
Johnson City TN 37601-

General Mail Facility
1237 E. Weisgarber Rd.
Knoxville TN
37950-9608

Colonial Finance Unit
4695 Southern Ave.
Memphis TN 38124-

Downtown Station
510 Guadalupe
Memphis TN
38701-3725

901 Broadway
Nashville TN 37202-

Texas
341 Pine St.
Abilene TX 79604-

2301 Ross St.
Amarillo TX 79120-

300 E. South St.
Arlington TX 76010-

Downtown Station -
Philatelic Store
510 Guadalupe
Austin TX 78701-

300 Willow
Beaumont TX 77704-

1535 Los Ebanos
Brownsville TX 78520-

2121 E. Wm. J. Bryan
Pky.
Bryan TX 77801-

2201 Hilltop Dr.
College Station TX
77840-

809 Nueces Bay Blvd.
Corpus Christi TX
78469-0703

Byran St. and Ervay St.
Dallas TX 75221-

Olla Podrida Finance
Station
12215 Coit Rd.
Dallas TX 75251-

5300 E. Paisano Dr.
El Paso TX 79910-

251 W. Lancaster
Fort Worth TX 76102-

Postique
401 Franklin Ave.
Houston TX
77201-9718

Central Station
2300 W. Story Rd.
Irving TX 75038-

300 N. 10th
Killeen TX 76541-

411 Ave. L
Lubbock TX 79408-

620 E. Pecan
McAllen TX 78501-

100 E. Wall
Midland TX 79702-

433 Belle Grove
Richardson TX 75080-

1 N. Bryant
San Angelo TX 76902-

Downtown Station
615 E. Houston St.
San Antonio TX 78205-

10410 Perrin Beitel Rd.
San Antonio TX 78284-

1411 Wunsche Loop
Spring TX 77373-

2211 N. Robinson
Texarkana TX 75501-

221 W. Ferguson
Tyler TX 75702-

800 Franklin
Waco TX 76701-

1000 Lamar St.
Wichita Falls TX 76307-

Utah
3680 Pacific Ave.
Ogden UT 84401-

1760 W. 2100 S.
Salt Lake City UT
84199-9811

Vermont
204 Main St.
Brattleboro VT 05301-

1 Elmwood Ave.
Burlington VT 05401-

White River
Junction VT 05001-

151 West St.
Rutland VT 05701-2859

Virginia
111 Sixth St.
Bristol VA 24201-

1155 Seminole Trail
Charlottesville VA
22906-

1425 Battlefield Blvd. N.
Chesapeake VA 23320-

700 Main St.
Danville VA 24541-

Merrifield Branch
8409 Lee Hwy.
Fairfax VA 22116-

809 Aberdeen Rd.
Hampton VA 23670-

3300 Odd Fellows Rd.
Lynchburg VA 24506-

Denbigh Station
14104 Warwick Blvd.
Newport News VA
23602-

600 Church St.
Norfolk VA 23501-

Thomas Corner Station
190 Janaf Shopping
Center
Norfolk VA 23502-

1801 Brook Rd.
Richmond VA 23232-

419 Rutherford Ave. NE.
Roanoke VA 24022-

1430 N. Augusta
Staunton VA 24401-

501 Viking Dr.
Virginia Beach VA
23452-

Washington
11 3rd St. NW.
Auburn WA 98001-

Main Office
1171 Bellevue Way N.E.
Bellevue WA 98009-

315 Prospect St.
Bellingham WA 98225-

3102 Hoyt
Everett WA 98201-

3500 W. Court
Pasco WA 99301-4532

424 E. 1st St.
Port Angeles WA
98362-

301 Union St.
Seattle WA 98101-

W. 904 Riverside
Spokane WA 99210-

1102 A St.
Tacoma WA 98402-

205W. Washington
Yakima WA 98903-

West Virginia
301 North St.
Bluefield WV
24701-4307

Town Center Station
1057 Charleston Town
Center
Charleston WV
25389-1057

500 W. Pike St.
Clarksburg WV
26301-2664

1000 Virginia Ave.W.
Huntington WV
25704-1726

217 King St.
Martinsburg WV
25401-

Wisconsin
126 N. Barstow St.
Eau Claire WI 54703-

325 E. Walnut
Green Bay WI 54301-

425 State St.
La Crosse WI 54601-

P.O. Box 7333
Madison WI
53707-7333

345 W. St. Paul Ave.
Milwaukee WI 53203-

1025 W. 20th Ave.
Oshkosh WI 54901-

235 Forrest St.
Wausau WI 54401-

Wyoming
150 E. B Street
Casper WY 82601-

2120 Capitol Ave.
Cheyenne WY 82001-

FOREIGN CENTERS
U.S. Postal Service stamps and products are available at face value from agencies in foreign countries, as follows:

Australia
Max Stern & Co.
Port Phillip Arcade
234 Flinders St.
Melbourne 3000

Denmark
Nordfrim
DK 5450 Otterup

France
Theodore Champion
8 Rue des Messageries
75010 Paris

Germany
Hermann W. Sieger
Venusberg 3234
73545 Lorch/
Wurttemberg

Great Britain
Harry Allen
P. O. Box 5
Watford, Herts
WD2 5SW

Japan
Japan Philatelic Agency
P. O. Box 350
Shinjuku
Tokyo 163-91

Netherlands
J.A. Visser
P. O. Box 184
3300 Ad Dordrecht

Switzerland
De Rosa International
S.A.
Av Du Tribunal
Federal 34
Ch-1005 Lausanne

Your local Post Office may be able to direct you to the nearest "Philatelic" Window, Philatelic Center or Postal Store (new, state-of-the-art facilities formerly called "Store of the Future").

Explanation of Catalog Prices

The United States Postal Service sells only the commemoratives released during the past few years, current regular and special stamps, and current postal stationery.

Prices in this book are called "catalog prices" by stamp collectors. Collectors use catalog prices as guidelines when buying or trading stamps. It is important to remember the prices are simply guidelines to the stamp values. Stamp condition (see pp 10-11) is very important in determining the actual value of a stamp.

Condition Affects Value

The catalog prices are given for unused (mint) stamps and used (canceled) stamps, which have been hinged and are in Fine – Very Fine condition. Stamps in Superb condition that have never been hinged may cost more than the listed price. Stamps in less than Fine condition may cost less.

The prices for used stamps are based on a light cancellation; a heavy cancellation lessens a stamp's value. Canceled stamps may be worth more than uncanceled stamps. This happens if the cancellation is of a special type or for a significant date. Therefore, it is important to study an envelope before removing a stamp and discarding its "cover."

Prices Are Estimated

Listed prices are estimates of how much you can expect to pay for a stamp from a dealer. A 15-cent minimum valuation has been established which represents a fair-market price to have a dealer locate and provide a single stamp to a customer. Dealers may charge less per stamp to provide a group of such stamps, and may charge less for such a single stamp. Similarly, a $1.00 minimum has been established for First Day Covers (FDCs). If you sell a stamp to a dealer, he or she may offer you much less than the catalog price. Dealers pay based on their interest in owning a particular stamp. If they already have a full supply, they may only buy additional stamps at a low price.

Sample Listing

		Un	U	PB/LP/PNC	#	FDC	Q
2636	29¢ Kentucky Statehood, June 1	.00	.00	0.00	( )	0.00	000,000,000

Scott Catalog Number (bold type indicates stamp is pictured)

Description Denomination

First Day of Issue

Unused Catalog Price

Used Catalog Price

Plate Block Price, Line Pair Price or Plate Number Coil Price

# of stamps in Plate Block, Line Pair or Plate Number Coil

First Day Cover Price

Quantity Issued (where known)

29 USA Kentucky 1792
My Old Kentucky Home State Park

#2636

Understanding the Listings

- Prices in regular type for single unused and used stamps are taken from the *Scott 1996 Standard Postage Stamp Catalogue*, Volume 1A, ©1995, whose editors have based these prices on **actual retail values** as they found them in the marketplace. The Scott numbering system for stamps is used in this book. Prices quoted for unused and used stamps are for "Fine" condition, except where Fine is not available.

- Stamp values in *italic* generally refer to items difficult to value accurately.

- A dash (—) in a value column means the item is known to exist but information is insufficient for establishing a value.

- The stamp listings contain a number of additions designated "a," "b," "c," etc. These represent recognized variations of stamps as well as errors. These listings are as complete as space permits.

- Occasionally, a new stamp or major variation may be inserted by the catalog editors into a series or sequence where it was not originally anticipated. These additions are identified by capital letters "A," "B" and so forth. For example, a new stamp which logically belonged between #1044 and 1045 is designated 1044A, even though it is entirely different from 1044. The insertion was preferable to a complete renumbering of the series.

- Prices for Plate Blocks, First Day Covers, American Commemorative Panels and Souvenir Pages are taken from *Scott 1995 Specialized Catalogue of U.S. Stamps*, ©1994.

Sample Variation Listing

			Un	U	PB/LP/PNC	#	FDC	Q
2281	25¢	Honeybee, Sept. 2	.45	.15	3.75	(3)	1.00	000,000,000
a		Imperf. pair	*45.00*					
b		Black omitted	*100.00*					
d		Pair, imperf. between	—					

Scott Catalog Number (bold type indicates stamp is pictured)

Denomination

Description

First Day of Issue

Unused Catalog Price

Used Catalog Price

Plate Block Price, Line Pair Price or Plate Number Coil Price

# of stamps in Plate Block, Line Pair or Plate Number Coil

First Day Cover Price

Quantity Issued (where known)

25 USA

#2281

Commemorative and Definitive Stamps

1847-1861

 1

 2

 3

 4

5 11

12 14 17

*For additional details and distinguishing characteristics
of stamps, see pages 64 and 65. This information has
now been positioned near the appropriate stamp listings
for better, quicker reference.*

Issues of 1847	Un	U
Thin, Bluish Wove Paper, July 1, Imperf., Unwmkd.		
1 5¢ Benjamin Franklin	4,500.00	425.00
b 5¢ orange brown	5,000.00	525.00
c 5¢ red orange	10,000.00	4,000.00
Pen cancel	—	225.00
Double transfer of top, or top and bottom, or bottom and lower left frame lines		525.00
Double transfer of top, bottom and left frame lines and numerals		900.00
2 10¢ George Washington	20,000.00	1050.00
Pen cancel	—	450.00
Vertical line through second "F" of "OFFICE," or with "stick pin" in tie, or with "harelip," or double transfer in lower right "X," or in "POST OFFICE," or of left and bottom frame lines	—	1,150.00

Issues of 1875, Reproductions of 1 and 2, Bluish Paper, Without Gum

3 5¢ Franklin	700.00	—
4 10¢ Washington	900.00	—

5¢. On the original, the left side of the white shirt frill touches the oval on a level with the top of the "F" of "Five." On the reproduction, it touches the oval about on a level with the top of the figure "5."

10¢. On the reproduction, line of coat at left points to right of "X" and line of coat at right points to center of "S" of CENTS. On the original, line of coat points to "T" of TEN and between "T" and "S" of CENTS.

On the reproduction, the eyes have a sleepy look, the line of the mouth is straighter and in the curl of hair near the left cheek is a strong black dot, while the original has only a faint one.

Issues of 1851-57, Imperf.		
5 1¢ Franklin, type I	175,000.00	17,500.00
5A 1¢ blue, type Ib	9,000.00	4,000.00
#6-9: Franklin (5), 1851		
6 1¢ dark blue, type Ia	22,500.00	6,000.00
7 1¢ blue, type II	575.00	115.00
Cracked plate	750.00	275.00
8 1¢ blue, type III	7,000.00	1,600.00
8A 1¢ pale blue, type IIIa	2,500.00	650.00
9 1¢ blue, type IV	425.00	90.00
Triple transfer, one inverted	550.00	125.00

#10-11, 25-26a all had plates on which at least four outer frame lines (and usually much more) were recut, adding to their value.

Issues of 1851-57 Imperf.	Un	U
10 3¢ orange brown Washington, type I (11)	1,600.00	45.00
3¢ copper brown	1,500.00	75.00
On part-India paper		250.00
11 3¢ Washington, type I	130.00	7.00
3¢ deep claret	185.00	13.50
Double transfer, "GENTS" for "CENTS"	200.00	25.00
12 5¢ Jefferson, type I	11,000.00	875.00
13 10¢ green Washington, type I (14)	9,500.00	575.00
14 10¢ green, type II	2,200.00	190.00
15 10¢ Washington, type III	2,200.00	190.00
16 10¢ green, type IV (14)	12,500.00	1,200.00
17 12¢ Washington	2,800.00	225.00

Issues of 1857-61, Perf. 15.5 (Issued in 1857 except #18, 27, 28A, 29, 30, 30A, 35, 36b, 37, 38, 39)

#18-24: Franklin (5)		
18 1¢ blue, type I	800.00	325.00
19 1¢ blue, type Ia	11,500.00	3,250.00
20 1¢ blue, type II	500.00	160.00
21 1¢ blue, type III	5,000.00	1,100.00
22 1¢ blue, type IIIa	850.00	300.00
23 1¢ blue, type IV	3,000.00	375.00
24 1¢ blue, type V	120.00	25.00
"Curl" on shoulder	150.00	37.50
"Earring" below ear	200.00	52.50
Long double "curl" in hair	185.00	42.50
b Laid paper		—
#25-26a: Washington (11)		
25 3¢ rose, type I	1,050.00	35.00
Cracked plate	1,200.00	175.00
26 3¢ dull red, type II	40.00	3.00
3¢ brownish carmine	75.00	10.00
3¢ claret	90.00	12.50
Left or right frame line double	60.00	8.75
Cracked plate	475.00	150.00
26a 3¢ dull red, type IIa	125.00	25.00
Double transfer	175.00	45.00
Left frame line double	—	65.00

1¢ Franklin Types I–V, series 1851-57, 1857-61, 1875

5

Bust of Benjamin Franklin

Detail of **#5, 18, 40** Type I

Has curved, unbroken lines outside labels. Scrollwork is substantially complete at top, forms little balls at bottom.

Detail of **#6, 19** Type Ia

Same as Type I at bottom but top ornaments and outer line partly cut away. Lower scrollwork is complete.

Detail of **#5A** Type Ib

Lower scrollwork is incomplete, the little balls are not so clear.

Detail of **#7, 20** Type II

Lower scrollwork incomplete (lacks little balls and lower plume ornaments). Side ornaments are complete.

Detail of **#8, 21** Type III

Outer lines broken in the middle. Side ornaments are substantially complete.

Detail of **#8A, 22** Type IIIa

Outer lines broken top or bottom but not both.

Detail of **#9, 23** Type IV

Similar to Type II, but outer lines recut top, bottom or both.

Detail of **#24** Type V

Similar to Type III of 1851-57 but with side ornaments partly cut away.

3¢ Washington Types I-IIa, series 1851-57, 1857-61, 1875

10

Bust of George Washington

Detail of **#26** Type II

The outer frame line has been removed at top and bottom. The side frame lines were recut so as to be continuous from the top to the bottom of the plate.

Detail of **#26a** Type IIa

The side frame lines extended only to the bottom of the stamp design.

Detail of **#10, 11, 25, 41** Type I

There is an outer frame line at top and bottom.

5¢ Jefferson Types I-II, Series 1851-57, 1857-61

12

Portrait of Thomas Jefferson

Detail of **#12, 27-29** Type I

There are projections on all four sides.

Detail of **#30-30A** Type II

The projections at top and bottom are partly cut away.

10¢ Washington Types I-IV, series 1851-57, 1857-61, 1875

Portrait of George Washington

15

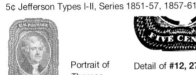

Detail of **#14, 32** Type II

The design is complete at the top. The outer line at the bottom is broken in the middle. The shells are partly cut away.

Detail of **#16, 34** Type IV

The outer lines have been re-cut at top or bottom or both. Types I, II, III and IV have complete ornaments at the sides of the stamps and three pearls at each outer edge of the bottom panel.

Detail of **#15, 33** Type III

The outer lines are broken above the top label and the "X" numerals. The outer line at the bottom and the shells are partly cut away, as in Type II.

Detail of **#13, 31, 43** Type I

The "shells" at the lower corners are practically complete. The outer line below the label is very nearly complete. The outer lines are broken above the middle of the top label and the "X" in each upper corner.

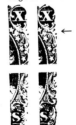

Detail of **#35** Type V

(Two typical examples). Side ornaments slightly cut away. Outer lines complete at top except over right "X". Outer lines complete at bottom and shells nearly so.

Issues of 1857-61	Un	U
Perf. 15.5		
#27-29: Jefferson (12)		
27 5¢ brick red, type I	*9,000.00*	625.00
28 5¢ red brown, type I	1,500.00	275.00
b 5¢ brt. red brn., type I	1,850.00	400.00
28A 5¢ Indian red, type I	*12,500.00*	1,800.00
29 5¢ brown, type I	950.00	200.00
Defective transfer	—	—
30 5¢ orange brown, type II	775.00	1,050.00
30A 5¢ brown, type II (30)	650.00	185.00
b Printed on both sides	*3,750.00*	*4,000.00*
#31-35: Washington (15)		
31 10¢ green, type I	8,000.00	500.00
32 10¢ green, type II	2,800.00	190.00
33 10¢ green, type III	2,800.00	190.00
"Curl" on forehead or in left "X"	—	225.00
34 10¢ green, type IV	*17,500.00*	1,400.00
35 10¢ green, type V	200.00	50.00
Small "curl" on forehead	235.00	60.00
"Curl" in "e" or "t" of "Cents"	250.00	70.00
Plate I—Outer frame lines complete.		
36 12¢ blk. Washington (17), plate I	400.00	105.00
Triple transfer	525.00	—
36b 12¢ black, plate III	350.00	100.00
Vertical line through rosette	450.00	145.00
37 24¢ gray lilac	700.00	210.00
a 24¢ gray	675.00	200.00
b 24¢ red lilac	1,000.00	
38 30¢ orange Franklin	850.00	300.00
Recut at bottom	900.00	400.00
39 90¢ blue Washington	1,250.00	*5,000.00*
Double transfer at top or bottom	1,250.00	—
90¢ Same, with pen cancel		1,100.00

Note: Beware of forged cancellations of #39. Genuine cancellations are rare.

Issues of 1875-61	Un	U
Issues of 1875, Government Reprints, White Paper, Without Gum, Perf. 12		
40 1¢ bright blue Franklin (5)	*450.00*	
41 3¢ scarlet Wash. (11)	*1,800.00*	
42 5¢ orange brown Jefferson (30)	*800.00*	
43 10¢ blue green Washington (14)	*1,750.00*	
44 12¢ greenish black Washington (17)	*2,000.00*	
45 24¢ blackish violet Washington (37)	*2,000.00*	
46 30¢ yellow orange Franklin (38)	*2,000.00*	
47 90¢ deep blue Washington (39)	*3,250.00*	
48-54 Not assigned		
Issue of 1861, Thin, Semi-Transparent Paper		
#55-62 are no longer considered postage stamps. Many experts consider them to be essays and/or trial color proofs.		
55 1¢ Franklin (see #63)		
56 3¢ Washington (see #65)		
58 10¢ Washington (see #68)		
59 12¢ Washington (see #69)		
60 24¢ Washington (see #70)		
61 30¢ Franklin (see #71)		
62 90¢ Washington (see #72)		
62B 10¢ dark green Washington (58)	*4,500.00*	450.00
Double transfer	*5,500.00*	525.00

More stamps than anyone in history

"First in war, first in peace, and first in the hearts of his countrymen," wrote Henry Lee in his famous eulogy of George Washington, his confidant and fellow soldier. Washington (1732-1799) is also first in stamp annals. You'll find his likeness on more U.S. stamps than that of any other individual. Celebrated as "Father of His Country," his leadership made the American Revolution and the new republic possible. Chosen unanimously as first President of the United States (1789-1797), Washington served two terms and refused a third term. **(#62, #72)**

30

37

38

39

40

62B

Have you noticed? The Perf listings have changed from fractions to decimals. For example, Perf 10-1/2 is now 10.5. This is the first step taken toward giving you a more precise perf gauge which currently may only be precise to the nearest 0.5.

63   **64**   **65**   **67**

68   **69**   **70**   **71**

72   **73**   **77**

Details

Issues of 1861-62, 1861-66, 1867 and 1875

Detail of **#63, 86, 92**

There is a dash in 63, 86 and 92 added under the tip of the ornament at the right of the numeral in upper left corner.

Detail of **#67, 75, 80, 95**

There is a leaf in 67, 75, 80 and 95 added to the foliated ornaments at each corner.

Detail of **#69, 85E, 90, 97**

In 69, 85E, 90 and 97, ovals and scrolls have been added at the corners.

Detail of **#64-66, 74, 79, 82-83, 85, 85C, 88, 94**

In 64-66, 74, 79, 82-83, 85, 85C, 88 and 94, ornaments at corners have been enlarged and end in a small ball.

Detail of **#68, 85D, 89, 96**

There is an outer line in 68, 85D, 89 and 96 cut below the stars and an outer line added to the ornaments above them.

Detail of **#72, 101**

In 72 and 101, parallel lines form an angle above the ribbon containing "U.S. Postage"; between these lines a row of dashes has been added, along with a point of color to the apex of the lower line.

Issues of 1861-62		Un	U
Perf. 12			
63	1¢ blue Franklin	150.00	15.00
a	1¢ ultramarine	400.00	125.00
b	1¢ dark blue	350.00	40.00
c	Laid paper	—	—
d	Vert. pair, imperf. horiz.		—
e	Printed on both sides	—	2,500.00
	Double transfer		22.50
	Dot in "U"	150.00	17.50
64	3¢ pink Washington	4,500.00	450.00
a	3¢ pigeon blood pink	10,000.00	2,500.00
b	3¢ rose pink	300.00	90.00
65	3¢ rose Washington	90.00	1.00
b	Laid paper	—	—
d	Vertical pair, imperf. horizontally	3,500.00	750.00
e	Printed on both sides	1,650.00	1,000.00
f	Double impression		6,000.00
	Cracked plate	—	—
	Double transfer	85.00	2.50
66	3¢ lake Washington	1,650.00	
	Double transfer	2,000.00	
67	5¢ buff Jefferson	9,000.00	425.00
68	10¢ yellow green Washington	300.00	30.00
	10¢ deep yellow green on thin paper	350.00	40.00
a	10¢ dark green	325.00	32.50
b	Vert. pair, imperf. horiz.		3,500.00
	Double transfer	325.00	40.00
69	12¢ blk. Washington	550.00	60.00
	12¢ intense black	575.00	60.00
	Double transfer of top or bottom frame line	575.00	65.00
	Double transfer of top and bottom frame lines	600.00	70.00
70	24¢ red lilac Washington	850.00	90.00
a	24¢ brown lilac	750.00	80.00
b	24¢ steel blue	5,000.00	300.00
c	24¢ violet	7,000.00	650.00
d	24¢ grayish lilac	1,400.00	350.00
	Scratch under "A" of "POSTAGE"		—
71	30¢ orange Franklin	650.00	72.50
a	Printed on both sides		—
72	90¢ bl. Washington	1,450.00	250.00
b	90¢ dark blue	1,600.00	300.00
73	2¢ blk. Andrew Jackson	175.00	22.50
	Double transfer	200.00	25.00
	Major double transfer of top left corner and "POSTAGE"		6,000.00
	Cracked plate	—	—

Issues of 1861-66		Un	U
Perf. 12			
	#74 was not regularly issued.		
74	3¢ scarlet Washington (65)	6,500.00	
75	5¢ red brown Jefferson (67)	2,000.00	250.00
76	5¢ brown Jefferson (67)	500.00	72.50
a	5¢ dark brown	600.00	90.00
	Double transfer of top or bottom frame line	425.00	80.00
77	15¢ blk. Abraham Lincoln	700.00	75.00
	Double transfer	600.00	75.00
78	24¢ lilac Washington (70)	425.00	60.00
c	24¢ black violet	17,500.00	1,100.00
	Scratch under "A" of "POSTAGE"	—	—

Grills on U.S. Stamps

Between 1867 and 1870, postage stamps were embossed with pyramid-shaped grills that absorbed cancellation ink to prevent reuse of canceled stamps.

Issues of 1867, With Grills

Grills A, B, C: Points Up

A. Grill Covers Entire Stamp			
79	3¢ rose Washington (56)	2,25.00	575.00
b	Printed on both sides		—
80	5¢ brown Jefferson (57)	—	—
a	5¢ dark brown		50,000.00
81	30¢ orange Franklin (61)		—
B. Grill about 18 x 15mm			
82	3¢ rose Washington (56)		95,000.00
C. Grill about 13 x 16mm			
83	3¢ rose Washington (56)	3,000.00	600.00
	Double grill	4,000.00	1,500.00
	Grills, D, Z, E, F: Points Down		
D. Grill about 12 x 14mm			
84	2¢ black Jackson (73)	9,500.00	1,500.00
85	3¢ rose Washington (56)	3,000.00	475.00
	Split grill		500.00
Z. Grill about 11 x 14mm			
85A	1¢ blue Franklin (55)		—
85B	2¢ black Jackson (73)	3,000.00	400.00
	Double transfer	2,000.00	425.00
85C	3¢ rose Washington (56)	5,000.00	1,200.00
	Double grill	6,000.00	
85D	10¢ grn. Washington (58)		45,000.00
85E	12¢ blk. Washington (59)	4,000.00	600.00
	Double transfer of top frame line		625.00
85F	15¢ black Lincoln (77)		100,000.00
E. Grill about 11 x 13mm			
86	1¢ blue Franklin (55)	1,100.00	275.00
	Double grill	—	375.00
	Split grill	1,050.00	275.00

Issues of 1867	Un	U
With Grills, Perf. 12		
87	2¢ black Jackson (73)	500.00	70.00
	2¢ intense black	475.00	75.00
	Double grill	—	—
	Double transfer	475.00	75.00
88	3¢ rose Washington (65)	375.00	10.00
a	3¢ lake red	425.00	12.50
	Double grill	—	—
	Very thin paper	375.00	11.00
89	10¢ grn. Washington (68)	2,000.00	200.00
	Double grill	2,500.00	300.00
90	12¢ blk. Washington (69)	2,250.00	200.00
	Double transfer of top or bottom frame line	2,100.00	220.00
91	15¢ black Lincoln (77)	4,250.00	450.00
	Double grill	—	700.00

F. Grill about 9 x 13mm		
92	1¢ blue Franklin (63)	525.00	110.00
	Double transfer	475.00	120.00
	Double grill	—	200.00
93	2¢ black Jackson (73)	200.00	25.00
	Double grill	—	100.00
	Very thin paper	190.00	30.00
94	3¢ red Washington (65)	175.00	2.50
c	Vertical pair, imperf. horizontally	1,000.00	
d	Printed on both sides	1,100.00	
	Double grill	—	—
	End roller grill		200.00
	Quadruple split grill	275.00	75.00
95	5¢ brown Jefferson (67)	1,500.00	300.00
a	5¢ dark brown	1,750.00	325.00
	Double transfer of top frame line	—	—
	Double grill	—	—
96	10¢ yellow green Washington (68)	1,200.00	110.00
	Double transfer	—	—
	Quadruple split grill		350.00
97	12¢ blk. Washington (69)	1,500.00	125.00
	Double transfer of top or bottom frame line	950.00	135.00
	Triple grill	—	
98	15¢ black Lincoln (77)	1,500.00	185.00
	Double transfer of upper right corner	—	—
	Double grill	—	250.00
	Quadruple split grill	1,750.00	350.00
99	24¢ gray lilac Washington (70)	2,000.00	450.00
100	30¢ orange Franklin (71)	2,750.00	425.00
	Double grill	3,000.00	700.00
101	90¢ bl. Washington (72)	5,000.00	800.00
	Double grill	7,000.00	

Issues of 1875	Un	U
Reissue of 1861-66 Issue, Without Grill, Perf. 12		
102	1¢ blue Franklin (63)	500.00	800.00
103	2¢ black Jackson (73)	2,000.00	4,000.00
104	3¢ brown red Washington (65)	2,250.00	4,250.00
105	5¢ brown Jefferson (67)	1,750.00	2,250.00
106	10¢ grn. Washington (68)	2,000.00	3,750.00
107	12¢ blk. Washington (69)	2,750.00	4,500.00
108	15¢ black Lincoln (77)	2,750.00	4,750.00
109	24¢ deep violet Washington (70)	3,250.00	6,000.00
110	30¢ brownish orange Franklin (71)	3,500.00	6,000.00
111	90¢ bl. Washington (72)	4,750.00	20,000.00

Issues of 1869, With Grill		
G. Grill about 9 1/2 x 9mm		
112	1¢ Franklin, Mar. 27	275.00	65.00
b	Without grill	850.00	
	Double grill	450.00	150.00
113	2¢ br. Post Rider, Mar. 27	225.00	25.00
	Split grill	225.00	35.00
	Double transfer		30.00
114	3¢ Locomotive, Mar. 27	175.00	7.00
a	Without grill	600.00	
d	Double impression		3,500.00
	Triple grill	—	—
	Sextuple grill	2,000.00	
	Gray paper	—	—
115	6¢ Washington	950.00	100.00
	Quadruple split grill	—	400.00
116	10¢ Shield and Eagle	1,000.00	90.00
	End roller grill	—	—
117	12¢ S.S. Adriatic, Apr. 5	950.00	100.00
	Split grill	850.00	105.00
118	15¢ Columbus Landing, type I, Apr. 2	2,750.00	400.00
119	15¢ type II (118)	1,100.00	150.00
b	Center inverted	220,000.00	16,000.00
c	Center double, one inverted		—
120	24¢ Declaration of Independence, Apr. 7	4,000.00	500.00
b	Center inverted	220,000.00	15,000.00
121	30¢ Shield, Eagle and Flags, May 15	3,000.00	475.00
b	Flags inverted	165,000.00	55,000.00
	Double grill	—	500.00
122	90¢ Lincoln	5,000.00	1,200.00
	Split grill	—	

Issues of 1875, Reissue of 1869 Issue, Without Grill, Hard, White Paper		
123	1¢ buff (112)	325.00	250.00
124	2¢ brown (113)	375.00	350.00
125	3¢ blue (114)	3,000.00	10,000.00
126	6¢ blue (115)	850.00	600.00

112

113

114

115

116

117

118

120

121

122

Details

15¢ Landing of Columbus, Types I-III, Series 1869-75

Detail of **#118** Type I

Picture unframed.

Detail of **#119** Type II

Picture framed.

#129 Type III

Same as Type I but without fringe of brown shading lines around central vignette.

134

135

136

137

138

139

140

141

142

143

144

156

157

158

Details

Detail of #**134, 145**

Detail of #**135, 146**

Detail of #**136, 147**

Detail of #**156, 167, 182, 192**

Detail of #**157, 168, 178, 180, 183, 193**

Detail of #**158, 169, 184, 194**

1¢. In the pearl at the left of the numeral "1" there is a small crescent.

2¢. Under the scroll at the left of "U.S." there is small diagonal line. This mark seldom shows clearly.

3¢. The under part of the upper tail of the left ribbon is heavily shaded.

	Issues of 1875, Perf. 12	Un	U
127	10¢ yellow (116)	1,400.00	1,300.00
128	12¢ green (117)	1,500.00	1,300.00
129	15¢ brown and blue, type III (118)	1,300.00	750.00
a	Imperf. horizontally	1,600.00	—
130	24¢ grn. & violet (120)	1,250.00	950.00
131	30¢ bl. & carmine (121)	1,750.00	1,600.00
132	90¢ car. & black (122)	4,000.00	4,500.00
	Issue of 1880, Reissue of 1869 Issue, Soft, Porous Paper		
133	1¢ buff (112)	200.00	160.00
a	1¢ brown orange, issued without gum	175.00	140.00
	Issues of 1870-71		
	With Grill, White Wove Paper, No Secret Marks		
	H. Grill about 10 x 12mm		
134	1¢ Franklin, April 1870	900.00	65.00
	End roller grill		300.00
135	2¢ Jackson, April 1870	525.00	40.00
136	3¢ Washington	400.00	11.00
	Cracked plate	—	50.00
137	6¢ Lincoln, April 1870	2,100.00	300.00
	Double grill	—	500.00
138	7¢ Edwin M. Stanton	1,500.00	275.00
139	10¢ Jefferson	2,000.00	475.00
140	12¢ Henry Clay	13,000.00	2,100.00
141	15¢ Daniel Webster	3,000.00	750.00
142	24¢ Gen. Winfield Scott	—	9,000.00
143	30¢ Alexander Hamilton	6,000.00	1,000.00
144	90¢ Commodore Perry	8,000.00	900.00
	Split grill		825.00

	Issues of 1870-71	Un	U
	Without Grill, White Wove Paper, No Secret Marks		
145	1¢ ultra. Franklin (134)	225.00	8.00
146	2¢ red brn. Jackson (135)	160.00	5.00
147	3¢ grn. Washington (136)	175.00	.60
148	6¢ carmine Lincoln (137)	325.00	12.50
	6¢ violet carmine	350.00	15.00
149	7¢ verm. Stanton (138)	425.00	55.00
150	10¢ brown Jefferson (139)	325.00	12.50
151	12¢ dull violet Clay (140)	750.00	80.00
152	15¢ brt. or. Webster (141)	725.00	90.00
153	24¢ purple Scott (142)	775.00	85.00
154	30¢ black Hamilton (143)	1,600.00	110.00
155	90¢ carmine Perry (144)	1,800.00	200.00

Comparison of Issue of 1870-71: Printed by National Bank Note Company. Issued without secret marks (134-41, 145-52, 187) and Issues of 1873-80: Printed by Continental and American Bank Note Companies. Issued with secret marks (156-63, 167-74, 178, 180, 182-184, 186, 188-90, 192-99).

	Issues of 1873, Without Grill, White Wove Paper, Thin to Thick, Secret Marks		
156	1¢ ultra. Franklin	120.00	1.75
	Paper with silk fibers	—	15.00
f	Imperf. pair	—	500.00
157	2¢ br. Jackson	250.00	10.00
	Double paper	325.00	20.00
c	With grill	1,100.00	600.00
158	3¢ gr. Washington	75.00	.15
	3¢ olive green	90.00	2.50
	Cracked plate	—	27.50

1873-1879

Issues of 1873	Un	U
Without Grill, White Wove Paper, Thin to Thick, Secret Marks		
159 6¢ dull pk. Lincoln	275.00	10.00
b With grill	*1,000.00*	
160 7¢ or. verm. Stanton	600.00	57.50
Ribbed paper	—	70.00
161 10¢ br. Jefferson	350.00	11.50
162 12¢ bl. vio. Clay	950.00	70.00
163 15¢ yel. or. Webster	875.00	67.50
a With grill	*3,000.00*	
164 24¢ pur. Scott		
165 30¢ gray blk. Hamilton	950.00	65.00
166 90¢ rose carm. Perry	1,800.00	200.00
Issues of 1875, Special Printing, Hard, White Wove Paper, Without Gum, Secret Marks		
Although perforated, these stamps were usually cut apart with scissors. As a result, the perforations are often much mutilated and the design is frequently damaged.		
167 1¢ ultra. Franklin (156)	*8,000.00*	
168 2¢ dk. br. Jackson (157)	*3,500.00*	
169 3¢ blue green Washington (158)	*9,500.00*	—
170 6¢ dull rose Lincoln (159)	*8,500.00*	
171 7¢ reddish vermilion Stanton (160)	*2,000.00*	
172 10¢ pale brown Jefferson (161)	*8,250.00*	
173 12¢ dark vio. Clay (162)	*3,000.00*	

Issues of 1875	Un	U
174 15¢ bright orange Webster (163)	*8,250.00*	
175 24¢ dull pur. Scott (142)	*1,850.00*	—
176 30¢ greenish black Hamilton (143)	*6,000.00*	
177 90¢ vio. car. Perry (144)	*7,500.00*	
Regular Issue, Yellowish Wove Paper		
178 2¢ verm. Jackson (157)	225.00	5.00
c With grill	*325.00*	
179 5¢ Zachary Taylor, June	275.00	10.00
Cracked plate	—	*100.00*
Double paper	*325.00*	
c With grill	625.00	
Paper with silk fibers	—	15.00
Special Printing, Hard, White Wove Paper, Without Gum		
180 2¢ carmine vermilion Jackson (157)	*22,500.00*	
181 5¢ br. bl. Taylor (179)	*35,000.00*	
Issues of 1879, Soft, Porous Paper, Thin to Thick		
182 1¢ dark ultramarine Franklin (156)	175.00	1.25
183 2¢ verm. Jackson (157)	80.00	1.25
a Double impression	—	*500.00*

159

160

161

162

163

179

Details

Detail of **#137, 148**

Detail of **#138, 149**

Detail of **#139, 150, 187**

Detail of **#159, 170, 186, 195**

6¢. The first four vertical lines of the shading in the lower part of the left ribbon have been strengthened.

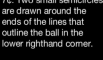

Detail of **#160, 171, 196**

7¢. Two small semicircles are drawn around the ends of the lines that outline the ball in the lower righthand corner.

Detail of **#161, 172, 188, 197**

10¢. There is a small semi-circle in the scroll at the right end of the upper label.

Detail of **#140, 151**

Detail of **#141, 152**

Detail of **#143, 154, 165, 176**

Detail of **#162, 173, 198**

2¢. The balls of the figure "2" are crescent-shaped.

Detail of **#163, 174, 189, 199**

15¢. In the lower part of the triangle in the upper left corner two lines have been made heavier, forming a "V". This mark can be found on some of the Continental and American (1879) printings, but not all stamps show it.

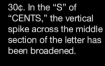

Detail of **#190**

30¢. In the "S" of "CENTS," the vertical spike across the middle section of the letter has been broadened.

205

206

207

208

209

210

211

212

219

220

221

222

223

224

225

226

227

228

229

Details

Issues of 1881-82, Re-engravings of 1873 Designs

Detail of **#206**

1¢. Upper vertical lines have been deepened, creating a solid effect in parts of background. Upper arabesques shaded.

Detail of **#207**

3¢. Shading at sides of central oval is half its previous width. A short horizontal dash has been cut below th "TS" of "CENTS."

Detail of **#208**

6¢. Has three vertical lines instead of four between the edge of the panel and the outside of the stamp.

Detail of **#209**

10¢. Has four vertical lines instead of five between left side of oval and edge of the shield. Horizontal lines in lower part of background strengthened.

	Issues of 1879, Perf. 12	Un	U
184	3¢ grn. Washington (158)	60.00	.15
	Double transfer	—	4.00
	Short transfer	—	5.00
185	5¢ blue Taylor (179)	325.00	8.00
186	6¢ pink Lincoln (159)	600.00	15.00
187	10¢ brown Jefferson (139) (no secret mark)	1,000.00	15.00
188	10¢ brown Jefferson (161) (with secret mark)	750.00	16.00
	10¢ black brown	750.00	25.00
	Double transfer		30.00
189	15¢ red or. Webster (163)	225.00	15.00
190	30¢ full blk. Hamilton (143)	650.00	35.00
191	90¢ carmine Perry (144)	1,400.00	155.00
	Issues of 1880, Special Printing, Soft, Porous Paper, Without Gum		
192	1¢ dark ultramarine Franklin (156)	10,000.00	
193	2¢ blk. br. Jackson (157)	6,000.00	
194	3¢ blue green Washington (158)	15,000.00	
195	6¢ dull rose Lincoln (159)	11,000.00	
196	7¢ scarlet vermilion Stanton (160)	2,250.00	
197	10¢ deep brown Jefferson (161)	10,000.00	
198	12¢ blk. pur. Clay (162)	3,500.00	
199	15¢ or. Webster (163)	11,000.00	
200	24¢ dk. vio. Scott (142)	3,500.00	
201	30¢ greenish black Hamilton (143)	8,500.00	
202	90¢ dull carmine Perry (144)	9,000.00	
203	2¢ scarlet vermilion Jackson (157)	18,000.00	
204	5¢ dp. bl. Taylor (179)	30,000.00	
	Issues of 1882		
205	5¢ Garfield, Apr. 10	135.00	4.50
	Special Printing, Soft, Porous Paper, Without Gum		
205C	5¢ gray brown Garfield (205)	18,000.00	
	Issues of 1881-82, Designs of 1873 Re-engraved		
206	1¢ Franklin, Aug. 1881	40.00	.40
	Double transfer	52.50	4.00
207	3¢ Washington, July 16, 1881	45.00	.15
	Double transfer	—	7.50
	Cracked plate	—	
208	6¢ Lincoln, June 1882	275.00	45.00
a	6¢ brown red	225.00	65.00
209	10¢ Jefferson, Apr. 1882	95.00	2.50
	10¢ pur. or olive brown	90.00	2.50
b	10¢ black brown	200.00	20.00

	Issues of 1883, Perf. 12	Un	U
210	2¢ Washington, Oct. 1	37.50	.15
	Double transfer	40.00	1.25
211	4¢ Jackson, Oct. 1	160.00	8.00
	Cracked plate	—	
	Special Printing, Soft, Porous Paper		
211B	2¢ pale red brown Washington (210)	500.00	—
c	Horizontal pair, imperf. between	2,000.00	
211D	4¢ deep blue green Jackson (211) no gum	15,000.00	
	Issues of 1887		
212	1¢ Franklin, June	65.00	.75
	Double transfer		—
213	2¢ green Washington (210), Sept. 10	25.00	.15
b	Printed on both sides		—
	Double transfer	—	3.00
214	3¢ vermilion Washington (207), Oct. 3	50.00	37.50
	Issues of 1888		
215	4¢ carmine Jackson (211), Nov.	160.00	11.00
216	5¢ indigo Garfield (205), Feb.	160.00	6.50
217	30¢ orange brown Hamilton (165), Jan.	375.00	75.00
218	90¢ pur. Perry (166), Feb.	850.00	150.00
	Issues of 1890-93		
219	1¢ Franklin, Feb. 22, 1890	20.00	.15
	Double transfer	—	—
219D	2¢ lake Washington (220), Feb. 22, 1890	160.00	.45
	Double transfer	—	—
220	2¢ Washington, 1890	15.00	.15
a	Cap on left "2"	35.00	1.00
c	Cap on both "2s"	150.00	10.00
	Double transfer	—	3.00
221	3¢ Jackson, Feb. 22, 1890	55.00	4.50
222	4¢ Lincoln, June 2, 1890	60.00	1.50
	Double transfer	65.00	—
223	5¢ Grant, June 2, 1890	55.00	1.50
	Double transfer	65.00	1.75
224	6¢ Garfield, Feb. 22, 1890	60.00	15.00
225	8¢ Sherman, Mar. 21, 1893	45.00	8.50
226	10¢ Webster, Feb. 22, 1890	120.00	1.75
	Double transfer	—	—
227	15¢ Clay, Feb. 22, 1890	160.00	15.00
	Double transfer	—	—
	Triple transfer	—	—
228	30¢ Jefferson, Feb. 22, 1890	250.00	20.00
	Double transfer	—	—
229	90¢ Perry, Feb. 22, 1890	400.00	95.00
	Short transfer at bottom	—	—

	Issues of 1893, Perf. 12	Un	U	PB	#	FDC	Q
	Columbian Exposition Issue, Printed by The American Bank Note Co., Jan. 2 (8¢ March)						
230	1¢ Columbus in Sight of Land	21.00	.25	300.00	(6)	*3,500.00*	449,195,550
	Double transfer	25.00	.50				
	Cracked plate	80.00					
231	2¢ Landing of Columbus	19.00	.15	250.00	(6)	*2,600.00*	1,464,588,750
	Double transfer	22.50	.25				
	Triple transfer	57.50	—				
	Quadruple transfer	85.00					
	Broken hat on third figure left of Columbus	50.00	.20				
	Broken frame line	20.00	.15				
	Recut frame lines	20.00	—				
	Cracked plate	80.00	—				
232	3¢ *Santa Maria,* Flagship	50.00	12.50	650.00	(6)	*6,000.00*	11,501,250
	Double transfer	67.50	—				
233	4¢ ultramarine, Fleet	70.00	5.50	1,000.00	(6)	*6,000.00*	19,181,550
a	4¢ blue (error)	*15,000.00*	*4,000.00*	*45,000.00*	(4)		
	Double transfer	100.00	—				
234	5¢ Columbus Soliciting Aid from Isabella	75.00	6.50	1,250.00	(6)	*6,250.00*	35,248,250
	Double transfer	120.00	—				
235	6¢ Columbus Welcomed at Barcelona	70.00	18.00			*6,750.00*	4,707,550
a	6¢ red violet	70.00	18.00	1,100.00	(6)		
	Double transfer	90.00	25.00				
236	8¢ Restored to Favor	60.00	8.00	725.00	(6)		10,656,550
	Double transfer	70.00	—				
237	10¢ Presenting Natives	115.00	5.50	2,750.00	(6)	*7,500.00*	16,516,950
	Double transfer	150.00	10.00				
	Triple transfer	—					
238	15¢ Columbus Announcing His Discovery	190.00	50.00	*3,500.00*	(6)		1,576,950
	Double transfer	—	—				
239	30¢ Columbus at La Rábida	260.00	70.00	*7,000.00*	(6)		617,250
240	50¢ Recall of Columbus	450.00	120.00	*10,500.00*	(6)		243,750
	Double transfer	—	—				
	Triple transfer	—	—				
241	$1 Isabella Pledging Her Jewels	1,350.00	525.00	*35,000.00*	(6)		55,050
	Double transfer	—	—				
242	$2 Columbus in Chains	1,400.00	450.00	*40,000.00*	(6)	*18,000.00*	45,550
243	$3 Columbus Describing His Third Voyage	2,000.00	800.00				27,650
a	$3 olive green	2,000.00	800.00	*60,000.00*	(6)		
244	$4 Isabella and Columbus	2,600.00	1,000.00				26,350
a	$4 rose carmine	2,600.00	1,000.00	*165,000.00*	(6)		
245	$5 Portrait of Columbus	3,000.00	1,200.00	*150,000.00*	(6)		27,350

230   231   232

233   234   235

236   237   238

239   240   241

242   243   244

245

246

248

253

246

248

253

254

255

256

257

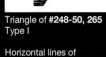
258

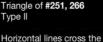
259

Details

2¢ Washington Types I-III, Series 1894-98

Triangle of **#248-50, 265**
Type I

Horizontal lines of
uniform thickness run
across the triangle.

Triangle of **#251, 266**
Type II

Horizontal lines cross the
triangle, but are thinner
within than without.

Triangle of **#252, 267,
279B-279Be** Type III

The horizontal lines do
not cross the double
frame lines of the triangle.

Issues of 1894	Un	U	PB	#
Unwmkd., Perf. 12				

Bureau Issues Starting in 1894 and continuing until 1979, the Bureau of Engraving and Printing in Washington produced all U.S. postage stamps except #909-21, 1335, 1355, 1410-18 and 1789. Beginning in 1979, security printers in addition to the Bureau of Engraving and Printing started producing postage stamps under contract with the U.S. Postal Service.

#		Un	U	PB	#
246	1¢ Franklin, Oct.	17.00	2.50	200.00	(6)
	Double transfer	21.00	3.00		
247	1¢ blue Franklin (246)	42.50	1.05	400.00	(6)
	Double transfer	—	2.50		
248	2¢ pink Washington, type I, Oct.	15.00	1.80	145.00	(6)
	Double transfer	—	—		
249	2¢ carmine lake, type I (248)	82.50	1.20	850.00	(6)
	Double transfer	—	1.50		
250	2¢ carmine, type I (248)	16.00	.30	200.00	(6)
a	Vertical pair, imperf. horizontally	1,500.00			
b	Horizontal pair, imperf. between	1,500.00			
	Double transfer	—	1.10		
251	2¢ carmine, type II (248)	135.00	1.80	1,450.00	(6)
252	2¢ carmine, type III (248)	75.00	2.50	950.00	(6)
b	Horizontal pair, imperf. between	1,500.00			
253	3¢ Jackson, Sept.	60.00	5.25	700.00	(6)
254	4¢ Lincoln, Sept.	75.00	2.50	850.00	(6)
255	5¢ Grant, Sept.	52.50	3.00	575.00	(6)
c	Vertical pair, imperf. horiz.	1,350.00			
	Worn plate, diagonal lines missing in oval background	60.00	3.00		
	Double transfer	67.50	3.00		
256	6¢ Garfield, July	95.00	15.00	1,500.00	(6)
a	Vertical pair, imperf. horizontally	850.00			
257	8¢ Sherman, Mar.	85.00	9.75	800.00	(6)
258	10¢ Webster, Sept.	140.00	6.50	1,600.00	(6)
	Double transfer	150.00	6.00		
259	15¢ Clay, Oct.	200.00	37.50	2,750.00	(6)

Not elected president under his real name

Born Hiram Ulysses Grant in Clermont County, Ohio, the future 18th president's name was revised when his appointment to West Point in 1839 was made out mistakenly to "Ulysses Simpson Grant." The error remained uncorrected.

Grant was commissioned colonel of the Twenty-First Illinois Volunteers. He displayed exceptional energy, determination and strategic aptitude. In 1864, Grant was appointed by President Lincoln as general-in-chief of the struggling Union Army. Elected President in 1868 and again in 1872, Grant's administrations were considered among the most corrupt in the nation's history. **(#255)**

	Issues of 1894, Unwmkd., Perf. 12	Un	U	PB	#
260	50¢ Jefferson, Nov.	300.00	75.00	4,250.00	(6)
261	$1 Perry, type I, Nov.	675.00	200.00	11,000.00	(6)
261A	$1 black Perry, type II (261), Nov.	1,650.00	450.00	18,500.00	(6)
262	$2 James Madison, Dec.	2,300.00	600.00	26,000.00	(6)
263	$5 John Marshall, Dec.	3,500.00	1,000.00	10,000.00	(4)
	Issues of 1895, Wmkd. (191)				
264	1¢ blue Franklin (246), Apr.	4.00	.16	130.00	(6)
265	2¢ carmine Washington, type I (248), May	22.50	.45	225.00	(6)
	Double transfer	27.50	3.00		
266	2¢ carmine, type II (248)	22.50	1.90	200.00	(6)
267	2¢ carmine, type III (248)	3.25	.16	90.00	(6)
	Triple transfer	—			
	Triangle at right without shading	17.50	5.00		
268	3¢ purple Jackson (253), Oct.	25.00	.70	375.00	(6)
	Double transfer	32.50	2.25		
269	4¢ dark brown Lincoln (254), June	27.50	.80	400.00	(6)
	Double transfer	25.00	2.25		
270	5¢ chocolate Grant (255), June 11	25.00	1.30	400.00	(6)
	Double transfer	32.50	2.50		
	Worn plate, diagonal lines missing in oval background	25.00	1.60		
271	6¢ dull brown Garfield (256), Aug.	55.00	2.75	1,100.00	(6)
	Very thin paper	47.50	2.50		
a	Wmkd. USIR	2,250.00	350.00		
272	8¢ violet brown Sherman (257), July	40.00	.70	475.00	(6)
a	Wmkd. USIR	1,750.00	110.00	5,500.00	(3)
	Double transfer	50.00	2.00		
273	10¢ dark green Webster (258), June	50.00	.90	800.00	(6)
	Double transfer	65.00	2.75		
274	15¢ dark blue Clay (259), Sept.	140.00	6.00	2,100.00	(6)
275	50¢ orange Jefferson (260), Nov.	200.00	16.00	4,000.00	(6)
a	50¢ red orange	225.00	17.50		
276	$1 black Perry, type I (261), Aug.	500.00	50.00	7,500.00	(6)
276A	$1 black Perry, type II (261)	1,050.00	105.00	15,000.00	(6)
277	$2 bright blue Madison (262), Aug.	850.00	250.00	14,000.00	(6)
a	$2 dark blue	825.00	260.00		
278	$5 dark green Marshall (263), Aug.	1,750.00	325.00	50,000.00	(6)

Fighting Great Britain on a Great Lake

"We have met the enemy, and they are ours," is the famous message U.S. Naval Lieutenant Oliver Hazard Perry (1785-1819) sent after defeating the British fleet on Lake Erie on Sept. 10, 1813, during the War of 1812. Though outgunned, his courageous and daring command of nine tiny naval vessels led to a victory that gave the Americans control of Lake Erie, and led to an American invasion of Upper Canada then under British control. **(#261)**

260   261

262   263

277

**Watermark 191
Double-line "USPS"
in capital letters;
detail at right.**

Details

$1 Perry, Types I-II, Series 1894

Detail of **#261, 276** Type I

The circles enclosing $1
are broken.

Detail of **#261A, 276A**
Type I

The circles enclosing $1
are complete.

	Issues of 1898-1900	Un	U	PB	#	FDC	Q
	Wmkd. (191), Perf. 12 (279e issued in 1900, rest in 1898)						
279	1¢ dp. grn. Franklin (246), Jan.	6.50	.15	110.00	(6)		
	Double transfer	9.00	.75				
279B	2¢ red Washington, type III (248)	6.50	.15	120.00	(6)		
c	2¢ rose carmine, type III	185.00	25.00	1,750.00	(6)		
d	2¢ orange red, type III	6.50	.15	120.00	(6)		
e	Booklet pane of 6, Apr. 16, 1900	375.00					
f	2¢ deep red, type III	12.50	.80				
280	4¢ rose brn. Lincoln (254), Oct.	22.50	.50				
a	4¢ lilac brown	22.50	.50				
b	4¢ orange brown	20.00	.50	400.00	(6)		
	Extra frame line at top	32.50	3.50				
281	5¢ dark blue Grant (255), Mar.	25.00	.45	425.00	(6)		
	Double transfer	32.50	1.75				
	Worn plate, diagonal lines missing in oval background	26.00	.55				
282	6¢ lake Garfield (256), Dec.	32.50	1.60	650.00	(6)		
a	6¢ purple lake	40.00	1.80	750.00	(6)		
	Double transfer	42.50	2.50				
282C	10¢ brown Webster (258), type I, Nov.	140.00	1.35	1,600.00	(6)		
	Double transfer	150.00	3.00				
283	10¢ orange brown Webster (258), type II	85.00	1.10	950.00	(6)		
284	15¢ olive grn. Clay (259), Nov.	120.00	5.00	1,600.00	(6)		
	Issues of 1898, Trans-Mississippi Exposition Issue, June 17						
285	1¢ Marquette on the Mississippi	22.50	4.00	250.00	(6)	5,500.00	70,993,400
	Double transfer	30.00	5.25				
286	2¢ Farming in the West	20.00	1.00	210.00	(6)	5,000.00	159,720,800
	Double transfer	27.50	1.75				
	Worn plate	21.00	1.25				
287	4¢ Indian Hunting Buffalo	115.00	16.00	1,150.00	(6)		4,924,500
288	5¢ Frémont on the Rocky Mountains	100.00	14.00	1,000.00	(6)	6,250.00	7,694,180
289	8¢ Troops Guarding Wagon Train	150.00	30.00	2,250.00	(6)	9,250.00	2,927,200
a	Vertical pair, imperf. horizontally	13,500.00		55,000.00	(4)		
290	10¢ Hardships of Emigration	135.00	18.00	2,500.00	(6)		4,629,760
291	50¢ Western Mining Prospector	450.00	150.00	13,000.00	(6)	11,000.00	530,400
292	$1 Western Cattle in Storm	1,050.00	400.00	37,500.00	(6)	15,000.00	56,900
293	$2 Mississippi River Bridge	1,700.00	700.00	90,000.00	(6)		56,200

282C

285

286

287

288

289

290

291

292

293

Details

10¢ Webster Types I-II, Series 1898

Detail of **#282C** Type I

The tips of the foliate ornaments do not impinge on the white curved line below "TEN CENTS."

Detail of **#283** Type II

The tips of the ornaments break the curved line below the "E" of "TEN" and the "T" of "CENTS."

Greatest Hits of the USA

- U.S. commemorative stamps issued during the year
- Large-format, informative book for displaying stamps
- Clear acetate mounts to protect stamps

A Tribute to America's Best

Whether it's people, places, ideals or events, you'll meet America's winners through U.S. commemorative stamps.

Fun, Informative and Valuable

Commemorative Stamp Collections gather the year's honorees in one convenient, collectible and colorful package. The upcoming Collection will contain 1995 commemoratives, including the following: Civil War; Marilyn Monroe; Carousel Horses; Lighthouses; Kids Care; the fifth and final World War II miniature sheet of 10; Jazz Musicians and more.

The 1995 Commemorative Stamp Collection is available (approximately November 1995) for $39.95.

1994 Collection Includes:

Legends of the West; Moon Landing; Wonders of the Sea; Locomotives; Summer Garden Flowers; the fourth World War II miniature sheet of 10; Popular Singers; Jazz and Blues Singers; Norman Rockwell; Endangered Birds; World Cup Soccer; Legends of the Silent Screen; Buffalo Soldiers; Winter Olympics; etc. ($29.95)

To Obtain a Commemorative Stamp Collection

The 1995 Collection and one or two earlier sets may be obtained at your local post office or Philatelic Center. You may also fill out the postage-paid request card in this book or call toll-free:

1-800-STAMP24

294 **295** **296**

297 **298** **299**

300 **301** **302** **303**

304 **305** **306** **307**

308 **309** **310**

311 **312** **313**

	Issues of 1901-03	Un	U	PB/LP	#	FDC	
	Issues of 1901, Pan-American Exposition Issue, May 1						
294	1¢ Great Lakes Steamer	16.00	2.50	210.00	(6)	*3,750.00*	91,401,500
a	Center inverted	*10,000.00*	*5,500.00*	*40,000.00*	(3)		
295	2¢ An Early Locomotive	15.00	.75	210.00	(6)	*3,250.00*	209,759,700
a	Center inverted	*32,500.00*	*13,500.00*	*210,000.00*	(4)		
296	4¢ Automobile	75.00	12.50	2,250.00	(6)	*4,250.00*	5,737,100
a	Center inverted	*12,500.00*		*55,000.00*	(4)		
297	5¢ Bridge at Niagara Falls	90.00	11.00	2,600.00	(6)	*4,500.00*	7,201,300
298	8¢ Canal Locks at Sault Ste. Marie	100.00	45.00	4,250.00	(6)		4,921,700
299	10¢ American Line Steamship	160.00	20.00	6,500.00	(6)		5,043,700
	Wmkd. (191), Perf. 12 (All issued in 1903 except #300b, 306, 308)						
300	1¢ Franklin, Feb.	6.50	.15	130.00	(6)		
b	Booklet pane of 6, Mar. 6, 1907	450.00	—				
	Double transfer	10.00	1.00				
	Worn plate	7.50	.25				
	Cracked plate	—	—				
301	2¢ Washington, Jan. 17	8.50	.15	130.00	(6)	*2,750.00*	
c	Booklet pane of 6, Jan. 24	375.00	—				
	Double transfer	14.00	.90				
	Cracked plate	—					
302	3¢ Jackson, Feb.	35.00	2.00	535.00	(6)		
	Double transfer	52.50	3.00				
	Cracked plate	—					
303	4¢ Grant, Feb.	37.50	.90	535.00	(6)		
	Double transfer	47.50	2.50				
304	5¢ Lincoln, Jan.	40.00	1.10	600.00	(6)		
305	6¢ Garfield, Feb.	45.00	2.00	625.00	(6)		
	6¢ brownish lake	47.50	2.00				
	Double transfer	60.00	2.50				
306	8¢ M. Washington, Dec. 1902	30.00	1.50	450.00	(6)		
	8¢ lavender	35.00	1.75				
307	10¢ Webster, Feb.	37.50	.70	700.00	(6)		
308	13¢ B. Harrison, Nov. 18, 1902	30.00	5.00	425.00	(6)		
309	15¢ Clay, May 27	110.00	3.75	2,000.00	(6)		
	Double transfer	135.00	7.50				
310	50¢ Jefferson, Mar. 23	300.00	17.50	4,750.00	(6)		
311	$1 David G. Farragut, June 5	575.00	45.00	10,000.00	(6)		
312	$2 Madison, June 5	850.00	140.00	17,500.00	(6)		
313	$5 Marshall, June 5	2,250.00	550.00	45,000.00	(6)		
	For listings of #312 and 313 with perf. 10, see #479 and 480.						

	Issues of 1906	Un	U	PB/LP	#	FDC	Q
	Issues of 1906-08, Imperf. (All issued in 1908 except #314)						
314	1¢ bl. grn. Franklin (300), Oct. 2, 1906	20.00	15.00	150.00	(6)		
314A	4¢ brown Grant (303), Apr.	22,500.00	16,000.00				
	#314A was issued imperforate, but all copies were privately perforated at the sides.						
315	5¢ blue Lincoln (304), May 12	300.00	400.00	2,900.00	(6)		
	Coil Stamps, Perf. 12 Horizontally						
316	1¢ bl. grn. pair Franklin (300), Feb. 18	75,000.00	—	100,000.00	(2)		
317	5¢ blue pair Lincoln (304), Feb. 24	9,000.00	—	9,000.00	(2)		
	Coil Stamp, Perf. 12 Vertically						
318	1¢ bl. grn. pair Franklin (300), July 31	5,500.00	—	7,500.00	(2)		
	Issues of 1903, Perf. 12						
319	2¢ Washington, Nov. 12	4.00	.15	67.50	(6)		
a	2¢ lake, type I	—	—				
b	2¢ carmine rose, type I	6.00	.20	125.00	(6)		
c	2¢ scarlet, type I	4.00	.15	60.00	(6)		
d	Vertical pair, imperf. horizontally	2,000.00					
f	2¢ lake, type II	5.00	.20				
g	Booklet pane of 6, carm., type I, Dec. 3	75.00	125.00				
h	Booklet pane of 6, carm., type II	135.00					
i	2¢ carmine, type II	17.50	—				
q	Booklet pane of 6, lake, type II	130.00					
	Washington (319), Imperf.						
320	2¢ carmine, Oct. 2	17.50	11.00	200.00	(6)		
a	2¢ lake, die II	50.00	40.00	625.00	(6)		
b	2¢ scarlet	16.00	12.00	175.00	(6)		
	Double transfer	24.00	15.00				
	Issues of 1908, Coil Stamp (319), Perf. 12 Horizontally						
321	2¢ carmine pair, Feb. 18	95,000.00	—				
	Coil Stamp, Perf. 12 Vertically						
322	2¢ carmine pair, July 31	6,500.00	5,000.00	8,000.00	(2)		
	Issues of 1904, Louisiana Purchase Exposition Issue, Apr. 30, Perf. 12						
323	1¢ Robert R. Livingston	20.00	3.00	200.00	(6)	3,000.00	79,779,200
	Diagonal line through left "1"	35.00	10.00				
324	2¢ Thomas Jefferson	17.00	1.00	200.00	(6)	3,250.00	192,732,400
325	3¢ James Monroe	65.00	24.00	750.00	(6)	3,750.00	4,542,600
326	5¢ William McKinley	70.00	15.00	800.00	(6)	5,500.00	6,926,700
327	10¢ Map of Louisiana Purchase	130.00	21.00	1,600.00	(6)	8,000.00	4,011,200
	Issues of 1907, Jamestown Exposition Issue, Apr. 26, Wmkd. (191), Perf. 12						
328	1¢ Captain John Smith	13.00	2.00	175.00	(6)	3,750.00	77,728,794
	Double transfer	16.00	3.00				
329	2¢ Founding of Jamestown, 1607	17.00	1.75	250.00	(6)	5,500.00	149,497,994
330	5¢ Pocahontas	72.50	16.00	1,600.00	(6)		7,980,594

319

323

324

325

326

327

328

329

330

Details

2¢ Washington Die I-II, Series 1903

Detail of #319a, 319b, 319g Die I

Detail of #319c, 319f, 319h, 319i Die II

331

332

333

334

335

336

337

338

339

340

341

342

Details

3¢ Washington Types I-IV, Series 1908-19

Detail of #**333, 345, 359, 376, 389, 394, 426, 445, 456, 464, 483, 493, 501-01b** Type I

Top line of toga rope is weak and rope shading lines are thin. Fifth line from left is missing. Line between lips is thin.

Detail of #**484, 494, 502, 541** Type II

Top line of toga rope is strong and rope shading lines are heavy and complete. Line between lips is heavy.

Detail of #**529** Type III

Top row of toga rope is strong but fifth shading line is missing as in Type I. Toga button center shading line consists of two dashes, central dot. "P," "O" of "POSTAGE" are separated by line of color.

Detail of #**530, 535** Type IV

Toga rope shading lines are complete. Second, fourth toga button shading lines are broken in middle, third line is continuous with dot in center. "P," "O" of "POSTAGE" are joined.

	Issues of 1908-09	Un	U	PB/LP	#
	Wmkd. (191) Perf. 126 (All issued in 1908 except #336, 338-42, 345-47)				
331	1¢ Franklin, Dec.	5.00	.15	45.00	(6)
a	Booklet pane of 6, Dec. 2	130.00	90.00		
	Double transfer	6.75	.60		
332	2¢ Washington, Nov.	4.50	.15	42.50	(6)
a	Booklet pane of 6, Nov. 16	115.00	90.00		
	Double transfer	9.00	—		
	Cracked plate	—	—		
333	3¢ Washington, type I, Dec.	22.50	1.75	200.00	(6)
334	4¢ Washington, Dec.	28.00	.55	250.00	(6)
	Double transfer	40.00	—		
335	5¢ Washington, Dec.	35.00	1.50	345.00	(6)
336	6¢ Washington, Jan. 1909	45.00	3.50	550.00	(6)
337	8¢ Washington, Dec.	32.50	1.75	300.00	(6)
	Double transfer	40.00	—		
338	10¢ Washington, Jan. 1909	50.00	1.00	650.00	(6)
a	"China Clay" paper	1,250.00			
	Very thin paper	—			
339	13¢ Washington, Jan. 1909	30.00	14.00	300.00	(6)
	Line through "TAG" of "POSTAGE"	47.50	—		
340	15¢ Washington, Jan. 1909	45.00	3.75	400.00	(6)
a	"China Clay" paper	1,500.00			
341	50¢ Washington, Jan. 13, 1909	200.00	10.00	4,500.00	(6)
342	$1 Washington, Jan. 29, 1909	360.00	50.00	10,000.00	(6)
	Imperf.				
343	1¢ green Franklin (331), Dec.	6.00	4.00	47.50	(6)
	Double transfer	11.50	5.50		
344	2¢ carmine Washington (332), Dec. 10	7.50	2.50	90.00	(6)
	Double transfer	12.50	3.50		
	Double transfer, design of 1¢	1,250.00	1,000.00		
	#345-47: Washington (333-35)				
345	3¢ deep violet, type I, Mar. 3, 1909	14.00	17.50	180.00	(6)
	Double transfer	22.50	—		
346	4¢ orange brown, Feb. 25, 1909	24.00	17.50	210.00	(6)
	Double transfer	42.50	—		
347	5¢ blue, Feb. 25, 1909	42.50	30.00	350.00	(6)
	Cracked plate	—			
	Issues of 1908-10, Coil Stamps, Perf. 12 Horizontally				
	#350-51, 354-56: Washington (Designs of 334-35, 338)				
348	1¢ green Franklin (331), Dec. 29, 1908	21.00	10.00	150.00	(2)
349	2¢ carmine Washington (332), Jan. 1909	37.50	6.00	265.00	(2)
	Double transfer, design of 1¢	—	1,750.00		
350	4¢ orange brown, Aug. 15, 1910	85.00	60.00	575.00	(2)
351	5¢ blue, Jan. 1909	95.00	90.00	575.00	(2)
	Issues of 1909, Coil Stamps, Perf. 12 Vertically				
352	1¢ green Franklin (331), Jan.	40.00	25.00	275.00	(2)
	Double transfer	—	—		

	Issues of 1909	Un	U	PB/LP	#	FDC	Q
	Coil Stamps, Perf. 12 Vertically						
353	2¢ carmine Washington (332), Jan. 12	40.00	6.00	275.00	(2)		
354	4¢ orange brown, Feb. 23	100.00	45.00	700.00	(2)		
355	5¢ blue, Feb. 23	110.00	65.00	725.00	(2)		
356	10¢ yellow, Jan. 7	1,750.00	750.00	7,000.00	(2)		
	Issues of 1909, Bluish Paper, Perf. 12, #359-66: Washington (Designs of 333-40)						
357	1¢ green Franklin (331), Feb. 16	80.00	65.00	875.00	(6)		
358	2¢ carmine Washington (332), Feb. 16	75.00	55.00	850.00	(6)		
	Double transfer	—					
359	3¢ deep violet, type I	1,600.00	*1,300.00*	*15,000.00*	(6)		
360	4¢ orange brown	*15,000.00*		*75,000.00*	(3)		
361	5¢ blue	3,750.00	*3,500.00*	*30,000.00*	(6)		
362	6¢ red orange	1,150.00	900.00	*13,000.00*	(6)		
363	8¢ olive green	*16,000.00*		*75,000.00*	(3)		
364	10¢ yellow	1,350.00	1,000.00	*13,500.00*	(6)		
365	13¢ blue green	2,500.00	*1,400.00*	*18,500.00*	(6)		
366	15¢ pale ultramarine	1,150.00	900.00	*10,000.00*	(6)		
	Lincoln Memorial Issue, Feb. 12, Wmkd. (191)						
367	2¢ Bust of Abraham Lincoln	4.25	1.40	100.00	(6)	*350.00*	148,387,191
	Double transfer	6.75	2.50				
	Imperf.						
368	2¢ carmine (367)	20.00	16.00	175.00	(6)	7,000.00	1,273,900
	Double transfer	40.00	24.00				
	Bluish Paper						
369	2¢ carmine (367)	170.00	175.00	*2,400.00*	(6)		637,000
	Alaska-Yukon Pacific Exposition Issue, June 1						
370	2¢ Willam H. Seward	7.50	1.25	175.00	(6)	*1,800.00*	152,887,311
	Double transfer	10.00	4.00				
	Imperf.						
371	2¢ carmine (370)	27.50	20.00	200.00	(6)		525,400
	Double transfer	40.00	25.00				
	Hudson-Fulton Celebration Issue, Sept. 25, Wmkd. (191)						
372	2¢ *Half Moon* & *Clermont*	11.00	3.25	250.00	(6)	800.00	72,634,631
	Double transfer	14.00	4.25				
	Imperf.						
373	2¢ carmine (372)	32.50	22.50	235.00	(6)	—	216,480
	Double transfer	45.00	27.50				
	Issues of 1910-11, Wmkd. (190) #376-82: Washington (Designs of 333-38, 340)						
374	1¢ green Franklin (331), Nov. 23, 1910	5.00	.15	65.00	(6)		
a	Booklet pane of 6, Oct. 7, 1910	90.00	*75.00*				
	Double transfer	12.50	—				
	Cracked plate	—	—				
375	2¢ carmine Washington (332), Nov. 23, 1910	5.00	.15	70.00	(6)		
	2¢ lake	*150.00*					
a	Booklet pane of 6, Nov. 30, 1910	75.00	*60.00*				
	Cracked plate	—	—				
	Double transfer	10.00	—				
	Double transfer, design of 1¢	—	*1,000.00*				
376	3¢ dp. vio., type I, Jan. 16, 1911	12.00	1.00	100.00	(6)		

367

370

372

USPS

Watermark 190
Single-line "USPS"
in capital letters;
detail at right.

Have you noticed? We expanded the
stamp listings. They are now grouped
according to historical eras.

397

398

399

400

We redesigned and expanded the new issues just for you! Read about the newest issues in the "New Issues" section.

	Issues of 1910-11	Un	U	PB/LP	#	FDC	Q
	Wmkd. (190), Perf. 12						
377	4¢ brown, Jan. 20, 1911	20.00	.30	130.00	(6)		
	Double transfer	—	—				
378	5¢ blue, Jan. 25, 1911	20.00	.30	160.00	(6)		
	Double transfer	—	—				
379	6¢ red orange, Jan. 25, 1911	25.00	.40	325.00	(6)		
380	8¢ olive green, Feb. 8, 1911	75.00	8.50	775.00	(6)		
381	10¢ yellow, Jan. 24, 1911	70.00	2.50	775.00	(6)		
382	15¢ pale ultramarine, Mar. 1, 1911	190.00	11.50	1,750.00	(6)		
	Issues of 1910, Jan. 3, Imperf.						
383	1¢ green Franklin (331)	2.25	2.00	37.50	(6)		
	Double transfer	5.75	—				
384	2¢ carmine Washington (332)	3.50	2.50	115.00	(6)		
	Dbl. transfer, design of 1¢	1,250.00					
	Double transfer	7.00	—				
	Cracked plate	17.50	—				
	Issues of 1910, Nov.1, Coil Stamps, Perf. 12 Horizontally						
385	1¢ green Franklin (331)	20.00	10.00	200.00	(2)		
386	2¢ carmine Washington (332)	35.00	12.50	375.00	(2)		
	Issues of 1910-11, Coil Stamps, Wmkd. (190), Perf. 12 Vertically						
387	1¢ green Franklin (331), Nov. 1, 1910	80.00	30.00	275.00	(2)		
388	2¢ carmine Washington (332), Nov. 1, 1910	550.00	200.00	3,750.00	(2)		
389	3¢ deep violet Washington, type I (333), Jan. 24, 1911	15,000.00	8,500.00				
	Issues of 1910-13, Coil Stamps, Perf. 8.5 Horizontally						
390	1¢ green Franklin (331), Dec. 12, 1910	3.25	4.00	20.00	(2)		
	Double transfer	—	—				
391	2¢ carmine Washington (332), Dec. 23, 1910	22.50	6.75	115.00	(2)		
	Coil Stamps, Perf. 8.5 Vertically #394-96: Washington (Designs of 333-35)						
392	1¢ green Franklin (331), Dec.12, 1910	12.50	14.00	85.00	(2)		
	Double transfer	—	—				
393	2¢ carmine Washington (332), Dec. 16, 1910	25.00	5.50	140.00	(2)		
394	3¢ deep violet, type I, Sept. 18, 1911	35.00	40.00	210.00	(2)		
395	4¢ brown, Apr. 15, 1912	35.00	35.00	210.00	(2)		
396	5¢ blue, Mar. 1913	35.00	35.00	210.00	(2)		
	Issues of 1913, Panama Pacific Exposition Issue, Wmkd. (190), Perf. 12						
397	1¢ Vasco Nunez de Balboa, Jan. 1	12.50	.85	110.00	(6)	3,500.00	167,398,463*
	Double transfer	17.50	2.00				
398	2¢ Pedro Miguel Locks, Panama Canal, Jan.	14.00	.30	210.00	(6)		251,856,543*
	2¢ carmine lake	400.00					
	Double transfer	35.00	2.00				
399	5¢ Golden Gate, Jan. 1	55.00	6.50	1,500.00	(6)	4,000.00	14,544,363*
400	10¢ yellow Discovery of San Francisco Bay, Jan. 1	100.00	14.00	2,000.00	(6)	—	8,484,182*
400A	10¢ orange (400), Aug.	185.00	10.50	7,750.00	(6)		
	*Includes perf. 10 printing quantities.						

	Issues of 1914-15, Perf. 10	Un	U	PB/LP	#
401	1¢ green (397), Dec. 1914	17.50	4.00	225.00	(6)
402	2¢ carmine (398), Jan. 1915	60.00	1.00	1,150.00	(6)
403	5¢ blue (399), Feb. 1915	130.00	11.00	3,250.00	(6)
404	10¢ orange (400), July 1915	825.00	42.50	10,000.00	(6)
	Issues of 1912-14, Wmkd. (190), Perf. 12				
405	1¢ green, Feb. 1912	4.00	.15	55.00	(6)
a	Vertical pair, imperf. horizontally	650.00	—		
b	Booklet pane of 6, Feb. 8, 1912	50.00	25.00		
	Cracked plate	12.00	—		
	Double transfer	5.75	—		
406	2¢ carmine, type I, Feb. 1912	3.75	.15	85.00	(6)
	2¢ lake	200.00	—		
a	Booklet pane of 6, Feb. 8, 1912	50.00	40.00		
b	Double impression	—			
	Double transfer	6.50	—		
407	7¢ black, Apr. 1914	65.00	8.00	900.00	(6)
	Imperf. #408-13: Washington (Designs of 405-6)				
408	1¢ green, Mar. 1912	1.00	.50	15.00	(6)
	Double transfer	2.50	1.00		
	Cracked plate	—	—		
409	2¢ carmine, type I, Feb. 1912	1.10	.50	30.00	(6)
	Cracked plate	15.00	—		
	Coil Stamps, Perf. 8.5 Horizontally				
410	1¢ green, Mar. 1912	5.00	3.00	25.00	(2)
	Double transfer	—	—		
411	2¢ carmine, type I, Mar. 1912	6.75	2.50	30.00	(2)
	Double transfer	9.00	—		
	Coil Stamps, Perf. 8.5 Vertically				
412	1¢ green, Mar. 18, 1912	16.00	3.75	65.00	(2)
413	2¢ carmine, type I, Mar. 1912	27.50	.75	130.00	(2)
	Double transfer	40.00	—		
	Perf. 12				
414	8¢ Franklin, Feb. 1912	30.00	.85	325.00	(6)
415	9¢ Franklin, Apr. 1914	37.50	9.50	500.00	(6)
416	10¢ Franklin, Jan. 1912	32.50	.25	365.00	(6)

405

406

407

414

415

416

2¢ Washington, Types I-VII, Series 1912-21

Detail of #406-06a, 411, 413, 425-25e, 442, 444, 449, 453, 461, 463-63a, 482, 499-99f Type I

One shading line in first curve of ribbon above left "2" and one in second curve of ribbon above right "2". Toga button has only a faint outline. Top line of toga rope, from button to front of the throat, is very faint. Shading lines of face end in the front of the ear, with little or no joining, to form lock of hair.

Detail of #482a, 500 Type Ia

Similar to Type I but all lines are stronger.

Detail of #454, 487, 491, 539Type II

Shading lines in ribbons as in Type I. Toga button, rope and rope shading lines are heavy. Shading lines of face at lock of hair end in strong vertical curved line.

Detail of #450, 455, 488, 492, 540, 546 Type III

Two lines of shading in curves of ribbons.

Detail of #526, 532 Type IV

Top line of toga rope is broken. Toga button shading lines form "DID". Line of color in left "2" is very thin and usually broken.

Detail of #527, 533 Type V

Top line of toga is complete. Toga button has five vertical shading lines. Line of color in left "2" is very thin and usually broken. Nose shading dots are as shown.

Detail of #528, 534 Type Va

Same as Type V except third row from bottom of nose shading dots has four dots instead of six. Overall height of design is 1/3mm shorter than Type V.

Detail of #528A, 534A Type VI

Generally same as Type V except line of color in left "2" is very heavy.

Detail of #528B, 534B Type VII

Line of color in left "2" is continuous, clearly defined and heavier than in Type V or Va but not as heavy as Type VI. An additional vertical row of dots has been added to upper lip. Numerous additional dots appear in hair at top of head.

417

418

419

420

421

423

434

After 1915 (from 1916 to date), all
postage stamps except #519 and 832b
are on unwatermarked paper.

	Issues of 1912-14, Perf. 12	Un	U	PB	#
417	12¢ Franklin, Apr. 1914	32.50	3.00	350.00	(6)
	Double transfer	40.00	—		
	Triple transfer	55.00	—		
418	15¢ Franklin, Feb. 1912	60.00	2.00	475.00	(6)
	Double transfer	—	—		
419	20¢ Franklin, Apr. 1914	140.00	9.00	1,300.00	(6)
420	30¢ Franklin, Apr. 1914	100.00	10.00	1,150.00	(6)
421	50¢ Franklin, Aug. 1914	350.00	10.00	5,750.00	(6)
	Wmkd. (191)				
422	50¢ Franklin (421), Feb. 12, 1912	190.00	9.50	3,750.00	(6)
423	$1 Franklin, Feb. 12, 1912	425.00	40.00	*8,000.00*	(6)
	Double transfer	450.00	—		
	Issues of 1914-15, Wmkd. (190), Perf.10 #424-30: Wash. (Designs of 405-06, 333-36, 407)				
424	1¢ green, Sept. 5, 1914	1.60	.15	35.00	(6)
	Cracked plate	—	—		
	Double transfer	4.25	—		
	Experimental precancel, New Orleans		—		
a	Perf. 12 x 10	*600.00*	*500.00*		
b	Perf. 10 x 12		*250.00*		
c	Vertical pair, imperf. horizontally	*425.00*	*250.00*		
d	Booklet pane of 6	3.00	.75		
e	Vertical pair, imperf. between and at top	—			
425	2¢ rose red, type I, Sept. 5, 1914	1.50	.15	22.50	(6)
	Cracked plate	9.00	—		
	Double transfer	—	—		
c	Perf. 10 x 12		—		
d	Perf. 12 x 10	—	*600.00*		
e	Booklet pane of 6, Jan. 6, 1914	12.50	*3.00*		
426	3¢ deep violet, type I, Sept. 18, 1914	10.00	.90	150.00	(6)
427	4¢ brown, Sept. 7, 1914	26.00	.30	475.00	(6)
	Double transfer	40.00	—		
428	5¢ blue, Sept. 14, 1914	25.00	.30	325.00	(6)
a	Perf. 12 x 10		*2,000.00*		
429	6¢ red orange, Sept. 28, 1914	35.00	.90	475.00	(6)
430	7¢ black, Sept. 10, 1914	65.00	2.50	875.00	(6)
	#431-33, 435, 437-40: Franklin (414-21, 423)				
431	8¢ pale olive green, Sept. 26, 1914	27.50	1.10	475.00	(6)
	Double impression	—			
432	9¢ salmon red, Oct. 6, 1914	37.50	5.00	650.00	(6)
433	10¢ orange yellow, Sept. 9, 1914	35.00	.20	650.00	(6)
434	11¢ Franklin, Aug. 11, 1915	17.50	5.50	225.00	(6)
435	12¢ claret brown, Sept. 10, 1914	18.00	2.75	260.00	(6)
a	12¢ copper red	19.00	2.75	290.00	(6)
	Double transfer	27.50	—		
	Triple transfer	32.50	—		
436	Not assigned				
437	15¢ gray, Sept. 16, 1914	95.00	4.50	825.00	(6)
438	20¢ ultramarine, Sept. 19, 1914	165.00	2.50	2,750.00	(6)
439	30¢ orange red, Sept. 19, 1914	225.00	10.00	3,500.00	(6)
440	50¢ violet, Dec. 10, 1915	500.00	10.00	13,500.00	(6)

	Issues of 1914	Un	U	PB/LB	#
	Coil Stamps, Perf. 10 Horizontally #441-59: Wash. (Designs of 405-06, 333-35; Flat Press, 18½-19 x 22mm)				
441	1¢ green, Nov. 14	.60	.80	4.25	(2)
442	2¢ carmine, type I, July 22	6.50	4.50	35.00	(2)
	Coil Stamps, Perf. 10 Vertically				
443	1¢ green, May 29	17.50	4.00	80.00	(2)
444	2¢ carmine, type I, Apr. 25	22.50	1.00	120.00	(2)
445	3¢ violet, type I, Dec. 18	190.00	100.00	875.00	(2)
446	4¢ brown, Oct. 2	100.00	30.00	450.00	(2)
447	5¢ blue, July 30	35.00	20.00	165.00	(2)
	Issues of 1915-16, Coil Stamps, Perf. 10 Horizontally (Rotary Press, Designs 18½–19 x 22½mm)				
448	1¢ green, Dec. 12, 1915	4.50	2.50	25.00	(2)
449	2¢ red, type I, Dec. 5, 1915	1,900.00	300.00	8,500.00	(2)
450	2¢ carmine, type III, Feb. 1916	8.00	2.25	35.00	(2)
451	Not assigned				
	Issues of 1914-16, Coil Stamps, Perf. 10 Vertically (Rotary Press, Designs 19½–20 x 22mm)				
452	1¢ green, Nov. 11, 1914	8.00	1.40	50.00	(2)
453	2¢ carmine rose, type I, July 3, 1914	95.00	3.25	425.00	(2)
	Cracked plate	—	—		
454	2¢ red, type II, June 1915	77.50	7.50	350.00	(2)
455	2¢ carmine, type III, Dec. 1915	7.50	.75	37.50	(2)
456	3¢ violet, type I, Feb. 2, 1916	210.00	75.00	825.00	(2)
457	4¢ brown, Feb. 18, 1916	20.00	15.00	100.00	(2)
	Cracked plate	35.00	—		
458	5¢ blue, Mar. 9, 1916	25.00	15.00	125.00	(2)
	Issue of 1914, Horizontal Coil Stamp, Imperf.				
459	2¢ carmine, type I, June 30	300.00	*750.00*	1,250.00	(2)
	Issues of 1915, Wmkd. (191), Perf. 10				
460	$1 violet black Franklin (423), Feb. 8	700.00	55.00	*10,000.00*	(6)
	Double transfer	650.00	—		
	Perf. 11				
461	2¢ pale carmine red Washington (406), type I, June 17	80.00	*175.00*	*1,000.00*	(6)
	Privately perforated copies of #409 have been made to resemble #461.				
	Issues of 1916-17, Unwmkd., Perf. 10 #462-69: Wash. (Designs of 405-06, 333-36, 407)				
462	1¢ green, Sept. 27, 1916	5.00	.15	125.00	(6)
	Experimental precancel, Springfield, MA, or New Orleans, LA		10.00		
a	Booklet pane of 6, Oct. 15, 1916	7.50	*1.00*		
463	2¢ carmine, type I, Sept. 25, 1916	3.50	.15	115.00	(6)
	Experimental precancel, Springfield, MA		22.50		
a	Booklet pane of 6, Oct. 8, 1916	62.50	*20.00*		
	Double transfer	5.75	—		
464	3¢ violet, type I, Nov. 11, 1916	57.50	8.00	1,200.00	(6)
	Double transfer in "CENTS"	*75.00*	—		
465	4¢ orange brown, Oct. 7, 1916	35.00	1.00	600.00	(6)
466	5¢ blue, Oct. 17, 1916	60.00	1.00	825.00	(6)
	Experimental precancel, Springfield, MA		150.00		
467	5¢ carmine (error in plate of 2¢)	475.00	525.00		
468	6¢ red orange, Oct. 10, 1916	75.00	5.00	1,100.00	(6)
	Experimental precancel, Springfield, MA		175.00		
469	7¢ black, Oct. 10, 1916	95.00	7.50	1,300.00	(6)
	Experimental precancel, Springfield, MA		175.00		

	Issues of 1916-17, Perf. 10	Un	U	PB/LP	#	FDC
	#470-78: Franklin (Designs of 414-16, 434, 417-21, 423)					
470	8¢ olive green, Nov. 13, 1916	45.00	3.75	500.00	(6)	
	Experimental precancel, Springfield, MA		165.00			
471	9¢ salmon red, Nov. 16, 1916	45.00	9.50	650.00	(6)	
472	10¢ orange yellow, Oct. 17, 1916	85.00	.75	1,200.00	(6)	
473	11¢ dark green, Nov. 16, 1916	27.50	11.00	300.00	(6)	
	Experimental precancel, Springfield, MA		*650.00*			
474	12¢ claret brown, Oct. 10, 1916	42.50	3.50	575.00	(6)	
	Double transfer	50.00	5.25			
	Triple transfer	65.00	8.50			
475	15¢ gray, Nov. 16, 1916	150.00	7.00	2,500.00	(6)	
476	20¢ light ultramarine, Dec. 5, 1916	210.00	7.50	3,250.00	(6)	
476A	30¢ orange red	*3,500.00*	—			
477	50¢ light violet, Mar. 2, 1917	900.00	40.00	*40,000.00*	(6)	
478	$1 violet black, Dec. 22, 1916	650.00	11.00	*13,000.00*	(6)	
	Double transfer	700.00	15.00			
479	$2 dark blue Madison (312), Mar. 22, 1917	290.00	30.00	4,000.00	(6)	
480	$5 light green Marshall (313), Mar. 22, 1917	225.00	32.50	2,750.00	(6)	
	Issues of 1916-17, Imperf.					
	#481-96: Washington (Designs of 405-06, 333-35)					
481	1¢ green, Nov. 1916	.80	.45	9.75	(6)	
	Double transfer	2.50	1.25			
482	2¢ carmine, type I, Dec. 8, 1916	1.35	1.00	20.00	(6)	
482A	2¢ deep rose, type Ia		*7,500.00*			
483	3¢ violet, type I, Oct. 13, 1917	12.50	6.50	110.00	(6)	
	Double transfer	16.00	—			
484	3¢ violet, type II	9.00	3.00	87.50	(6)	
	Double transfer	12.50	—			
485	5¢ carmine (error in plate of 2¢), Mar. 1917	*9,000.00*				
	Issues of 1916-22, Coil Stamps, Perf. 10 Horizontally					
486	1¢ green, Jan. 1918	.70	.20	3.25	(2)	
	Double transfer	2.25	—			
487	2¢ carmine, type II, Nov. 15, 1916	12.50	2.50	87.50	(2)	
488	2¢ carmine, type III, 1919	2.25	1.35	12.00	(2)	
	Cracked plate	12.00	7.50			
489	3¢ violet, type I, Oct. 10, 1917	4.25	1.00	22.50	(2)	
	Coil Stamps, Perf. 10 Vertically					
490	1¢ green, Nov. 17, 1916	.45	.15	2.50	(2)	
	Cracked plate (horizontal)	7.50	—			
	Cracked plate (vertical) retouched	9.00	—			
	Rosette crack	*35.00*	—			
491	2¢ carmine, type II, Nov. 17, 1916	1,500.00	450.00	7,250.00	(2)	
492	2¢ carmine, type III	6.75	.15	35.00	(2)	
493	3¢ violet, type I, July 23, 1917	14.00	2.00	90.00	(2)	
494	3¢ violet, type II, Feb. 4, 1918	8.00	1.00	50.00	(2)	
495	4¢ orange brown, Apr. 15, 1917	8.00	3.00	55.00	(2)	
	Cracked plate	25.00	—			
496	5¢ blue, Jan. 15, 1919	3.00	.90	20.00	(2)	
497	10¢ orange yellow Franklin (416), Jan. 31, 1922	16.00	9.00	100.00	(2)	*2,000.00*

	Issue of 1917-19	Un	U	PB	#	FDC
	Perf. 11, #498-507: Washington (Designs of 405-06, 333-36, 407)					
498	1¢ green, Mar. 1917	.30	.15	13.00	(6)	
a	Vertical pair, imperf. horizontally	175.00				
b	Horizontal pair, imperf. between	75.00				
d	Double impression	175.00				
e	Booklet pane of 6, Apr. 6, 1917	1.60	.35			
f	Booklet pane of 30, Sept. 1917	*750.00*				
g	Perf. 10 top or bottom	*500.00*	—			
	Cracked plate	7.50	—			
499	2¢ rose, type I, Mar. 1917	.35	.15	14.00	(6)	
a	Vertical pair, imperf. horizontally	150.00				
b	Horizontal pair, imperf. vertically	200.00	*100.00*			
e	Booklet pane of 6, Mar. 31, 1917	2.75	.50			
f	Booklet pane of 30, Sept. 1917	*15,000.00*				
g	Double impression	150.00	—			
	Double transfer	6.00	—			
500	2¢ deep rose, type Ia	200.00	150.00	1,650.00	(6)	
	Pair, types I and Ia	*1,000.00*				
501	3¢ light violet, type I, Mar. 1917	8.50	.15	80.00	(6)	
b	Booklet pane of 6, Oct. 17, 1917	50.00	*15.00*			
d	Double impression	200.00				
502	3¢ dark violet, type II	11.50	.15	120.00	(6)	
b	Booklet pane of 6	35.00	*10.00*			
c	Vertical pair, imperf. horizontally	250.00	125.00			
e	Perf. 10, top or bottom	*425.00*	—			
503	4¢ brown, Mar. 1917	7.75	.15	110.00	(6)	
504	5¢ blue, Mar. 1917	7.00	.15	110.00	(6)	
	Double transfer	10.00	—			
505	5¢ rose (error in plate of 2¢)	350.00	400.00			
506	6¢ red orange, Mar. 1917	10.50	.20	135.00	(6)	
507	7¢ black, Mar. 1917	22.50	.85	200.00	(6)	
	#508-12, 514-18: Franklin (Designs of 414-16, 434, 417-21, 423)					
508	8¢ olive bister, Mar. 1917	9.50	.40	130.00	(6)	
c	Perf. 10 top or bottom		*500.00*			
509	9¢ salmon red, Mar. 1917	11.50	1.40	125.00	(6)	
510	10¢ orange yellow, Mar. 1917	13.50	.15	160.00	(6)	
511	11¢ light green, May 1917	7.50	2.00	115.00	(6)	
	Double transfer	12.50	3.00			
512	12¢ claret brown, May 1917	7.50	.30	105.00	(6)	
a	12¢ brown carmine	8.00	.35			
b	Perf. 10, top or bottom	—	*450.00*			
513	13¢ apple green, Jan. 10, 1919	9.00	4.75	115.00	(6)	
	13¢ deep apple green	9.75	5.25			
514	15¢ gray, May 1917	30.00	.80	425.00	(6)	
515	20¢ light ultramarine, May 1917	40.00	.20	475.00	(6)	
	20¢ deep ultramarine	39.00	.20			
b	Vertical pair, imperf. between	*325.00*				
516	30¢ orange red, May 1917	32.50	.60	475.00	(6)	
a	Perf. 10 top or bottom	*850.00*	—			
517	50¢ red violet, May 1917	60.00	.45	1,500.00	(6)	
c	Perf. 10, top or bottom		*700.00*			
518	$1 violet brown, May 1917	45.00	1.20	1,200.00	(6)	
b	$1 deep brown	*1,250.00*	*600.00*			

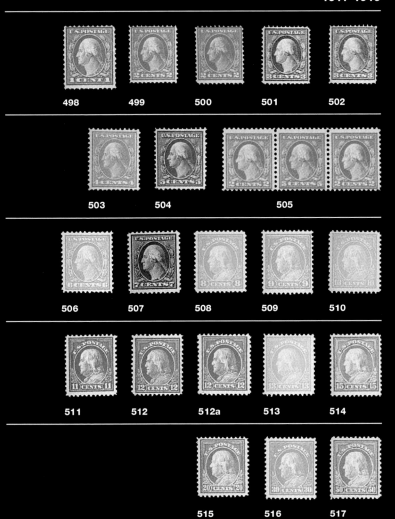

498   499   500   501   502

503   504   505

506   507   508   509   510

511   512   512a   513   514

515   516   517

We redesigned and expanded the new issues just for you! Read about the newest issues in the "1995 Issues—New U.S. Postage Stamps" section.

523   **524**

537

Now, there are more stamps than ever before and dozens of new illustrations of your favorite stamps!

	Issue of 1917, Wmkd. (191), Perf. 11	Un	U	PB	#	FDC	Q
519	2¢ carm. Washington (332), Oct. 10	250.00	*450.00*	2,000.00	(6)		
	Privately perforated copies of #344 have been made to resemble #519.						
520-22	Not assigned						
	Issues of 1918, Unwmkd.						
523	$2 Franklin, Aug. 19	600.00	200.00	*12,500.00*	(8)		
524	$5 Franklin, Aug. 19	200.00	30.00	*4,000.00*	(8)		
	Issues of 1918-20 #525-35: Washington (Designs of 405-06, 333)						
525	1¢ gray green, Dec. 1918	1.50	.35	15.00	(6)		
	1¢ Emerald	2.50	.85				
a	1¢ dark green	1.65	.75				
d	Double impression	15.00	15.00				
526	2¢ carmine, type IV, Mar. 15, 1920	21.00	2.75	160.00	(6)	*800.00*	
	Gash on forehead	30.00	—				
	Malformed "2" at left	27.50	5.25				
527	2¢ carmine, type V	15.00	.60	85.00	(6)		
a	Double impression	55.00	10.00				
	Line through "2" and "EN"	20.00	—				
528	2¢ carmine, type Va	6.25	.15	42.50	(6)		
c	Double impression	25.00					
528A	2¢ carmine, type VI	45.00	1.00	235.00	(6)		
d	Double impression	150.00	—				
528B	2¢ carmine, type VII	15.00	.30	100.00	(6)		
e	Double impression	55.00					
	Retouched on check	—	—				
529	3¢ violet, type III, Mar. 1918	2.25	.15	40.00	(6)		
a	Double impression	30.00	—				
b	Printed on both sides	*350.00*					
530	3¢ purple, type IV	1.00	.15	10.00	(6)		
a	Double impression	20.00	6.00				
b	Printed on both sides	250.00					
	"Blister" under "U.S."	4.00	—				
	Recut under "U.S."	4.00	—				
	Imperf.						
531	1¢ green, Jan. 1919	7.00	7.00	60.00	(6)		
532	2¢ carmine rose, type IV	37.50	25.00	225.00	(6)		
533	2¢ carmine, type V	175.00	75.00	1,300.00	(6)		
534	2¢ carmine, type Va	9.00	6.00	75.00	(6)		
534A	2¢ carmine, type VI	32.50	20.00	250.00	(6)		
534B	2¢ carmine, type VII	1,250.00	700.00	*10,000.00*	(6)		
535	3¢ violet, type IV, 1918	7.00	4.50	50.00	(6)		
a	Double impression	100.00	—				
	Issues of 1919, Perf. 12.5						
536	1¢ gray green Washington (405), Aug.	12.00	14.00	120.00	(6)		
a	Horizontal pair, imperf. vertically	*500.00*					
	Perf. 11						
537	3¢ Allied Victory, Mar. 3	7.75	2.75	85.00	(6)		99,585,200
a	deep red violet	*350.00*	*100.00*	*2,500.00*	(6)		
c	red violet	32.50	7.50				
	Double transfer	—	—				

	Issues of 1919, Perf. 11 x 10	Un	U	PB	#	FDC	Q
	#538-46: Washington (Designs of 405-06, 333; 19¹/₂–20 x 22-22¹/₄ mm)						
538	1¢ green, June	7.75	6.00	72.50	(4)		
a	Vertical pair, imperf. horizontally	50.00	100.00	750.00	(4)		
	Double transfer	15.00	—				
539	2¢ carmine rose, type II	3,000.00	3,000.00	15,000.00	(4)		
540	2¢ carmine rose, type III, June 14	7.75	6.00	70.00	(4)		
	Double transfer	20.00	—				
a	Vertical pair, imperf. horizontally	50.00	100.00				
b	Horizontal pair, imperf. vertically	550.00					
541	3¢ violet, type II, June	27.50	20.00	265.00	(4)		
	Issue of 1920, Perf. 10 x 11 (Design 19 x 22¹/₂–22³/₄mm)						
542	1¢ green, May 26	9.00	.65	100.00	(6)	950.00	
	Issues of 1921, Perf. 10 (Design 19 x 22¹/₂mm)						
543	1¢ green, May	.35	.15	1.40	(4)		
a	Horizontal pair, imperf. between	550.00					
	Double transfer		—				
	Triple transfer	—	—				
	Issue of 1922, Perf. 11 (Design 19 x 22¹/₂mm)						
544	1¢ green	12,500.00	3,000.00				
	Issues of 1921 (Designs 19¹/₂–20 x 22mm)						
545	1¢ green, May	110.00	110.00	750.00	(4)		
546	2¢ carmine rose, type III, May	70.00	110.00	525.00	(4)		
a	Perf. 10 at left	—					
	Recut in hair	85.00	150.00				
	Issues of 1920, Perf. 11						
547	$2 Franklin, Nov. 1	175.00	32.50	4,000.00	(8)		
	Pilgrim Tercentenary Issue, Dec. 21						
548	1¢ The Mayflower	3.75	1.65	40.00	(6)	800.00	137,978,207
	Double transfer	—	—				
549	2¢ Landing of the Pilgrims	5.50	1.25	50.00	(6)	650.00	196,037,327
550	5¢ Signing of the Compact	37.50	10.00	400.00	(6)	—	11,321,607
	Issues of 1922-25, Perf. 11 (See also #581-91, 594-606, 622-23, 631-42, 658-79, 684-87, 692-701, 723)						
551	¹/₂¢ Nathan Hale, Apr. 4, 1925	.15	.15	4.25	(6)	15.00 (4)	
	"Cap" on fraction bar	.45	.15				
552	1¢ Franklin, Jan. 17, 1923	1.35	.15	17.50	(6)	20.00 (2)	
a	Booklet pane of 6, Aug. 11, 1923	5.00	.50				
	Double transfer	3.50	—				
553	1¹/₂¢ Harding, Mar. 19, 1925	2.25	.15	25.00	(6)	25.00 (2)	
554	2¢ Washington, Jan. 15, 1923	1.25	.15	17.50	(6)	35.00	
a	Horizontal pair, imperf. vertically	200.00					
b	Vertical pair, imperf. horizontally	500.00					
c	Booklet pane of 6, Feb. 10, 1923	6.00	1.00				
	Double transfer	2.25	.60				
555	3¢ Lincoln, Feb. 12, 1923	15.00	.85	125.00	(6)	27.50	
556	4¢ M. Washington, Jan. 15, 1923	15.00	.20	125.00	(6)	50.00	
b	Perf. 10, top or bottom	425.00	—				
557	5¢ T. Roosevelt, Oct. 27, 1922	15.00	.15	150.00	(6)	125.00	
a	Imperf. pair	1,500.00					
c	Perf. 10, top or bottom	—	500.00				
558	6¢ Garfield, Nov. 20, 1922	30.00	.75	325.00	(6)	225.00	
	Double transfer	40.00	2.00				
	Same, recut	40.00	2.00				

547

548

549

550

551

552

553

554

555

556

557

558

559

560

561

562

563

564

565

566

567

568

569

570

571

572

573

	Issues of 1922-25, Perf. 11	Un	U	PB	#	FDC
559	7¢ McKinley, May 1, 1923	7.00	.45	50.00	(6)	140.00
	Double transfer	—	—			
560	8¢ Grant, May 1, 1923	37.50	.35	500.00	(6)	175.00
	Double transfer	—	—			
561	9¢ Jefferson, Jan. 15, 1923	12.00	.90	115.00	(6)	175.00
	Double transfer	—	—			
562	10¢ Monroe, Jan. 15, 1923	16.00	.15	150.00	(6)	160.00
a	Vertical pair, imperf. horizontally	1,250.00				
b	Imperf. pair	1,250.00				
c	Perf. 10 at top or bottom		750.00			
563	11¢ Hayes, Oct. 4, 1922	1.25	.25	22.50	(6)	600.00
564	12¢ Cleveland, Mar. 20, 1923	5.50	.15	62.50	(6)	175.00
a	Horizontal pair, imperf. vertically	1,000.00				
b	Imperf. pair					
565	14¢ American Indian, May 1, 1923	3.50	.65	45.00	(6)	375.00
	Double transfer	—	—			
566	15¢ Statue of Liberty, Nov. 11, 1922	19.00	.15	225.00	(6)	500.00
567	20¢ Golden Gate, May 1, 1923	19.00	.15	165.00	(6)	500.00
a	Horizontal pair, imperf. vertically	1,500.00				
568	25¢ Niagara Falls, Nov. 11, 1922	17.00	.38	175.00	(6)	675.00
b	Vertical pair, imperf. horizontally	850.00				
c	Perf. 10 at one side	—				
569	30¢ Buffalo, Mar. 20, 1923	30.00	.30	235.00	(6)	825.00
	Double transfer	45.00	2.50			
570	50¢ Arlington Amphitheater, Nov. 11, 1922	50.00	.15	600.00	(6)	1,200.00
571	$1 Lincoln Memorial, Feb. 12, 1923	42.50	.35	350.00	(6)	5,500.00
	Double transfer	80.00	1.50			
572	$2 U.S. Capitol, Mar. 20, 1923	90.00	8.00	800.00	(6)	11,000.00
573	$5 Head of Freedom, Capitol Dome, Mar. 20, 1923	150.00	12.50	2,600.00	(8)	16,000.00
574	Not assigned					
	Issues of 1923-25, Imperf.					
575	1¢ green Franklin (552), Mar. 20, 1923	7.00	4.00	70.00	(6)	
576	1½¢ yel. brn. Harding (553), Apr. 4, 1925	1.50	1.50	17.00	(6)	45.00
577	2¢ carmine Washington (554)	1.50	1.25	25.00	(6)	
	Issues of 1923, Perf. 11 x 10					
578	1¢ green Franklin (552)	70.00	110.00	600.00	(4)	
579	2¢ carmine Washington (554)	60.00	100.00	450.00	(4)	
	Recut in eye	85.00	125.00			
	Issues of 1923-26, Perf. 10 (See also #551-73, 622-23, 631-42, 658-79, 684-87, 692-701, 723)					
580	Not assigned					
581	1¢ green Franklin (552), Apr. 21, 1923	7.00	.55	75.00	(4)	2,000.00
582	1½¢ brn. Harding (553), Mar. 19, 1925	3.50	.45	27.50	(4)	40.00
	Pair with full horiz. gutter between	135.00				
583	2¢ carm. Wash. (554), Apr. 14, 1924	1.75	.15	17.00	(4)	
a	Booklet pane of 6, Aug. 27, 1926	75.00	25.00			1,500.00
584	3¢ violet Lincoln (555), Aug. 1, 1925	19.00	1.75	160.00	(4)	55.00
585	4¢ yellow brown Martha Washington (556), Mar. 1925	11.50	.30	140.00	(4)	55.00
586	5¢ blue T. Roosevelt (557), Dec. 1924	12.00	.18	135.00	(4)	57.50
587	6¢ red orange Garfield (558), Mar. 1925	5.50	.25	60.00	(4)	60.00
588	7¢ black McKinley (559), May 29, 1926	8.00	4.25	67.50	(4)	70.00

	Issues of 1923-26, Perf. 11 x 10	Un	U	PB/LP	#	FDC	Q
589	8¢ olive grn. Grant (560), May 29, 1926	17.50	2.75	150.00	(4)	72.50	
590	9¢ rose Jefferson (561), May 29, 1926	3.75	1.90	30.00	(4)	72.50	
591	10¢ orange Monroe (562), June 8, 1925	47.50	.15	350.00	(4)	95.00	
592-93	Not assigned						
	Perf. 11						
594	1¢ green Franklin (552), design 19¾ x 22¼mm	16,000.00	4,250.00				
595	2¢ carmine Washington (554), design 19¾ x 22¼mm	225.00	250.00	900.00	(4)		
596	1¢ green Franklin (552), design 19¼ x 22¾mm		27,500.00				
	Issues of 1923-29, Coil Stamps, Perf. 10 Vertically						
597	1¢ green Franklin (552), July 18, 1923	.25	.15	1.65	(2)	*550.00*	
	Gripper cracks or double transfer	2.25	1.00				
598	1½¢ brown Harding (553), Mar. 19, 1925	.75	.15	2.85	(2)	50.00	
599	2¢ carmine Washington type I, Jan. 1923	.30	.15	1.65	(2)	*600.00*	
	Double transfer	1.65	1.00				
	Gripper cracks	2.00	2.00				
599A	2¢ carmine Washington (554), type II, Mar. 1929	105.00	9.50	550.00	(2)		
600	3¢ violet Lincoln (555), May 10, 1924	5.50	.15	18.50	(2)	60.00	
601	4¢ yellow brown M. Washington (556), Aug. 5, 1923	3.25	.30	17.50	(2)		
602	5¢ dark blue T. Roosevelt (557), Mar. 5, 1924	1.30	.15	7.25	(2)	82.50	
603	10¢ orange Monroe (562), Dec. 1, 1924	3.00	.15	17.50	(2)	100.00	
	Coil Stamps, Perf. 10 Horizontally						
604	1¢ yel. grn. Franklin (552), July 19, 1924	.25	.15	2.15	(2)	90.00	
605	1½¢ yel. brn. Harding (553), May 9, 1925	.25	.15	1.65	(2)	70.00	
606	2¢ carmine Washington (554), Dec. 31, 1923	.25	.15	1.25	(2)	100.00	
607-09	Not assigned						
	Issues of 1923, Harding Memorial Issue, Perf. 11						
610	2¢ blk. Harding, Sept. 1	.55	.15	18.00	(6)	30.00	1,459,487,085
a	Horizontal pair, imperf. vertically	1,100.00					
	Double transfer	1.75	.50				
	Imperf.						
611	2¢ blk. Harding (610), Nov. 15	6.50	4.25	85.00	(6)	90.00	770,000
	Perf. 10						
612	2¢ blk. Harding (610), Sept. 12	14.00	1.50	225.00	(4)	100.00	99,950,300
	Perf. 11						
613	2¢ black Harding (610)		15,000.00				
	Issues of 1924, Huguenot-Walloon Tercentary Issue, May 1						
614	1¢ Ship *Nieu Nederland*	2.75	3.00	30.00	(6)	30.00	51,378,023
615	2¢ Walloons' Landing at Fort Orange (Albany)	5.50	2.00	60.00	(6)	32.50	77,753,423
	Double transfer	12.50	3.50				
616	5¢ Huguenot Monument to Jan Ribault at Mayport, Florida	27.50	12.50	265.00	(6)	50.00	5,659,023

599   610

614   615   616

Details

2¢ Washington Types I-II, Series 1923-29

Detail of **#599, 634** Type I

No heavy hair lines at top center of head.

Detail of **#599A, 634A** Type II

Three heavy hair lines at top center of head.

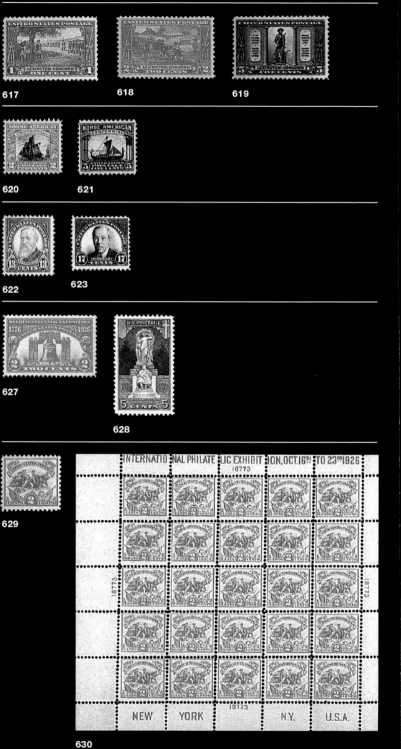

617

618

619

620

621

622

623

627

628

629

630

	Issues of 1925, Perf. 11	Un	U	PB	#	FDC	Q
	Issues of 1925, Lexington-Concord Issue, April 4						
617	1¢ Washington at Cambridge	2.50	2.25	40.00	(6)	27.50	15,615,000
618	2¢ "The Birth of Liberty," by Henry Sandham	5.00	3.75	67.50	(6)	30.00	26,596,600
619	5¢ "The Minute Man," by Daniel Chester French	24.00	12.50	235.00	(6)	65.00	5,348,800
	Line over head	50.00	18.50				
	Norse-American Issue, May 18						
620	2¢ Sloop *Restaurationen*	3.75	2.75	200.00	(8)	20.00	9,104,983
621	5¢ Viking Ship	14.00	10.50	650.00	(8)	30.00	1,900,983
	Issues of 1925-26 (See also #551-79, 581-91, 594-606, 631-42, 658-79, 684-87, 692-701, 723)						
622	13¢ B. Harrison, Jan. 11, 1926	12.00	.40	150.00	(6)	20.00	
623	17¢ Wilson, Dec. 28, 1925	13.00	.20	165.00	(6)	25.00	
624-26	Not assigned						
	Issues of 1926						
627	2¢ Independence Sesquicentennial Exposition, May 10	2.75	.40	35.00	(6)	10.00	307,731,900
628	5¢ John Ericsson Memorial, May 29	5.50	2.75	75.00	(6)	22.50	20,280,500
629	2¢ Battle of White Plains, Oct. 18	1.75	1.50	35.00	(6)	6.25	40,639,485
a	Vertical pair, imperf. between	—					
	International Philatelic Exhibition Souvenir Sheet, Oct. 18						
630	2¢ Battle of White Plains, sheet of 25 with selvage inscription (629)	350.00	375.00			1,400.00	107,398
	Dot over first "S" of "States"	375.00	400.00				
	Imperf. (See also #551-79, 581-91, 594-606, 622-23, 658-79, 684-87, 692-701, 723)						
631	1¹/₂¢ yellow brown Harding (553), Aug. 27	1.75	1.60	42.50	(4)	30.00	
	Issues of 1926-34, Perf. 11 x 10.5 (See also #551-73, 575-79, 581-91, 594-606, 622-23, 631-42, 684-87, 692-701, 723)						
632	1¢ green Franklin (552), June 10, 1927	.15	.15	1.65	(4)	45.00	
a	Booklet pane of 6, Nov. 2, 1927	4.50	*.25*			*3,000.00*	
b	Vertical pair, imperf. between	200.00	*125.00*				
	Pair with full vertical gutter between	150.00	—				
	Cracked plate	—	—				
633	1¹/₂¢ yellow brown Harding (553), May 17, 1927	1.60	.15	50.00	(4)	45.00	
634	2¢ carmine Washington (554), type I, Dec. 10, 1926	.15	.15	1.00	(4)	47.50	
	Pair with full vertical gutter between	200.00					
b	2¢ carmine lake, type I	—	—	—			
c	Horizontal pair, imperf. between	*2,000.00*					
d	Booklet pane of 6, Feb. 25, 1927	1.40	*.15*				
634A	2¢ carmine Washington (554), type II, Dec. 1928	300.00	12.50	1,550.00	(4)		
	Pair with full vertical or horizontal gutter between	1,000.00					
635	3¢ violet Lincoln (555), Feb. 3, 1927	.35	.15	5.00	(4)	47.50	
a	3¢ bright violet Lincoln, Feb. 7, 1934	.25	.15	3.25	(4)	25.00	
	Gripper cracks	3.25	2.00				
636	4¢ yellow brown Martha Washington (556), May 17, 1927	2.00	.15	60.00	(4)	50.00	
	Pair with full vertical gutter between	*200.00*					
637	5¢ dark blue Theodore Roosevelt (557), Mar. 24, 1927	1.90	.15	12.00	(4)	50.00	
	Pair with full vertical gutter between	*275.00*					

	Issues of 1926-34	Un	U	PB/LB	#	FDC	Q
	Perf. 11 x 10.5						
638	6¢ red orange Garfield (558), July 27, 1927	2.00	.15	12.00	(4)	57.50	
	Pair with full vert. gutter between	*200.00*					
639	7¢ black McKinley (559), Mar. 24, 1927	2.00	.15	21.00	(4)	57.50	
a	Vertical pair, imperf. between	150.00	80.00				
640	8¢ olive green Grant (560), June 10, 1927	2.00	.15	12.00	(4)	62.50	
641	9¢ orange red Jefferson (561), 1931	2.00	.15	12.00	(4)	72.50	
642	10¢ orange Monroe (562), Feb. 3, 1927	3.25	.15	23.50	(4)	90.00	
	Double transfer	—	—				
	Issues of 1927, Perf. 11						
643	2¢ Vermont Sesquicentennial, Aug. 3	1.25	.75	35.00	(6)	5.00	39,974,900
644	2¢ Burgoyne Campaign, Aug. 3	3.00	1.90	35.00	(6)	12.50	25,628,450
	Issues of 1928						
645	2¢ Valley Forge, May 26	.90	.35	22.50	(6)	4.00	101,330,328
	Perf. 11 x 10.5						
646	2¢ Battle of Monmouth/ Molly Pitcher, Oct. 20	.95	.95	25.00	(4)	15.00	9,779,896
	Wide spacing, vertical pair	20.00	—				
	Hawaii Sesquicentennial Issue, Aug. 13						
647	2¢ Washington (554)	3.75	3.75	90.00	(4)	15.00	5,519,897
	Wide spacing, vertical pair	75.00					
648	5¢ Theodore Roosevelt (557)	11.00	11.00	225.00	(4)	22.50	1,459,897
	Aeronautics Conference Issue, Dec. 12, Perf. 11						
649	2¢ Wright Airplane	1.00	.75	11.50	(6)	7.00	51,342,273
650	5¢ Globe and Airplane	4.50	3.00	50.00	(6)	10.00	10,319,700
	Plate flaw, "prairie dog"	27.50	12.50				
	Issues of 1929						
651	2¢ George Rogers Clark, Feb. 25	.55	.40	8.50	(6)	6.00	16,684,674
	Double transfer	4.00	2.00				
652	Not assigned						
	Perf. 11 x 10.5						
653	1/2¢ olive brown Nathan Hale (551), May 25	.15	.15	1.00	(4)	25.00	
	Electric Light's Golden Jubilee Issue, June 5, Perf. 11						
654	2¢ Thomas Edison's First Lamp	.60	.60	25.00	(6)	10.00	31,679,200
	Perf. 11 x 10.5						
655	2¢ carmine rose (654), June 11	.55	.15	30.00	(4)	80.00	210,119,474
	Coil Stamp, Perf. 10 Vertically						
656	2¢ carmine rose (654), June 11	12.50	1.25	50.00	(2)	90.00	133,530,000
	Perf. 11						
657	2¢ Sullivan Expedition, June 17	.60	.50	24.00	(6)	4.00	51,451,880
	2¢ lake	50.00	—				

643

644

645

646

647

648

649

650

651

654

657

658

669

680

681

682

683

684

685

	Issues of 1929	Un	U	PB/LP	#	FDC	Q
	#658-68 overprinted "Kans.," May 1, Perf. 11 x 10.5 (See also #551-73, 575-79, 581-91, 594-606, 622-23, 631-42, 684-87, 692-701, 723)						
658	1¢ Franklin	1.50	1.35	25.00	(4)	35.00	13,390,000
a	Vertical pair, one without overprint	300.00					
659	1¹/₂¢ brown Harding (553)	2.50	1.90	35.00	(4)	35.00	8,240,000
	Wide spacing, pair	65.00					
660	2¢ carmine Washington (554)	2.75	.75	30.00	(4)	35.00	87,410,000
661	3¢ violet Lincoln (555)	13.00	10.00	115.00	(4)	37.50	2,540,000
662	4¢ yellow brown Martha Washington (556)	13.00	6.00	120.00	(4)	40.00	2,290,000
663	5¢ deep blue T. Roosevelt (557)	9.00	6.50	92.50	(4)	40.00	2,700,000
664	6¢ red orange Garfield (558)	20.00	12.00	275.00	(4)	50.00	1,450,000
665	7¢ black McKinley (559)	19.00	18.00	350.00	(4)	50.00	1,320,000
666	8¢ olive green Grant (560)	65.00	50.00	525.00	(4)	95.00	1,530,000
667	9¢ light rose Jefferson (561)	10.00	7.50	110.00	(4)	95.00	1,130,000
668	10¢ orange yel. Monroe (562)	16.00	8.00	200.00	(4)	100.00	2,860,000
	#669-79 overprinted "Nebr.," May 1						
669	1¢ Franklin	2.25	1.50	30.00	(4)	35.00	8,220,000
a	Vertical pair, one without overprint	275.00					
670	1¹/₂¢ brown Harding (553)	2.00	1.65	32.50	(4)	35.00	8,990,000
671	2¢ carmine Washington (554)	2.00	.85	25.00	(4)	35.00	73,220,000
672	3¢ violet Lincoln (555)	8.50	7.50	87.50	(4)	40.00	2,110,000
673	4¢ yellow brown Martha Washington (556)	13.00	9.50	140.00	(4)	47.50	1,600,000
	Wide spacing, pair	110.00					
674	5¢ deep blue T. Roosevelt (557)	11.00	9.50	150.00	(4)	47.50	1,860,000
675	6¢ red orange Garfield (558)	27.50	15.00	300.00	(4)	70.00	980,000
676	7¢ black McKinley (559)	15.00	11.50	180.00	(4)	75.00	850,000
677	8¢ olive green Grant (560)	21.00	16.00	275.00	(4)	75.00	1,480,000
678	9¢ light rose Jefferson (561)	24.00	18.00	350.00	(4)	85.00	530,000
679	10¢ orange yel. Monroe (562)	75.00	14.00	750.00	(4)	95.00	1,890,000
	Warning: Excellent forgeries of the Kansas and Nebraska overprints exist.						
	Perf. 11						
680	2¢ Battle of Fallen Timbers, Sept. 14	.65	.65	21.00	(6)	3.50	29,338,274
681	2¢ Ohio River Canalization, Oct. 19	.50	.50	16.00	(6)	3.50	32,680,900
	Issues of 1930						
682	2¢ Mass. Bay Colony, Apr. 8	.50	.38	20.00	(6)	3.50	74,000,774
683	2¢ Carolina-Charleston, Apr. 10	1.00	.90	35.00	(6)	3.50	25,215,574
	Perf. 11 x 10.5						
684	1¹/₂¢ Warren G. Harding, Dec. 1	.25	.15	1.40	(4)	4.50	
	Pair with full horizontal gutter between	175.00					
	Pair with full vert. gutter between —						
685	4¢ William H. Taft, June 4	.75	.15	9.00	(4)	6.00	
	Gouge on right "4"	2.00	.60				
	Recut right "4"	2.00	.65				
	Pair with full horizontal gutter between	—					
	Coil Stamps, Perf. 10 Vertically						
686	1¹/₂¢ brn. Harding (684), Dec. 1	1.50	.15	5.00	(2)	5.00	
687	4¢ brown Taft (685), Sept. 18	2.75	.38	10.00	(2)	20.00	

	Issues of 1930, Perf. 11	Un	U	PB	#	FDC		Q
688	2¢ Battle of Braddock's Field, July 9	.85	.75	28.50	(6)	4.00		25,609,470
689	2¢ Gen. von Steuben, Sept. 17	.45	.45	17.00	(6)	4.00		66,487,000
a	Imperf. pair	2,500.00		12,000.00	(6)			
	Issues of 1931							
690	2¢ General Pulaski, Jan. 16	.20	.15	10.00	(6)	4.00		96,559,400
691	Not assigned							
	Perf. 11 x 10.5 (See also #551-73, 575-79, 581-91, 594-606, 622-23, 631-42, 658-79, 684-87, 723)							
692	11¢ light bl. Hayes (563), Sept. 4	2.00	.15	10.50	(4)	100.00		
	Retouched forehead	6.50	1.00					
693	12¢ brown violet Cleveland (564), Aug. 25	4.00	.15	17.50	(4)	100.00		
694	13¢ yellow green Harrison (622), Sept. 4	1.75	.15	11.50	(4)	100.00		
695	14¢ dark blue American Indian (565), Sept. 8	2.75	.22	13.50	(4)	100.00		
696	15¢ gray Statue of Liberty (566), Aug. 27	6.50	.15	30.00	(4)	125.00		
	Perf. 10.5 x 11							
697	17¢ black Wilson (623), July 25	3.50	.15	16.50	(4)	400.00		
698	20¢ carmine rose Golden Gate (567), Sept. 8	7.75	.15	35.00	(4)	325.00		
	Double transfer	20.00	—					
699	25¢ blue green Niagara Falls (568), July 25	7.25	.15	35.00	(4)	450.00		
700	30¢ brown Buffalo (569), Sept. 8	11.50	.15	60.00	(4)	325.00		
	Cracked plate	22.50	.85					
701	50¢ lilac Arlington Amphitheater (570), Sept. 4	35.00	.15	185.00	(4)	450.00		
	Perf. 11							
702	2¢ Red Cross, May 21	.16	.15	1.60	(4)	3.00		99,074,600
	Red cross omitted	—						
703	2¢ Yorktown, Oct. 19	.35	.25	2.25	(4)	3.50		25,006,400
a	2¢ lake and black	4.00	.65					
b	2¢ dark lake and black	375.00		1,750.00	(4)			
c	Pair, imperf. vertically	4,000.00						
	Issues of 1932, Washington Bicentennial Issue, Jan. 1, Perf. 11 x 10.5							
704	½¢ Portrait by Charles W. Peale	.15	.15	3.00	(4)	5.00 (4)		87,969,700
	Broken circle	.60	.15					
705	1¢ Bust by Jean Antoine Houdon	.15	.15	4.00	(4)	4.00 (2)		1,265,555,100
706	1½¢ Portrait by Charles W. Peale	.32	.15	13.00	(4)	4.00 (2)		304,926,800
707	2¢ Portrait by Gilbert Stuart	.15	.15	1.50	(4)	4.00		4,222,198,300
	Gripper cracks	1.50	.50					
708	3¢ Portrait by Charles W. Peale	.40	.15	10.50	(4)	4.00		456,198,500
709	4¢ Portrait by Charles P. Polk	.22	.15	4.25	(4)	4.00		151,201,300
	Broken bottom frame line	1.50	.50					
710	5¢ Portrait by Charles W. Peale	1.40	.15	14.50	(4)	4.00		170,565,100
	Cracked plate	5.00	1.00					
711	6¢ Portrait by John Trumbull	2.75	.15	50.00	(4)	4.00		111,739,400
712	7¢ Portrait by John Trumbull	.22	.15	4.25	(4)	4.00		83,257,400
713	8¢ Portrait by Charles B.J.F. Saint Memin	2.50	.50	50.00	(4)	4.50		96,506,100
	Pair, full vert. gutter between	—						
714	9¢ Portrait by W. Williams	2.00	.15	30.00	(4)	4.50		75,709,200
715	10¢ Portrait by Gilbert Stuart	8.50	.15	95.00	(4)	4.50		147,216,000

688   **689**   **690**

702   **703**

704   **705**   **706**

707   **708**   **709**

710   **711**   **712**

713   **714**   **715**

1932-1933

716

717

718

719

720

724

725

726

727

728

729

730

731

732

733

	Issues of 1932, Perf. 11	Un	U	PB/LP	#	FDC	Q
	Olympic Winter Games Issue, Jan. 25						
716	2¢ Ski Jumper	.35	.16	10.00	(6)	6.00	51,102,800
	Recut	3.50	1.50				
	Colored "snowball"	25.00	5.00				
	Perf. 11 x 10.5						
717	2¢ Arbor Day, Apr. 22	.15	.15	6.50	(4)	4.00	100,869,300
	Olympic Summer Games Issue, June 15						
718	3¢ Runner at Starting Mark	1.25	.15	9.50	(4)	6.00	168,885,300
	Gripper cracks	4.00	.75				
719	5¢ Myron's Discobolus	2.00	.20	18.00	(4)	8.00	53,376,100
	Gripper cracks	4.00	1.00				
720	3¢ Washington, June 16	.15	.15	1.20	(4)	7.50	
	Pair with full vertical or horizontal gutter between	200.00					
b	Booklet pane of 6, July 25	27.50	5.00			100.00	
c	Vertical pair, imperf. between	300.00	250.00				
	Recut lines on nose	2.00	.75				
	Coil Stamp, Perf. 10 Vertically						
721	3¢ deep violet (720), June 24	2.25	.15	8.25	(2)	15.00	
	Recut lines around eyes	—	—				
	Coil Stamp, Perf. 10 Horizontally						
722	3¢ deep violet (720), Oct. 12	1.25	.30	5.00	(2)	15.00	
	Coil Stamp, Perf. 10 Vertically (See also #551-73, 575-79, 581-91, 594-606, 622-23, 631-42, 684-87, 692-701)						
723	6¢ deep orange Garfield (558), Aug. 18	8.50	.25	42.50	(2)	15.00	
	Perf. 11						
724	3¢ William Penn, Oct. 24	.25	.15	8.00	(6)	3.25	49,949,000
a	Vertical pair, imperf. horizontally	—					
725	3¢ Daniel Webster, Oct. 24	.30	.24	16.50	(6)	3.25	49,538,500
	Issues of 1933						
726	3¢ Georgia Settlement, Feb. 12	.25	.18	10.00	(6)	3.25	61,719,200
	Perf. 10.5 x 11						
727	3¢ Peace of 1783, Apr. 19	.15	.15	4.00	(4)	3.50	73,382,400
	Century of Progress Issue, May 25						
728	1¢ Restoration of Fort Dearborn	.15	.15	2.00	(4)	3.00	348,266,800
	Gripper cracks	2.00	—				
729	3¢ Federal Building at Chicago	.15	.15	2.00	(4)	3.00	480,239,300
	American Philatelic Society Issue Souvenir Sheets, Aug. 25, Without Gum, Imperf.						
730	1¢ sheet of 25 (728)	24.00	24.00			100.00	456,704
a	Single stamp from sheet	.65	.35			3.25 (3)	11,417,600
731	3¢ sheet of 25 (729)	22.50	22.50			100.00	441,172
a	Single stamp from sheet	.50	.35			3.25	11,029,300
	Perf. 10.5 x 11						
732	3¢ NRA, Aug. 15	.15	.15	1.50	(4)	3.25	1,978,707,300
	Gripper cracks	1.50	—				
	Recut at right	2.00					
	Perf. 11						
733	3¢ Byrd Antarctic Expedition II, Oct. 9	.40	.48	15.00	(6)	7.00	5,735,944
	Double transfer	2.50	1.00				
734	5¢ Kosciuszko, Oct. 13	.50	.22	27.50	(6)	4.50	45,137,700
a	Horizontal pair, imperf. vertically	2,000.00					

	Issues of 1934, Imperf.	Un	U	PB	#	FDC	Q
	National Stamp Exhibition Issue Souvenir Sheet, Feb. 10, Without Gum						
735	3¢ sheet of 6 (733)	12.50	10.00			40.00	811,404
a	Single stamp from sheet	2.00	1.65			5.00	4,868,424
	Perf. 11						
736	3¢ Maryland Tercentenary, Mar. 23	.15	.15	7.50	(6)	1.60	46,258,300
	Double transfer	—	—				
	Mothers of America Issue, May 2, Perf. 11 x 10.5						
737	3¢ Portrait of his Mother, by James A. McNeill Whistler	.15	.15	1.00	(4)	1.60	193,239,100
	Perf. 11						
738	3¢ deep violet (737)	.15	.15	4.25	(6)	1.60	15,432,200
739	3¢ Wisconsin Tercentenary, July 7	.15	.15	3.00	(6)	1.10	64,525,400
a	Vert. pair, imperf. horiz.	250.00					
b	Horiz. pair, imperf. vert.	325.00					
	National Parks Issue, Unwmkd.						
740	1¢ El Capitan, Yosemite (California), July 16	.15	.15	1.00	(6)	2.25	84,896,350
	Recut	1.50	.50				
a	Vertical pair, imperf. horizontally, with gum	450.00					
741	2¢ Grand Canyon (Ariz.), July 24	.15	.15	1.25	(6)	2.25	74,400,200
a	Vertical pair, imperf. horizontally, with gum	300.00					
b	Horizontal pair, imperf. vertically, with gum	300.00					
	Double transfer	1.25	—				
742	3¢ Mirror Lake, Mt. Rainier (Washington), Aug. 3	.15	.15	1.75	(6)	2.50	95,089,000
a	Vertical pair, imperf. horizontally, with gum	350.00					
743	4¢ Cliff Palace, Mesa Verde (Colorado), Sept. 25	.35	.32	7.00	(6)	2.25	19,178,650
a	Vertical pair, imperf. horizontally, with gum	500.00					
744	5¢ Old Faithful, Yellowstone (Wyoming), July 30	.60	.55	8.75	(6)	2.25	30,980,100
a	Horizontal pair, imperf. vertically, with gum	400.00					
745	6¢ Crater Lake (Oregon), Sept. 5	1.00	.75	15.00	(6)	3.00	16,923,350
746	7¢ Great Head, Acadia Park (Maine), Oct. 2	.55	.65	10.00	(6)	3.00	15,988,250
a	Horizontal pair, imperf. vertically, with gum	550.00					
747	8¢ Great White Throne, Zion Park (Utah), Sept. 18	1.40	1.65	15.00	(6)	3.25	15,288,700
748	9¢ Glacier National Park (Montana), Aug. 27	1.50	.55	15.00	(6)	3.50	17,472,600
749	10¢ Great Smoky Mountains (North Carolina), Oct. 8	2.75	.90	25.00	(6)	6.00	18,874,300
	American Philatelic Society Issue Souvenir Sheet, Aug. 28, Imperf.						
750	3¢ sheet of 6 (742)	27.50	25.00			40.00	511,391
a	Single stamp from sheet	3.25	3.00			3.25	3,068,346
	Trans-Mississippi Philatelic Exposition Issue Souvenir Sheet, Oct. 10						
751	1¢ sheet of 6 (740)	12.00	12.00			35.00	793,551
a	Single stamp from sheet	1.35	1.50			3.25 (3)	4,761,306

735

736

737

739

740

741

742

744

743

745

746

747

748

749

750

751

1935

Examples of Special Printing Position Blocks

Gutter Block 752

Centerline Block 754

Line Block 756

Arrow Block 763

	Issues of 1935	Un	U	PB	#	FDC	Q
	Special Printing (#752-71), March 15, Without Gum, Perf. 10.5 x 11						
752	3¢ violet Peace of 1783 (727)	.15	.15	11.00	(4)	5.00	3,274,556
	Perf. 11						
753	3¢ blue Byrd Expedition II (733)	.40	.40	15.00	(6)	6.00	2,040,760
	Imperf.						
754	3¢ dp. vio. Whistler's Mother (737)	.50	.50	16.50	(6)	6.00	2,389,288
755	3¢ deep violet Wisconsin (739)	.50	.50	16.50	(6)	6.00	2,294,948
756	1¢ green Yosemite (740)	.20	.20	3.65	(6)	6.00	3,217,636
757	2¢ red Grand Canyon (741)	.22	.22	4.50	(6)	6.00	2,746,640
	Double transfer	—					
758	3¢ deep violet Mt. Rainier (742)	.45	.40	12.50	(6)	6.00	2,168,088
759	4¢ brown Mesa Verde (743)	.90	.90	16.50	(6)	6.50	1,822,684
760	5¢ blue Yellowstone (744)	1.40	1.25	18.50	(6)	6.50	1,724,576
	Double transfer	—					
761	6¢ dark blue Crater Lake (745)	2.25	2.00	30.00	(6)	6.50	1,647,696
762	7¢ black Acadia (746)	1.40	1.25	25.00	(6)	6.50	1,682,948
	Double transfer	—					
763	8¢ sage green Zion (747)	1.50	1.40	30.00	(6)	7.50	1,638,644
764	9¢ red orange Glacier (748)	1.75	1.50	32.50	(6)	7.50	1,625,224
765	10¢ gray black Smoky Mts. (749)	3.50	3.00	41.50	(6)	7.50	1,644,900
766	1¢ yellow grn. (728), pane of 25	24.00	24.00			250.00	98,712
a	Single stamp from pane	.65	.35			5.50	2,467,800
767	3¢ violet (729), pane of 25	22.50	22.50			250.00	85,914
a	Single stamp from pane	.50	.35			5.50 (3)	2,147,850
768	3¢ dark blue (733), pane of 6	18.00	12.50			250.00	267,200
a	Single stamp from pane	2.50	2.00			6.50	1,603,200
769	1¢ green (740), pane of 6	12.00	9.00			250.00	279,960
a	Single stamp from pane	1.75	1.50			4.00	1,679,760
770	3¢ deep violet (742), pane of 6	27.50	22.50			250.00	215,920
a	Single stamp from pane	3.00	3.00			5.00	1,295,520
771	16¢ dark blue Great Seal of U.S.	2.00	2.00	43.50	(6)	12.50	1,370,560
	For perforate variety, see #CE2.						

A number of position pieces can be collected from the panes or sheets of the 1935 Special Printing issues, including horizontal and vertical gutter (#752, 766-70) or line (#753-65, 771) blocks of four (HG/L and VG/L), arrow-and-guideline blocks of four (AGL) and crossed-gutter or centerline blocks of four (CG/L). Pairs sell for half the price of blocks of four.

	HG/L	VG/L	AGL	CG/L			HG/L	VG/L	AGL	CG/L
752	9.00	15.00		35.00		762	6.00	6.00	6.50	10.00
753	3.50	37.50	40.00	42.50		763	6.50	6.50	7.00	11.00
754	2.10	2.10	2.25	5.00		764	7.50	7.50	8.00	21.00
755	2.10	2.10	2.25	5.00		765	14.50	14.50	15.00	21.50
756	.90	.90	1.00	2.35		766	8.50	9.75		11.50
757	.95	.95	1.00	2.75		767	7.50	8.75		11.50
758	1.95	1.95	2.00	4.00		768	12.00	13.00		15.00
759	3.75	3.75	4.00	5.50		769	11.00	11.00		12.00
760	6.50	6.50	7.00	11.00		770	20.00	20.00		21.50
761	9.25	9.25	9.50	14.50		771	8.75	8.75	10.00	36.50

	Issues of 1935	Un	U	PB	#	FDC	Q
	Perf. 11 x 10.5						
	Beginning with #772, unused values are for never-hinged stamps.						
772	3¢ Connecticut, Apr. 26	.15	.15	1.40	(4)	8.00	70,726,800
	Defect in cent design	1.00	.25				
773	3¢ California Pacific International Expo, May 29	.15	.15	1.40	(4)	8.00	100,839,600
	Pair with full vertical gutter between	—					
	Perf. 11						
774	3¢ Boulder Dam, Sept. 30	.15	.15	1.85	(6)	10.00	73,610,650
	Perf. 11 x 10.5						
775	3¢ Michigan Statehood, Nov. 1	.15	.15	1.40	(4)	8.00	75,823,900
	Issues of 1936						
776	3¢ Republic of Texas, Mar. 2	.15	.15	1.40	(4)	17.50	124,324,500
	Perf. 10.5 x 11						
777	3¢ Rhode Island, May 4	.15	.15	1.40	(4)	8.00	67,127,650
	Pair with full gutter between *200.00*						
	Third International Philatelic Exhibition Issue Souvenir Sheet, May 9, Imperf.						
778	Sheet of 4 different stamps (#772, 773, 775 and 776)	1.75	1.75			13.00	2,809,039
a-d	Single stamp from sheet	.40	.30				2,809,039
779-81	Not assigned						
	Perf. 11 x 10.5						
782	3¢ Arkansas Statehood, June 15	.15	.15	1.40	(4)	8.00	72,992,650
783	3¢ Oregon Territory, July 14	.15	.15	1.40	(4)	8.50	74,407,450
	Double transfer	1.00	.50				
784	3¢ Susan B. Anthony, Aug. 26	.15	.15	.75	(4)	5.00	269,522,200
	Period missing after "B"	.75	.25				

The stamps you couldn't get apart

Printed to commemorate the Third Philatelic Exhibition of 1936, this souvenir sheet **(#778)** is especially notable as being the first to feature multiple designs without any perforations.

Interesting Fact: Postmaster General James A. Farley (1888-1976) later became chairman of the Coca-Cola Company.

772

773

774

775

776

777

778

782

783

784

785

786

787

788

789

790

791

792

793

794

795

796

798

799

800

801

802

	Issues of 1936-37	Un	U	PB	#	FDC	Q
	Perf. 11 x 10.5, Army Issue						
785	1¢ George Washington, Nathanael Green and Mount Vernon, Dec. 15, 1936	.15	.15	.85	(4)	5.00	105,196,150
	Pair with full vertical gutter between	—					
786	2¢ Andrew Jackson, Winfield Scott and The Hermitage, Jan. 15, 1937	.15	.15	.85	(4)	5.00	93,848,500
787	3¢ Generals Sherman, Grant and Sheridan, Feb. 18, 1937	.15	.15	1.10	(4)	5.00	87,741,150
788	4¢ Generals Robert E. Lee and "Stonewall" Jackson and Stratford Hall, Mar. 23, 1937	.30	.15	8.00	(4)	5.50	35,794,150
789	5¢ U.S. Military Academy at West Point, May 26, 1937	.60	.15	8.50	(4)	5.50	36,839,250
	Navy Issue						
790	1¢ John Paul Jones, John Barry, *Bon Homme Richard* and *Lexington,* Dec. 15, 1936	.15	.15	.85	(4)	5.00	104,773,450
791	2¢ Stephen Decatur, Thomas Macdonough and *Saratoga,* Jan. 15, 1937	.15	.15	.80	(4)	5.00	92,054,550
792	3¢ David G. Farragut and David D. Porter, *Hartford* and *Powhatan,* Feb. 18, 1937	.15	.15	1.00	(4)	5.00	93,291,650
793	4¢ Admirals William T. Sampson, George Dewey and Winfield S. Schley, Mar. 23, 1937	.30	.15	8.00	(4)	5.50	34,552,950
794	5¢ Seal of U.S. Naval Academy and Naval Cadets, May 26, 1937	.60	.15	8.50	(4)	5.50	36,819,050
	Issues of 1937						
795	3¢ Northwest Territory Ordinance, July 13	.15	.15	1.10	(4)	6.00	84,825,250
	Perf. 11						
796	5¢ Virginia Dare, Aug. 18	.20	.18	7.00	(6)	7.00	25,040,400
	Society of Philatelic Americans Issue Souvenir Sheet, Aug. 26, Imperf.						
797	10¢ blue green (749)	.60	.40			6.00	5,277,445
	Perf. 11 x 10.5						
798	3¢ Constitution Sesquicentennial, Sept. 17	.15	.15	1.00	(4)	6.50	99,882,300
	Territorial Issues, Perf. 10.5 x 11						
799	3¢ Hawaii, Oct. 18	.15	.15	1.25	(4)	7.00	78,454,450
	Perf. 11 x 10.5						
800	3¢ Alaska, Nov. 12	.15	.15	1.25	(4)	7.00	77,004,200
	Pair with full gutter between	—					
801	3¢ Puerto Rico, Nov. 25	.15	.15	1.25	(4)	7.00	81,292,450
802	3¢ Virgin Islands, Dec. 15	.15	.15	1.25	(4)	7.00	76,474,550
	Pair with full vertical gutter between	275.00					

	Issues of 1938-54, Perf. 11 x 10.5	Un	U	PB	#	FDC
	Presidential Issue (#804b, 806b, 807a issued in 1939, 832b in 1951, 832c in 1954, rest in 1938; see also 839-51)					
803	1/2¢ Benjamin Franklin, May 19	.15	.15	.35	(4)	1.75
804	1¢ George Washington, Apr. 25	.15	.15	.35	(4)	2.00
b	Booklet pane of 6, Jan. 27, 1939	1.50	.20			15.00
	Pair with full vertical gutter between	125.00	—			
805	1 1/2¢ Martha Washington, May 5	.15	.15	.30	(4)	2.00
b	Horizontal pair, imperf. between	150.00	25.00			
	Pair with full horizontal gutter between	150.00				
806	2¢ John Adams, June 3	.15	.15	.35	(4)	2.00
b	Booklet pane of 6, Jan. 27, 1939	3.50	.50			15.00
	Recut at top of head	3.00	1.50			
807	3¢ Thomas Jefferson, June 16	.15	.15	.35	(4)	2.00
a	Booklet pane of 6, Jan. 27, 1939	7.00	.50			18.00
b	Horizontal pair, imperf. between	650.00	—			
c	Imperf. pair	2,500.00				
808	4¢ James Madison, July 1	.60	.15	4.00	(4)	2.00
809	4 1/2¢ The White House, July 11	.15	.15	1.60	(4)	2.00
810	5¢ James Monroe, July 21	.20	.15	1.25	(4)	2.00
811	6¢ John Quincy Adams, July 28	.20	.15	1.75	(4)	2.00
812	7¢ Andrew Jackson, Aug. 4	.25	.15	1.75	(4)	2.00
813	8¢ Martin Van Buren, Aug. 11	.28	.15	1.75	(4)	2.00
814	9¢ William H. Harrison, Aug. 18	.32	.15	1.90	(4)	3.00
	Pair with full vertical gutter between	—				
815	10¢ John Tyler, Sept. 2	.25	.15	1.40	(4)	3.00
816	11¢ James K. Polk, Sept. 8	.65	.15	3.25	(4)	3.00
817	12¢ Zachary Taylor, Sept. 14	.90	.15	4.50	(4)	3.00
818	13¢ Millard Fillmore, Sept. 22	1.25	.15	6.75	(4)	3.00
819	14¢ Franklin Pierce, Oct. 6	.90	.15	4.50	(4)	3.00
820	15¢ James Buchanan, Oct. 13	.38	.15	2.50	(4)	3.00
821	16¢ Abraham Lincoln, Oct. 20	.90	.25	4.50	(4)	5.00
822	17¢ Andrew Johnson, Oct. 27	.85	.15	4.25	(4)	5.00
823	18¢ Ulysses S. Grant, Nov. 3	1.50	.15	7.50	(4)	5.00
824	19¢ Rutherford B. Hayes, Nov. 10	1.25	.35	6.25	(4)	5.00
825	20¢ James A. Garfield, Nov. 10	.70	.15	3.50	(4)	5.00
826	21¢ Chester A. Arthur, Nov. 22	1.25	.15	7.50	(4)	5.00
827	22¢ Grover Cleveland, Nov. 22	1.00	.40	9.50	(4)	5.00
828	24¢ Benjamin Harrison, Dec. 2	3.50	.18	18.75	(4)	5.00
829	25¢ William McKinley, Dec. 2	.60	.15	4.00	(4)	6.00
830	30¢ Theodore Roosevelt, Dec. 8	4.25	.15	24.00	(4)	7.50
831	50¢ William Howard Taft, Dec. 8	6.00	.15	37.50	(4)	10.00

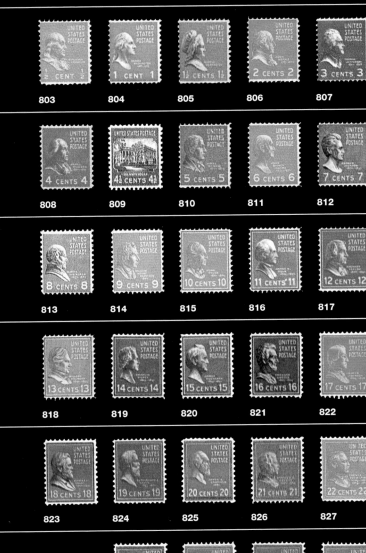

803   804   805   806   807

808   809   810   811   812

813   814   815   816   817

818   819   820   821   822

823   824   825   826   827

828   829   830   831

832

833

834

835

836

837

838

852

853

854

855

856

857

858

	Issues of 1938-54, Perf. 11	Un	U	PB/LP	#	FDC	Q
832	$1 Woodrow Wilson, Aug. 29	7.00	.15	35.00	(4)	45.00	
a	Vertical pair, imperf. horizontally	1,500.00					
b	Watermarked "USIR" (1951)	300.00	70.00	1,850.00	(4)		
c	$1 red violet and black, Aug. 31, 1954	6.00	.15	30.00	(4)	25.00	
d	As "c," vert. pair, imperf. horiz.	1,100.00					
e	Vertical pair, imperf. between	2,500.00					
f	As "c," vert. pair, imperf. between	7,000.00					
833	$2 Warren G. Harding, Sept. 29	21.00	3.75	110.00	(4)	90.00	
834	$5 Calvin Coolidge, Nov. 17	95.00	3.00	425.00	(4)	140.00	
a	$5 red, brown and black	2,250.00	1,500.00				
	Issues of 1938, Perf. 11 x 10.5						
835	3¢ Constitution Ratification, June 21	.22	.15	3.50	(4)	6.50	73,043,650
	Perf. 11						
836	3¢ Swedish-Finnish Tercentenary, June 27	.15	.15	2.75	(6)	6.00	58,564,368
	Perf. 11 x 10.5						
837	3¢ Northwest Territory, July 15	.15	.15	8.00	(4)	6.00	65,939,500
838	3¢ Iowa Territorial Centennial, Aug. 24	.15	.15	4.50	(4)	6.00	47,064,300
	Pair with full vertical gutter between	—					
	Issues of 1939, Coil Stamps, Jan. 20, Perf. 10 Vertically						
839	1¢ green Washington (804)	.20	.15	.90	(2)	5.00	
840	1½¢ bister brn. Martha Washington (805)	.24	.15	.95	(2)	5.00	
841	2¢ rose carmine, John Adams (806)	.24	.15	1.25	(2)	5.00	
842	3¢ deep violet Jefferson (807)	.42	.15	1.50	(2)	5.00	
	Gripper cracks	—					
	Thin, translucent paper	2.00	—				
843	4¢ red violet Madison (808)	6.00	.35	22.50	(2)	5.00	
844	4½¢ dark gray White House (809)	.50	.35	3.25	(2)	5.00	
845	5¢ bright blue Monroe (810)	4.50	.30	20.00	(2)	5.00	
846	6¢ red orange John Quincy Adams (811)	.80	.15	7.00	(2)	7.00	
847	10¢ brown red Tyler (815)	10.00	.40	35.00	(2)	9.00	
	Coil Stamps, Jan. 27, Perf. 10 Horizontally						
848	1¢ green Washington (804)	.55	.15	2.00	(2)	5.00	
849	1½¢ bister brn. Martha Washington (805)	1.10	.30	3.00	(2)	5.00	
850	2¢ rose carmine John Adams (806)	2.00	.40	6.00	(2)	5.00	
851	3¢ deep violet Jefferson (807)	1.75	.35	5.00	(2)	6.00	
	Perf. 10.5 x 11						
852	3¢ Golden Gate Exposition, Feb. 18	.15	.15	1.40	(4)	6.00	114,439,600
853	3¢ New York World's Fair, Apr. 1	.15	.15	1.90	(4)	8.00	101,699,550
	Perf. 11						
854	3¢ Washington's Inauguration, Apr. 30	.40	.15	3.50	(6)	6.00	72,764,550
	Perf. 11 x 10.5						
855	3¢ Baseball, June 12	1.25	.15	6.75	(4)	25.00	81,269,600
	Perf. 11						
856	3¢ Panama Canal, Aug. 15	.18	.15	3.00	(6)	5.00	67,813,350
	Perf. 10.5 x 11						
857	3¢ Printing, Sept. 25	.15	.15	1.00	(4)	5.00	71,394,750
	Perf. 11 x 10.5						
858	3¢ 50th Anniversary of Statehood (Montana, North Dakota, South Dakota, Washington), Nov. 2	.15	.15	1.25	(4)	5.00	66,835,000

	Issues of 1940, Perf. 10.5 x 11	Un	U	PB	#	FDC	Q
	Famous Americans Issue						
	Authors						
859	1¢ Washington Irving, Jan. 29	.15	.15	.90	(4)	1.50	56,348,320
860	2¢ James Fenimore Cooper, Jan. 29	.15	.15	.90	(4)	1.50	53,177,110
861	3¢ Ralph Waldo Emerson, Feb. 5	.15	.15	1.25	(4)	1.50	53,260,270
862	5¢ Louisa May Alcott, Feb. 5	.28	.20	8.50	(4)	2.25	22,104,950
863	10¢ Samuel L. Clemens (Mark Twain), Feb. 13	1.50	1.35	35.00	(4)	3.75	13,201,270
	Poets						
864	1¢ Henry W. Longfellow, Feb. 16	.15	.15	1.65	(4)	1.50	51,603,580
865	2¢ John Greenleaf Whittier, Feb. 16	.15	.15	1.75	(4)	1.50	52,100,510
866	3¢ James Russell Lowell, Feb. 20	.15	.15	2.00	(4)	1.50	51,666,580
867	5¢ Walt Whitman, Feb. 20	.32	.18	9.00	(4)	4.00	22,207,780
868	10¢ James Whitcomb Riley, Feb. 24	1.65	1.40	35.00	(4)	6.00	11,835,530
	Educators						
869	1¢ Horace Mann, Mar. 14	.15	.15	1.90	(4)	1.50	52,471,160
870	2¢ Mark Hopkins, Mar. 14	.15	.15	1.00	(4)	1.50	52,366,440
871	3¢ Charles W. Eliot, Mar. 28	.15	.15	2.00	(4)	1.50	51,636,270
872	5¢ Frances E. Willard, Mar. 28	.38	.25	9.50	(4)	4.00	20,729,030
873	10¢ Booker T. Washington, Apr. 7	1.10	1.25	25.00	(4)	6.00	14,125,580
	Scientists						
874	1¢ John James Audubon, Apr. 8	.15	.15	.90	(4)	1.50	59,409,000
875	2¢ Dr. Crawford W. Long, Apr. 8	.15	.15	.75	(4)	1.50	57,888,600
876	3¢ Luther Burbank, Apr. 17	.15	.15	1.00	(4)	2.00	58,273,180
877	5¢ Dr. Walter Reed, Apr. 17	.25	.15	5.75	(4)	2.50	23,779,000
878	10¢ Jane Addams, Apr. 26	1.00	.95	22.50	(4)	5.00	15,112,580
	Composers						
879	1¢ Stephen Collins Foster, May 3	.15	.15	.90	(4)	1.50	57,322,790
880	2¢ John Philip Sousa, May 3	.15	.15	.90	(4)	1.50	58,281,580
881	3¢ Victor Herbert, May 13	.15	.15	1.10	(4)	1.50	56,398,790
882	5¢ Edward A. MacDowell, May 13	.40	.22	8.75	(4)	2.50	21,147,000
883	10¢ Ethelbert Nevin, June 10	3.50	1.35	32.50	(4)	5.00	13,328,000
	Artists						
884	1¢ Gilbert Charles Stuart, Sept. 5	.15	.15	1.00	(4)	1.50	54,389,510
885	2¢ James A. McNeill Whistler, Sept. 5	.15	.15	.90	(4)	1.50	53,636,580
886	3¢ Augustus Saint-Gaudens, Sept. 16	.15	.15	.90	(4)	1.50	55,313,230
887	5¢ Daniel Chester French, Sept. 16	.48	.22	8.00	(4)	1.75	21,720,580
888	10¢ Frederic Remington, Sept. 30	1.75	1.40	30.00	(4)	5.00	13,600,580
	Inventors						
889	1¢ Eli Whitney, Oct. 7	.15	.15	1.75	(4)	1.50	47,599,580
890	2¢ Samuel F.B. Morse, Oct. 7	.15	.15	.90	(4)	1.50	53,766,510
891	3¢ Cyrus Hall McCormick, Oct. 14	.25	.15	1.65	(4)	1.50	54,193,580
892	5¢ Elias Howe, Oct. 14	1.00	.32	13.00	(4)	3.00	20,264,580
893	10¢ Alexander Graham Bell, Oct. 28	10.00	2.25	70.00	(4)	7.50	13,726,580

| 859 | 860 | 861 | 862 | 863 |

| 864 | 865 | 866 | 867 | 868 |

| 869 | 870 | 871 | 872 | 873 |

| 874 | 875 | 876 | 877 | 878 |

| 879 | 880 | 881 | 882 | 883 |

| 884 | 885 | 886 | 887 | 888 |

| 889 | 890 | 891 | 892 | 893 |

894

895

896

898

897

899

900

901

903

904

902

905

906

907

908

	Issues of 1940, Perf. 11 x 10.5	Un	U	PB	#	FDC	Q
894	3¢ Pony Express, Apr. 3	.25	.15	3.00	(4)	5.00	46,497,400
	Perf. 10.5 x 11						
895	3¢ Pan American Union, Apr. 14	.20	.15	2.75	(4)	4.50	47,700,000
	Perf. 11 x 10.5						
896	3¢ Idaho Statehood, July 3	.15	.15	1.75	(4)	4.50	50,618,150
	Perf. 10.5 x 11						
897	3¢ Wyoming Statehood, July 10	.15	.15	1.50	(4)	4.50	50,034,400
	Perf. 11 x 10.5						
898	3¢ Coronado Expedition, Sept. 7	.15	.15	1.50	(4)	4.50	60,943,700
	National Defense Issue, Oct. 16						
899	1¢ Statue of Liberty	.15	.15	.45	(4)	4.25	
a	Vertical pair, imperf. between	*500.00*	—				
b	Horizontal pair, imperf. between	40.00	—				
	Pair with full vertical gutter between	*200.00*					
	Cracked plate	3.00					
	Gripper cracks	3.00					
900	2¢ 90mm Antiaircraft Gun	.15	.15	.50	(4)	4.25	
a	Horizontal pair, imperf. between	40.00	—				
	Pair with full vertical gutter between	*275.00*					
901	3¢ Torch of Enlightenment	.15	.15	.60	(4)	4.25	
a	Horizontal pair, imperf. between	30.00	—				
	Pair with full vertical gutter between	—					
	Perf. 10.5 x 11						
902	3¢ Thirteenth Amendment, Oct. 20	.16	.15	3.00	(4)	5.00	44,389,550
	Issue of 1941, Perf. 11 x 10.5						
903	3¢ Vermont Statehood, Mar. 4	.15	.15	1.75	(4)	6.00	54,574,550
	Issues of 1942						
904	3¢ Kentucky Statehood, June 1	.15	.15	1.10	(4)	4.00	63,558,400
905	3¢ Win the War, July 4	.15	.15	.40	(4)	3.75	
b	3¢ purple	—	—				
	Pair with full vertical or horizontal gutter between	*175.00*					
906	5¢ Chinese Resistance, July 7	.22	.16	9.50	(4)	6.00	21,272,800
	Issues of 1943						
907	2¢ Allied Nations, Jan. 14	.15	.15	.35	(4)	3.50	1,671,564,200
	Pair with full vertical or horizontal gutter between	*225.00*					
908	1¢ Four Freedoms, Feb. 12	.15	.15	.50	(4)	3.50	1,227,334,200

	Issues of 1943-44, Perf. 12	Un	U	PB	#	FDC	Q
	Overrun Countries Issue (#921 issued in 1944, rest in 1943)						
909	5¢ Poland, June 22	.16	.15	6.00*	(4)	5.00	19,999,646
910	5¢ Czechoslovakia, July 12	.16	.15	3.00*	(4)	4.00	19,999,646
911	5¢ Norway, July 27	.15	.15	1.50*	(4)	4.00	19,999,646
912	5¢ Luxembourg, Aug. 10	.15	.15	1.40*	(4)	4.00	19,999,646
913	5¢ Netherlands, Aug. 24	.15	.15	1.40*	(4)	4.00	19,999,646
914	5¢ Belgium, Sept. 14	.15	.15	1.25*	(4)	4.00	19,999,646
915	5¢ France, Sept. 28	.15	.15	1.40*	(4)	4.00	19,999,646
916	5¢ Greece, Oct. 12	.35	.25	13.00*	(4)	4.00	14,999,646
917	5¢ Yugoslavia, Oct. 26	.25	.15	6.50*	(4)	4.00	14,999,646
918	5¢ Albania, Nov. 9	.18	.15	6.00*	(4)	4.00	14,999,646
919	5¢ Austria, Nov. 23	.18	.15	4.00*	(4)	4.00	14,999,646
920	5¢ Denmark, Dec. 7	.18	.15	5.75*	(4)	4.00	14,999,646
921	5¢ Korea, Nov. 2, 1944	.15	.15	5.00*	(4)	5.00	14,999,646
	"KORPA" plate flaw	17.50	12.50				
	*Instead of plate numbers, the selvage is inscribed with the name of the country.						
	Issues of 1944, Perf. 11 x 10.5						
922	3¢ Transcontinental Railroad, May 10	.20	.15	1.50	(4)	5.00	61,303,000
923	3¢ Steamship, May 22	.15	.15	1.25	(4)	4.00	61,001,450
924	3¢ Telegraph, May 24	.15	.15	.90	(4)	3.50	60,605,000
925	3¢ Philippines, Sept. 27	.15	.15	1.10	(4)	3.50	50,129,350
926	3¢ Motion Pictures, Oct. 31	.15	.15	.90	(4)	3.50	53,479,400

Bringing the Atlantic and Pacific coasts together

Around and through great mountain ranges, across blistering deserts and endless prairie, the first transcontinental rail took shape with the toil of thousands of immigrants and Civil War veterans. The Union Pacific, building westward from Nebraska, and the Central Pacific, building eastward from California, met at Promontory Point, Utah, on May 10, 1869. A golden spike was driven into the last rail to commemorate the completion of the first chain of railroads to span the North American continent. Trains have always been a favorite subject for U.S. stamps. You can find the newest train stamp in the New Issues section (beginning on page 20). Other train-related stamps are: #295, 993, 1006, 1506, 1573, 1755, 1897A, 1905, 2226, 2362-2366, 2402 and 2843-2847. **(#922)**

Interesting Fact: Until tracks were standardized in the mid-1880s, railroad tracks often varied in width, preventing trains from passing from one line to another.

COMPLETION OF FIRST TRANSCONTINENTAL RAILROAD
UNITED STATES OF AMERICA

909

910

911

912

913

914

915

916

917

918

919

920

921

922

923

924

925

926

927

928

929

930

931

932

933

934

935

936

937

938

939

940

941

942

943

944

945

946

947

	Issues of 1945, Perf. 11 x 10.5	Un	U	PB	#	FDC	Q
927	3¢ Florida Statehood, Mar. 3	.15	.15	.55	(4)	3.50	61,617,350
928	5¢ United Nations Conference, Apr. 25	.15	.15	.45	(4)	4.00	75,500,000
	Perf. 10¹/₂ x 11						
929	3¢ Iwo Jima (Marines), July 11	.15	.15	.38	(4)	6.75	137,321,000
	Issues of 1945-46, Franklin D. Roosevelt Issue, Perf. 11 x 10.5						
930	1¢ Roosevelt and Hyde Park Residence, July 26, 1945	.15	.15	.16	(4)	2.50	128,140,000
931	2¢ Roosevelt and "The Little White House" at Warm Springs, Ga., Aug. 24, 1945	.15	.15	.24	(4)	2.50	67,255,000
932	3¢ Roosevelt and White House, June 27, 1945	.15	.15	.28	(4)	2.50	133,870,000
933	5¢ Roosevelt, Map of Western Hemisphere and Four Freedoms, Jan. 30, 1946	.15	.15	.40	(4)	3.00	76,455,400
934	3¢ Army, Sept. 28	.15	.15	.30	(4)	4.75	128,357,750
935	3¢ Navy, Oct. 27	.15	.15	.30	(4)	4.75	135,863,000
936	3¢ Coast Guard, Nov. 10	.15	.15	.30	(4)	4.75	111,616,700
937	3¢ Alfred E. Smith, Nov. 26	.15	.15	.30	(4)	2.50	308,587,700
	Pair with full vertical gutter between	—					
938	3¢ Texas Statehood, Dec. 29	.15	.15	.30	(4)	4.00	170,640,000
	Issues of 1946						
939	3¢ Merchant Marine, Feb. 26	.15	.15	.30	(4)	4.75	135,927,000
940	3¢ Veterans of World War II, May 9	.15	.15	.30	(4)	1.75	260,339,100
941	3¢ Tennessee Statehood, June 1	.15	.15	.30	(4)	1.50	132,274,500
942	3¢ Iowa Statehood, Aug. 3	.15	.15	.30	(4)	1.50	132,430,000
943	3¢ Smithsonian Institution, Aug. 10	.15	.15	.30	(4)	1.50	139,209,500
944	3¢ Kearny Expedition, Oct. 16	.15	.15	.30	(4)	1.50	114,684,450
	Issues of 1947, Perf. 10.5 x 11						
945	3¢ Thomas A. Edison, Feb. 11	.15	.15	.30	(4)	2.00	156,540,510
	Perf. 11 x 10.5						
946	3¢ Joseph Pulitzer, Apr. 10	.15	.15	.30	(4)	1.50	120,452,600
947	3¢ Postage Stamps Centenary, May 17	.15	.15	.30	(4)	1.50	127,104,300

Minimum value listed for a stamp is 15 cents; for a First Day Cover (FDC), $1.00. This minimum represents a fair-market price for having a dealer locate and provide a single stamp or cover from his or her stock. Dealers may charge less per stamp or cover for a group of such stamps or covers, or less for a single stamp or cover.

Add Stamps Automatically

- Automatic shipment of new stamps, stationery and/or philatelic products you want via mail order
- Quality guaranteed

Richard Nixon

Convenient and Complete

Armchair collectors need never leave the comfort of home to use the U.S. Postal Service's Standing Order Service subscription program. Sign up once, make an advance deposit, and all postal items you desire will be shipped to you automatically every few months.

Guaranteed Quality

Subscribers to the Standing Order Service receive mint-condition postal items of exceptional quality—the best available centering, color and printing registration. If you are not completely satisfied, return the item within 30 days for a full refund or replacement.

All products are sold at face value—there are no markups, extra fees or shipping and handling charges. Just make an advance deposit based on the items and quantities you plan to select. You will be notified when you need to replenish your deposit account.

For Information

Send in the postage-paid request card in this book or call toll-free:

1-800-STAMP24

	Issues of 1947, Imperf.	Un	U	PB	#	FDC	Q
	Centenary International Philatelic Exhibition Issue Souvenir Sheet, May 19						
948	Souvenir sheet of 2 stamps (#1-2)	.60	.45			2.00	10,299,600
a	5¢ single stamp from sheet	.25	.20				
b	10¢ single stamp from sheet	.30	.25				
	Perf. 11 x 10.5						
949	3¢ Doctors, June 9	.15	.15	.30	(4)	1.00	132,902,000
950	3¢ Utah Settlement, July 24	.15	.15	.30	(4)	1.00	131,968,000
951	3¢ U.S. Frigate *Constitution*, Oct. 21	.15	.15	.30	(4)	1.50	131,488,000
	Perf. 10.5 x 11						
952	3¢ Everglades National Park, Dec. 5	.15	.15	.30	(4)	1.00	122,362,000
	Issues of 1948, Perf. 10¹/₂ x 11						
953	3¢ Dr. G.W. Carver, Jan. 5	.15	.15	.30	(4)	1.00	121,548,000
	Perf. 11 x 10.5						
954	3¢ California Gold, Jan. 24	.15	.15	.30	(4)	1.00	131,109,500
955	3¢ Mississippi Territory, Apr. 7	.15	.15	.30	(4)	1.00	122,650,500
956	3¢ Four Chaplains, May 28	.15	.15	.30	(4)	1.00	121,953,500
957	3¢ Wisconsin Statehood, May 29	.15	.15	.30	(4)	1.00	115,250,000
958	5¢ Swedish Pioneer, June 4	.15	.15	.45	(4)	1.00	64,198,500
959	3¢ Progress of Women, July 19	.15	.15	.30	(4)	1.00	117,642,500
	Perf. 10.5 x 11						
960	3¢ William Allen White, July 31	.15	.15	.30	(4)	1.00	77,649,600
	Perf. 11 x 10.5						
961	3¢ U.S.-Canada Friendship, Aug. 2	.15	.15	.30	(4)	1.00	113,474,500
962	3¢ Francis Scott Key, Aug. 9	.15	.15	.30	(4)	1.00	120,868,500
963	3¢ Salute to Youth, Aug. 11	.15	.15	.30	(4)	1.00	77,800,500
964	3¢ Oregon Territory, Aug. 14	.15	.15	.30	(4)	1.00	52,214,000
	Perf. 10.5 x 11						
965	3¢ Harlan F. Stone, Aug. 25	.15	.15	.60	(4)	1.00	53,958,100
966	3¢ Palomar Observatory, Aug. 30	.15	.15	1.10	(4)	1.50	61,120,100
a	Vertical pair, imperf. between	500.00					
	Perf. 11 x 10.5						
967	3¢ Clara Barton, Sept. 7	.15	.15	.30	(4)	.90	57,823,000

A salute to suffrage

Elizabeth Stanton, Carrie Chapman Catt and Lucretia Mott were instrumental in gaining women the right to vote. In August 1995, the Postal Service issued a new stamp honoring Women's Suffrage by recognizing the contributions of the movement. For a visual of this horizontal stamp, designed by April Greiman, see the 1995 Issues section. **(#959)**

Elizabeth Stanton   **Carrie Chapman Catt**   **Lucretia Mott**

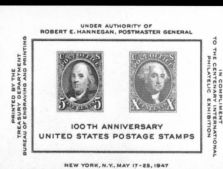

948

949

950

951

952

953

954

955

956

957

958

959

960

961

962

963

964

965

966

967

968

969

970

971

971

972

973

974

975

976

977

978

979

980

981

982

983

984

985

986

987

988

	Issues of 1948, Perf. 11 x 10.5	Un	U	PB	#	FDC	Q
968	3¢ Poultry Industry, Sept. 9	.15	.15	.35	(4)	.90	52,975,000
	Perf. 10.5 x 11						
969	3¢ Gold Star Mothers, Sept. 21	.15	.15	.35	(4)	1.00	77,149,000
	Perf. 11 x 10.5						
970	3¢ Fort Kearny, Sept. 22	.15	.15	.35	(4)	1.00	58,332,000
971	3¢ Volunteer Firemen, Oct. 4	.15	.15	.35	(4)	1.50	56,228,000
972	3¢ Indian Centennial, Oct. 15	.15	.15	.35	(4)	1.00	57,832,000
973	3¢ Rough Riders, Oct. 27	.15	.15	.35	(4)	1.00	53,875,000
974	3¢ Juliette Gordon Low, Oct. 29	.15	.15	.35	(4)	1.00	63,834,000
	Perf. 10.5 x 11						
975	3¢ Will Rogers, Nov. 4	.15	.15	.40	(4)	1.00	67,162,200
976	3¢ Fort Bliss, Nov. 5	.15	.15	1.25	(4)	1.00	64,561,000
	Perf. 11 x 10.5						
977	3¢ Moina Michael, Nov. 9	.15	.15	.35	(4)	1.00	64,079,500
978	3¢ Gettysburg Address, Nov. 19	.15	.15	.35	(4)	1.00	63,388,000
	Perf. 10.5 x 11						
979	3¢ American Turners, Nov. 20	.15	.15	.35	(4)	1.00	62,285,000
980	3¢ Joel Chandler Harris, Dec. 9	.15	.15	.55	(4)	1.00	57,492,600
	Issues of 1949, Perf. 11 x 10.5						
981	3¢ Minnesota Territory, Mar. 3	.15	.15	.30	(4)	1.00	99,190,000
982	3¢ Washington and Lee University, Apr. 12	.15	.15	.30	(4)	1.00	104,790,000
983	3¢ Puerto Rico Election, Apr. 27	.15	.15	.30	(4)	1.00	108,805,000
984	3¢ Annapolis Tercentenary, May 23	.15	.15	.30	(4)	1.00	107,340,000
985	3¢ Grand Army of the Republic, Aug. 29	.15	.15	.30	(4)	1.00	117,020,000
	Perf. 10.5 x 11						
986	3¢ Edgar Allan Poe, Oct. 7	.15	.15	.45	(4)	1.00	122,633,000
	Thin outer frame line at top, inner frame line missing	6.00					
	Issues of 1950, Perf. 11 x 10.5						
987	3¢ American Bankers, Jan. 3	.15	.15	.30	(4)	1.00	130,960,000
	Perf. 10.5 x 11						
988	3¢ Samuel Gompers, Jan. 27	.15	.15	.30	(4)	1.00	128,478,000

	Issues of 1950	Un	U	PB	#	FDC	Q
	National Capital Sesquicentennial Issue, Perf. 10.5 x 11, 11 x 10.5						
989	3¢ Statue of Freedom on Capitol Dome, Apr. 20	.15	.15	.30	(4)	1.00	132,090,000
990	3¢ Executive Mansion, June 12	.15	.15	.38	(4)	1.00	130,050,000
991	3¢ Supreme Court, Aug. 2	.15	.15	.30	(4)	1.00	131,350,000
992	3¢ U.S. Capitol, Nov. 22	.15	.15	.38	(4)	1.00	129,980,000
	Gripper cracks	1.00	.50				
	Perf. 11 x 10.5						
993	3¢ Railroad Engineers, Apr. 29	.15	.15	.30	(4)	1.00	122,315,000
994	3¢ Kansas City, MO, June 3	.15	.15	.30	(4)	1.00	122,170,000
995	3¢ Boy Scouts, June 30	.15	.15	.35	(4)	3.00	131,635,000
996	3¢ Indiana Territory, July 4	.15	.15	.30	(4)	1.00	121,860,000
997	3¢ California Statehood, Sept. 9	.15	.15	.30	(4)	1.00	121,120,000
	Issues of 1951						
998	3¢ United Confederate Veterans, May 30	.15	.15	.30	(4)	1.00	119,120,000
999	3¢ Nevada Settlement, July 14	.15	.15	.30	(4)	1.00	112,125,000
1000	3¢ Landing of Cadillac, July 24	.15	.15	.30	(4)	1.00	114,140,000
1001	3¢ Colorado Statehood, Aug. 1	.15	.15	.30	(4)	1.00	114,490,000
1002	3¢ American Chemical Society, Sept. 4	.15	.15	.30	(4)	1.00	117,200,000
1003	3¢ Battle of Brooklyn, Dec. 10	.15	.15	.30	(4)	1.00	116,130,000
	Issues of 1952						
1004	3¢ Betsy Ross, Jan. 2	.15	.15	.35	(4)	1.00	116,175,000
1005	3¢ 4-H Club, Jan. 15	.15	.15	.30	(4)	1.00	115,945,000
1006	3¢ B&O Railroad, Feb. 28	.15	.15	.35	(4)	1.25	112,540,000
1007	3¢ American Automobile Association, Mar. 4	.15	.15	.30	(4)	1.00	117,415,000

She put the stars on the flag

As the story goes, in June 1776, General George Washington came to Betsy Ross's house in Philadelphia with a highly secret and dangerous request: to make a flag for a country that was about to declare its independence from England. Ross suggested a design using five-pointed stars and sewed the first flag of the United States of America in her back parlor. Congress approved that flag on June 14, 1777. **(#1004)**

Interesting Fact: Ross's house, on Arche Street, still stands as a historic landmark in what is now downtown Philadelphia.

989

990

991

992

993

994

995

996

997

998

999

1000

1001

1002

1003

1004

1005

1006

1007

1008

1009

1010

1011

1012

1013

1014

1015

1016

1017

1018

1019

1020

1021

1022

1023

1024

1025

1026

1027

1028

1029

	Issues of 1952, Perf. 11 x 10.5	Un	U	PB	#	FDC	Q
1008	3¢ NATO, Apr. 4	.15	.15	.30	(4)	1.00	2,899,580,000
1009	3¢ Grand Coulee Dam, May 15	.15	.15	.30	(4)	1.00	114,540,000
1010	3¢ Arrival of Lafayette, June 13	.15	.15	.30	(4)	1.00	113,135,000
	Perf. 10.5 x 11						
1011	3¢ Mt. Rushmore Memorial, Aug. 11	.15	.15	.35	(4)	1.00	116,255,000
	Perf. 11 x 10.5						
1012	3¢ Engineering, Sept. 6	.15	.15	.30	(4)	1.00	113,860,000
1013	3¢ Service Women, Sept. 11	.15	.15	.30	(4)	1.00	124,260,000
1014	3¢ Gutenberg Bible, Sept. 30	.15	.15	.30	(4)	1.00	115,735,000
1015	3¢ Newspaper Boys, Oct. 4	.15	.15	.30	(4)	1.00	115,430,000
1016	3¢ International Red Cross, Nov. 21	.15	.15	.30	(4)	1.00	136,220,000
	Issues of 1953						
1017	3¢ National Guard, Feb. 23	.15	.15	.35	(4)	1.00	114,894,600
1018	3¢ Ohio Statehood, Mar. 2	.15	.15	.35	(4)	1.00	118,706,000
1019	3¢ Washington Territory, Mar. 2	.15	.15	.30	(4)	1.00	114,190,000
1020	3¢ Louisiana Purchase, Apr. 30	.15	.15	.30	(4)	1.00	113,990,000
1021	5¢ Opening of Japan, July 14	.15	.15	.90	(4)	1.00	89,289,600
1022	3¢ American Bar Association, Aug. 24	.15	.15	.30	(4)	1.00	114,865,000
1023	3¢ Sagamore Hill, Sept. 14	.15	.15	.30	(4)	1.00	115,780,000
1024	3¢ Future Farmers, Oct. 13	.15	.15	.30	(4)	1.00	115,244,600
1025	3¢ Trucking Industry, Oct. 27	.15	.15	.30	(4)	1.00	123,709,600
1026	3¢ General George S. Patton, Nov. 11	.15	.15	.40	(4)	1.75	114,798,600
1027	3¢ New York City, Nov. 20	.15	.15	.35	(4)	1.00	115,759,600
1028	3¢ Gadsden Purchase, Dec. 30	.15	.15	.30	(4)	1.00	116,134,600
	Issue of 1954						
1029	3¢ Columbia University, Jan. 4	.15	.15	.30	(4)	1.00	118,540,000

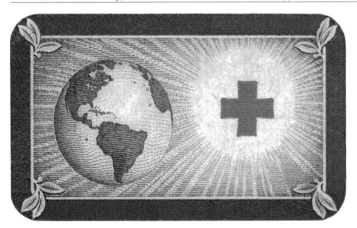

The flag shared by over 100 countries

After witnessing 40,000 casualties at the Battle of Solferino in Italy in 1859, Swiss citizen Jean Henry Dunant helped found the Red Cross. The "red cross" symbolizes neutral aid and pays homage to the flag of Switzerland, where the two international Red Cross organizations are located. This issue is one of the few two-color stamps of its era. **(#1016)**

Interesting Fact: Clara Barton (1821-1912), called the Angel of the Battlefield for her heroic work as a nurse during the Civil War, founded the American Red Cross in 1881. See stamp #967, as well as the new Civil War "Classic Collection" stamps in the 1995 Issues section.

	Issues of 1954-67, Perf. 11 x 10.5	Un	U	PB	#	FDC
	Liberty Issue					
1030	1/2¢ Franklin, Oct. 20, 1954	.15	.15	.25	(4)	1.00
1031	1¢ Washington, Aug. 26, 1954	.15	.15	.20	(4)	1.00
	Pair with full vertical or horizontal gutter between	150.00				
b	Wet printing	.15	.15	.20		
	Perf. 10.5 x 11					
1031A	1 1/4¢ Palace of the Governors, June 17, 1960	.15	.15	.45	(4)	1.00
1032	1 1/2¢ Mt. Vernon, Feb. 22, 1956	.15	.15	2.00	(4)	1.00
	Perf. 11 x 10.5					
1033	2¢ Jefferson, Sept. 15, 1954	.15	.15	.22	(4)	1.00
	Pair with full vertical or horizontal gutter between	—				
1034	2 1/2¢ Bunker Hill, June 17, 1959	.15	.15	.50	(4)	1.00
1035	3¢ Statue of Liberty, June 24, 1954	.15	.15	.30	(4)	1.00
a	Booklet pane of 6, June 30, 1954	4.00	*.50*			5.00
b	Tagged, July 6, 1966	.25	.25	5.00	(4)	15.00
c	Imperf. pair	1,750.00				
d	Horizontal pair, imperf. between	—				
e	Wet printing	.15	.15	.30		
f	As "a," dry printing	4.75	*.60*			
1036	4¢ Lincoln, Nov. 19, 1954	.15	.15	.35	(4)	1.00
a	Booklet pane of 6, July 31, 1958	2.50	*.50*			4.00
b	Tagged, Nov. 2, 1963	.48	.40	6.50	(4)	50.00
	Perf. 10.5 x 11					
1037	4 1/2¢ The Hermitage, Mar. 16, 1959	.15	.15	.65	(4)	1.00
	Perf. 11 x 10.5					
1038	5¢ James Monroe, Dec. 2, 1954	.15	.15	.50	(4)	1.00
	Pair with full vertical gutter between	200.00				
1039	6¢ T. Roosevelt, Nov. 18, 1955	.25	.15	1.10	(4)	1.00
a	Wet printing	.42	.15			
1040	7¢ Wilson, Jan. 10, 1956	.20	.15	1.00	(4)	1.00
	Perf. 11					
1041	8¢ Statue of Liberty, Apr. 9, 1954	.24	.15	2.25	(4)	1.00
a	Carmine double impression	650.00				
1042	8¢ Statue of Liberty, redrawn, Mar. 22, 1958	.20	.15	.95	(4)	1.00
	Perf. 11 x 10.5					
1042A	8¢ Gen. John J. Pershing, Nov. 17, 1961	.22	.15	.95	(4)	1.00
	Perf. 10.5 x 11					
1043	9¢ The Alamo, June 14, 1956	.28	.15	1.40	(4)	1.50
1044	10¢ Independence Hall, July 4, 1956	.22	.15	1.10	(4)	1.00
b	Tagged, July 6, 1966	2.00	1.00	*20.00*	(4)	15.00
	Perf. 11					
1044A	11¢ Statue of Liberty, June 15, 1961	.28	.15	1.25	(4)	1.00
c	Tagged, Jan. 11, 1967	2.00	1.60	*35.00*	(4)	22.50

1030

1031

1031A

1032

1033

1034

1035

1036

1037

1038

1039

1040

1041

1042

1042A

1043

1044

1044A

1045 **1046**

1047

1048 **1049**

1050 **1051**

1052 **1053**

	Issues of 1954-67, Perf. 11 x 10.5	Un	U	PB/LP	#	FDC
1045	12¢ Benjamin Harrison, June 6, 1959	.32	.15	1.50	(4)	1.00
a	Tagged, 1968	.45	.15	3.00	(4)	25.00
1046	15¢ John Jay, Dec. 12, 1958	.90	.15	3.00	(4)	1.00
a	Tagged, July 6, 1966	1.00	.35	7.50	(4)	20.00
	Perf. 10.5 x 11					
1047	20¢ Monticello, Apr. 13, 1956	.40	.15	1.80	(4)	1.20
	Perf. 11 x 10.5					
1048	25¢ Paul Revere, Apr. 18, 1958	1.10	.15	5.60	(4)	1.30
1049	30¢ Robert E. Lee, Sept. 21, 1955	.70	.15	5.65	(4)	1.50
a	Wet printing	1.75	.15	5.65	(4)	
1050	40¢ John Marshall, Sept. 24, 1955	1.50	.15	8.00	(4)	1.75
a	Wet printing	2.50	.25	8.00	(4)	
1051	50¢ Susan B. Anthony, Aug. 25, 1955	1.50	.15	6.75	(4)	6.00
a	Wet printing	2.50	.15	6.75	(4)	
1052	$1 Patrick Henry, Oct. 7, 1955	5.00	.15	24.00	(4)	10.00
a	Wet printing	6.50	.15	24.00	(4)	
	Perf. 11					
1053	$5 Alexander Hamilton, Mar. 19, 1956	75.00	6.75	325.00	(4)	55.00
	Issues of 1954-73, Coil Stamps, Perf. 10 Vertically					
1054	1¢ dark green Washington (1031), Oct. 8, 1954	.18	.15	.75	(2)	1.00
b	Imperf. pair	2,000.00	—			
c	Wet printing	.35	.16			
	Coil Stamp, Perf. 10 Horizontally					
1054A	1¹/₄¢ turquoise Palace of the Governors (1031A), June 17, 1960	.15	.15	2.25	(2)	1.00
	Coil Stamps, Perf. 10 Vertically					
1055	2¢ rose carmine Jefferson (1033), Oct. 22, 1954	.15	.15	.75	(2)	1.00
a	Tagged, May 6, 1968	.15	.15			11.00
b	Imperf. pair (Bureau precanceled)		450.00			
c	As "a," imperf. pair	475.00				
d	Wet printing	.20	.15			
1056	2¹/₂¢ gray blue Bunker Hill (1034), Sept. 9, 1959	.25	.25	3.50	(2)	2.00
1057	3¢ deep violet Statue of Liberty (1035), July 20, 1954	.15	.15	.55	(2)	1.00
a	Imperf. pair	1,350.00	—	1,650.00	(2)	
b	Tagged, Oct. 1966	1.00	.50	65.00		
c	Wet printing	.24	.15			
1058	4¢ red violet Lincoln (1036), July 31, 1958	.15	.15	.60	(2)	1.00
a	Imperf. pair	90.00	70.00	200.00	(2)	
b	Wet printing (Bureau precanceled)		.50			
	Coil Stamp, Perf. 10 Horizontally					
1059	4¹/₂¢ blue green The Hermitage (1037), May 1, 1959	1.50	1.20	14.00	(2)	1.75
	Coil Stamp, Perf. 10 Vertically					
1059A	25¢ green Revere (1048), Feb. 25, 1965	.50	.30	1.75	(2)	1.25
b	Tagged, Apr. 3, 1973	.55	.20			14.00
	Dull finish gum	.55				
c	Imperf. pair	40.00		75.00	(2)	

	Issues of 1954, Perf. 11 x 10.5	Un	U	PB	#	FDC	Q
1060	3¢ Nebraska Territory, May 7	.15	.15	.30	(4)	1.00	115,810,000
1061	3¢ Kansas Territory, May 31	.15	.15	.30	(4)	1.00	113,603,700
	Perf. 10.5 x 11						
1062	3¢ George Eastman, July 12	.15	.15	.35	(4)	1.00	128,002,000
	Perf. 11 x 10.5						
1063	3¢ Lewis and Clark Expedition, July 28	.15	.15	.35	(4)	1.00	116,078,150
	Issues of 1955, Perf. 10.5x 11						
1064	3¢ Pennsylvania Academy of the Fine Arts, Jan. 15	.15	.15	.30	(4)	1.00	116,139,800
	Perf. 11 x 10.5						
1065	3¢ Land-Grant Colleges, Feb. 12	.15	.15	.30	(4)	1.00	120,484,800
1066	8¢ Rotary International, Feb. 23	.16	.15	.85	(4)	1.75	53,854,750
1067	3¢ Armed Forces Reserve, May 21	.15	.15	.30	(4)	1.00	176,075,000
	Perf. 10.5 x 11						
1068	3¢ New Hampshire, June 21	.15	.15	.35	(4)	1.00	125,944,400
	Perf. 11 x 10.5						
1069	3¢ Soo Locks, June 28	.15	.15	.30	(4)	1.00	122,284,600
1070	3¢ Atoms for Peace, July 28	.15	.15	.35	(4)	1.00	133,638,850
1071	3¢ Fort Ticonderoga, Sept. 18	.15	.15	.35	(4)	1.00	118,664,600
1072	3¢ Andrew W. Mellon, Dec. 20	.15	.15	.30	(4)	1.00	112,434,000

Walking across the American continent

The expedition led by Meriwether Lewis (1774-1809) and William Clark (1770-1838) was conceived by President Thomas Jefferson to explore the Louisiana Purchase. Taking over two years (1804-1806), Lewis and Clark developed maps and collected mineral and botanical specimens. The total expedition covered 8000 miles. **(#1063)**

Interesting Fact: In what is now North Dakota, the expedition met up with Sacagawea (1787?-1812?), a Shoshoni Indian married to a French Canadian trapper. Engaged as a guide and interpreter, she became the only woman on the expedition and was central to its ultimate success. See #2869, Legends of the West, 1994.

1060

1061

1062

1063

1064

1065

1066

1067

1068

1069

1070

1071

1072

1073

1074

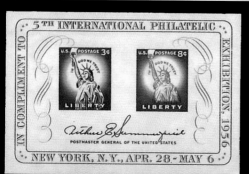

1075

1076

1077

1078

1079

1080

1081

1082

1083

1084

1085

	Issues of 1956, Perf. 10.5 x 11	Un	U	PB/LP	#	FDC	Q
1073	3¢ Benjamin Franklin, Jan. 17	.15	.15	.30	(4)	1.00	129,384,550
	Perf. 11 x 10.5						
1074	3¢ Booker T. Washington, Apr. 5	.15	.15	.30	(4)	1.00	121,184,600
	Fifth International Philatelic Exhibition Issues Souvenir Sheet, Imperf.						
1075	Sheet of 2 stamps (1035, 1041), Apr. 28	2.25	2.00			5.00	2,900,731
a	3¢ (1035), single stamp from sheet	.90	.80				
b	8¢ (1041), single stamp from sheet	1.25	1.00				
	Perf. 11 x 10.5						
1076	3¢ New York Coliseum and Columbus Monument, Apr. 30	.15	.15	.30	(4)	1.00	119,784,200
	Wildlife Conservation Issue						
1077	3¢ Wild Turkey, May 5	.15	.15	.35	(4)	1.10	123,159,400
1078	3¢ Pronghorn Antelope, June 22	.15	.15	.35	(4)	1.10	123,138,800
1079	3¢ King Salmon, Nov. 9	.15	.15	.35	(4)	1.10	109,275,000
	Perf. 10.5 x 11						
1080	3¢ Pure Food and Drug Laws, June 27	.15	.15	.30	(4)	1.00	112,932,200
	Perf. 11 x 10.5						
1081	3¢ Wheatland, Aug. 5	.15	.15	.30	(4)	1.00	125,475,000
	Perf. 10.5 x 11						
1082	3¢ Labor Day, Sept. 3	.15	.15	.30	(4)	1.00	117,855,000
	Perf. 11 x 10.5						
1083	3¢ Nassau Hall, Sept. 22	.15	.15	.30	(4)	1.00	122,100,000
	Perf. 10.5 x 11						
1084	3¢ Devils Tower, Sept. 24	.15	.15	.30	(4)	1.00	118,180,000
	Pair with full horizontal gutter between	—					
	Perf. 11 x 10.5						
1085	3¢ Children's Stamp, Dec. 15	.15	.15	.30	(4)	1.00	100,975,000

Is the Pronghorn Antelope Really an Antelope?

More similar to the deer than the antelope, the North American Pronghorn Antelope has pronged or branching hollow horns, which it sheds annually after breeding season. True antelope have nonbranching horns and do not shed them periodically; they are permanent.

The Pronghorn Antelope roams Alberta's grasslands, the eastern plains of Colorado and the western desert valleys of Utah. One of the fastest mammals on the North American continent, the Pronghorn is able to run at speeds up to 45 mph. **(#1078)**

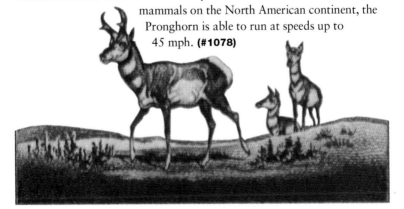

	Issues of 1957, Perf. 11 x 10.5	Un	U	PB	#	FDC	Q
1086	3¢ Alexander Hamilton, Jan. 11	.15	.15	.30	(4)	1.00	115,299,450
	Perf. 10.5 x 11						
1087	3¢ Polio, Jan. 15	.15	.15	.30	(4)	1.00	186,949,600
	Perf. 11 x 10.5						
1088	3¢ Coast and Geodetic Survey, Feb. 11	.15	.15	.30	(4)	1.00	115,235,000
1089	3¢ American Institute of Architects, Feb. 23	.15	.15	.30	(4)	1.00	106,647,500
	Perf. 10.5 x 11						
1090	3¢ Steel Industry, May 22	.15	.15	.30	(4)	1.00	112,010,000
	Perf. 11 x 10.5						
1091	3¢ International Naval Review-Jamestown Festival, June 10	.15	.15	.30	(4)	1.00	118,470,000
1092	3¢ Oklahoma Statehood, June 14	.15	.15	.35	(4)	1.00	102,230,000
1093	3¢ School Teachers, July 1	.15	.15	.30	(4)	1.00	102,410,000
	Perf. 11						
1094	4¢ Flag, July 4	.15	.15	.35	(4)	1.00	84,054,400
	Perf. 10.5 x 11						
1095	3¢ Shipbuilding, Aug. 15	.15	.15	.30	(4)	1.00	126,266,000
	Champion of Liberty Issue, Ramon Magsaysay, Aug. 31, Perf. 11						
1096	8¢ Bust of Magsaysay on Medal	.16	.15	.70	(4)	1.00	39,489,600
	Plate block of 4, ultramarine P# omitted	—					
	Perf. 10.5 x 11						
1097	3¢ Lafayette, Sept. 6	.15	.15	.30	(4)	1.00	122,990,000
	Perf. 11						
1098	3¢ Wildlife Conservation, Nov. 22	.15	.15	.35	(4)	1.00	174,372,800
	Perf. 10 1/2 x 11						
1099	3¢ Religious Freedom, Dec. 27	.15	.15	.30	(4)	1.00	114,365,000
	Issues of 1958						
1100	3¢ Gardening-Horticulture, Mar. 15	.15	.15	.30	(4)	1.00	122,765,200
1101-03	Not assigned						
	Perf. 11 x 10.5						
1104	3¢ Brussels Universal and International Exhibition, Apr. 17	.15	.15	.30	(4)	1.00	113,660,200
1105	3¢ James Monroe, Apr. 28	.15	.15	.30	(4)	1.00	120,196,580
1106	3¢ Minnesota Statehood, May 11	.15	.15	.30	(4)	1.00	120,805,200
	Perf. 11						
1107	3¢ International Geophysical Year, May 31	.15	.15	.35	(4)	1.00	125,815,200
	Perf. 11 x 10.5						
1108	3¢ Gunston Hall, June 12	.15	.15	.30	(4)	1.00	108,415,200

Minimum value listed for a stamp is 15 cents; for a First Day Cover (FDC), $1.00. This minimum represents a fair-market price for having a dealer locate and provide a single stamp or cover from his or her stock. Dealers may charge less per stamp or cover for a group of such stamps or covers, or less for a single stamp or cover.

1086

1087

1088

1089

1090

1091

1092

1093

1094

1095

1096

1097

1098

1099

1100

1104

1105

1106

1107

1108

163

1109

1110

1111

1112

1113

1114

1115

1116

1117

1118

1120

1119

1121

1122

1123

1124

1125

1126

1127

1128

1129

1130

1131

	Issues of 1958, Perf. 10.5 x 11	Un	U	PB	#	FDC	Q
1109	3¢ Mackinac Bridge, June 25	.15	.15	.30	(4)	1.00	107,195,200
	Champion of Liberty Issue, Simon Bolivar, July 24						
1110	4¢ Bust of Bolivar on Medal	.15	.15	.35	(4)	1.00	115,745,280
	Perf. 11						
1111	8¢ Bust of Bolivar on Medal	.16	.15	1.40	(4)	1.00	39,743,670
	Plate block of four, ocher P# only	—					
	Perf. 11 x 10.5						
1112	4¢ Atlantic Cable, Aug. 15	.15	.15	.40	(4)	1.00	114,570,200
	Issues of 1958-59, Lincoln Sesquicentennial Issue, Perf. 10.5 x 11						
1113	1¢ Portrait by George Healy, Feb. 12, 1959	.15	.15	.25	(4)	1.00	120,400,200
1114	3¢ Sculptured Head by Gutzon Borglum, Feb. 27, 1959	.15	.15	.30	(4)	1.00	91,160,200
	Perf. 11 x 10.5						
1115	4¢ Lincoln and Stephen Douglas Debating, by Joseph Boggs Beale, Aug. 27, 1958	.15	.15	.40	(4)	1.00	114,860,200
1116	4¢ Statue in Lincoln Memorial by Daniel Chester French, May 30, 1959	.15	.15	.40	(4)	1.00	126,500,000
	Champion of Liberty Issue, Lajos Kossuth, Sept. 19, Perf. 10.5 x 11						
1117	4¢ Bust of Kossuth on Medal	.15	.15	.40	(4)	1.00	120,561,280
	Perf. 11						
1118	8¢ Bust of Kossuth on Medal	.16	.15	1.25	(4)	1.00	44,064,580
	Perf. 10.5 x 11						
1119	4¢ Freedom of the Press, Sept. 22	.15	.15	.40	(4)	1.00	118,390,200
	Perf. 11 x 10.5						
1120	4¢ Overland Mail, Oct. 10	.15	.15	.40	(4)	1.00	125,770,200
	Perf. 10.5 x 11						
1121	4¢ Noah Webster, Oct. 16	.15	.15	.40	(4)	1.00	114,114,280
	Perf. 11						
1122	4¢ Forest Conservation, Oct. 27	.15	.15	.40	(4)	1.00	156,600,200
	Perf. 11 x 10.5						
1123	4¢ Fort Duquesne, Nov. 25	.15	.15	.40	(4)	1.00	124,200,200
	Issues of 1959						
1124	4¢ Oregon Statehood, Feb. 14	.15	.15	.40	(4)	1.00	120,740,200
	Champion of Liberty Issue, José de San Martin, Feb. 25, Perf. 10.5 x 11						
1125	4¢ Bust of San Martin on Medal	.15	.15	.40	(4)	1.00	133,623,280
a	Horizontal pair, imperf. between	1,100.00					
	Perf. 11						
1126	8¢ Bust of San Martin on Medal	.16	.15	.80	(4)	1.00	45,568,000
	Perf. 10.5 x 11						
1127	4¢ NATO, Apr. 1	.15	.15	.40	(4)	1.00	122,493,280
	Perf. 11 x 10.5						
1128	4¢ Arctic Explorations, Apr. 6	.15	.15	.40	(4)	1.00	131,260,200
1129	8¢ World Peace Through World Trade, Apr. 20	.16	.15	.75	(4)	1.00	47,125,200
1130	4¢ Silver Centennial, June 8	.15	.15	.40	(4)	1.00	123,105,000
	Perf. 11						
1131	4¢ St. Lawrence Seaway, June 26	.15	.15	.40	(4)	1.00	126,105,050
	Pair with full horizontal gutter between	—					

	Issues of 1959, Perf. 11	Un	U	PB	#	FDC	Q
1132	4¢ 49-Star Flag, July 4	.15	.15	.40	(4)	1.00	209,170,000
1133	4¢ Soil Conservation, Aug. 26	.15	.15	.40	(4)	1.00	120,835,000
	Perf. 10.5 x 11						
1134	4¢ Petroleum Industry, Aug. 27	.15	.15	.40	(4)	1.00	115,715,000
	Perf. 11 x 10.5						
1135	4¢ Dental Health, Sept. 14	.15	.15	.40	(4)	1.00	118,445,000
	Champion of Liberty Issue, Ernst Reuter, Sept. 29, Perf. 10.5 x 11						
1136	4¢ Bust of Reuter on Medal	.15	.15	.40	(4)	1.00	111,685,000
	Perf. 11						
1137	8¢ Bust of Reuter on Medal	.16	.15	.80	(4)	1.00	43,099,210
	Perf. 10.5 x 11						
1138	4¢ Dr. Ephraim McDowell, Dec. 3	.15	.15	.40	(4)	1.00	115,444,000
a	Vertical pair, imperf. between	400.00					
b	Vertical pair, imperf. horizontally	275.00					
	Issues of 1960-61, American Credo Issue, Perf. 11						
1139	4¢ Quotation from Washington's Farewell Address, Jan. 20, 1960	.15	.15	.40	(4)	1.00	126,470,000
1140	4¢ Benjamin Franklin Quotation, Mar. 31, 1960	.15	.15	.40	(4)	1.00	124,560,000
1141	4¢ Thomas Jefferson Quotation, May 18, 1960	.15	.15	.45	(4)	1.00	115,455,000
1142	4¢ Francis Scott Key Quotation, Sept. 14, 1960	.15	.15	.45	(4)	1.00	122,060,000
1143	4¢ Abraham Lincoln Quotation, Nov. 19, 1960	.15	.15	.48	(4)	1.00	120,540,000
	Pair with full horizontal gutter between	—					
1144	4¢ Patrick Henry Quotation, Jan. 11, 1961	.15	.15	.50	(4)	1.00	113,075,000
	Issues of 1960						
1145	4¢ Boy Scouts, Feb. 8	.15	.15	.40	(4)	1.75	139,325,000
	Olympic Winter Games Issue, Feb. 18, Perf. 10.5 x 11						
1146	4¢ Olympic Rings and Snowflake	.15	.15	.40	(4)	1.00	124,445,000
	Champion of Liberty Issue, Thomas G. Masaryk, Mar. 7						
1147	4¢ Bust of Masaryk on Medal	.15	.15	.35	(4)	1.00	113,792,100
a	Vertical pair, imperf. between	3,250.00					
	Perf. 11						
1148	8¢ Bust of Masaryk on Medal	.16	.15	1.00	(4)	1.00	44,215,500
a	Horizontal pair, imperf. between	—					
	Perf. 11 x 10.5						
1149	4¢ World Refugee Year, Apr. 7	.15	.15	.40	(4)	1.00	113,195,000
	Perf. 11						
1150	4¢ Water Conservation, Apr. 18	.15	.15	.40	(4)	1.00	121,805,000
	Perf. 10.5 x 11						
1151	4¢ SEATO, May 31	.15	.15	.40	(4)	1.00	115,353,000
a	Vertical pair, imperf. between	150.00					

1132

1133

1134

1135

1136

1137

1138

1139

1140

1141

1142

1143

1144

1145

1146

1147

1148

1149

1150

1151

1152

1153

1154

1155

1156

1157

1158

1159

1160

1161

1162

1163

1164

1165

1166

1167

1168

1169

1170

1171

1172

1173

	Issues of 1960, Perf. 11 x 10.5	Un	U	PB	#	FDC	Q
1152	4¢ American Woman, June 2	.15	.15	.40	(4)	1.00	111,080,000
	Perf. 11						
1153	4¢ 50-Star Flag, July 4	.15	.15	.40	(4)	1.00	153,025,000
	Perf. 11 x 10.5						
1154	4¢ Pony Express, July 19	.15	.15	.40	(4)	1.00	119,665,000
	Perf. 10.5 x 11						
1155	4¢ Employ the Handicapped, Aug. 28	.15	.15	.40	(4)	1.00	117,855,000
1156	4¢ 5th World Forestry Congress, Aug. 29	.15	.15	.40	(4)	1.00	118,185,000
	Perf. 11						
1157	4¢ Mexican Independence, Sept. 16	.15	.15	.40	(4)	1.00	112,260,000
1158	4¢ U.S.-Japan Treaty, Sept. 28	.15	.15	.40	(4)	1.00	125,010,000
	Champion of Liberty Issue, Ignacy Jan Paderewski, Oct. 8, Perf. 10.5 x 11						
1159	4¢ Bust of Paderewski on Medal	.15	.15	.40	(4)	1.00	119,798,000
	Perf. 11						
1160	8¢ Bust of Paderewski on Medal	.16	.15	1.10	(4)	1.00	42,696,050
	Perf. 10.5 x 11						
1161	4¢ Sen. Robert A. Taft Memorial, Oct. 10	.15	.15	.40	(4)	1.00	106,610,000
	Perf. 11 x 10.5						
1162	4¢ Wheels of Freedom, Oct. 15	.15	.15	.40	(4)	1.00	109,695,000
	Perf. 11						
1163	4¢ Boys' Clubs of America, Oct. 18	.15	.15	.40	(4)	1.00	123,690,000
1164	4¢ First Automated Post Office, Oct. 20	.15	.15	.40	(4)	1.00	123,970,000
	Champion of Liberty Issue, Gustaf Mannerheim, Oct. 26, Perf. 10.5 x 11						
1165	4¢ Bust of Mannerheim on Medal	.15	.15	.40	(4)	1.00	124,796,000
	Perf. 11						
1166	8¢ Bust of Mannerheim on Medal	.16	.15	.80	(4)	1.00	42,076,720
1167	4¢ Camp Fire Girls, Nov. 1	.15	.15	.40	(4)	1.00	116,210,000
	Champion of Liberty Issue, Giusseppe Garibaldi, Nov. 2, Perf. 10.5 x 11						
1168	4¢ Bust of Garibaldi on Medal	.15	.15	.40	(4)	1.00	126,252,000
	Perf. 11						
1169	8¢ Bust of Garibaldi on Medal	.16	.15	.80	(4)	1.00	42,746,200
	Perf. 10.5 x 11						
1170	4¢ Sen. Walter F. George Memorial, Nov. 5	.15	.15	.40	(4)	1.00	124,117,000
1171	4¢ Andrew Carnegie, Nov. 25	.15	.15	.40	(4)	1.00	119,840,000
1172	4¢ John Foster Dulles Memorial, Dec. 6	.15	.15	.40	(4)	1.00	117,187,000
	Perf. 11 x 10.5						
1173	4¢ Echo I-Communications for Peace, Dec. 15	.18	.15	.75	(4)	2.00	124,390,000

	Issues of 1961, Perf. 10.5 x 11	Un	U	PB	#	FDC	Q
	Champion of Liberty Issue, Mahatma Gandhi, Jan. 26						
1174	4¢ Bust of Gandhi on Medal	.15	.15	.40	(4)	1.00	112,966,000
	Perf. 11						
1175	8¢ Bust of Gandhi on Medal	.16	.15	1.00	(4)	1.00	41,644,400
1176	4¢ Range Conservation, Feb. 2	.15	.15	.40	(4)	1.00	110,850,000
	Perf. 10.5 x 11						
1177	4¢ Horace Greeley, Feb. 3	.15	.15	.40	(4)	1.00	98,616,000
	Issues of 1961-65, Civil War Centennial Issue, Perf. 11 x 10.5						
1178	4¢ Fort Sumter, Apr. 12, 1961	.16	.15	.60	(4)	1.25	101,125,000
1179	4¢ Shiloh, Apr. 7, 1962	.15	.15	.48	(4)	1.25	124,865,000
	Perf. 11						
1180	5¢ Gettysburg, July 1, 1963	.15	.15	.55	(4)	1.25	79,905,000
1181	5¢ The Wilderness, May 5, 1964	.15	.15	.55	(4)	1.25	125,410,000
1182	5¢ Appomattox, Apr. 9, 1965	.25	.15	1.15	(4)	1.25	112,845,000
a	Horizontal pair, imperf. vertically	4,500.00					
1183	4¢ Kansas Statehood, May 10	.15	.15	.40	(4)	1.00	106,210,000
	Perf. 11 x 10.5						
1184	4¢ Sen. George W. Norris, July 11	.15	.15	.40	(4)	1.00	110,810,000
1185	4¢ Naval Aviation, Aug. 20	.15	.15	.40	(4)	1.00	116,995,000
	Pair with full vertical gutter between	150.00					
	Perf. 10.5 x 11						
1186	4¢ Workmen's Compensation, Sept. 4	.15	.15	.40	(4)	1.00	121,015,000
	With plate # inverted			.60	(4)		
	Perf. 11						
1187	4¢ Frederic Remington, Oct. 4	.15	.15	.40	(4)	1.00	111,600,000
	Perf. 10.5 x 11						
1188	4¢ Republic of China, Oct. 10	.15	.15	.40	(4)	1.00	110,620,000
1189	4¢ Naismith-Basketball, Nov. 6	.15	.15	.40	(4)	2.00	109,110,000
	Perf. 11						
1190	4¢ Nursing, Dec. 28	.15	.15	.40	(4)	1.00	145,350,000
	Issues of 1962						
1191	4¢ New Mexico Statehood, Jan. 6	.15	.15	.40	(4)	1.00	112,870,000
1192	4¢ Arizona Statehood, Feb. 14	.15	.15	.40	(4)	1.00	121,820,000
1193	4¢ Project Mercury, Feb. 20	.15	.15	.40	(4)	3.00	289,240,000
1194	4¢ Malaria Eradication, Mar. 30	.15	.15	.40	(4)	1.00	120,155,000
	Perf. 10.5 x 11						
1195	4¢ Charles Evans Hughes, Apr. 11	.15	.15	.40	(4)	1.00	124,595,000

1174

1175

1176

1177

1178

1179

1180

1181

1182

1183

1184

1185

1186

1187

1188

1189

1190

1191

1192

1193

1194

1195

1196

1197

1198

1199

1200

1201

1202

1203

1204

1205

1206

1207

1208

1209

1213

1230

1231

1232

1233

1234

	Issues of 1962, Perf. 11	Un	U	PB/LP	#	FDC	Q
1196	4¢ Seattle World's Fair, Apr. 25	.15	.15	.40	(4)	1.00	147,310,000
1197	4¢ Louisiana Statehood, Apr. 30	.15	.15	.40	(4)	1.00	118,690,000
	Perf. 11 x 10.5						
1198	4¢ Homestead Act, May 20	.15	.15	.40	(4)	1.00	122,730,000
1199	4¢ Girl Scout Jubilee, July 24	.15	.15	.40	(4)	1.00	126,515,000
	Pair with full vertical gutter between *250.00*						
1200	4¢ Sen. Brien McMahon, July 28	.15	.15	.40	(4)	1.00	130,960,000
1201	4¢ Apprenticeship, Aug. 31	.15	.15	.40	(4)	1.00	120,055,000
	Perf. 11						
1202	4¢ Sam Rayburn, Sept. 16	.15	.15	.40	(4)	1.00	120,715,000
1203	4¢ Dag Hammarskjold, Oct. 23	.15	.15	.40	(4)	1.00	121,440,000
1204	4¢ black, brown and yellow (yellow inverted), Dag Hammarskjold, special printing, Nov. 16	.15	.15	1.25	(4)	6.00	40,270,000
	Christmas Issue, Nov. 1						
1205	4¢ Wreath and Candles	.15	.15	.40	(4)	1.00	861,970,000
1206	4¢ Higher Education, Nov. 14	.15	.15	.40	(4)	1.00	120,035,000
1207	4¢ Winslow Homer, Dec. 15	.15	.15	.48	(4)	1.00	117,870,000
a	Horizontal pair, imperf. between	*6,750.00*					
	Issue of 1963-66						
1208	5¢ Flag over White House, Jan. 9, 1963	.15	.15	.50	(4)	1.00	
a	Tagged, Aug. 25, 1966	.16	.15	.80	(4)	11.50	
b	Horizontal pair, imperf. between	*1,500.00*					
	Pair with full horizontal gutter between	—					
	Issues of 1962-66, Perf. 11 x 10.5						
1209	1¢ Andrew Jackson, Mar. 22, 1963	.15	.15	.20	(4)	1.00	
a	Tagged, July 6, 1966	.15	.15	.30	(4)	5.75	
b	Horizontal pair, imperf. between, tagged	—					
1210-12	Not assigned						
1213	5¢ George Washington, Nov. 23, 1962	.15	.15	.45	(4)	1.00	
a	Booklet pane of 5 + label	2.75	*1.50*			4.00	
b	Tagged, Oct. 28, 1963	.50	.22	3.00	(4)	5.75	
c	As "a," tagged	1.75	*1.50*				
1214-24	Not assigned						
	Coil Stamps, Perf. 10 Vertically						
1225	1¢ green Jackson (1209), May 31, 1963	.15	.15	1.75	(2)	1.00	
a	Tagged, July 6, 1966	.15	.15	5.75	(2)	5.00	
1226-28	Not assigned						
1229	5¢ dark blue gray Washington (1213), Nov. 23, 1962	1.25	.15	3.50	(2)	1.00	
a	Tagged, Oct. 28, 1963	1.25	.15			20.00	
b	Imperf. pair	*325.00*		*1,150.00*	(2)		
	Issues of 1963, Perf. 11						
1230	5¢ Carolina Charter, Apr. 6	.15	.15	.50	(4)	1.00	129,945,000
1231	5¢ Food for Peace-Freedom from Hunger, June 4	.15	.15	.50	(4)	1.00	135,620,000
1232	5¢ West Virginia Statehood, June 20	.15	.15	.50	(4)	1.00	137,540,000
1233	5¢ Emancipation Proclamation, Aug. 16	.15	.15	.50	(4)	1.00	132,435,000
1234	5¢ Alliance for Progress, Aug. 17	.15	.15	.50	(4)	1.00	135,520,000

	Issues of 1963, Perf. 10.5 x 11	Un	U	PB	#	FDC	Q
1235	5¢ Cordell Hull, Oct. 5	.15	.15	.50	(4)	1.00	131,420,000
	Perf. 11 x 10.5						
1236	5¢ Eleanor Roosevelt, Oct. 11	.15	.15	.50	(4)	1.00	133,170,000
	Perf. 11						
1237	5¢ The Sciences, Oct. 14	.15	.15	.50	(4)	1.00	130,195,000
1238	5¢ City Mail Delivery, Oct. 26	.15	.15	.50	(4)	1.00	128,450,000
1239	5¢ International Red Cross, Oct. 29	.15	.15	.50	(4)	1.00	118,665,000
	Christmas Issue, Nov. 1						
1240	5¢ National Christmas Tree and White House	.15	.15	.50	(4)	1.00	1,291,250,000
a	Tagged, Nov. 2	.65	.40	5.00	(4)	60.00	
	Pair with full horizontal gutter between	—					
1241	5¢ John James Audubon, Dec. 7 (See also #C71)	.15	.15	.50	(4)	1.00	175,175,000
	Issues of 1964, Perf. 10.5 x 11						
1242	5¢ Sam Houston, Jan. 10	.15	.15	.50	(4)	1.00	125,995,000
	Perf. 11						
1243	5¢ Charles M. Russell, Mar. 19	.15	.15	.50	(4)	1.00	128,025,000
	Perf. 11 x 10.5						
1244	5¢ New York World's Fair, Apr. 22	.15	.15	.50	(4)	1.00	145,700,000
	Perf. 11						
1245	5¢ John Muir, Apr. 29	.15	.15	.50	(4)	1.00	120,310,000
	Perf. 11 x 10.5						
1246	5¢ President John Fitzgerald Kennedy Memorial, May 29	.15	.15	.50	(4)	1.00	511,750,000
	Perf. 10.5 x 11						
1247	5¢ New Jersey Settlement, June 15	.15	.15	.50	(4)	1.00	123,845,000
	Perf. 11						
1248	5¢ Nevada Statehood, July 22	.15	.15	.50	(4)	1.00	122,825,000
1249	5¢ Register and Vote, Aug. 1	.15	.15	.50	(4)	1.00	453,090,000
	Perf. 10.5 x 11						
1250	5¢ Shakespeare, Aug. 14	.15	.15	.50	(4)	1.00	123,245,000
1251	5¢ Doctors William and Charles Mayo, Sept. 11	.15	.15	.50	(4)	1.00	123,355,000
	Perf. 11						
1252	5¢ American Music, Oct. 15	.15	.15	.50	(4)	1.00	126,970,000
a	Blue omitted	1,250.00					
1253	5¢ Homemakers, Oct. 26	.15	.15	.50	(4)	1.00	121,250,000

1235

1236

1237

1238

1239

1240

1241

1242

1243

1244

1245

1246

1247

1248

1249

1250

1251

1252

1253

1254   1255

5¢

5¢

5¢

5¢

1256   1257   1257b

1258

1259

1260

1261

1262

1263

1264

1265

1266

1267

1268

1269

1270

1271

1272

1273

1274

1275

1276

	Issues of 1964, Perf. 11	Un	U	PB	#	FDC	Q
	Christmas Issue, Nov. 9						
1254	5¢ Holly	.30	.15			1.00	351,940,000
1255	5¢ Mistletoe	.30	.15			1.00	351,940,000
1256	5¢ Poinsettia	.30	.15			1.00	351,940,000
1257	5¢ Sprig of Conifer	.30	.15			1.00	351,940,000
b	Block of four, #1254-57	1.25	1.25	1.50	(4)	3.00	
c	As "b," tagged, Nov. 10	3.25	2.00			57.50	
	Perf. 10.5 x 11						
1258	5¢ Verrazano-Narrows Bridge, Nov. 21	.15	.15	.50	(4)	1.00	120,005,000
	Perf. 11						
1259	5¢ Fine Arts, Dec. 2	.15	.15	.50	(4)	1.00	125,800,000
	Perf. 10.5 x 11						
1260	5¢ Amateur Radio, Dec. 15	.15	.15	.50	(4)	1.00	122,230,000
	Issues of 1965, Perf. 11						
1261	5¢ Battle of New Orleans, Jan. 8	.15	.15	.50	(4)	1.00	115,695,000
1262	5¢ Physical Fitness-Sokol, Feb. 15	.15	.15	.50	(4)	1.00	115,095,000
1263	5¢ Crusade Against Cancer, Apr. 1	.15	.15	.50	(4)	1.00	119,560,000
	Perf. 10.5 x 11						
1264	5¢ Winston Churchill Memorial, May 13	.15	.15	.50	(4)	1.00	125,180,000
	Perf. 11						
1265	5¢ Magna Carta, June 15	.15	.15	.50	(4)	1.00	120,135,000
	Corner block of four, black PB# omitted	—					
1266	5¢ International Cooperation Year—United Nations, June 26	.15	.15	.50	(4)	1.00	115,405,000
1267	5¢ Salvation Army, July 2	.15	.15	.50	(4)	1.00	115,855,000
	Perf. 10.5 x 11						
1268	5¢ Dante Alighieri, July 17	.15	.15	.50	(4)	1.00	115,340,000
1269	5¢ President Herbert Hoover Memorial, Aug. 10	.15	.15	.50	(4)	1.00	114,840,000
	Perf. 11						
1270	5¢ Robert Fulton, Aug. 19	.15	.15	.50	(4)	1.00	116,140,000
1271	5¢ Florida Settlement, Aug. 28	.15	.15	.50	(4)	1.00	116,900,000
a	Yellow omitted	475.00					
1272	5¢ Traffic Safety, Sept. 3	.15	.15	.50	(4)	1.00	114,085,000
1273	5¢ John Singleton Copley, Sept. 17	.15	.15	.50	(4)	1.00	114,880,000
1274	11¢ International Telecommunication Union, Oct. 6	.35	.16	5.75	(4)	1.00	26,995,000
1275	5¢ Adlai E. Stevenson Memorial, Oct. 23	.15	.15	.50	(4)	1.00	128,495,000
	Christmas Issue, Nov. 2						
1276	5¢ Angel with Trumpet (1840 Weather Vane)	.15	.15	.50	(4)	1.00	1,139,930,000
a	Tagged, Nov. 15	.75	.25	7.50	(4)	42.50	
1277	Not assigned						

The stamp listings contain a number of "a," "b," "c," etc. additions which include recognized varieties and errors. These listings are as complete as space permits.

	Issues of 1965-78	Un	U	PB	#	FDC
	Prominent Americans Issue, Perf. 11 x 10.5, 10.5 x 11 (See also #1299, 1303-05C)					
1278	1¢ Jefferson, Jan. 12, 1968	.15	.15	.20	(4)	1.00
a	Booklet pane of 8	1.00	.25			2.50
b	Bklt. pane of 4 + 2 labels, May 10, 1971	.75	.20			12.50
c	Untagged (Bureau precanceled)		.15			
1279	1¼¢ Albert Gallatin, Jan. 30, 1967	.15	.15	10.00	(4)	1.00
1280	2¢ Frank Lloyd Wright, Jan. 8, 1968	.15	.15	.25	(4)	1.00
a	Booklet pane of 5 + label	1.20	.40			4.00
b	Untagged (Bureau precanceled)		.15			
c	Booklet pane of 6, May 7, 1971	1.00	.35			15.00
	Pair with full vertical gutter between	—				
1281	3¢ Francis Parkman, Sept. 16, 1967	.15	.15	.30	(4)	1.00
a	Untagged (Bureau precanceled)		.15			
1282	4¢ Lincoln, Nov. 19, 1965	.15	.15	.38	(4)	1.00
a	Tagged, Dec. 1, 1965	.15	.15	.38	(4)	20.00
	Pair with full horizontal gutter between	—				
1283	5¢ Washington, Feb. 22, 1966	.15	.15	.50	(4)	1.00
a	Tagged, Feb. 23, 1966	.15	.15	.50	(4)	22.50
1283B	5¢ redrawn, Nov. 17, 1967	.15	.15	.50	(4)	1.00
	Dull finish gum	.20		1.00	(4)	
d	Untagged (Bureau precanceled)		.15			
1284	6¢ Roosevelt, Jan. 29, 1966	.15	.15	.60	(4)	1.00
a	Tagged, Dec. 29, 1966	.15	.15	.80	(4)	20.00
b	Booklet pane of 8, Dec. 28, 1967	1.50	.50			3.00
c	Booklet pane of 5 + label, Jan. 9, 1968	1.25	.50			100.00
1285	8¢ Albert Einstein, Mar. 14, 1966	.20	.15	.85	(4)	1.50
a	Tagged, July 6, 1966	.16	.15	.75	(4)	14.00
1286	10¢ Jackson, Mar. 15, 1967	.20	.15	1.00	(4)	1.00
b	Untagged (Bureau precanceled)		.20			
1286A	12¢ Henry Ford, July 30, 1968	.25	.15	1.00	(4)	1.00
c	Untagged (Bureau precanceled)		.25			
1287	13¢ John F. Kennedy, May 29, 1967	.25	.15	1.20	(4)	1.50
a	Untagged (Bureau precanceled)		.25			
1288	15¢ Oliver Wendell Holmes, Mar. 8, 1968	.30	.15	1.25	(4)	1.00
a	Untagged (Bureau precanceled)		.30			
	Booklet Stamp, Perf. 10					
1288B	15¢ dark rose claret Holmes (1288), Single from booklet	.28	.15			1.00
c	Booklet pane of 8, June 14, 1978	2.25	1.25			3.00
e	As "c," vert. imperf. between	—				
	Perf. 11 x 10.5, 10.5 x 11					
1289	20¢ George C. Marshall, Oct. 24, 1967	.42	.15	1.90	(4)	1.00
a	Tagged, Apr. 3, 1973	.40	.15	1.75	(4)	12.50
1290	25¢ Frederick Douglass, Feb. 14, 1967	.55	.15	2.25	(4)	1.25
a	Tagged, Apr. 3, 1973	.45	.15	2.00	(4)	14.00
1291	30¢ John Dewey, Oct. 21, 1968	.58	.15	3.00	(4)	1.25
a	Tagged, Apr. 3, 1973	.52	.15	2.75	(4)	14.00
1292	40¢ Thomas Paine, Jan. 29, 1968	.85	.15	3.25	(4)	1.60
a	Tagged, Apr. 3, 1973	.65	.15	3.00	(4)	15.00
1293	50¢ Lucy Stone, Aug. 13, 1968	.90	.15	4.50	(4)	3.25
a	Tagged, Apr. 3, 1973	.80	.15	3.75	(4)	20.00
1294	$1 Eugene O'Neill, Oct. 16, 1967	2.25	.15	10.00	(4)	7.50
a	Tagged, Apr. 3, 1973	1.65	.15	8.00	(4)	22.50

1278

1279

1280

1281

1282

1283

1283B

1284

1285

1286

1286A

1287

1288

1289

1290

1291

1292

1293

1294

1295   **1305**

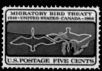 

1306   **1307**

1310

1308   **1309**

1311

1314

1312   **1313**

	Issues of 1965-78	Un	U	PB/LP	#	FDC	Q
	Perf. 11 x 10.5, 10.5 x 11						
1295	$5 John Bassett Moore, Dec. 3, 1966	12.50	2.25	50.00	(4)	40.00	
a	Tagged, Apr. 3, 1973	8.00	2.00	35.00	(4)	65.00	
1296	Not assigned						
	Issues of 1966-81, Coil Stamps, Perf. 10 Horizontally						
1297	3¢ violet Parkman (1281), Nov. 4, 1975	.15	.15	.45	(2)	1.00	
a	Imperf. pair	30.00		25.00	(2)		
b	Untagged (Bureau precanceled)		.15				
c	As "b," imperf. pair		6.00	25.00	(2)		
1298	6¢ Roosevelt (1284), Dec. 28, 1967	.15	.15	1.25	(2)	1.00	
a	Imperf. pair	2,000.00					
	Coil Stamps, Perf. 10 Vertically (See also #1279-96)						
1299	1¢ green Jefferson (1278), Jan. 12, 1968	.15	.15	.20	(2)	1.00	
a	Untagged (Bureau precanceled)		.15				
b	Imperf. pair	30.00	—	65.00	(2)		
1300-02 Not assigned							
1303	4¢ blk. Lincoln (1282), May 28, 1966	.15	.15	.75	(2)	1.00	
a	Untagged (Bureau precanceled)		.15				
b	Imperf. pair	800.00		1,500.00	(2)		
1304	5¢ bl. Washington (1283), Sept. 8, 1966	.15	.15	.40	(2)	1.00	
a	Untagged (Bureau precanceled)		.15				
b	Imperf. pair	150.00		900.00	(2)		
e	As "a," imperf. pair		450.00				
1304C	5¢ redrawn (1283B), 1981	.15	.15	.60	(2)		
d	Imperf. pair	1,250.00					
1305	6¢ gray brown Roosevelt, Feb. 28, 1968	.15	.15	.55	(2)	1.00	
a	Imperf. pair	70.00		120.00	(2)		
b	Untagged (Bureau precanceled)		.20				
1305E	15¢ rose claret Holmes (1288), June 14, 1978	.25	.15	1.25	(2)	1.00	
	Dull finish gum	.60					
f	Untagged (Bureau precanceled)		.30				
g	Imperf. pair	25.00		90.00	(2)		
h	Pair, imperf. between	200.00		600.00	(2)		
1305C	$1 dull purple Eugene O'Neill (1294), Jan. 12, 1973	1.75	.20	5.00	(2)	5.00	
d	Imperf. pair	2,250.00		4,000.00	(2)		
	Issues of 1966, Perf. 11						
1306	5¢ Migratory Bird Treaty, Mar. 16	.15	.15	.50	(4)	1.00	116,835,000
1307	5¢ Humane Treatment of Animals, Apr. 9	.15	.15	.50	(4)	1.00	117,470,000
1308	5¢ Indiana Statehood, Apr. 16	.15	.15	.50	(4)	1.00	123,770,000
1309	5¢ American Circus, May 2	.20	.15	.50	(4)	2.50	131,270,000
	Sixth International Philatelic Exhibition Issue						
1310	5¢ Stamped Cover, May 21	.15	.15	.50	(4)	1.00	122,285,000
	Souvenir Sheet, Imperf.						
1311	5¢ Stamped Cover (1310) and Washington, D.C., Scene, May 23	.15	.15			1.00	14,680,000
	Perf. 11						
1312	5¢ The Bill of Rights, July 1	.15	.15	.50	(4)	1.00	114,160,000
	Perf. 10.5 x 11						
1313	5¢ Poland's Millennium, July 30	.15	.15	.50	(4)	1.00	128,475,000
	Perf. 11						
1314	5¢ National Park Service, Aug. 25	.15	.15	.50	(4)	1.00	119,535,000
a	Tagged, Aug. 26	.30	.25	2.00	(4)	20.00	

	Issues of 1966, Perf. 11	Un	U	PB	#	FDC	Q
1315	5¢ Marine Corps Reserve, Aug. 29	.15	.15	.50	(4)	1.00	125,110,000
a	Tagged	.30	.20	2.00	(4)	20.00	
b	Black and bister omitted	—					
1316	5¢ Women's Clubs, Sept. 12	.15	.15	.50	(4)	1.00	114,853,200
a	Tagged, Sept. 13	.30	.20	2.00	(4)	22.50	
	American Folklore Issue, Johnny Appleseed, Sept. 24						
1317	5¢ Johnny Appleseed and Apple	.15	.15	.50	(4)	1.00	124,290,000
a	Tagged, Sept. 26	.30	.20	2.00	(4)	22.50	
1318	5¢ Beautification of America, Oct. 5	.15	.15	.50	(4)	1.00	128,460,000
a	Tagged	.30	.20	1.50	(4)	20.00	
1319	5¢ Great River Road, Oct. 21	.15	.15	.50	(4)	1.00	127,585,000
a	Tagged, Oct. 22	.30	.20	2.00	(4)	22.50	
1320	5¢ Savings Bond-Servicemen, Oct. 26	.15	.15	.50	(4)	1.00	115,875,000
a	Tagged, Oct. 27	.30	.20	2.00	(4)	22.50	
b	Red, dark bl. and blk. omitted	4,250.00					
c	Dark blue omitted	8,000.00					
	Christmas Issue, Nov. 1						
1321	5¢ Madonna and Child, by Hans Memling	.15	.15	.50	(4)	1.00	1,173,547,400
a	Tagged, Nov. 2	.30	.20	1.90	(4)	9.50	
1322	5¢ Mary Cassatt, Nov. 17	.15	.15	.60	(4)	1.00	114,015,000
a	Tagged	.30	.25	2.00	(4)	20.00	
	Issues of 1967						
1323	5¢ National Grange, Apr. 17	.15	.15	.50	(4)	1.00	121,105,000
a	Tagging omitted	3.50					
1324	5¢ Canada, May 25	.15	.15	.50	(4)	1.00	132,045,000
1325	5¢ Erie Canal, July 4	.15	.15	.50	(4)	1.00	118,780,000
1326	5¢ Search for Peace, July 5	.15	.15	.50	(4)	1.00	121,985,000
1327	5¢ Henry David Thoreau, July 12	.15	.15	.50	(4)	1.00	111,850,000
1328	5¢ Nebraska Statehood, July 29	.15	.15	.50	(4)	1.00	117,225,000
a	Tagging omitted	4.00					
1329	5¢ Voice of America, Aug. 1	.15	.15	.50	(4)	1.00	111,515,000
	American Folklore Issue, Davy Crockett, Aug. 17						
1330	5¢ Davy Crockett	.15	.15	.50	(4)	1.00	114,270,000
a	Vertical pair, imperf. between	6,000.00					
b	Green omitted	—					
c	Black and green omitted	—					
d	Yellow and green omitted	—					
	Accomplishments in Space Issue, Sept. 29						
1331	5¢ Space-Walking Astronaut	.65	.15			1.10	60,432,500
a	Attached pair, #1331-32	1.50	1.50	3.50	(4)	8.00	
1332	5¢ Gemini 4 Capsule and Earth	.65	.15	3.00	(4)		60,432,500
1333	5¢ Urban Planning, Oct. 2	.15	.15	.50	(4)	1.00	110,675,000
1334	5¢ Finland Independence, Oct. 6	.15	.15	.50	(4)	1.00	110,670,000

Minimum value listed for a stamp is 15 cents; for a First Day Cover (FDC), $1.00. This minimum represents a fair-market price for having a dealer locate and provide a single stamp or cover from his or her stock. Dealers may charge less per stamp or cover for a group of such stamps or covers, or less for a single stamp or cover.

1315

1316

1317

1318

1319

1320

1321

1322

1323

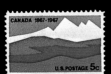

1324

1325

1326

1327

1328

1329

1330

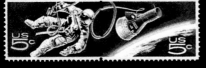

1331   **1332**   **1331a**

1333   **1334**

1335

1336

1337

1338

1339

1340

1341

1342

1343

1344

1355

1345

1346

1347

1348

1349

1350

1351

1352

1353

1354

1354a

	Issues of 1967, Perf. 12	Un	U	PB	#	FDC	Q
1335	5¢ Thomas Eakins, Nov. 2	.15	.15	.50	(4)	1.00	113,825,000
	Christmas Issue, Nov. 6, Perf. 11						
1336	5¢ Madonna and Child, by Hans Memling	.15	.15	.45	(4)	1.00	1,208,700,000
1337	5¢ Mississippi Statehood, Dec. 11	.15	.15	.50	(4)	1.00	113,330,000
	Issues of 1968-1971						
1338	6¢ Flag over White House (design 19 x 22mm), Jan. 24, 1968	.15	.15	.45	(4)	1.00	
k	Vertical pair, imperf. between	500.00					
	Coil Stamp, Perf. 10 Vertically						
1338A	6¢ dark blue, red and green (1338), May 30, 1969	.15	.15	.28		1.00	
b	Imperf. pair	450.00					
	Perf. 11 x 10.5						
1338D	6¢ dark blue, red and green (1338, design 18¼ x 21mm), Aug. 7, 1970	.15	.15	2.60	(20)	1.00	
e	Horizontal pair, imperf. between	175.00					
1338F	8¢ dark blue, red and slate green (1338), May 10, 1971	.15	.15	3.50	(20)	1.00	
i	Imperf., vertical pair	50.00					
j	Horizontal pair, imperf. between	50.00					
	Coil Stamp, Perf. 10 Vertically						
1338G	8¢ dark blue, red and slate green (1338), May 10, 1971	.20	.15	.36		1.00	
h	Imperf. pair	55.00					
	Issues of 1968, Perf. 11						
1339	6¢ Illinois Statehood, Feb. 12	.15	.15	.50	(4)	1.00	141,350,000
1340	6¢ HemisFair '68, Mar. 30	.15	.15	.50	(4)	1.00	144,345,000
a	White omitted	1,400.00					
1341	$1 Airlift, Apr. 4	2.50	1.25	12.50	(4)	6.50	
	Pair with full horizontal gutter between		—				
1342	6¢ Support Our Youth-Elks, May 1	.15	.15	.50	(4)	1.00	147,120,000
1343	6¢ Law and Order, May 17	.15	.15	.50	(4)	1.00	130,125,000
1344	6¢ Register and Vote, June 27	.15	.15	.50	(4)	1.00	158,700,000
	Historic Flag Issue, July 4						
1345	6¢ Ft. Moultrie Flag, 1776	.50	.25			3.00	22,804,000
1346	6¢ Ft. McHenry (U.S.) Flag, 1795-1818	.35	.25			3.00	22,804,000
1347	6¢ Washington's Cruisers Flag, 1775	.30	.25			3.00	22,804,000
1348	6¢ Bennington Flag, 1777	.30	.25			3.00	22,804,000
1349	6¢ Rhode Island Flag, 1775	.30	.25			3.00	22,804,000
1350	6¢ First Stars and Stripes, 1777	.30	.25			3.00	22,804,000
1351	6¢ Bunker Hill Flag, 1775	.30	.25			3.00	22,804,000
1352	6¢ Grand Union Flag, 1776	.30	.25			3.00	22,804,000
1353	6¢ Philadelphia Light Horse Flag, 1775	.30	.25			3.00	22,804,000
1354	6¢ First Navy Jack, 1775	.30	.25			3.00	22,804,000
a	Strip of 10, #1345-54	3.25	3.25	6.75	(20)	15.00	
	Perf. 12						
1355	6¢ Walt Disney, Sept. 11	.16	.15	.70	(4)	2.50	153,015,000
a	Ocher omitted	700.00	—				
b	Vertical pair, imperf. horizontally	750.00					
c	Imperf. pair	675.00					
d	Black omitted	2,000.00					
e	Horizontal pair, imperf. between	4,750.00					
f	Blue omitted	2,100.00					

	Issues of 1968, Perf. 11	Un	U	PB	#	FDC	Q
1356	6¢ Father Marquette, Sept. 20	.15	.15	.50	(4)	1.00	132,560,000
	American Folklore Issue, Daniel Boone, Sept. 26						
1357	6¢ Pennsylvania Rifle, Powder Horn, Tomahawk, Pipe and Knife	.15	.15	.50	(4)	1.00	130,385,000
a	Tagging omitted	—					
1358	6¢ Arkansas River Navigation, Oct. 1	.15	.15	.50	(4)	1.00	132,265,000
1359	6¢ Leif Erikson, Oct. 9	.15	.15	.50	(4)	1.00	128,710,000
	Perf. 11 x 10.5						
1360	6¢ Cherokee Strip, Oct. 15	.15	.15	.55	(4)	1.00	124,775,000
a	Tagging omitted	4.50					
	Perf. 11						
1361	6¢ John Trumbull, Oct. 18	.15	.15	.60	(4)	1.00	128,295,000
1362	6¢ Waterfowl Conservation, Oct. 24	.15	.15	.70	(4)	1.00	142,245,000
a	Vertical pair, imperf. between	550.00					
b	Red and dark blue omitted	1,000.00					
	Christmas Issue, Nov. 1						
1363	6¢ Angel Gabriel, from "The Annunciation," by Jan Van Eyck	.15	.15	2.00	(10)	1.00	1,410,580,000
a	Untagged, Nov. 2	.15	.15	2.00	(10)	6.50	
b	Imperf. pair tagged	250.00					
c	Light yellow omitted	100.00					
d	Imperf. pair (untagged)	325.00					
1364	6¢ American Indian, Nov. 4	.16	.15	.70	(4)	1.00	125,100,000
	Issues of 1969, Beautification of America Issue, Jan. 16						
1365	6¢ Capitol, Azaleas and Tulips	.45	.15			1.00	48,142,500
1366	6¢ Washington Monument, Potomac River and Daffodils	.45	.15			1.00	48,142,500
1367	6¢ Poppies and Lupines along Highway	.45	.15			1.00	48,142,500
1368	6¢ Blooming Crabapple Trees Lining Avenue	.45	.15	2.25	(4)	1.00	48,142,500
a	Block of 4, #1365-68	2.00	2.00	2.25	(4)	4.00	
b	As "a," tagging omitted	—					
1369	6¢ American Legion, Mar. 15	.15	.15	.50	(4)	1.00	148,770,000
	American Folklore Issue, Grandma Moses, May 1						
1370	6¢ "July Fourth," by Grandma Moses	.15	.15	.50	(4)	1.00	139,475,000
a	Horizontal pair, imperf. between	225.00					
b	Black and Prussian blue omitted	900.00					
1371	6¢ Apollo 8, May 5	.15	.15	.65	(4)	3.00	187,165,000
a	Imperf. pair	—					
1372	6¢ W.C. Handy, May 17	.15	.15	.50	(4)	1.00	125,555,000
a	Tagging omitted	4.50					
1373	6¢ California Settlement, July 16	.15	.15	.50	(4)	1.00	144,425,000
1374	6¢ John Wesley Powell, Aug. 1	.15	.15	.50	(4)	1.00	135,875,000
1375	6¢ Alabama Statehood, Aug. 2	.15	.15	.50	(4)	1.00	151,110,000

1356

1357

1358

1359

1360

1361

1362

1363

1364

1365   **1366**

1367   **1368**   **1368a**

1369

1370

1371

1372

1373

1374   **1375**

1376   **1377**

1380

1378   **1379**   **1379a**

1381   **1382**

1383

1384

1384 Precancel

1385

1386

1387   **1388**

AMERICAN BALD EAGLE   AFRICAN ELEPHANT HERD

1391

HAIDA CEREMONIAL CANOE   THE AGE OF REPTILES

1392

1389   **1390**   **1390a**

	Issues of 1969, Perf. 11	Un	U	PB	#	FDC	Q
	Botanical Congress Issue, Aug. 23						
1376	6¢ Douglas Fir (Northwest)	.75	.15			1.00	39,798,750
1377	6¢ Lady's Slipper (Northeast)	.75	.15			1.00	39,798,750
1378	6¢ Ocotillo (Southwest)	.75	.15			1.00	39,798,750
1379	6¢ Franklinia (Southeast)	.75	.15			1.00	39,798,750
a	Block of 4, #1376-79	3.25	3.25	3.75	(4)	5.00	
	Perf. 10.5 x 11						
1380	6¢ Dartmouth College Case, Sept. 22	.15	.15	.50	(4)	1.00	129,540,000
	Perf. 11						
1381	6¢ Professional Baseball, Sept. 24	.65	.15	2.70	(4)	6.00	130,925,000
a	Black omitted	1,100.00					
1382	6¢ College Football, Sept. 26	.15	.15	.80	(4)	3.00	139,055,000
1383	6¢ Dwight D. Eisenhower, Oct. 14	.15	.15	.50	(4)	1.00	150,611,200
	Christmas Issue, Nov. 3, Perf. 11 x 10.5						
1384	6¢ Winter Sunday in Norway, Maine	.15	.15	1.40	(10)	1.00	1,709,795,000
	Precanceled	.50	.15				
b	Imperf. pair	1,100.00					
c	Light green omitted	25.00					
d	Light green and yellow omitted	1,000.00	—				
e	Yellow omitted	—					
f	Tagging omitted	1.50					
	Precanceled versions issued on an experimental basis in four cities whose names appear on the stamps: Atlanta, GA; Baltimore, MD; Memphis, TN; and New Haven, CT.						
	Perf. 11						
1385	6¢ Hope for the Crippled, Nov. 20	.15	.15	.50	(4)	1.00	127,545,000
1386	6¢ William M. Harnett, Dec. 3	.15	.15	.50	(4)	1.00	145,788,800
	Issues of 1970, Natural History Issue, May 6						
1387	6¢ American Bald Eagle	.15	.15			1.50	50,448,550
1388	6¢ African Elephant Herd	.15	.15			1.50	50,448,550
1389	6¢ Tlingit Chief in Haida Ceremonial Canoe	.15	.15			1.50	50,448,550
1390	6¢ Brontosaurus, Stegosaurus and Allosaurus from Jurassic Period	.15	.15			1.50	50,448,550
a	Block of 4, #1387-90	.50	.50	.65	(4)	4.00	
1391	6¢ Maine Statehood, July 9	.15	.15	.50	(4)	1.00	171,850,000
	Perf. 11 x 10.5						
1392	6¢ Wildlife Conservation, July 20	.15	.15	.50	(4)	1.00	142,205,000

	Issues of 1970-74, Perf. 11 x 10.5	Un	U	PB/LP	#	FDC	Q
1393	6¢ Eisenhower, Aug. 6, 1970	.15	.15	.50	(4)	1.00	
a	Booklet pane of 8	1.25	*.50*			3.00	
b	Booklet pane of 5 + label	1.25	*.50*			1.50	
c	Untagged (Bureau precanceled)		.15				
	Perf. 10.5 x 11						
1393D	7¢ Franklin, Oct. 20, 1972	.15	.15	.60	(4)	1.00	
e	Untagged (Bureau precanceled)		.15				
	Perf. 11						
1394	8¢ Eisenhower, May 10, 1971	.16	.15	.60	(4)	1.00	
	Pair with full vertical gutter between	—					
	Perf. 11 x 10.5						
1395	8¢ deep claret Eisenhower (1394), Single from booklet	.20	.15			1.00	
a	Booklet pane of 8, May 10, 1971	1.80	*1.25*			3.00	
b	Booklet pane of 6, May 10, 1971	1.25	.75			3.00	
c	Booklet pane of 4 + 2 labels, Jan. 28, 1972	1.65	*.50*			2.25	
d	Booklet pane of 7 + label, Jan. 28, 1972	1.75	*1.00*			2.00	
1396	8¢ U.S. Postal Service, July 1, 1971	.15	.15	2.00	(12)	1.00	
1397	14¢ Fiorello H. LaGuardia, Apr. 24, 1972	.25	.15	1.15	(4)	1.00	
a	Untagged (Bureau precanceled)		.25				
1398	16¢ Ernie Pyle, May 7, 1971	.28	.15	1.25	(4)	1.00	
a	Untagged (Bureau precanceled)		.35				
1399	18¢ Dr. Elizabeth Blackwell, Jan. 23, 1974	.32	.15	1.40	(4)	1.00	
1400	21¢ Amadeo P. Giannini, June 27, 1973	.32	.15	1.50	(4)	1.00	
	Coil Stamps, Perf. 10 Vertically						
1401	6¢ dark blue gray Eisenhower (1393), Aug. 6, 1970	.15	.15	.50	(2)	1.00	
a	Untagged (Bureau precanceled)		.15				
b	Imperf. pair	*1,500.00*		—	(2)		
1402	8¢ deep claret Eisenhower (1394), May 10, 1971	.15	.15	.45	(2)	1.00	
a	Imperf. pair	45.00		70.00	(2)		
b	Untagged (Bureau precanceled)		.15				
c	Pair, imperf. between	*6,250.00*					
1403-04	Not assigned						
	Issues of 1970, Perf. 11						
1405	6¢ Edgar Lee Masters, Aug. 22	.15	.15	.50	(4)	1.00	137,660,000
a	Tagging omitted	7.50					
1406	6¢ Woman Suffrage, Aug. 26	.15	.15	.50	(4)	1.00	135,125,000
1407	6¢ South Carolina Settlement, Sept. 12	.15	.15	.50	(4)	1.00	135,895,000
1408	6¢ Stone Mountain Memorial, Sept. 19	.15	.15	.50	(4)	1.00	132,675,000
1409	6¢ Ft. Snelling, Oct. 17	.15	.15	.50	(4)	1.00	134,795,000
	Anti-Pollution Issue, Oct. 28, Perf. 11 x 10.5						
1410	6¢ Save Our Soil— Globe and Wheat Field	.25	.15			1.25	40,400,000
1411	6¢ Save Our Cities— Globe and City Playground	.25	.15			1.25	40,400,000
1412	6¢ Save Our Water— Globe and Bluegill Fish	.25	.15			1.25	40,400,000
1413	6¢ Save Our Air— Globe and Seagull	:25	.15			1.25	40,400,000
a	Block of 4, #1410-13	1.25	1.25	2.50	(10)	3.00	

1393
1393D
1394
1396

1397
1398
1399
1400

1405
1406
1407

1408
1409

1410
1411

1412
1413
1413a

Christmas 6US

1414

Christmas 6US

1414a

1417

1418

1418b

1419

1420

1421

1422   1421a

1425

1426

AMERICA'S WOOL

1423

DOUGLAS MacARTHUR

1424

1427

1428

1429

1430

1430a

	Issues of 1970, Perf. 10.5 x 11	Un	U	PB	#	FDC	Q
	Christmas Issue, Nov. 5						
1414	6¢ Nativity, by Lorenzo Lotto	.15	.15	1.15	(8)	1.40	638,730,000*
a	Precanceled	.15	.15	1.90	(8)		358,245,000
b	Black omitted	650.00					
c	As "a," blue omitted	1,500.00					
	#1414a-18a were furnished to 68 cities. Unused prices are for copies with gum and used prices are for copies with or without gum but with an additional cancellation. *Includes #1414a.						
	Perf. 11 x 10.5						
1415	6¢ Tin and Cast-iron Locomotive	.40	.15			1.40	122,313,750
a	Precanceled	.90	.15				109,912,500
b	Black omitted	2,500.00					
1416	6¢ Toy Horse on Wheels	.40	.15			1.40	122,313,750
a	Precanceled	.90	.15				109,912,500
b	Black omitted	2,500.00					
c	Imperf. pair		4,000.00				
1417	6¢ Mechanical Tricycle	.40	.15			1.40	122,313,750
a	Precanceled	.90	.15				109,912,500
b	Black omitted	2,500.00					
1418	6¢ Doll Carriage	.40	.15	3.75	(8)	1.40	122,313,750
a	Precanceled	.90	.15	3.75	(8)		109,912,500
b	Block of 4, #1415-18	1.75	1.25	3.75	(8)	3.50	
c	Block of 4, #1415a-18a	3.75	3.50	9.00	(8)		
d	Black omitted	2,500.00					
	Perf. 11						
1419	6¢ United Nations, Nov. 20	.15	.15	.50	(4)	1.00	127,610,000
	Pair with full horizontal gutter between	—					
1420	6¢ Landing of the Pilgrims, Nov. 21	.15	.15	.50	(4)	1.00	129,785,000
a	Orange and yellow omitted	850.00					
	Disabled American Veterans and Servicemen Issue, Nov. 24						
1421	6¢ Disabled American Veterans Emblem	.15	.15			1.00	67,190,000
a	Attached pair, #1421-22	.25	.25	1.00	(4)	1.25	
1422	6¢ U.S. Servicemen	.15	.15			1.00	67,190,000
	Issues of 1971						
1423	6¢ American Wool Industry, Jan. 19	.15	.15	.50	(4)	1.00	136,305,000
a	Tagging omitted	3.50	—				
1424	6¢ Gen. Douglas MacArthur, Jan. 26	.15	.15	.50	(4)	1.00	134,840,000
1425	6¢ Blood Donor, Mar. 12	.15	.15	.50	(4)	1.00	130,975,000
a	Tagging omitted	4.50					
	Perf. 11 x 10.5						
1426	8¢ Missouri Statehood, May 8	.15	.15	2.00	(12)	1.00	161,235,000
	Wildlife Conservation Issue, June 12, Perf. 11						
1427	8¢ Trout	.16	.15			1.25	43,920,000
1428	8¢ Alligator	.16	.15			1.25	43,920,000
1429	8¢ Polar Bear	.16	.15			1.25	43,920,000
1430	8¢ California Condor	.16	.15			1.25	43,920,000
a	Block of 4, #1427-30	.65	.65	.75	(4)	3.00	
b	As "a," light green and dark green omitted from #1427-28	3,500.00					
c	As "a," red omitted from #1427, 1429-30	9,000.00					

	Issues of 1971, Perf. 11	Un	U	PB	#	FDC	Q
1431	8¢ Antarctic Treaty, June 23	.15	.15	.70	(4)	1.00	138,700,000
a	Tagging omitted	4.00					
	American Revolution Bicentennial Issue, July 4						
1432	8¢ Bicentennial Commission Emblem	.16	.15	.85	(4)	1.00	138,165,000
a	Gray and black omitted	650.00					
b	Gray omitted	1,100.00					
1433	8¢ John Sloan, Aug. 2	.15	.15	.70	(4)	1.00	152,125,000
a	Tagging omitted	—					
	Space Achievement Decade Issue, Aug. 2						
1434	8¢ Earth, Sun and Landing Craft on Moon	.15	.15				88,147,500
a	Attached pair, #1434-35	.30	.25	.70	(4)	2.50	
b	As "a," blue and red omitted	1,500.00					
1435	8¢ Lunar Rover and Astronauts	.15	.15				88,147,500
a	Tagging omitted	6.00					
1436	8¢ Emily Dickinson, Aug. 28	.15	.15	.70	(4)	1.00	142,845,000
a	Black and olive omitted	850.00					
b	Pale rose omitted	7,500.00					
1437	8¢ San Juan, Puerto Rico, Sept. 12	.15	.15	.70	(4)	1.00	148,755,000
a	Tagging omitted	5.00					
	Perf. 10.5 x 11						
1438	8¢ Prevent Drug Abuse, Oct. 4	.15	.15	1.00	(6)	1.00	139,080,000
1439	8¢ CARE, Oct. 27	.15	.15	1.25	(8)	1.00	130,755,000
a	Black omitted	4,500.00					
b	Tagging omitted	2.50					
	Historic Preservation Issue, Oct. 29, Perf. 11						
1440	8¢ Decatur House, Washington, D.C.	.16	.15			1.25	42,552,000
1441	8¢ Whaling Ship *Charles W. Morgan*, Mystic, Connecticut	.16	.15			1.25	42,552,000
1442	8¢ Cable Car, San Francisco	.16	.15			1.25	42,552,000
1443	8¢ San Xavier del Bac Mission, Tucson, Arizona	.16	.15			1.25	42,552,000
a	Block of 4, #1440-43	.65	.65	.75	(4)	3.00	
b	As "a," black brown omitted	2,400.00					
c	As "a," ocher omitted	—					
	Christmas Issue, Nov. 10, Perf. 10.5 x 11						
1444	8¢ Adoration of the Shepherds, by Giorgione	.15	.15	2.00	(12)	1.00	1,074,350,000
a	Gold omitted	500.00					
1445	8¢ Partridge in a Pear Tree	.15	.15	2.00	(12)	1.00	979,540,000

The stamp listings contain a number of "a," "b," "c," etc. additions which include recognized varieties and errors. These listings are as complete as space permits.

1431

1432

1433

1434   **1435**   **1434a**

1436   **1437**   **1438**   **1439**

1440   **1441**

1442   **1443**   **1443a**

1972

1446

1447

1448   **1449**

1450   **1451 1451a**

1452

1454

1453

Family Planning

1455

1456   **1457**

1458   **1459**   **1459a**

1460

1461

1462

1463

	Issues of 1972, Perf. 11	Un	U	PB	#	FDC	Q
1446	8¢ Sidney Lanier, Feb. 3	.15	.15	.70	(4)	1.00	137,355,000
	Perf. 10.5 x 11						
1447	8¢ Peace Corps, Feb. 11	.15	.15	1.00	(6)	1.00	150,400,000
	National Parks Centennial Issue, Cape Hatteras, Apr. 5 (See also #C84)						
1448	2¢ Ship at Sea	.15	.15				43,182,500
1449	2¢ Cape Hatteras Lighthouse	.15	.15				43,182,500
1450	2¢ Laughing Gulls on Driftwood	.15	.15				43,182,500
1451	2¢ Laughing Gulls and Dune	.15	.15				43,182,500
a	Block of 4, #1448-51	.20	.20	.45	(4)	1.25	
b	As "a," black omitted	2,250.00					
	Wolf Trap Farm, June 26						
1452	6¢ Performance at Shouse Pavilion	.15	.15	.55	(4)	1.00	104,090,000
1453	8¢ Old Faithful, Yellowstone, Mar. 1	.15	.15	.70	(4)	1.00	164,096,000
a	Tagging omitted	10.00					
	Mount McKinley, July 28						
1454	15¢ View of Mount McKinley in Alaska	.30	.18	1.30	(4)	1.00	53,920,000

Note: Beginning with this National Parks Centennial issue, the USPS began to offer stamp collectors first day cancellations affixed to 8" x 10½" souvenir pages. The pages are similar to the stamp announcements that have appeared on Post Office bulletin boards beginning with Scott #1132. See "Souvenir Pages" listed in the back of this book (see Table of Contents).

		Un	U	PB	#	FDC	Q
1455	8¢ Family Planning, Mar. 18	.15	.15	.70	(4)	1.00	153,025,000
a	Yellow omitted	—					
b	Dark brown and olive omitted	—					
	American Bicentennial Issue, Colonial American Craftsmen, July 4, Perf. 11 x 10.5						
1456	8¢ Glassblower	.16	.15			1.00	50,472,500
1457	8¢ Silversmith	.16	.15			1.00	50,472,500
1458	8¢ Wigmaker	.16	.15			1.00	50,472,500
1459	8¢ Hatter	.16	.15			1.00	50,472,500
a	Block of 4, #1456-59	.65	.65	.75	(4)	2.50	
	Olympic Games Issue, Aug. 17 (See also #C85)						
1460	8¢ Bicycling and Olympic Rings	.15	.15	1.25	(10)	1.00	67,335,000
	Plate flaw (broken red ring)	7.50					
1461	8¢ Bobsledding and Olympic Rings	.15	.15	1.60	(10)	1.00	179,675,000
1462	15¢ Running and Olympic Rings	.28	.18	3.00	(10)	1.00	46,340,000
1463	8¢ Parent Teachers Association, Sept. 15	.15	.15	.70	(4)	1.00	180,155,000

	Issues of 1972, Perf. 11 x 10.5	Un	U	PB	#	FDC	Q
	Wildlife Conservation Issue, Sept. 20, Perf. 11						
1464	8¢ Fur Seals	.16	.15			1.50	49,591,200
1465	8¢ Cardinal	.16	.15			1.50	49,591,200
1466	8¢ Brown Pelican	.16	.15			1.50	49,591,200
1467	8¢ Bighorn Sheep	.16	.15			1.50	49,591,200
a	Block of 4, #1464-67	.65	.65	.75	(4)	3.00	
b	As "a," brown omitted	3,750.00					
c	As "a," green and blue omitted	—					

Note: With this Wildlife Conservation issue the USPS introduced the "American Commemorative Series" Stamp Panels. Each panel contains a block of four or more mint stamps with text and background illustrations. See pages 426-431 for a complete listing.

		Un	U	PB	#	FDC	Q
1468	8¢ Mail Order Business, Sept. 27	.15	.15	1.90	(12)	1.00	185,490,000
	Perf. 10.5 x 11						
1469	8¢ Osteopathic Medicine, Oct. 9	.15	.15	1.00	(6)	1.00	162,335,000
	American Folklore Issue, Tom Sawyer, Oct. 13, Perf. 11						
1470	8¢ Tom Sawyer Whitewashing a Fence, by Norman Rockwell	.15	.15	.70	(4)	1.00	162,789,950
a	Horizontal pair, imperf. between	4,500.00					
b	Red and black omitted	2,000.00					
c	Yellow and tan omitted	2,200.00					
	Christmas Issue, Nov. 9, Perf. 10.5 x 11						
1471	8¢ Angels from "Mary, Queen of Heaven," by the Master of the St. Lucy Legend	.15	.15	1.90	(12)	1.00	1,003,475,000
a	Pink omitted	200.00					
b	Black omitted	4,000.00					
1472	8¢ Santa Claus	.15	.15	1.90	(12)	1.00	1,017,025,000
	Perf. 11						
1473	8¢ Pharmacy, Nov. 10	.15	.15	.70	(4)	1.00	165,895,000
a	Blue and orange omitted	900.00					
b	Blue omitted	2,250.00					
c	Orange omitted	2,000.00					
1474	8¢ Stamp Collecting, Nov. 17	.15	.15	.65	(4)	1.00	166,508,000
a	Black omitted	900.00					
	Issues of 1973, Perf. 11 x 10.5						
1475	8¢ Love, Jan. 26	.15	.15	1.00	(6)	1.00	320,055,000
	American Bicentennial Issue, Communications in Colonial Times, Perf. 11						
1476	8¢ Printer and Patriots Examining Pamphlet, Feb. 16	.15	.15	.65	(4)	1.00	166,005,000
1477	8¢ Posting a Broadside, Apr. 13	.15	.15	.65	(4)	1.00	163,050,000
	Pair with full horizontal gutter between	—					
1478	8¢ Postrider, June 22	.15	.15	.65	(4)	1.00	159,005,000
1479	8¢ Drummer, Sept. 28	.15	.15	.70	(4)	1.00	147,295,000
	Boston Tea Party, July 4						
1480	8¢ British Merchantman	.15	.15			1.00	49,068,750
1481	8¢ British Three-Master	.15	.15			1.00	49,068,750
1482	8¢ Boats and Ship's Hull	.15	.15			1.00	49,068,750
1483	8¢ Boat and Dock	.15	.15			1.00	49,068,750
a	Block of 4, #1480-83	.60	.45	.70	(4)	3.00	
b	As "a," blk. (engraved) omitted	1,750.00					
c	As "a," blk. (lithographed) omitted	1,650.00					

1464 **1465**

1468

1466 **1467** **1467a**

1469 **1470**

1473

1471 **1472**

1474

1475 **1476** **1477**

1478 **1479**

1480 **1481**

1482 **1483** **1483a**

1484

1485

1486

1487

1488

1489　　**1490**　　**1491**　　**1492**　　**1493**

Nearly 27 billion
U.S. stamps
are sold yearly
to carry
your letters to
every corner
of the world.

People Serving You

Mail is
picked up
from nearly
a third of a million
local collection
boxes, as well
as your mailbox.

People Serving You

More than
87 billion letters
and packages
are handled
yearly—almost
300 million every
delivery day.

People Serving You

The People
in your
Postal Service
handle and
deliver more
than 500 million
packages yearly.

People Serving You

Thousands of
machines, buildings,
and vehicle
must be operated
and maintained
to keep your
mail moving.

People Serving You

1494　　**1495**　　**1496**　　**1497**　　**1498**

The skill
of sorting mail
manually
is still vital
to delivery of
your mail.

People Serving You

Employees
use modern, high-
speed equipment
to sort and process
huge volumes of
mail in central
locations.

People Serving You

Thirteen billion
pounds of mail are
handled yearly by
postal employees
as they speed
your letters and
packages.

People Serving You

Our customers
include
54 million urban
and 12 million
rural families,
plus 9 million
businesses.

People Serving You

Employees
cover
4 million miles
each delivery day
to bring mail to
your home or
business.

People Serving You

Issues of 1973, Perf. 11	Un	U	PB	#	FDC	Q
American Arts Issue						
1484 8¢ George Gershwin and Scene from "Porgy and Bess," Feb. 28	.15	.15	1.75	(12)	1.00	139,152,000
a Vertical pair, imperf. horizontally	250.00					
1485 8¢ Robinson Jeffers, Man and Children of Carmel with Burro, Aug. 13	.15	.15	1.75	(12)	1.00	128,048,000
a Vertical pair, imperf. horizontally	250.00					
1486 8¢ Henry Ossawa Tanner, Palette and Rainbow, Sept. 10	.15	.15	1.75	(12)	1.00	146,008,000
1487 8¢ Willa Cather, Pioneer Family and Covered Wagon, Sept. 20	.15	.15	1.75	(12)	1.00	139,608,000
a Vertical pair, imperf. horizontally	300.00					
1488 8¢ Nicolaus Copernicus, Apr. 23	.15	.15	.65	(4)	1.00	159,475,000
a Orange omitted	900.00					
b Black omitted	1,500.00					
Postal Service Employees Issue, Apr. 30, Perf. 10.5 x 11						
1489 8¢ Stamp Counter	.15	.15			1.00	48,602,000
1490 8¢ Mail Collection	.15	.15			1.00	48,602,000
1491 8¢ Letter Facing on Conveyor	.15	.15			1.00	48,602,000
1492 8¢ Parcel Post Sorting	.15	.15			1.00	48,602,000
1493 8¢ Mail Canceling	.15	.15			1.00	48,602,000
1494 8¢ Manual Letter Routing	.15	.15			1.00	48,602,000
1495 8¢ Electronic Letter Routing	.15	.15			1.00	48,602,000
1496 8¢ Loading Mail on Truck	.15	.15			1.00	48,602,000
1497 8¢ Carrier Delivering Mail	.15	.15			1.00	48,602,000
1498 8¢ Rural Mail Delivery	.15	.15			1.00	48,602,000
a Strip of 10, #1489-98	1.50	1.00	3.10	(20)	5.00	

#1489-98 were the first United States postage stamps to have printing on the back.
(See also #1559-62.)

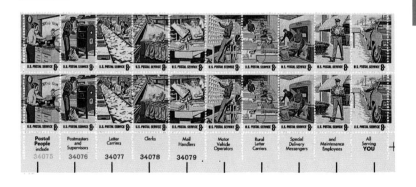

#1498a plate block (above). As shown on the bottom row, when these stamps are turned over, the inscriptions appear in the reverse order from the designs (each appearing on the back of the appropriate image).

	Issues of 1973, Perf. 11	Un	U	PB	#	FDC	Q
1499	8¢ Harry S. Truman, May 8	.15	.15	.55	(4)	1.00	157,052,800
	Progress in Electronics Issue, July 10 (See also #C86)						
1500	6¢ Marconi's Spark Coil and Gap	.15	.15	.55	(4)	1.00	53,005,000
1501	8¢ Transistors and Printed Circuit Board	.15	.15	.70	(4)	1.00	159,775,000
a	Black omitted	650.00					
b	Tan and lilac omitted	1,500.00					
1502	15¢ Microphone, Speaker, Vacuum Tube, TV Camera Tube	.28	.15	1.20	(4)	1.00	39,005,000
a	Black omitted	1,500.00					
1503	8¢ Lyndon B. Johnson, Aug. 27	.15	.15	1.75	(12)	1.00	152,624,000
a	Horizontal pair, imperf. vertically	300.00					
	Issues of 1973-74, Rural America Issue						
1504	8¢ Angus and Longhorn Cattle, by F.C. Murphy, Oct. 5, 1973	.15	.15	.65	(4)	1.00	145,840,000
a	Green and red brown omitted	1,000.00					
b	Vertical pair, imperf. between		—				
1505	10¢ Chautauqua Tent and Buggies, Aug. 6, 1974	.18	.15	.80	(4)	1.00	151,335,000
1506	10¢ Wheat Fields and Train, Aug. 16, 1974	.18	.15	.80	(4)	1.00	141,085,000
a	Black and blue omitted	750.00					
	Issues of 1973, Christmas Issue, Nov. 7, Perf. 10.5 x 11						
1507	8¢ Small Cowper Madonna, by Raphael	.15	.15	1.85	(12)	1.00	885,160,000
	Pair with full vertical gutter between	—					
1508	8¢ Christmas Tree in Needlepoint	.15	.15	1.85	(12)	1.00	939,835,000
a	Vertical pair, imperf. between	400.00					
	Pair with full horizontal gutter between	—					
	Issues of 1973-74, Perf. 11 x 10.5						
1509	10¢ 50-Star and 13-Star Flags, Dec. 8, 1973	.18	.15	3.75	(20)	1.00	
a	Horizontal pair, imperf. between	50.00					
b	Blue omitted	160.00					
c	Imperf. pair	1,150.00					
1510	10¢ Jefferson Memorial, Dec. 14, 1973	.18	.15	.80	(4)	1.00	
a	Untagged (Bureau precanceled)		.18				
b	Booklet pane of 5 + label	1.50	.30			2.25	
c	Booklet pane of 8	1.65	.30			2.50	
d	Booklet pane of 6, Aug. 5, 1974	5.25	.30			3.00	
e	Vertical pair, imperf. horizontally	350.00					
f	Vertical pair, imperf. between	—					

1499

1500   1501   1502

1503

1504   1505   1506

1509   1510

1507   1508

1511

1518

1525

1526

1527

1528

1529

1530   **1531**   **1532**   **1533**

1534   **1535**   **1536**   **1537**   **1537a**

	Issues of 1973-74, Perf. 11 x 10.5	Un	U	PB/LP	#	FDC	Q
1511	10¢ ZIP Code, Jan. 4, 1974	.22	.15	1.50	(8)	1.00	
a	Yellow omitted	50.00					
	Pair with full horizontal gutter between	—					
1512-17	Not assigned						
	Coil Stamps, Perf. 10 Vertically						
1518	6.3¢ Liberty Bell, Oct. 1, 1974	.15	.15	.65	(2)	1.00	
a	Untagged (Bureau precanceled)		.15	.80	(2)		
b	Imperf. pair	175.00		400.00	(2)		
c	As "a," imperf. pair		100.00	200.00	(2)		
1519	10¢ red and blue Flags (1509), Dec. 8, 1973	.20	.15			1.00	
a	Imperf. pair	30.00					
1520	10¢ blue Jefferson Memorial (1510), Dec. 14, 1973	.25	.15	.55	(2)	1.00	
a	Untagged (Bureau precanceled)		.25				
b	Imperf. pair	40.00		65.00	(2)		
1521-24	Not assigned						
	Issues of 1974, Perf. 11						
1525	10¢ Veterans of Foreign Wars, Mar. 11	.16	.15	.75	(4)	1.00	149,930,000
	Perf. 10.5 x 11						
1526	10¢ Robert Frost, Mar. 26	.16	.15	.75	(4)	1.00	145,235,000
	Perf. 11						
1527	10¢ Expo '74 World's Fair, Apr. 18	.16	.15	2.20	(12)	1.00	135,052,000
	Perf. 11 x 10.5						
1528	10¢ Horse Racing, May 4	.16	.15	2.20	(12)	1.00	156,750,000
a	Blue omitted	900.00					
b	Red omitted	—					
	Perf. 11						
1529	10¢ Skylab, May 14	.18	.15	.80	(4)	1.50	164,670,000
a	Vertical pair, imperf. between	—					
	Universal Postal Union Issue, June 6						
1530	10¢ Michelangelo, from "School of Athens," by Raphael	.20	.15			1.00	23,769,600
1531	10¢ "Five Feminine Virtues," by Hokusai	.20	.15			1.00	23,769,600
1532	10¢ "Old Scraps," by John Fredrick Peto	.20	.15			1.00	23,769,600
1533	10¢ "The Lovely Reader," by Jean Etienne Liotard	.20	.15			1.00	23,769,600
1534	10¢ "Lady Writing Letter," by Gerard Terborch	.20	.15			1.00	23,769,600
1535	10¢ Inkwell and Quill, from "Boy with a Top," by Jean-Baptiste Simeon Chardin	.20	.15			1.00	23,769,600
1536	10¢ Mrs. John Douglas, by Thomas Gainsborough	.20	.15			1.00	23,769,600
1537	10¢ Don Antonio Noriega, by Francisco de Goya	.20	.15			1.00	23,769,600
a	Block of 8, #1530-37	1.60	1.50	3.50	(16)	4.00	
b	As "a," imperf. vertically	7,500.00					

	Issues of 1974, Perf. 11	Un	U	PB	#	FDC	Q
	Mineral Heritage Issue, June 13						
1538	10¢ Petrified Wood	.16	.15			1.00	41,803,200
a	Light blue and yellow omitted	—					
1539	10¢ Tourmaline	.16	.15			1.00	41,803,200
a	Light blue omitted	—					
b	Black and purple omitted	—					
1540	10¢ Amethyst	.16	.15			1.00	41,803,200
a	Light blue and yellow omitted	—					
1541	10¢ Rhodochrosite	.16	.15			1.00	41,803,200
a	Block of 4, #1538-41	.75	.80	.85	(4)	2.50	
b	As "a," light blue and yellow omitted	2,000.00					
c	Light blue omitted	—					
d	Black and red omitted	—					
1542	10¢ First Kentucky Settlement-Ft. Harrod, June 15	.16	.15	.75	(4)	1.00	156,265,000
a	Dull black omitted	700.00					
b	Green, black and blue omitted	3,250.00					
c	Green omitted	—					
d	Green and black omitted	—					
	American Bicentennial Issue, First Continental Congress, July 4						
1543	10¢ Carpenters' Hall	.18	.15			1.00	48,896,250
1544	10¢ "We Ask but for Peace, Liberty and Safety"	.18	.15			1.00	48,896,250
1545	10¢ "Deriving Their Just Powers from the Consent of the Governed"	.18	.15			1.00	48,896,250
1546	10¢ Independence Hall	.18	.15			1.00	48,896,250
a	Block of 4, #1543-46	.75	.75	.85	(4)	2.75	
1547	10¢ Energy Conservation, Sept. 23	.18	.15	.75	(4)	1.00	148,850,000
a	Blue and orange omitted	800.00					
b	Orange and green omitted	800.00					
c	Green omitted	900.00					
	American Folklore Issue, The Legend of Sleepy Hollow, Oct. 10						
1548	10¢ Headless Horseman and Ichabod Crane	.16	.15	.75	(4)	1.00	157,270,000
1549	10¢ Retarded Children, Oct. 12	.16	.15	.75	(4)	1.00	150,245,000
	Christmas Issue, Perf. 10.5 x 11						
1550	10¢ Angel from Perussis Altarpiece, Oct. 23	.16	.15	1.75	(10)	1.00	835,180,000
	Perf. 11 x 10.5						
1551	10¢ "The Road-Winter," by Currier and Ives, Oct. 23	.16	.15	2.00	(12)	1.00	882,520,000
	Precanceled Self-Adhesive, Imperf.						
1552	10¢ Dove Weather Vane atop Mount Vernon, Nov. 15	.16	.15	3.50	(20)	1.00	213,155,000
	Issues of 1975, American Arts Issue, Perf. 10.5 x 11						
1553	10¢ Benjamin West, Self-Portrait, Feb. 10	.18	.15	1.85	(10)	1.00	156,995,000
	Perf. 11						
1554	10¢ Paul Laurence Dunbar and Lamp, May 1	.18	.15	1.85	(10)	1.00	146,365,000
a	Imperf. pair	1,250.00					
1555	10¢ D.W. Griffith and Motion-Picture Camera, May 27	.16	.15	.75	(4)	1.00	148,805,000
a	Brown omitted	750.00					

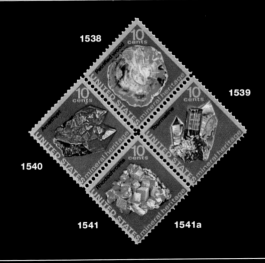

1538
1539
1540
1541
1541a

1542

1543
1544
1545
1546
1546a

1547

1548

1549

1550

1551

1552

1553

1554

1555

1556

1557

1558

1559

1560

1561

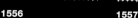

YOUTHFUL HEROINE
On the dark night of April 26, 1777, 16-year-old Sybil Ludington rode her horse "Star" alone through the Connecticut countryside rallying her father's militia to repel a raid by the British on Danbury.

GALLANT SOLDIER
The conspicuously courageous actions of black foot soldier Salem Poor at the Battle of Bunker Hill on June 17, 1775, earned him citations for his bravery and leadership ability.

FINANCIAL HERO
Businessman and broker Haym Salomon was responsible for raising most of the money needed to finance the American Revolution and later to save the new nation from collapse.

1562

1563

1564

FIGHTER EXTRAORDINARY
Peter Francisco's strength and bravery made him a legend around campfires. He fought with distinction at Brandywine, Yorktown and Guilford Court House.

1565   **1566**   **1569**

1567   **1568**   **1568a**

1570   **1569a**

Issues of 1975, Perf. 11	Un	U	PB	#	FDC	Q
Space Issues						
1556 10¢ Pioneer 10 Passing Jupiter, Feb. 28	.16	.15	.75	(4)	2.00	173,685,000
a Red and yellow omitted	1,400.00					
b Blue omitted	800.00					
1557 10¢ Mariner 10, Venus and Mercury, Apr. 4	.16	.15	.75	(4)	2.00	158,600,000
a Red omitted	600.00					
b Ultramarine and bister omitted	1,800.00					
1558 10¢ Collective Bargaining, Mar. 13	.18	.15	1.60	(8)	1.00	153,355,000
Imperfs. of #1558 exist from printer's waste.						
American Bicentennial Issue, Contributors to the Cause, Mar. 25, Perf. 11 x 10.5						
1559 8¢ Sybil Ludington Riding Horse	.15	.15	1.50	(10)	1.00	63,205,000
a Back inscription omitted	275.00					
1560 10¢ Salem Poor Carrying Musket	.18	.15	1.85	(10)	1.00	157,865,000
a Back inscription omitted	225.00					
1561 10¢ Haym Salomon Figuring Accounts	.18	.15	1.85	(10)	1.00	166,810,000
a Back inscription omitted	275.00					
b Red omitted	225.00					
1562 18¢ Peter Francisco Shouldering Cannon	.35	.20	3.60	(10)	1.00	44,825,000
Battle of Lexington & Concord, Apr. 19, Perf. 11						
1563 10¢ "Birth of Liberty," by Henry Sandham	.18	.15	2.20	(12)	1.00	144,028,000
a Vertical pair, imperf. horizontally	400.00					
Battle of Bunker Hill, June 17						
1564 10¢ "Battle of Bunker Hill," by John Trumbull	.18	.15	2.20	(12)	1.00	139,928,000
Military Uniforms, July 4						
1565 10¢ Soldier with Flintlock Musket, Uniform Button	.18	.15			1.00	44,963,750
1566 10¢ Sailor with Grappling Hook, First Navy Jack, 1775	.18	.15			1.00	44,963,750
1567 10¢ Marine with Musket, Full-Rigged Ship	.18	.15			1.00	44,963,750
1568 10¢ Militiaman with Musket, Powder Horn	.18	.15			1.00	44,963,750
a Block of 4, #1565-68	.75	.75	2.30	(12)	2.50	
Apollo Soyuz Space Issue, July 15						
1569 10¢ Apollo and Soyuz after Docking and Earth	.18	.15			2.00	80,931,600
a Attached pair, #1569-70	.36	.25	2.20	(12)	4.00	
b As "a," vertical pair, imperf. horizontally	2,000.00					
Pair with full horizontal gutter between	—					
1570 10¢ Spacecraft before Docking, Earth and Project Emblem	.18	.15			2.00	80,931,600

	Issues of 1975, Perf. 11 x 10.5	Un	U	PB	#	FDC	Q
1571	10¢ International Women's Year, Aug. 26	.16	.15	1.10	(6)	1.00	145,640,000
	Postal Service Bicentennial Issue, Sept. 3						
1572	10¢ Stagecoach and Trailer Truck	.18	.15			1.00	42,163,750
1573	10¢ Old and New Locomotives	.18	.15			1.00	42,163,750
1574	10¢ Early Mail Plane and Jet	.18	.15			1.00	42,163,750
1575	10¢ Satellite for Mailgrams	.18	.15			1.00	42,163,750
a	Block of 4, #1572-75	.75	.80	2.30	(12)	1.25	
b	As "a," red "10¢" omitted	—					
	Perf. 11						
1576	10¢ World Peace Through Law, Sept. 29	.18	.15	.80	(4)	1.00	146,615,000
	Banking and Commerce Issue, Oct. 6						
1577	10¢ Engine Turning, Indian Head Penny and Morgan Silver Dollar	.18	.15			1.00	73,098,000
a	Attached pair, #1577-78	.36	.20	.80	(4)	1.25	
b	Brown and blue omitted	1,400.00					
c	As "a," brn., blue and yel. omitted	2,500.00					
1578	10¢ Seated Liberty Quarter, $20 Gold Piece and Engine Turning	.18	.15			1.00	73,098,000
	Christmas Issue, Oct. 14						
1579	(10¢) Madonna and Child, by Domenico Ghirlandaio	.18	.15	2.20	(12)	1.00	739,430,000
a	Imperf. pair	110.00					
	Plate flaw ("d" damaged)	5.00	—				
1580	(10¢) Christmas Card, by Louis Prang, 1878	.18	.15	2.20	(12)	1.00	878,690,000
a	Imperf. pair	120.00					
b	Perf. 10.5 x 11	.60	.15	9.50	(12)		
	Issues of 1975-81, Americana Issue, Perf. 11 x 10.5 (Designs 181/2 x 221/2mm; #1590-90a, 171/2 x 20mm; see also #1606, 1608, 1610-19, 1622-23, 1625, 1811, 1813, 1816)						
1581	1¢ Inkwell & Quill, Dec. 8, 1977	.15	.15	.25	(4)	1.00	
a	Untagged (Bureau precanceled)		.15				
1582	2¢ Speaker's Stand, Dec. 8, 1977	.15	.15	.25	(4)	1.00	
a	Untagged (Bureau precanceled)		.15				
1583	Not assigned						
1584	3¢ Early Ballot Box, Dec. 8, 1977	.15	.15	.30	(4)	1.00	
a	Untagged (Bureau precanceled)		.15				
1585	4¢ Books, Eyeglasses, Dec. 8, 1977	.15	.15	.40	(4)	1.00	
a	Untagged (Bureau precanceled)		1.25				
1586-89	Not assigned						
	Booklet Stamp						
1590	9¢ Capitol Dome (1591), single from booklet (1623a), Mar. 11, 1977	.50	.20			1.00	
	Booklet Stamp, Perf. 10						
a	Single (1591) from booklet (1623c)	20.00	12.50				
	#1590 is on white paper; #1591 is on gray paper.						
	Perf. 11 x 10.5						
1591	9¢ Capitol Dome, Nov. 24, 1975	.16	.15	.70	(4)	1.00	
a	Untagged (Bureau precanceled)		.18				
1592	10¢ Contemplation of Justice, Nov. 17, 1977	.18	.15	.90	(4)	1.00	
a	Untagged (Bureau precanceled)		.25				
1593	11¢ Printing Press, Nov. 13, 1975	.20	.15	.90	(4)	1.00	
1594	12¢ Torch, Apr. 8, 1981	.22	.15	1.25	(4)	1.00	

1571

1572   1573

1574   1575   1575a

1576

1577   1578   1577a

1579   1580

1581   1582

1584   1585

1591   1592

1593   1594

1596

1595

1597

1599

1603

1604

1605

1606

1608

1610

1611

1612

1613

1614

1615

1615C

	Issues of 1975-79, Perf. 11 x 10.5	Un	U	PB/LP	#	FDC
	Americana Issue (continued) (See also #1581-82, 1584-85, 1590-99, 1603-08, 1610-19, 1622-23, 1625, 1811, 1813, 1816)					
1595	13¢ Liberty Bell, single from booklet	.25	.15			1.00
a	Booklet pane of 6, Oct. 31, 1975	1.90	.50			2.00
b	Booklet pane of 7 + label	1.75	.50			2.75
c	Booklet pane of 8	2.00	.50			2.50
d	Booklet pane of 5 + label, Apr. 2, 1976	1.40	.50			2.25
	Perf. 11					
1596	13¢ Eagle and Shield, Dec. 1, 1975	.22	.15	2.75	(12)	1.00
a	Imperf. pair	50.00				
b	Yellow omitted	200.00				
1597	15¢ Ft. McHenry Flag, June 30, 1978	.28	.15	1.75	(6)	1.00
a	Imperf. pair	17.50				
b	Gray omitted	500.00				
	Booklet Stamp, Perf. 11 x 10.5					
1598	15¢ Ft. McHenry Flag (1597), single from booklet	.35	.15			1.00
a	Booklet pane of 8, June 30, 1978	3.50	.60			2.50
	Perf. 11 x 10.5					
1599	16¢ Head of Liberty, Mar. 31, 1978	.34	.15	1.90	(4)	1.00
1600-02	Not assigned					
1603	24¢ Old North Church, Nov. 14, 1975	.45	.15	1.90	(4)	1.00
1604	28¢ Ft. Nisqually, Aug. 11, 1978	.55	.15	2.30	(4)	1.25
	Dull finish gum	1.10				
1605	29¢ Sandy Hook Lighthouse, Apr. 14, 1978	.55	.15	2.75	(4)	1.25
	Dull finish gum	2.00				
1606	30¢ One-Rm. Schoolhouse, Aug. 27, 1979	.55	.15	2.30	(4)	1.25
1607	Not assigned					
	Perf. 11					
1608	50¢ Whale Oil Lamp, Sept. 11, 1979	.85	.15	3.75	(4)	1.50
a	Black omitted	300.00				
b	Vertical pair, imperf. horizontally	—				
1609	Not assigned					
1610	$1 Candle and Rushlight Holder, July 2, 1979	1.75	.20	7.50	(4)	3.00
a	Brown omitted	300.00				
b	Tan, orange and yellow omitted	350.00				
c	Brown inverted	15,000.00				
1611	$2 Kerosene Table Lamp, Nov. 16, 1978	3.25	.75	14.00	(4)	5.00
1612	$5 Railroad Lantern, Aug. 23, 1979	7.50	1.75	31.00	(4)	12.50
	Coil Stamps, Perf. 10 Vertically					
1613	3.1¢ Guitar, Oct. 25, 1979	.15	.15	1.50	(2)	1.00
a	Untagged (Bureau precanceled)		.50			
b	Imperf. pair	1,350.00		3,600.00	(2)	
1614	7.7¢ Saxhorns, Nov. 20, 1976	.20	.15	1.00	(2)	1.00
a	Untagged (Bureau precanceled)		.35			
b	As "a," imperf. pair		1,400.00	4,400.00	(2)	
1615	7.9¢ Drum, Apr. 23, 1976	.20	.15	.65	(2)	1.00
a	Untagged (Bureau precanceled)		.20			
b	Imperf. pair	600.00				
1615C	8.4¢ Piano, July 13, 1978	.22	.15	3.25	(2)	1.00
d	Untagged (Bureau precanceled)		.30			
e	As "d," pair, imperf. between		50.00	—	(2)	
f	As "d," imperf. pair		15.00	30.00	(2)	

	Issues of 1975-81, Perf. 10 Vertically	Un	U	PB/LP	#	FDC
	Americana Issue (continued) (See also #1581-82, 1584-85, 1590-99, 1603-05, 1811, 1813, 1816)					
1616	9¢ slate green Capitol Dome (1591), Mar. 5, 1976	.20	.15	.90	(2)	1.00
a	Imperf. pair	*125.00*		*250.00*	(2)	
b	Untagged (Bureau precanceled)		.35			
c	As "b," imperf. pair		*650.00*	—		
1617	10¢ purple Contemplation of Justice (1592), Nov. 4, 1977	.20	.15	1.10	(2)	1.00
a	Untagged (Bureau precanceled)		.25			
b	Imperf. pair	*70.00*		*125.00*	(2)	
	Dull finish gum	.20				
1618	13¢ brown Liberty Bell (1595), Nov. 25, 1975	.25	.15	.60	(2)	1.00
a	Untagged (Bureau precanceled)		.45			
b	Imperf. pair	25.00		*65.00*	(2)	
g	Pair, imperf. between	—				
1618C	15¢ Ft. McHenry Flag (1597), June 30, 1978	.40	.15			1.00
d	Imperf. pair	20.00				
e	Pair, imperf. between	*150.00*				
f	Gray omitted	*40.00*				
1619	16¢ blue Head of Liberty (1599), Mar. 31, 1978	.32	.15	1.50	(2)	1.00
a	Huck Press printing (white background with a bluish tinge, fraction of a millimeter smaller)	.50	.15			
	Perf. 11 x 10.5					
1620-21	Not assigned					
1622	13¢ Flag over Independence Hall, Nov. 15, 1975	.24	.15	5.75	(20)	1.00
a	Horizontal pair, imperf. between	50.00				
b	Imperf. pair	*1,250.00*				
c	Perf. 11, 1981	.65	.15	*75.00*	(20)	
d	As "c," vertical pair, imperf.	*150.00*				
e	Horizontal pair, imperf. vertically	—				
	Booklet Stamps					
1623	13¢ Flag over Capitol, single from booklet (1623a)	.22	.15			1.00
a	Booklet pane of 8, (1 #1590 and 7 #1623), Mar. 11, 1977	2.25	.60			25.00
	Booklet Stamps, Perf. 10					
b	13¢ Single from booklet	1.00	1.00			
c	Booklet pane of 8, (1 #1590a and 7 #1623b)	30.00	—			12.50
	#1623, 1623b issued only in booklets. All stamps are imperf. at one side or imperf. at one side and bottom.					
	Booklet Stamps, Perf. 11 x 10.5					
d	Attached pair, #1590 and 1623	.75	—			
	Booklet Stamps, Perf. 10					
e	Attached pair, #1590a and 1623b	22.50	—			
1624	Not assigned					
	Coil Stamp, Perf. 10 Vertically					
1625	13¢ Flag over Independence Hall (1622), Nov. 15, 1975	.25	.15			1.00
a	Imperf. pair	22.50				

1622

1623a

1632

1629　　　**1630**　　　**1631**　**1631a**

1633

1634

1635

1636

1637

1638

1639

1640

1641

1642

1643

1644

1645

1646

1647

	Issues of 1976, Perf. 11	Un	U	PB	#	FDC	Q
	American Bicentennial Issue, The Spirit of '76, Jan. 1						
1629	13¢ Drummer Boy	.20	.15			1.25	73,152,000
1630	13¢ Old Drummer	.20	.15			1.25	73,152,000
1631	13¢ Fife Player	.20	.15			1.25	73,152,000
a	Strip of 3, #1629-31	.60	.60	3.10	(12)	2.00	
b	As "a," imperf.	1,450.00					
c	Imperf. pair, #1631	750.00					
1632	13¢ Interphil 76, Jan. 17	.20	.15	1.00	(4)	1.00	157,825,000
	State Flags, Feb. 23						
1633	13¢ Delaware	.25	.20			1.25	8,720,100
1634	13¢ Pennsylvania	.25	.20			1.25	8,720,100
1635	13¢ New Jersey	.25	.20			1.25	8,720,100
1636	13¢ Georgia	.25	.20			1.25	8,720,100
1637	13¢ Connecticut	.25	.20			1.25	8,720,100
1638	13¢ Massachusetts	.25	.20			1.25	8,720,100
1639	13¢ Maryland	.25	.20			1.25	8,720,100
1640	13¢ South Carolina	.25	.20			1.25	8,720,100
1641	13¢ New Hampshire	.25	.20			1.25	8,720,100
1642	13¢ Virginia	.25	.20			1.25	8,720,100
1643	13¢ New York	.25	.20			1.25	8,720,100
1644	13¢ North Carolina	.25	.20			1.25	8,720,100
1645	13¢ Rhode Island	.25	.20			1.25	8,720,100
1646	13¢ Vermont	.25	.20			1.25	8,720,100
1647	13¢ Kentucky	.25	.20			1.25	8,720,100

From this state, the United States declared independence

The second state to join the Union, Pennsylvania means Penn's Woods and refers to land given William Penn by British King Charles II in 1681. Penn, a Quaker, established the colony as a place of religious freedom. The Declaration of Independence was adopted in Pennsylvania's State House, now Independence Hall. Philadelphia served as the nation's capital from 1790 to 1800. **(#1634)**

Issues of 1976, Perf. 11	Un	U	FDC	Q
American Bicentennial Issue (continued), State Flags, Feb. 23				
1648	13¢ Tennessee	.25	.20	1.25	8,720,100
1649	13¢ Ohio	.25	.20	1.25	8,720,100
1650	13¢ Louisiana	.25	.20	1.25	8,720,100
1651	13¢ Indiana	.25	.20	1.25	8,720,100
1652	13¢ Mississippi	.25	.20	1.25	8,720,100
1653	13¢ Illinois	.25	.20	1.25	8,720,100
1654	13¢ Alabama	.25	.20	1.25	8,720,100
1655	13¢ Maine	.25	.20	1.25	8,720,100
1656	13¢ Missouri	.25	.20	1.25	8,720,100
1657	13¢ Arkansas	.25	.20	1.25	8,720,100
1658	13¢ Michigan	.25	.20	1.25	8,720,100
1659	13¢ Florida	.25	.20	1.25	8,720,100
1660	13¢ Texas	.25	.20	1.25	8,720,100
1661	13¢ Iowa	.25	.20	1.25	8,720,100
1662	13¢ Wisconsin	.25	.20	1.25	8,720,100
1663	13¢ California	.25	.20	1.25	8,720,100
1664	13¢ Minnesota	.25	.20	1.25	8,720,100
1665	13¢ Oregon	.25	.20	1.25	8,720,100
1666	13¢ Kansas	.25	.20	1.25	8,720,100
1667	13¢ West Virginia	.25	.20	1.25	8,720,100

No going farther south than this

The southernmost state on the mainland, Florida was the 27th state admitted to the Union, on March 3, 1845. Its nickname is the Sunshine State. Florida (which means "flowery" in Spanish) was given its name by explorer Ponce de Leon, who arrived in 1513. Settled first by the Indian tribes Calusa, Tequestra, Timucua, Apalachee and Ais, Florida was subsequently ruled by the Spanish, French and British before being ceded by Spain to the U.S. in 1821. **(#1659)**

1648 **1649** **1650**

1651 **1652**

1653 **1654** **1655**

1656 **1657**

1658 **1659** **1660**

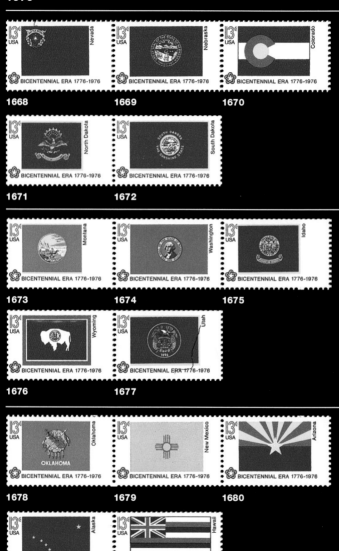

13¢ USA — Nevada — BICENTENNIAL ERA 1776-1976
1668

13¢ USA — Nebraska — BICENTENNIAL ERA 1776-1976
1669

13¢ USA — Colorado — BICENTENNIAL ERA 1776-1976
1670

13¢ USA — North Dakota — BICENTENNIAL ERA 1776-1976
1671

13¢ USA — South Dakota — BICENTENNIAL ERA 1776-1976
1672

13¢ USA — Montana — BICENTENNIAL ERA 1776-1976
1673

13¢ USA — Washington — BICENTENNIAL ERA 1776-1976
1674

13¢ USA — Idaho — BICENTENNIAL ERA 1776-1976
1675

13¢ USA — Wyoming — BICENTENNIAL ERA 1776-1976
1676

13¢ USA — Utah — BICENTENNIAL ERA 1776-1976
1677

13¢ USA — Oklahoma — OKLAHOMA — BICENTENNIAL ERA 1776-1976
1678

13¢ USA — New Mexico — BICENTENNIAL ERA 1776-1976
1679

13¢ USA — Arizona — BICENTENNIAL ERA 1776-1976
1680

13¢ USA — Alaska — BICENTENNIAL ERA 1776-1976
1681

13¢ USA — Hawaii — BICENTENNIAL ERA 1776-1976
1682

	Issues of 1976, Perf. 11	Un	U	PB	#	FDC	Q
	American Bicentennial Issue (continued), State Flags, Feb. 23						
1668	13¢ Nevada	.25	.20			1.25	8,720,100
1669	13¢ Nebraska	.25	.20			1.25	8,720,100
1670	13¢ Colorado	.25	.20			1.25	8,720,100
1671	13¢ North Dakota	.25	.20			1.25	8,720,100
1672	13¢ South Dakota	.25	.20			1.25	8,720,100
1673	13¢ Montana	.25	.20			1.25	8,720,100
1674	13¢ Washington	.25	.20			1.25	8,720,100
1675	13¢ Idaho	.25	.20			1.25	8,720,100
1676	13¢ Wyoming	.25	.20			1.25	8,720,100
1677	13¢ Utah	.25	.20			1.25	8,720,100
1678	13¢ Oklahoma	.25	.20			1.25	8,720,100
1679	13¢ New Mexico	.25	.20			1.25	8,720,100
1680	13¢ Arizona	.25	.20			1.25	8,720,100
1681	13¢ Alaska	.25	.20			1.25	8,720,100
1682	13¢ Hawaii	.25	.20			1.25	8,720,100
a	Pane of 50, #1633-82	13.00	—	13.00	(50)	27.50	

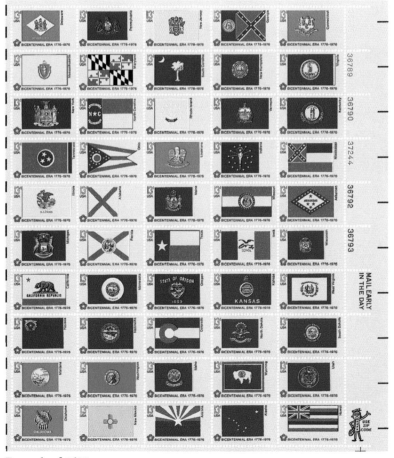

Example of 1682a

	Issues of 1976, Perf. 11	Un	U	PB	#	FDC	Q
1683	13¢ Telephone Centennial, Mar. 10	.22	.15	1.00	(4)	1.00	158,915,000
1684	13¢ Commercial Aviation, Mar. 19	.22	.15	2.25	(10)	1.00	156,960,000
1685	13¢ Chemistry, Apr. 6	.20	.15	2.75	(12)	1.00	158,470,000
	Pair with full vertical gutter between	—					
	American Bicentennial Issue Souvenir Sheets, May 29, 5 stamps each						
1686	13¢ The Surrender of Lord Cornwallis at Yorktown, by John Trumbull	3.25	—			6.00	1,990,000
a	13¢ Two American Officers	.45	.40				1,990,000
b	13¢ Gen. Benjamin Lincoln	.45	.40				1,990,000
c	13¢ George Washington	.45	.40				1,990,000
d	13¢ John Trumbull, Col. David Cobb, General Friedrich von Steuben, Marquis de Lafayette and Thomas Nelson	.45	.40				1,990,000
e	13¢ Alexander Hamilton, John Laurens and Walter Stewart	.45	.40				1,990,000
f	"USA/13¢" omitted on "b," "c" and "d," imperf.		— 2,000.00				
g	"USA/13¢" omitted on "a" and "e"	450.00	—				
h	Imperf. (untagged)		2,000.00				
i	"USA/13¢" omitted on "b," "c" and "d"	450.00					
j	"USA/13¢" double on "b"	—					
k	"USA/13¢" omitted on "c" and "d"	—					
l	"USA/13¢" omitted on "e"	500.00					
m	"USA/13¢" omitted, imperf. (untagged)	—	—				
1687	18¢ The Declaration of Independence, 4 July 1776 at Philadelphia, by John Trumbull	4.25	—			7.50	1,983,000
a	18¢ John Adams, Roger Sherman and Robert R. Livingston	.55	.55				1,983,000
b	18¢ Thomas Jefferson and Benjamin Franklin	.55	.55				1,983,000
c	18¢ Thomas Nelson, Jr., Francis Lewis, John Witherspoon and Samuel Huntington	.55	.55				1,983,000
d	18¢ John Hancock and Charles Thomson	.55	.55				1,983,000
e	18¢ George Read, John Dickinson and Edward Rutledge	.55	.55				1,983,000
f	Design and marginal inscriptions omitted	3,000.00					
g	"USA/18¢" omitted on "a" and "c"	800.00					
h	"USA/18¢" omitted on "b," "d" and "e"	500.00					
i	"USA/18¢" omitted on "d"	500.00	500.00				
j	Black omitted in design	1,750.00					
k	"USA/18¢" omitted, imperf. (untagged)	3,000.00					
m	"USA/18¢" omitted on "b" and "e"	500.00					

1683

1684

1685

The Surrender of Lord Cornwallis at Yorktown
From a Painting by John Trumbull

1686

The Declaration of Independence, 4 July 1776 at Philadelphia
From a Painting by John Trumbull

1687

Washington Crossing the Delaware
From a Painting by Emanuel Leutze / Eastman Johnson

Washington Reviewing His Ragged Army at Valley Forge
From a Painting by William T. Trego

Issues of 1976, Perf. 11	Un	U	FDC	Q
American Bicentennial Issue (continued) Souvenir Sheets, May 29, 5 stamps each				
1688 24¢ Washington Crossing the Delaware, by Emanuel Leutze/ Eastman Johnson	5.25	—	8.50	1,953,000
a 24¢ Boatmen	.70	.70		1,953,000
b 24¢ George Washington	.70	.70		1,953,000
c 24¢ Flagbearer	.70	.70		1,953,000
d 24¢ Men in Boat	.70	.70		1,953,000
e 24¢ Steersman and Men on Shore	.70	.70		1,953,000
f "USA/24¢" omitted, imperf.	3,250.00			
g "USA/24¢" omitted on "d" and "e"	—	450.00		
h Design and marginal inscriptions omitted	3,250.00			
i "USA/24¢" omitted on "a," "b" and "c"	500.00	—		
j Imperf. (untagged)	2,750.00			
k "USA/24¢" inverted on "d" and "e"	—			
1689 31¢ Washington Reviewing His Ragged Army at Valley Forge, by William T. Trego	6.25	—	9.50	1,903,000
a 31¢ Two Officers	.85	.85		1,903,000
b 31¢ George Washington	.85	.85		1,903,000
c 31¢ Officer and Brown Horse	.85	.85		1,903,000
d 31¢ White Horse and Officer	.85	.85		1,903,000
e 31¢ Three Soldiers	.85	.85		1,903,000
f "USA/31¢" omitted, imperf.	2,750.00			
g "USA/31¢" omitted on "a" and "c"	—			
h "USA/31¢" omitted on "b," "d" and "e"	—	—		
i "USA/31¢" omitted on "e"	500.00			
j Black omitted in design	1,500.00			
k Imperf. (untagged)		2,250.00		
l "USA/31¢" omitted on "b" and "d"	—			
m "USA/31¢" omitted on "a," "c" and "e"	—			
n As "m," imperf. (untagged)	—			
p As "h," imperf. (untagged)		2,500.00		
q As "g," imperf. (untagged)	2,750.00			

	Issues of 1976, Perf.11	Un	U	PB	#	FDC	Q
	American Bicentennial Issue, Benjamin Franklin, June 1						
1690	13¢ Bust of Franklin, Map of North America, 1776	.20	.15	.90	(4)	1.00	164,890,000
a	Light blue omitted	300.00					
	Declaration of Independence, by John Trumbull, July 4						
1691	13¢ Delegates	.20	.15			1.00	41,222,500
1692	13¢ Delegates and John Adams	.20	.15			1.00	41,222,500
1693	13¢ Roger Sherman, Robert R. Livingston, Thomas Jefferson and Benjamin Franklin	.20	.15			1.00	41,222,500
1694	13¢ John Hancock, Charles Thomson, George Read, John Dickinson and Edward Rutledge	.20	.15			1.00	41,222,500
a	Strip of 4, #1691-94	.85	.75	4.50	(20)	2.00	
	Olympic Games Issue, July 16						
1695	13¢ Diver and Olympic Rings	.28	.15			1.00	46,428,750
1696	13¢ Skier and Olympic Rings	.28	.15			1.00	46,428,750
1697	13¢ Runner and Olympic Rings	.28	.15			1.00	46,428,750
1698	13¢ Skater and Olympic Rings	.28	.15			1.00	46,428,750
a	Block of 4, #1695-98	1.15	.85	3.50	(12)	2.00	
b	As "a," imperf.	750.00					
1699	13¢ Clara Maass, Aug. 18	.20	.15	3.00	(12)	1.00	130,592,000
a	Horizontal pair, imperf. vertically	400.00					
1700	13¢ Adolph S. Ochs, Sept. 18	.20	.15	1.00	(4)	1.00	158,332,400
	Christmas Issue, Oct. 27						
1701	13¢ Nativity, by John Singleton Copley	.20	.15	2.75	(12)	1.00	809,955,000
a	Imperf. pair	100.00					
1702	13¢ "Winter Pastime," by Nathaniel Currier	.22	.15	2.25	(10)	1.00	481,685,000*
a	Imperf. pair	110.00					
	*Includes #1703 printing						
1703	13¢ as #1702	.22	.15	5.50	(20)	1.00	
a	Imperf. pair	125.00					
b	Vertical pair, imperf. between	—					

#1702 has overall tagging. Lettering at base is black and usually 1/2mm below design. As a rule, no "snowflaking" in sky or pond. Pane of 50 has margins on 4 sides with slogans. #1703 has block tagging the size of the printed area. Lettering at base is gray-black and usually 3/4mm below design. "Snowflaking" generally in sky and pond. Pane of 50 has margin only at right or left and no slogans.

	Issues of 1977, American Bicentennial Issue, Washington at Princeton, Jan. 3						
1704	13¢ Washington, Nassau Hall, Cannon and 13-star Flag, by Charles Willson Peale	.22	.15	2.25	(10)	1.00	150,328,000
a	Horizontal pair, imperf. vertically	500.00					
1705	13¢ Sound Recording, Mar. 23	.22	.15	1.00	(4)	1.00	176,830,000

1690

1691   1692   1693   1694   1694a

1695   1696

1699

1700

1697   1698   1698a

1701   1702   1703

1704

1705

1706   1707

1708   1709   1709a

1710

1711

1712   1713

1714   1715   1715a

1716

1717   1718

1719   1720   1720a

1721

Issues of 1977, Perf. 11	Un	U	PB	#	FDC	Q
American Folk Art Issue, Pueblo Pottery, Apr. 13						
1706 13¢ Zia Pot	.22	.15			1.00	48,994,000
1707 13¢ San Ildefonso Pot	.22	.15			1.00	48,994,000
1708 13¢ Hopi Pot	.22	.15			1.00	48,994,000
1709 13¢ Acoma Pot	.22	.15			1.00	48,994,000
a Block of 4, #1706-09	.90	.60	2.50	(10)	2.00	
b As "a," imperf. vertically	2,250.00					
1710 13¢ Solo Transatlantic Flight, May 20	.22	.15	2.75	(12)	1.00	208,820,000
a Imperf. pair	1,150.00					
1711 13¢ Colorado Statehood, May 21	.22	.15	2.75	(12)	1.00	192,250,000
a Horizontal pair, imperf. between	500.00					
b Horizontal pair, imperf. vertically	900.00					
c Perf. 11.2	.35	.25				
Butterfly Issue, June 6						
1712 13¢ Swallowtail	.22	.15			1.00	54,957,500
1713 13¢ Checkerspot	.22	.15			1.00	54,957,500
1714 13¢ Dogface	.22	.15			1.00	54,957,500
1715 13¢ Orange-Tip	.22	.15			1.00	54,957,500
a Block of 4, #1712-15	.90	.60	2.75	(12)	2.00	
b As "a," imperf. horizontally	15,000.00					
American Bicentennial Issue, Lafayette's Landing in South Carolina, June 13						
1716 13¢ Marquis de Lafayette	.22	.15	1.00	(4)	1.00	159,852,000
Skilled Hands for Independence, July 4						
1717 13¢ Seamstress	.22	.15			1.00	47,077,500
1718 13¢ Blacksmith	.22	.15			1.00	47,077,500
1719 13¢ Wheelwright	.22	.15			1.00	47,077,500
1720 13¢ Leatherworker	.22	.15			1.00	47,077,500
a Block of 4, #1717-20	.90	.80	2.75	(12)	1.75	
Perf. 11 x 10.5						
1721 13¢ Peace Bridge, Aug. 4	.22	.15	1.00	(4)	1.00	163,625,000

Pottery made only by women

Pueblo pottery, one of the finest of all Indian art forms, developed during the Classic Pueblo period (1050-1300 A.D.). Pueblo pots are traditionally made by hand and only by women of the tribe. Coils of clay are shaped and smoothed, coated with watery clay material called slip, polished, decorated and fired. Each Pueblo village has its own designs, which can include geometric, floral, animal and bird patterns. The designs may be multi-colored, black-on-white, or black with a black finish design. **(#1706-09)**

Join the Club for Collecting Adventure

- A Commemorative Stamp Club Album
- Custom-printed album pages featuring illustrations and mounting areas for individual stamp issues
- Stamps and mounts mailed conveniently to your home

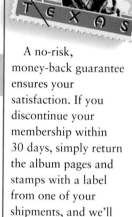

The Commemorative Stamp Club provides a convenient, comprehensive and attractive method for collecting and saving U.S. stamps. Your membership means the start of an exciting adventure, one that will introduce you to America's best—the places, people, events and ideals honored through commemorative stamps.

And if you're looking for further excitement, you can expand your horizons by choosing to receive definitive stamps, other special issues (such as the Music series and the World War II

sheets) and album pages. These are offered at the end of each year.

Other Membership Benefits

You'll receive clear acetate mounts to hold and protect your stamps and a free one-year subscription to *Stamps etc.*, a publication mailed four times a year with full-color illustrations of all stamps, postal cards, aerogrammes, stamped envelopes and other collectibles available through mail order.

A no-risk, money-back guarantee ensures your satisfaction. If you discontinue your membership within 30 days, simply return the album pages and stamps with a label from one of your shipments, and we'll send you a complete refund.

To Join

For more detailed information, use the postage-paid request card in this book or call toll-free:

1-800-STAMP24

Issue Date
April 26, 1995

First Day City
Yorba Linda,
California

Designer
Daniel Schwartz

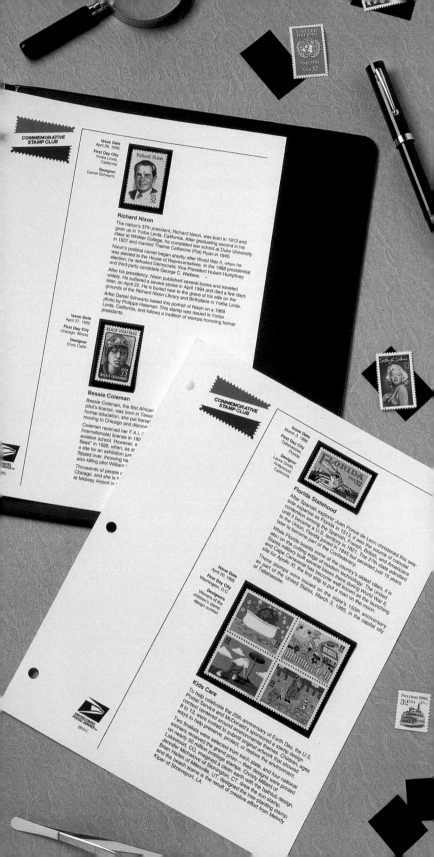

Richard Nixon

The nation's 37th president, Richard Nixon, was born in 1913 and grew up in Yorba Linda, California. After graduating second in his class at Whittier College, he completed law school at Duke University in 1937 and married Thelma Catherine (Pat) Ryan in 1940.

Nixon's political career began shortly after World War II, when he was elected to the House of Representatives. In the 1968 presidential election, he defeated Democratic Vice President Hubert Humphrey and third-party candidate George C. Wallace.

After his presidency, Nixon published several books and traveled widely. He suffered a severe stroke in April 1994 and died a few days later, on April 22. He is buried next to the grave of his wife on the grounds of the Richard Nixon Library and Birthplace in Yorba Linda.

Artist Daniel Schwartz based this portrait of Nixon on a 1969 photo by Philippe Halsman. This stamp was issued in Yorba Linda, California, and follows a tradition of stamps honoring former presidents.

Issue Date
April 27, 1995

First Day City
Chicago, Illinois

Designer
Chris Calle

Bessie Coleman

Bessie Coleman, the first African
pilot's license, was born in Texas
formal education, she put herse
moving to Chicago and discov

Coleman received her F.A.I. (
International) license in 192
aviation school. However, e
Bess" in 1926, when, as sh
a site for an exhibition jum
flipped over, throwing he
also killing pilot William

Thousands of people
Chicago, and she is h
at Midway Airport in

Issue Date
March 3, 1995

First Day City
Tallahassee,
Florida

Designer
Laura Smith
Hollywood,
California

Florida Statehood

After Spanish explorer Juan Ponce de Leon christened this sea-
side expanse as Florida in 1513, it was the source of colonial
contention among the Spanish, French, British, and Americans
until it became a U.S. territory in 1821. The 27th state admitted
to the Union, Florida joined in 1845 but seceded just 16 years
later to become part of the Confederacy.

While Florida boasts some of the country's oldest cities, it is
also on the cutting edge of modern technology. The United
States military built several bases there well known as the launching
and Cape Canaveral has become the first ship to put a man on the moon.
site for Apollo XI, the state's 150th anniversary

These stamps were issued on the state's 150th anniversary
as part of the United States, March 3, 1995, in the Capital city
of Tallahassee.

Issue Date
April 20, 1995

First Day City
Washington, D.C.

Designers
Winners of the
children's stamp
design contest

Kids Care

To help celebrate the 25th anniversary of Earth Day, the U.S.
Postal Service and McDonald's sponsored a stamp design
contest centered around environmental themes. Children, ages
6 to 13, were invited to submit original artwork that showed
ways to help preserve, protect, or restore the environment.

Two finalists were selected from each state, and four national
winners received the grand prize. Their designs were printed
on nearly 50 million postage stamps.

Lakewood, CO, imagined a clean earth with the bathtub design.
Jennifer Michahow of Stonington, CT, drew the sun stamp;
Brian Hailes of Maesville, UT, designed the tree planting stamp;
and the beach scene is the result of creative effort from Melody
Kiper of Shreveport, LA.

	Issues of 1977, Perf. 11	Un	U	PB	#	FDC	Q
	American Bicentennial Issue, Battle of Oriskany, Aug. 6						
1722	13¢ Herkimer at Oriskany, by Frederick Yohn	.22	.15	2.50	(10)	1.25	156,296,000
	Energy Issue, Oct. 20						
1723	13¢ Energy Conservation	.22	.15			1.00	79,338,000
a	Attached pair, #1723-24	.45	.40	2.75	(12)	1.25	
1724	13¢ Energy Development	.22	.15			1.00	79,338,000
1725	13¢ First Civil Settlement— Alta, California, Sept. 9	.22	.15	1.00	(4)	1.00	154,495,000
	American Bicentennial Issue, Articles of Confederation, Sept. 30						
1726	13¢ Members of Continental Congress in Conference	.22	.15	1.00	(4)	1.00	168,050,000
1727	13¢ Talking Pictures, Oct. 6	.22	.15	1.00	(4)	1.00	156,810,000
	American Bicentennial Issue, Surrender at Saratoga, Oct. 7						
1728	13¢ Surrender of Burgoyne, by John Trumbull	.22	.15	2.50	(10)	1.00	153,736,000
	Christmas Issue, Oct. 21						
1729	13¢ Washington at Valley Forge, by J.C. Leyendecker	.22	.15	5.75	(20)	1.00	882,260,000
a	Imperf. pair	75.00					
1730	13¢ Rural Mailbox	.22	.15	2.50	(10)	1.00	921,530,000
a	Imperf. pair	300.00					
	Issues of 1978						
1731	13¢ Carl Sandburg, Jan. 6	.22	.15	1.00	(4)	1.00	156,560,000
	Captain Cook Issue, Jan. 20						
1732	13¢ Capt. James Cook– Alaska, by Nathaniel Dance	.22	.15			1.00	101,077,500
a	Attached pair, #1732-33	.50	.30			1.50	
b	As "a," imperf. between	4,500.00					
1733	13¢ *Resolution* and *Discovery*– Hawaii, by John Webber	.22	.15			1.00	101,077,500
a	Vertical pair, imperf. horizontally	—					
1734	13¢ Indian Head Penny, Jan. 11	.24	.15	1.50	(4)	1.00	
	Pair with full horizontal gutter between	—					
a	Horizontal pair, imperf. vertically	300.00					
1735	(15¢) "A" Stamp, May 22	.24	.15	1.25	(4)	1.00	
a	Imperf. pair	75.00					
b	Vertical pair, imperf. horizontally	500.00					
	Booklet Stamp, Perf. 11 x 10.5						
1736	(15¢) "A" orange Eagle (1735), single from booklet	.25	.15			1.00	
a	Booklet pane of 8, May 22	2.25	.60			2.50	
	Roses Booklet Issue, July 11, Perf. 10						
1737	15¢ Roses, single from booklet	.25	.15			1.00	
a	Booklet pane of 8	2.25	.60			2.50	
b	As "a," imperf.	—					

#1736-37 issued only in booklets. All stamps are imperf. on one side or on one side and bottom.

1722

1723

1725

1724   **1723a**

1726

1727

US Bicentennial 13 cents

1728

1729   **1730**

1732

1731

1733   **1732a**

1734

1735

1737

1738 1739 1740 1741 1742 1742a

1744

1745 1746

1747 1748 1748a

1750

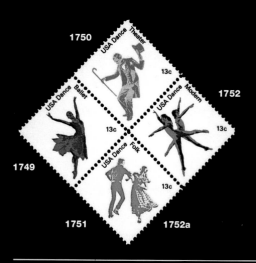

1749 1751 1752a

1752

1753

1754

1755 1756

	Issues of 1980, Perf. 11	Un	U	PB/LP	#	FDC	Q
	Windmills Booklet Issue, Feb. 7						
1738	15¢ Virginia, 1720	.30	.15			1.00	
1739	15¢ Rhode Island, 1790	.30	.15			1.00	
1740	15¢ Massachusetts, 1793	.30	.15			1.00	
1741	15¢ Illinois, 1860	.30	.15			1.00	
1742	15¢ Texas, 1890	.30	.15			1.00	
a	Booklet pane of 10, #1738-42	3.50	*.60*			3.50	
	#1737-42 issued only in booklets. All stamps are imperf. top or bottom, or top or bottom and right side.						
	Issues of 1978 (continued), Coil Stamp, Perf. 10 Vertically						
1743	(15¢) "A" orange Eagle (1735), May 22	.25	.15	.65	(2)	1.00	
a	Imperf. pair	*90.00*		—	(2)		
	Black Heritage Issue, Harriet Tubman, Feb. 1, Perf. 10.5 x 11						
1744	13¢ Harriet Tubman and Cart Carrying Slaves	.22	.15	3.00	(12)	1.00	156,525,000
	American Folk Art Issue, Quilts, Mar. 8, Perf. 11						
1745	13¢ Basket design, red and orange	.22	.15			1.00	41,295,600
1746	13¢ Basket design, red	.22	.15			1.00	41,295,600
1747	13¢ Basket design, orange	.22	.15			1.00	41,295,600
1748	13¢ Basket design, brown	.22	.15			1.00	41,295,600
a	Block of 4, #1745-48	.90	.60	3.00	(12)	2.00	
	American Dance Issue, Apr. 26						
1749	13¢ Ballet	.22	.15			1.00	39,399,600
1750	13¢ Theater	.22	.15			1.00	39,399,600
1751	13¢ Folk	.22	.15			1.00	39,399,600
1752	13¢ Modern	.22	.15			1.00	39,399,600
a	Block of 4, #1749-52	.90	.60	3.00	(12)	1.75	
	American Bicentennial Issue, French Alliance, May 4						
1753	13¢ King Louis XVI and Benjamin Franklin, by Charles Gabriel Sauvage	.22	.15	1.05	(4)	1.00	102,920,000
	Perf. 10.5 x 11						
1754	13¢ Early Cancer Detection, May 18	.24	.15	1.05	(4)	1.00	152,355,000
	Performing Arts Issue, Jimmie Rodgers, May 24, Perf. 11						
1755	13¢ Jimmie Rodgers with Locomotive, Guitar and Brakeman's Cap	.24	.15	3.00	(12)	1.00	94,625,000
	George M. Cohan, July 3						
1756	15¢ George M. Cohan, "Yankee Doodle Dandy" and Stars	.26	.15	3.50	(12)	1.00	151,570,000

Minimum value listed for a stamp is 15 cents; for a First Day Cover (FDC), $1.00. This minimum represents a fair-market price for having a dealer locate and provide a single stamp or cover from his or her stock. Dealers may charge less per stamp or cover for a group of such stamps or covers, or less for a single stamp or cover.

	Issues of 1978, Perf. 11	Un	U	PB	#	FDC	Q
	CAPEX '78 Souvenir Sheet, June 10						
1757	13¢ Souvenir sheet of 8	1.65	1.65	1.90	(8)	2.75	15,170,400
a	13¢ Cardinal	.20	.15				15,170,400
b	13¢ Mallard	.20	.15				15,170,400
c	13¢ Canada Goose	.20	.15				15,170,400
d	13¢ Blue Jay	.20	.15				15,170,400
e	13¢ Moose	.20	.15				15,170,400
f	13¢ Chipmunk	.20	.15				15,170,400
g	13¢ Red Fox	.20	.15				15,170,400
h	13¢ Raccoon	.20	.15				15,170,400
i	Yellow, green, red, brown and black (litho.) omitted	5,000.00					
1758	15¢ Photography, June 26	.26	.15	3.25	(12)	1.00	163,200,000
1759	15¢ Viking Missions to Mars, July 20	.26	.15	1.20	(4)	2.00	158,880,000
	Wildlife Conservation Issue, American Owls, Aug. 26						
1760	15¢ Great Gray Owl	.26	.15			1.00	46,637,500
1761	15¢ Saw-Whet Owl	.26	.15			1.00	46,637,500
1762	15¢ Barred Owl	.26	.15			1.00	46,637,500
1763	15¢ Great Horned Owl	.26	.15			1.00	46,637,500
a	Block of 4, #1760-63	1.05	.85	1.25	(4)	2.00	
	American Trees Issue, Oct. 9						
1764	15¢ Giant Sequoia	.26	.15			1.00	42,034,000
1765	15¢ White Pine	.26	.15			1.00	42,034,000
1766	15¢ White Oak	.26	.15			1.00	42,034,000
1767	15¢ Gray Birch	.26	.15			1.00	42,034,000
a	Block of 4, #1764-67	1.05	.85	3.50	(12)	2.00	
b	As "a," imperf. horizontally	12,500.00					

Customers could buy this full pane with six souvenir sheets. **(#1757)**

a   b   c   d

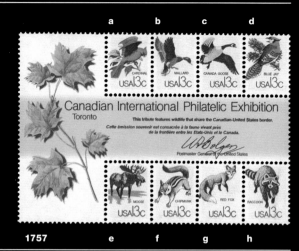

1757   e   f   g   h

1758

1759

1760   **1761**

1762   **1763**   **1763a**

1764   **1765**

1766   **1767**   **1767a**

1768

1769

1770

1771

1772

1775   **1776**

1773

1774

1777   **1778**   **1778a**

1779   **1780**   **1783**   **1784**

1781   **1782**   **1782a**

1785   **1786**   **1786a**

238

	Issues of 1978, Perf. 11	Un	U	PB	#	FDC	Q
	Christmas Issues, Oct. 18						
1768	15¢ Madonna and Child with Cherubim, by Andrea della Robbia	.26	.15	3.50	(12)	1.00	963,370,000
a	Imperf. pair	90.00					
1769	15¢ Child on Hobby Horse and Christmas Trees	.26	.15	3.50	(12)	1.00	916,800,000
a	Imperf. pair	100.00					
b	Vertical pair, imperf. horizontally	1,750.00					
	Pair with full horizontal gutter between	—					
	Issues of 1979, Perf. 11						
1770	15¢ Robert F. Kennedy, Jan. 12	.26	.15	1.20	(4)	2.00	159,297,600
	Black Heritage Issue, Martin Luther King, Jr., Jan. 13						
1771	15¢ Martin Luther King, Jr., and Civil Rights Marchers	.26	.15	3.50	(12)	1.00	166,435,000
a	Imperf. pair	—					
1772	15¢ International Year of the Child, Feb. 15	.26	.15	1.20	(4)	1.00	162,535,000
	Literary Arts Issue, John Steinbeck, Feb. 27, Perf. 10.5 x 11						
1773	15¢ John Steinbeck, by Philippe Halsman	.26	.15	1.20	(4)	1.00	155,000,000
1774	15¢ Albert Einstein, Mar. 4	.28	.15	1.20	(4)	1.50	157,310,000
	Pair with full horizontal gutter between	—					
	American Folk Art Issue, Pennsylvania Toleware, Apr. 19, Perf. 11						
1775	15¢ Straight-Spout Coffeepot	.28	.15			1.00	43,524,000
1776	15¢ Tea Caddy	.28	.15			1.00	43,524,000
1777	15¢ Sugar Bowl	.28	.15			1.00	43,524,000
1778	15¢ Curved-Spout Coffeepot	.28	.15			1.00	43,524,000
a	Block of 4, #1775-78	1.15	.85	2.90	(10)	2.00	
b	As "a," imperf. horizontally	4,250.00					
	American Architecture Issue, June 4						
1779	15¢ Virginia Rotunda, by Thomas Jefferson	.28	.15			1.00	41,198,400
1780	15¢ Baltimore Cathedral, by Benjamin Latrobe	.28	.15			1.00	41,198,400
1781	15¢ Boston State House, by Charles Bulfinch	.28	.15			1.00	41,198,400
1782	15¢ Philadelphia Exchange, by William Strickland	.28	.15			1.00	41,198,400
a	Block of 4, #1779-82	1.15	.85	1.35	(4)	2.00	
	Endangered Flora Issue, June 7						
1783	15¢ Persistent Trillium	.28	.15			1.00	40,763,750
1784	15¢ Hawaiian Wild Broadbean	.28	.15			1.00	40,763,750
1785	15¢ Contra Costa Wallflower	.28	.15			1.00	40,763,750
1786	15¢ Antioch Dunes Evening Primrose	.28	.15			1.00	40,763,750
a	Block of 4, #1783-86	1.15	.85	3.50	(12)	2.00	
b	As "a," imperf.	600.00					
	As "a," full vertical gutter between	—					

	Issues of 1979, Perf. 11	Un	U	PB	#	FDC	Q
1787	15¢ Seeing Eye Dogs, June 15	.28	.15	5.75	(20)	1.00	161,860,000
a	Imperf. pair	400.00					
1788	15¢ Special Olympics, Aug. 9	.28	.15	2.90	(10)	1.00	165,775,000
	American Bicentennial Issue, John Paul Jones, Sept. 23, Perf. 11 x 12						
1789	15¢ John Paul Jones, by Charles Willson Peale	.28	.15	2.90	(10)	1.00	160,000,000
a	Perf. 11	.30	.15	3.10	(10)		
b	Perf. 12	2,000.00	1,000.00				
c	Vertical pair, imperf. horizontally	200.00					
d	As "a," vertical pair, imperf. horizontal	150.00					
	Numerous varieties of printer's waste of #1789 exist.						
	Olympic Summer Games Issue, Sept. 5, Perf. 11 (See also #C97)						
1790	10¢ Javelin Thrower	.20	.20	3.00	(12)	1.00	67,195,000
	Sept. 28						
1791	15¢ Runner	.28	.15			1.00	46,726,250
1792	15¢ Swimmer	.28	.15			1.00	46,726,250
1793	15¢ Rowers	.28	.15			1.00	46,726,250
1794	15¢ Equestrian Contestant	.28	.15			1.00	46,726,250
a	Block of 4, #1791-94	1.15	.85	3.50	(12)	2.00	
b	As "a," imperf.	1,400.00					
	Issues of 1980, Olympic Winter Games Issue, Feb. 1, Perf. 11 x 10.5						
1795	15¢ Speed Skater	.32	.15			1.00	52,073,750
1796	15¢ Downhill Skier	.32	.15			1.00	52,073,750
1797	15¢ Ski Jumper	.32	.15			1.00	52,073,750
1798	15¢ Hockey Goaltender	.32	.15			1.00	52,073,750
a	Perf. 11	1.05	—	13.00	(12)		
b	Block of 4, #1795-98	1.30	1.00			2.00	
c	Block of 4, #1795a-98a	4.25	—				
	Issues of 1979 (continued), Christmas Issue, Oct. 18, Perf. 11						
1799	15¢ Virgin and Child with Cherubim, by Gerard David	.28	.15	3.40	(12)	1.00	873,710,000
a	Imperf. pair	100.00					
b	Vertical pair, imperf. horizontally	700.00					
c	Vertical pair, imperf. between	2,250.00					
1800	15¢ Santa Claus, Christmas Tree Ornament	.28	.15	3.40	(12)	1.00	931,880,000
a	Green and yellow omitted	500.00					
b	Green, yellow and tan omitted	650.00					
	Performing Arts Issue, Will Rogers, Nov. 4						
1801	15¢ Will Rogers Portrait and Rogers as a Cowboy Humorist	.28	.15	3.40	(12)	1.00	161,290,000
a	Imperf. pair	225.00					
1802	15¢ Vietnam Veterans, Nov. 11	.28	.15	2.90	(10)	2.50	172,740,000
	Issues of 1980 (continued), Performing Arts Issue, W.C. Fields, Jan. 29						
1803	15¢ W.C. Fields Portrait and Fields as a Juggler	.28	.15	3.40	(12)	1.25	168,995,000
	Black Heritage Issue, Benjamin Banneker, Feb. 15						
1804	15¢ Benjamin Banneker Portrait and Banneker as Surveyor	.28	.15	3.40	(12)	1.00	160,000,000
a	Horizontal pair, imperf. vertically	800.00					

1787

1788

1789

1791   1792

1790

1793   1794   1794a

1795   1796

1797   1798   1798b

1799   1800

1801

1802

1803   1804

1805

1807

1809

1813

1816

1806

1808

1810

1818

1821

1822

1823

1824

1825

1826

1827

1828

1829

1830 **1830a**

	Issues of 1980, Perf. 11	Un	U	PB/LP	#	FDC	Q
	Letter Writing Issue, Feb. 25						
1805	15¢ Letters Preserve Memories	.28	.15			1.00	38,933,000
1806	15¢ purple P.S. Write Soon	.28	.15			1.00	38,933,000
1807	15¢ Letters Lift Spirits	.28	.15			1.00	38,933,000
1808	15¢ green P.S. Write Soon	.28	.15			1.00	38,933,000
1809	15¢ Letters Shape Opinions	.28	.15			1.00	38,933,000
1810	15¢ red and blue P.S. Write Soon	.28	.15			1.00	38,933,000
a	Vertical Strip of 6, #1805-10	1.75	1.50	10.00	(36)	2.50	
	Issues of 1980-81, Americana Issue, Coil Stamps, Perf. 10 Vertically (See also #1581-82, 1584-85, 1590-99, 1603-06, 1608, 1610-19, 1622-23, 1625)						
1811	1¢ dark blue, greenish Inkwell and Quill (1581), Mar. 6, 1980	.15	.15	.30	(2)	1.00	
a	Imperf. pair	*175.00*		*325.00*	(2)		
1812	Not assigned						
1813	3.5¢ Weaer Violins, June 23, 1980	.15	.15	.90	(2)	1.00	
a	Untagged (Bureau precanceled)		.15				
b	Imperf. pair	*225.00*		—	(2)		
1814-15	Not assigned						
1816	12¢ red brown, *beige* Torch from Statue of Liberty (1594), Apr. 8, 1981	.24	.15	1.25	(2)	1.00	
a	Untagged (Bureau precanceled)		.25				
b	Imperf. pair	*175.00*		*300.00*	(2)		
1817	Not assigned						
	Issues of 1981, Perf. 11 x 10.5						
1818	(18¢) "B" Stamp, Mar. 15	.32	.15	1.50	(4)	1.00	
	Booklet Stamp, Perf. 10						
1819	(18¢) "B" Stamp (1818), single from booklet	40	.15			1.00	
a	Booklet pane of 8, Mar. 15	3.50	*1.50*			3.00	
	Coil Stamp, Perf. 10 Vertically						
1820	(18¢) "B" Stamp (1818), Mar. 15	.40	.15	1.60	(2)	1.00	
a	Imperf. pair	*125.00*		—	(2)		
	Issues of 1980 (continued), Perf. 10.5 x 11						
1821	15¢ Frances Perkins, April 10	.28	.15	1.20	(4)	1.00	163,510,000
	Perf. 11						
1822	15¢ Dolley Madison, May 20	.28	.15	1.40	(4)	1.00	256,620,000
1823	15¢ Emily Bissell, May 31	.28	.15	1.20	(4)	1.00	95,695,000
a	Vertical pair, imperf. horizontally	*350.00*					
1824	15¢ Helen Keller/Anne Sullivan, June 27	.28	.15	1.20	(4)	1.00	153,975,000
1825	15¢ Veterans Administration, July 21	.28	.15	1.20	(4)	1.00	160,000,000
a	Horizontal pair, imperf. vertically	*450.00*					
	American Bicentennial Issue, General Bernardo de Galvez, July 23						
1826	15¢ Gen. de Galvez, Battle of Mobile	.28	.15	1.20	(4)	1.00	103,855,000
a	Red, brown and blue omitted	*800.00*					
b	Bl., brn., red and yel. omitted	*1,400.00*					
	Coral Reefs Issue, Aug. 26						
1827	15¢ Brain Coral, Beaugregory Fish	.26	.15			1.00	51,291,250
1828	15¢ Elkhorn Coral, Porkfish	.26	.15			1.00	51,291,250
1829	15¢ Chalice Coral, Moorish Idol	.26	.15			1.00	51,291,250
1830	15¢ Finger Coral, Sabertooth Blenny	.26	.15			1.00	51,291,250
a	Block of 4, #1827-30	1.05	.85	3.50	(12)	2.00	
b	As "a," imperf.	*1,250.00*					
c	As "a," imperf. between, vertically	—					
d	As "a," imperf. vertically	*3,000.00*					

	Issues of 1980, Perf. 11	Un	U	PB	#	FDC	Q
1831	15¢ Organized Labor, Sept. 1	.28	.15	3.50	(12)	1.00	166,590,000
a	Imperf. pair	375.00					
	Literary Arts Issue, Edith Wharton, Sept. 5, Perf. 10.5 x 11						
1832	15¢ Edith Wharton Reading Letter	.28	.15	1.20	(4)	1.00	163,275,000
	Perf. 11						
1833	15¢ Education, Sept. 12	.28	.15	1.70	(6)	1.00	160,000,000
a	Horizontal pair, imperf. vertically	250.00					
	American Folk Art Issue, Pacific Northwest Indian Masks, Sept. 25						
1834	15¢ Heiltsuk, Bella Bella Tribe	.30	.15			1.00	38,101,000
1835	15¢ Chilkat Tlingit Tribe	.30	.15			1.00	38,101,000
1836	15¢ Tlingit Tribe	.30	.15			1.00	38,101,000
1837	15¢ Bella Coola Tribe	.30	.15			1.00	38,101,000
a	Block of 4, #1834-37	1.25	.85	3.25	(10)	2.00	
	American Architecture Issue, Oct. 9						
1838	15¢ Smithsonian Institution, by James Renwick	.30	.15			1.00	38,756,000
1839	15¢ Trinity Church, by Henry Hobson Richardson	.30	.15			1.00	38,756,000
1840	15¢ Pennsylvania Academy of Fine Arts, by Frank Furness	.30	.15			1.00	38,756,000
1841	15¢ Lyndhurst, by Alexander Jefferson Davis	.30	.15			1.00	38,756,000
a	Block of 4, #1838-41	1.25	.85	1.50	(4)	2.00	
	Christmas Issue, Oct. 31						
1842	15¢ Madonna and Child from Epiphany Window, Washington Cathedral	.28	.15	3.40	(12)	1.00	693,250,000
a	Imperf. pair	80.00					
	Pair with full vertical gutter between	—					
1843	15¢ Wreath and Toys	.28	.15	5.75	(20)	1.00	718,715,000
a	Imperf. pair	80.00					
b	Buff omitted	25.00					

Building American architecture

Frank Furness' eclectic yet highly original work in architecture has had considerable influence on the development of his country's architecture. Born in Philadelphia and best known for his design for the **Pennsylvania Academy of the Fine Arts,** Furness' design began a transition in American architecture away from the academic buildings of the previous generation. He is best known for his highly decorated and stridently colorful Victorian style.

(#1840)

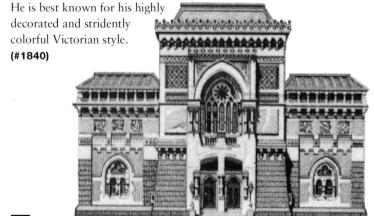

Organized Labor
Proud and Free
USA 15c

1831

1832

1834

1835

Heiltsuk, Bella Bella
Indian Art USA 15c

Chilkat Tlingit
Indian Art USA 15c

Learning never ends

edes by Josef Albers USA 15c

1833

Tlingit
Indian Art USA 15c

Bella Coola
Indian Art USA 15c

1836   **1837**   **1837a**

1838   1839

Renwick, 1815-1895 Smithsonian Washington
Architecture USA 15c

Richardson, 1838-1886 Trinity Church Boston
Architecture USA 15c

Furness, 1839-1912 Penn Academy Philadelphia
Architecture USA 15c

A.J Davis 1803-1892 Lyndhurst Tarrytown NY
Architecture USA 15c

1840   **1841**   **1841a**

Christmas USA 15c

USA 15c
Season's Greetings

1842   **1843**

Dorothea Dix USA 1c
1844

 Igor Stravinsky USA 2c
1845

 Henry Clay USA 3c
1846

Carl Schurz 4c USA
1847

 Pearl Buck USA 5c
1848

 Walter Lippmann 6 USA
1849

Abraham Baldwin USA 7
1850

Henry Knox USA 8
1851

 Sylvanus Thayer USA 9
1852

 Richard Russell USA 10c
1853

 Alden Partridge USA 11
1854

 USA 13c Crazy Horse
1855

Sinclair Lewis USA 14
1856

 Rachel Carson USA 17c
1857

George Mason USA 18c
1858

 USA 19c Sequoyah
1859

Ralph Bunche USA 20c
1860

 Thomas H. Gallaudet USA 20c
1861

 Harry S Truman USA 20c
1862

John J. Audubon USA 22
1863

Frank C. Laubach USA 30c
1864

 Charles R Drew MD USA 35c
1865

 Robert Millikan 37c USA
1866

 Grenville Clark USA 39
1867

 Lillian M. Gilbreth USA 40c
1868

 USA 50 Chester W. Nimitz
1869

	Issues of 1980-85, Perf. 11	Un	U	PB	#	FDC
	Great Americans Issue (See also #2168-73, 2176-80, 2182-86, 2188, 2190-92, 2194-97)					
1844	1¢ Dorothea Dix, Sept. 23, 1983	.15	.15	.35	(6)	1.00
a	Imperf. pair	350.00				
b	Vertical pair, imperf. between	—				
	Perf. 11 x 10.5					
1845	2¢ Igor Stravinsky, Nov. 18, 1982	.15	.15	.25	(4)	1.00
a	Vertical pair, full gutter between	—				
1846	3¢ Henry Clay, July 13, 1983	.15	.15	.35	(4)	1.00
1847	4¢ Carl Schurz, June 3, 1983	.15	.15	.40	(4)	1.00
1848	5¢ Pearl Buck, June 25, 1983	.15	.15	.50	(4)	1.00
	Perf. 11					
1849	6¢ Walter Lippman, Sept. 19, 1985	.15	.15	.75	(6)	1.00
a	Vertical pair, imperf. between	2,300				
1850	7¢ Abraham Baldwin, Jan. 25, 1985	.15	.15	.75	(6)	1.00
1851	8¢ Henry Knox, July 25, 1985	.15	.15	.80	(4)	1.00
1852	9¢ Sylvanus Thayer, June 7, 1985	.16	.15	1.00	(6)	1.00
1853	10¢ Richard Russell, May 31, 1984	.18	.15	1.10	(6)	1.00
a	Vertical pair, imperf. between	1,100.00				
b	Horizontal pair, imperf. between	2,250.00				
1854	11¢ Alden Partridge, Feb. 12, 1985	.20	.15	1.10	(4)	1.00
	Perf. 11 x 10.5					
1855	13¢ Crazy Horse, Jan. 15, 1982	.24	.15	1.40	(4)	1.00
	Perf. 11					
1856	14¢ Sinclair Lewis, Mar. 21, 1985	.25	.15	1.55	(6)	1.00
a	Vertical pair, imperf. horizontally	150.00				
b	Horizontal pair, imperf. between	8.50				
c	Vertical pair, imperf. between	1,750.00				
	Perf. 11 x 10.5					
1857	17¢ Rachel Carson, May 28, 1981	.32	.15	1.50	(4)	1.00
1858	18¢ George Mason, May 7, 1981	.32	.15	2.25	(4)	1.00
1859	19¢ Sequoyah, Dec. 27, 1980	.35	.15	2.00	(4)	1.00
1860	20¢ Ralph Bunche, Jan. 12, 1982	.40	.15	3.00	(4)	1.00
1861	20¢ Thomas H. Gallaudet, June 10, 1983	.38	.15	3.00	(4)	1.00
	Perf. 11					
1862	20¢ Harry S. Truman, Jan. 26, 1984	.38	.15	2.40	(6)	1.00
b	Overall tagging, 1990	—	—			
1863	22¢ John J. Audubon, Apr. 23, 1985	.40	.15	2.50	(6)	1.00
a	Vertical pair, imperf. horizontally	2,500.00				
b	Vertical pair, imperf. between	—				
c	Horizontal pair, imperf. between	2,250.00				
1864	30¢ Frank C. Laubach, Sept. 2, 1984	.55	.15	3.50	(6)	1.00
	Perf. 11 x 10.5					
1865	35¢ Charles R. Drew, MD, June 3, 1981	.65	.15	2.75	(4)	1.25
1866	37¢ Robert Millikan, Jan. 26, 1982	.70	.15	3.25	(4)	1.25
	Perf. 11					
1867	39¢ Grenville Clark, May 20, 1985	.70	.15	4.25	(6)	1.25
a	Vertical pair, imperf. horizontally	600.00				
b	Vertical pair, imperf. between	1,750.00				
1868	40¢ Lillian M. Gilbreth, Feb. 24, 1984	.70	.15	4.60	(6)	1.25
1869	50¢ Chester W. Nimitz, Feb. 22, 1985	.90	.15	4.50	(4)	1.25
1870-73 Not assigned						

	Issues of 1981, Perf. 11	Un	U	PB/PNC	#	FDC	Q
1874	15¢ Everett Dirksen, Jan. 4	.28	.15	1.25	(4)	1.00	160,155,000
	Black Heritage Issue, Whitney Moore Young, Jan. 30						
1875	15¢ Whitney Moore Young at Desk	.28	.15	1.40	(4)	1.00	159,505,000
	Flower Issue, April 23						
1876	18¢ Rose	.35	.15			1.00	52,654,000
1877	18¢ Camellia	.35	.15			1.00	52,654,000
1878	18¢ Dahlia	.35	.15			1.00	52,654,000
1879	18¢ Lily	.35	.15			1.00	52,654,000
a	Block of 4, #1876-79	1.40	.85	1.65	(4)	2.50	
	Wildlife Booklet Issue, May 14						
1880	18¢ Bighorn Sheep	.35	.15			1.00	
1881	18¢ Puma	.35	.15			1.00	
1882	18¢ Harbor Seal	.35	.15			1.00	
1883	18¢ Bison	.35	.15			1.00	
1884	18¢ Brown Bear	.35	.15			1.00	
1885	18¢ Polar Bear	.35	.15			1.00	
1886	18¢ Elk (Wapiti)	.35	.15			1.00	
1887	18¢ Moose	.35	.15			1.00	
1888	18¢ White-Tailed Deer	.35	.15			1.00	
1889	18¢ Pronghorn Antelope	.35	.15			1.00	
a	Booklet pane of 10, #1880-89	8.00	—			5.00	

#1880-89 issued only in booklets. All stamps are imperf. at one side or imperf. at one side and bottom.

	Flag and Anthem Issue, April 24						
1890	18¢ "...for amber waves of grain"	.32	.15	2.00	(6)	1.00	
a	Imperf. pair	100.00					
b	Vertical pair, imperf. horizontally	—					
	Coil Stamp, Perf. 10 Vertically						
1891	18¢ "...from sea to shining sea"	.36	.15	4.75	(3)	1.00	
a	Imperf. pair	20.00					

Beginning with #1891, all coil stamps except #1947 feature a small plate number at the bottom of the design at varying intervals in a roll, depending on the press used. The basic "plate number coil" (PNC) collecting unit is a strip of three stamps, with the plate number appearing on the middle stamp. PNC values are for the most common plate number.

	Booklet Stamps, Perf. 11						
1892	6¢ USA Circle of Stars, single from booklet (1893a)	.55	.15			1.00	
1893	18¢ "...for purple mountain majesties," single from booklet (1893a)	.32	.15			1.00	
a	Booklet pane of 8 (2 #1892 & 6 #1893)	3.00	—			2.50	
b	As "a," imperf. vertically between	*80.00*	—				

#1892-93 issued only in booklets. All stamps are imperf. at one side or imperf. at one side and bottom.

	Flag Over Supreme Court Issue, Dec. 17 (Except #1896b, issued June 1, 1982)						
1894	20¢ Flag Over Supreme Court	.35	.15	2.25	(6)	1.00	
a	Imperf. pair	40.00					
b	Vertical pair, imperf. horizontally	*650.00*					
c	Dark blue omitted	*90.00*					
d	Black omitted	*300.00*					
	Coil Stamp, Perf. 10 Vertically						
1895	20¢ Flag Over Supreme Court (1894)	.35	.15	4.00	(3)	1.00	
a	Imperf. pair	10.00					
b	Black omitted	50.00					
c	Blue omitted	—					
e	Untagged (Bureau precanceled)	.50	.50	45.00	(3)		

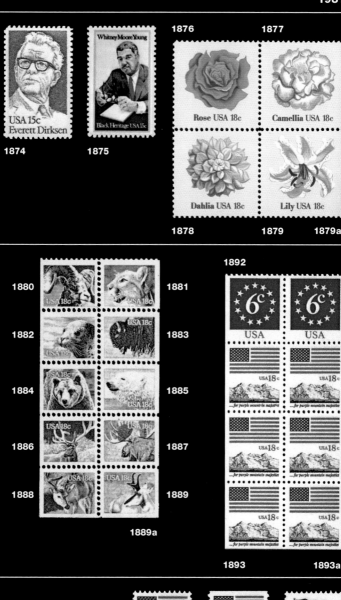

USA 15c
Everett Dirksen

1874

Whitney Moore Young

Black Heritage USA 15c

1875

1876   **1877**

Rose USA 18c   Camellia USA 18c

Dahlia USA 18c   Lily USA 18c

1878   **1879**   **1879a**

1880   **1881**

1882   **1883**

1884   **1885**

1886   **1887**

1888   **1889**

1889a

1892

6c USA   6c USA

USA 18c   USA 18c
...for purple mountain majesties   ...for purple mountain majesties

USA 18c   USA 18c
...for purple mountain majesties   ...for purple mountain majesties

USA 18c   USA 18c
...for purple mountain majesties   ...for purple mountain majesties

1893   **1893a**

USA 18c
...for amber waves of grain

1890

USA 18c
...from sea to shining sea

1891

USA 20c

1894

Omnibus 1880s
USA 1c

1897

Locomotive 1870s
USA 2c

1897A

Handcar 1880s
USA 3c

1898

Stagecoach 1890s
USA 4c

1898A

Motorcycle
1913
USA 5c

1899

Sleigh 1880s
Auth
USA 5.2c Nonprofit
Org.

1900

Bicycle 1870s
USA 5.9c
Auth.
Nonprofit
Org.

1901

Baby Buggy 1880s
USA 7.4c

1902

Mail Wagon 1880s
USA 9.3c
Bulk
Rate

1903

Hansom Cab 1890s
USA 10.9c
Bulk
Rate

1904

RR Caboose 1890s
USA 11c
Bulk Rate

1905

Electric Auto 1917
USA 17c

1906

Surrey 1890s
USA 18c

1907

Fire Pumper
1860s
USA 20c

1908

USA $9.35

1909

The Gift of Self
USA 18c
American Red Cross
1881-1981

1910

SAVINGS AND LOANS
SAVE
USA 18c

1911

	Issues of 1981, Perf. 11 x 10.5	Un	U	PB/PNC/LP	#	FDC	Q
	Booklet Stamp						
1896	20¢ Flag over Supreme Court (1894), single from booklet	.35	.15			1.00	
a	Booklet pane of 6	2.50	—			6.00	
b	Booklet pane of 10, June 1, 1982	4.25	—			10.00	
	Issues of 1981-84, Perf. 10 Vertically						
	Coil Stamps, Transportation Issue (See also #2123-36, 2225-26, 2228, 2231, 2252-66, 2452-53A, 2457, 2464, 2468)						
1897	1¢ Omnibus 1880s, Aug. 19, 1983	.15	.15	.55	(3)	1.00	
b	Imperf. pair	700.00		—	(3)		
1897A	2¢ Locomotive 1870s, May 20, 1982	.15	.15	.50	(3)	1.00	
e	Imperf. pair	50.00		—	(3)		
1898	3¢ Handcar 1880s, Mar. 25, 1983	.15	.15	.95	(3)	1.00	
1898A	4¢ Stagecoach 1890s, Aug. 19, 1982	.15	.15	1.65	(3)	1.00	
b	Untagged (Bureau precanceled)	.15	.15	4.75	(3)	1.00	
c	As "b," imperf. pair	700.00					
d	Imperf. pair	850.00	—				
1899	5¢ Motorcycle 1913, Oct. 10, 1983	.15	.15	.25	(3)	1.00	
a	Imperf. pair	—					
1900	5.2¢ Sleigh 1880s, Mar. 21, 1983	.15	.15	8.00	(3)	1.00	
a	Untagged (Bureau precanceled)	.15	.15	10.00	(3)	1.00	
1901	5.9¢ Bicycle 1870s, Feb. 17, 1982	.18	.15	9.00	(3)	1.00	
a	Untagged (Bureau precanceled)	.18	.18	20.00	(3)	1.00	
b	As "a," imperf. pair	200.00		—	(2)		
1902	7.4¢ Baby Buggy 1880s, April 7, 1984	.18	.15	8.50	(3)	1.00	
a	Untagged (Bureau precanceled)	.20	.20	3.75	(3)	1.00	
1903	9.3¢ Mail Wagon 1880s, Dec. 15, 1981	.25	.15	8.00	(3)	1.00	
a	Untagged (Bureau precanceled)	.22	.22	4.00	(3)	1.00	
b	As "a," imperf. pair	125.00		—	(2)		
1904	10.9¢ Hansom Cab 1890s, Mar. 26, 1982	.24	.15	16.00	(3)	1.00	
a	Untagged (Bureau precanceled)	.24	.24	27.50	(3)	1.00	
b	As "a," imperf. pair	150.00		—	(2)		
1905	11¢ RR Caboose 1890s, Feb. 3, 1984	.24	.15	4.00	(3)	1.00	
a	Untagged (Bureau precanceled)	.24	.15	3.25	(3)	1.00	
1906	17¢ Electric Auto 1917, June 25, 1981	.32	.15	3.00	(3)	1.00	
a	Untagged (Bureau precanceled)	.35	.35	4.75	(3)	1.00	
b	Imperf. pair	165.00		—	(2)		
c	As "a," imperf. pair	650.00		—	(2)		
1907	18¢ Surrey 1890s, May 18, 1981	.34	.15	4.00	(3)	1.00	
a	Imperf. pair	120.00		—	(2)		
1908	20¢ Fire Pumper 1860s, Dec. 10, 1981	.32	.15	3.00	(3)	1.00	
a	Imperf. pair	110.00		300.00	(2)		
	Values for plate # coil strips of 3 stamps for #1897-1908 are for the most common plate numbers. Other plate #s and strips of 5 stamps may have higher values.						
	Issue of 1983, Express Mail Booklet Issue, Aug. 12, Perf. 10 Vertically						
1909	$9.35 Eagle and Moon, single from booklet	22.50	14.00			45.00	
a	Booklet pane of 3	62.50	—			125.00	
	#1909 issued only in booklets. All stamps are imperf. at top and bottom or imperf. at top, bottom and right side.						
	Issues of 1981 (continued), Perf. 10.5 x 11						
1910	18¢ American Red Cross, May 1	.32	.15	1.35	(4)	1.00	165,175,000
	Perf. 11						
1911	18¢ Savings and Loans, May 8	.32	.15	1.50	(4)	1.00	107,240,000

	Issues of 1981, Perf. 11	Un	U	PB	#	FDC	Q
	Space Achievement Issue, May 21						
1912	18¢ Exploring the Moon—Moon Walk	.32	.15			1.00	42,227,375
1913	18¢ Benefiting Mankind (upper left)—Columbia Space Shuttle	.32	.15			1.00	42,227,375
1914	18¢ Benefiting Mankind—Space Shuttle Deploying Satellite	.32	.15			1.00	42,227,375
1915	18¢ Understanding the Sun—Skylab	.32	.15			1.00	42,227,375
1916	18¢ Probing the Planets—Pioneer 11	.32	.15			1.00	42,227,375
1917	18¢ Benefiting Mankind—Columbia Space Shuttle Lifting Off	.32	.15			1.00	42,227,375
1918	18¢ Benefiting Mankind—Space Shuttle Preparing to Land	.32	.15			1.00	42,227,375
1919	18¢ Comprehending the Universe—Telescope	.32	.15			1.00	42,227,375
a	Block of 8, #1912-19	3.00	2.75	3.00	(8)	3.00	
b	As "a," imperf.	9,000.00					
1920	18¢ Professional Management, June 18	.32	.15	1.40	(4)	1.00	99,420,000
	Preservation of Wildlife Habitats Issue, June 26						
1921	18¢ Save Wetland Habitats—Great Blue Heron	.35	.15			1.00	44,732,500
1922	18¢ Save Grassland Habitats—Badger	.35	.15			1.00	44,732,500
1923	18¢ Save Mountain Habitats—Grizzly Bear	.35	.15			1.00	44,732,500
1924	18¢ Save Woodland Habitats—Ruffled Grouse	.35	.15			1.00	44,732,500
a	Block of 4, #1921-24	1.40	1.00	1.90	(4)	2.50	
1925	18¢ International Year of the Disabled, June 29	.32	.15	1.40	(4)	1.00	100,265,000
a	Vertical pair, imperf. horizontally	2,750.00					
1926	18¢ Edna St. Vincent Millay, July 10	.32	.15	1.40	(4)	1.00	99,615,000
a	Black omitted	425.00	—				
1927	18¢ Alcoholism, Aug. 19	.42	.15	15.00	(6)	1.00	97,535,000
a	Imperf. pair	400.00					

Three billion miles from home

In 1973, NASA launched Pioneer 11, a spacecraft that joined Pioneer 10 and Voyagers 1 and 2 in searching for the heliopause, the edge of our solar system.

In December 1974, Pioneer 11 provided scientists with their first close-up pictures of Jupiter. The close approach and the spacecraft's speed of 107,373 miles per hour hurled Pioneer 11 1.5 billion miles across the solar system toward Saturn, by far the fastest speed ever reached by a man-made object.

In 1990, Pioneer 11 crossed Neptune's orbit 2.8 billion miles from the Earth, making transmission of readable data more difficult. **(#1916)**

1981

1912   **1913**   **1914**   **1915**

1916   **1917**   **1918**   **1919** **1919a**

1920

1921   **1922**

1923   **1924**   **1924a**

1925

1927

1928   **1929**

1930   **1931**   **1931a**

1932   **1933**

1934   **1935**   **1936**

1937   **1938**   **1938a**

1939   **1940**

1941

Issues of 1981, Perf. 11		Un	U	PB	#	FDC	Q
American Architecture Issue, Aug. 28							
1928	18¢ NYU Library, by Sanford White	.42	.15			1.00	41,827,000
1929	18¢ Biltmore House, by Richard Morris Hunt	.42	.15			1.00	41,827,000
1930	18¢ Palace of the Arts, by Bernard Maybeck	.42	.15			1.00	41,827,000
1931	18¢ National Farmer's Bank, by Louis Sullivan	.42	.15			1.00	41,827,000
a	Block of 4, #1928-31	1.75	1.00	2.00	(4)	2.50	
American Sports Issue, Babe Zaharias and Bobby Jones, Sept. 22, Perf. 10.5 x 11							
1932	18¢ Babe Zaharias Holding Trophy	.32	.15	1.75	(4)	1.00	101,625,000
1933	18¢ Bobby Jones Teeing off	.32	.15	1.50	(4)	1.00	99,170,000
	Perf. 11						
1934	18¢ Frederic Remington, Oct. 9	.32	.15	1.50	(4)	1.00	101,155,000
a	Vertical pair, imperf. between	275.00					
b	Brown omitted	550.00					
1935	18¢ James Hoban, Oct. 13	.32	.16	1.60	(4)	1.00	101,200,000
1936	20¢ James Hoban, Oct. 13	.35	.15	1.65	(4)	1.00	167,360,000
American Bicentennial Issue, Yorktown-Virginia Capes, Oct. 16							
1937	18¢ Battle of Yorktown 1781	.35	.15			1.00	81,210,000
1938	18¢ Battle of the Virginia Capes 1781	.35	.15			1.00	81,210,000
a	Attached pair, #1937-38	.90	.15	1.90	(4)	1.50	
b	As "a," black omitted	450.00					
Christmas Issue, Oct. 28							
1939	20¢ Madonna and Child, by Botticelli	.38	.15	1.60	(4)	1.00	597,720,000
a	Imperf. pair	125.00					
b	Vertical pair, imperf. horizontally	1,650.00					
1940	20¢ Felt Bear on Sleigh	.38	.15	1.60	(4)	1.00	792,600,000
a	Imperf. pair	275.00					
b	Vertical pair, imperf. horizontally	—					
1941	20¢ John Hanson, Nov. 5	.38	.15	1.60	(4)	1.00	167,130,000

The only grand-slam golfer in history

Robert Tyre Jones, Jr. (1902-71) single-handedly established golf's popularity in America. One of the finest golfers who ever lived, Bobby Jones captured 13 major championships by the time he retired at age 28. He was the only golfer ever to win what was then called "the grand slam of golf," capturing the open and amateur titles in both the U.S. and Great Britain in 1930. Golf is recognized as one of the country's most popular recreational sports; see the new stamps honoring those sports among the new issues in the front of this book. (**#1933**)

	Issues of 1981, Perf. 11	Un	U	PB/LP	#	FDC	Q
	Desert Plants Issue, Dec. 11						
1942	20¢ Barrel Cactus	.35	.15			1.00	47,890,000
1943	20¢ Agave	.35	.15			1.00	47,890,000
1944	20¢ Beavertail Cactus	.35	.15			1.00	47,890,000
1945	20¢ Saguaro	.35	.15			1.00	47,890,000
a	Block of 4, #1942-45	1.50	.15	1.60	(4)	2.50	
b	As "a," deep brown omitted	7,500.00					
c	#1945 vertical pair, imperf.	5,250.00					
	Perf. 11 x 10.5						
1946	(20¢) "C" Stamp, Oct. 11	.38	.15	1.85	(4)	1.00	
	Coil Stamp, Perf. 10 Vertically						
1947	(20¢) "C" brown Eagle (1946), Oct. 11	.60	.15	1.50	(2)	1.00	
a	Imperf. pair	1,750.00		—	(2)		
	Booklet Stamp, Perf. 11 x 10.5						
1948	(20¢) "C" brown Eagle (1946), single from booklet	.38	.15			1.00	
a	Booklet pane of 10, Oct. 11	4.50	—			3.50	
	Issues of 1982, Bighorn Sheep Booklet Issue, Jan. 8, Perf. 11						
1949	20¢ Bighorn Sheep, single from booklet	.50	.15			1.00	
a	Booklet pane of 10	5.00	—			6.00	
b	As "a," imperf. between	100.00					
	#1949 issued only in booklets. All stamps are imperf. at one side or imperf. at one side and bottom.						
1950	20¢ Franklin D. Roosevelt, Jan. 30	.38	.15	1.60	(4)	1.00	163,939,200
	Perf. 11 x 10.5						
1951	20¢ Love, Feb. 1	.38	.15	1.60	(4)	1.00	446,745,000
a	Perf. 11	.48	.15	2.00	(4)		
b	Imperf. pair	275.00					
c	Blue omitted	175.00					
	Perf. 11						
1952	20¢ George Washington, Feb. 22	.38	.15	1.60	(4)	1.00	180,700,000

These pointy leaves come in a variety of shapes and sizes

Found mostly in the Western hemisphere, cacti come in a wide variety of shapes and sizes. The beavertail cactus (*optunia basilaris*) belongs to the most widespread of all cactus genera, growing as far away as the Galapagos Islands, where Charles Darwin developed his theory of evolution. As with most cacti, the beavertail's stems are succulents, having fleshy tissues that are enlarged to store water. Cactus spines are actually leaves that have evolved to conserve water and to protect the plant from being eaten by desert animals. Once a year, the beavertail produces beautiful red blossoms that can sometimes be as large as a person's hand. **(#1944)**

1943

1942   **1944**   **1945** **1945a**

1946   **1949**

1950   **1951**

1952

1982

Alabama — USA 20c — Yellowhammer & Camellia — 1953
Alaska — USA 20c — Willow Ptarmigan & Forget-Me-Not — 1954
Arizona — USA 20c — Cactus Wren & Saguaro Cactus Blossom — 1955
Arkansas — USA 20c — Mockingbird & Apple Blossom — 1956
California — USA 20c — California Quail & California Poppy — 1957

Colorado — USA 20c — Lark Bunting & Rocky Mountain Columbine — 1958
Connecticut — USA 20c — Robin & Mountain Laurel — 1959
Delaware — USA 20c — Blue Hen Chicken & Peach Blossom — 1960
Florida — USA 20c — Mockingbird & Orange Blossom — 1961
Georgia — USA 20c — Brown Thrasher & Cherokee Rose — 1962

Hawaii — USA 20c — Hawaiian Goose & Hibiscus — 1963
Idaho — USA 20c — Mountain Bluebird & Syringa — 1964
Illinois — USA 20c — Cardinal & Violet — 1965
Indiana — USA 20c — Cardinal & Peony — 1966
Iowa — USA 20c — Eastern Goldfinch & Wild Rose — 1967

Kansas — USA 20c — Western Meadowlark & Sunflower — 1968
Kentucky — USA 20c — Cardinal & Goldenrod — 1969
Louisiana — USA 20c — Brown Pelican & Magnolia — 1970
Maine — USA 20c — Chickadee & White Pine Cone and Tassel — 1971
Maryland — USA 20c — Baltimore Oriole & Black-Eyed Susan — 1972

Massachusetts — USA 20c — Black-Capped Chickadee & Mayflower — 1973
Michigan — USA 20c — Robin & Apple Blossom — 1974
Minnesota — USA 20c — Common Loon & Showy Lady Slipper — 1975
Mississippi — USA 20c — Mockingbird & Magnolia — 1976
Missouri — USA 20c — Eastern Bluebird & Red Hawthorn — 1977

	Issues of 1982, Perf. 10.5 x 11	Un	U	FDC	Q
	State Birds & Flowers Issue, Apr. 14				
1953	20¢ Alabama: Yellowhammer and Camellia	.48	.25	1.25	13,339,000
1954	20¢ Alaska: Willow Ptarmigan and Forget-Me-Not	.48	.25	1.25	13,339,000
1955	20¢ Arizona: Cactus Wren and Saguaro Cactus Blossom	.48	.25	1.25	13,339,000
1956	20¢ Arkansas: Mockingbird and Apple Blossom	.48	.25	1.25	13,339,000
1957	20¢ California: California Quail and California Poppy	.48	.25	1.25	13,339,000
1958	20¢ Colorado: Lark Bunting and Rocky Mountain Columbine	.48	.25	1.25	13,339,000
1959	20¢ Connecticut: Robin and Mountain Laurel	.48	.25	1.25	13,339,000
1960	20¢ Delaware: Blue Hen Chicken and Peach Blossom	.48	.25	1.25	13,339,000
1961	20¢ Florida: Mockingbird and Orange Blossom	.48	.25	1.25	13,339,000
1962	20¢ Georgia: Brown Thrasher and Cherokee Rose	.48	.25	1.25	13,339,000
1963	20¢ Hawaii: Hawaiian Goose and Hibiscus	.48	.25	1.25	13,339,000
1964	20¢ Idaho: Mountain Bluebird and Syringa	.48	.25	1.25	13,339,000
1965	20¢ Illinois: Cardinal and Violet	.48	.25	1.25	13,339,000
1966	20¢ Indiana: Cardinal and Peony	.48	.25	1.25	13,339,000
1967	20¢ Iowa: Eastern Goldfinch and Wild Rose	.48	.25	1.25	13,339,000
1968	20¢ Kansas: Western Meadowlark and Sunflower	.48	.25	1.25	13,339,000
1969	20¢ Kentucky: Cardinal and Goldenrod	.48	.25	1.25	13,339,000
1970	20¢ Louisiana: Brown Pelican and Magnolia	.48	.25	1.25	13,339,000
1971	20¢ Maine: Chickadee and White Pine Cone and Tassel	.48	.25	1.25	13,339,000
1972	20¢ Maryland: Baltimore Oriole and Black-Eyed Susan	.48	.25	1.25	13,339,000
1973	20¢ Massachusetts: Black-Capped Chickadee and Mayflower	.48	.25	1.25	13,339,000
1974	20¢ Michigan: Robin and Apple Blossom	.48	.25	1.25	13,339,000
1975	20¢ Minnesota: Common Loon and Showy Lady Slipper	.48	.25	1.25	13,339,000
1976	20¢ Mississippi: Mockingbird and Magnolia	.48	.25	1.25	13,339,000
1977	20¢ Missouri: Eastern Bluebird and Red Hawthorn	.48	.25	1.25	13,339,000

	Issues of 1982, Perf. 10.5 x 11	Un	U	FDC	Q
	State Birds & Flowers Issue (continued), Apr. 14				
1978	20¢ Montana: Western Meadowlark & Bitterroot	.48	.25	1.25	13,339,000
1979	20¢ Nebraska: Western Meadowlark & Goldenrod	.48	.25	1.25	13,339,000
1980	20¢ Nevada: Mountain Bluebird & Sagebrush	.48	.25	1.25	13,339,000
1981	20¢ New Hampshire: Purple Finch & Lilac	.48	.25	1.25	13,339,000
1982	20¢ New Jersey: American Goldfinch & Violet	.48	.25	1.25	13,339,000
1983	20¢ New Mexico: Roadrunner & Yucca Flower	.48	.25	1.25	13,339,000
1984	20¢ New York: Eastern Bluebird & Rose	.48	.25	1.25	13,339,000
1985	20¢ North Carolina: Cardinal & Flowering Dogwood	.48	.25	1.25	13,339,000
1986	20¢ North Dakota: Western Meadowlark & Wild Prairie Rose	.48	.25	1.25	13,339,000
1987	20¢ Ohio: Cardinal & Red Carnation	.48	.25	1.25	13,339,000
1988	20¢ Oklahoma: Scissor-tailed Flycatcher & Mistletoe	.48	.25	1.25	13,339,000
1989	20¢ Oregon: Western Meadowlark & Oregon Grape	.48	.25	1.25	13,339,000
1990	20¢ Pennsylvania: Ruffed Grouse & Mountain Laurel	.48	.25	1.25	13,339,000
1991	20¢ Rhode Island: Rhode Island Red & Violet	.48	.25	1.25	13,339,000
1992	20¢ South Carolina: Carolina Wren & Carolina Jessamine	.48	.25	1.25	13,339,000
1993	20¢ South Dakota: Ring-Necked Pheasant & Pasqueflower	.48	.25	1.25	13,339,000
1994	20¢ Tennessee: Mockingbird & Iris	.48	.25	1.25	13,339,000
1995	20¢ Texas: Mockingbird & Bluebonnet	.48	.25	1.25	13,339,000
1996	20¢ Utah: California Gull & Sego Lily	.48	.25	1.25	13,339,000
1997	20¢ Vermont: Hermit Thrush & Red Clover	.48	.25	1.25	13,339,000
1998	20¢ Virginia: Cardinal & Flowering Dogwood	.48	.25	1.25	13,339,000
1999	20¢ Washington: American Goldfinch & Rhododendron	.48	.25	1.25	13,339,000
2000	20¢ West Virginia: Cardinal & Rhododendron Maximum	.48	.25	1.25	13,339,000
2001	20¢ Wisconsin: Robin & Wood Violet	.48	.25	1.25	13,339,000
2002	20¢ Wyoming: Western Meadowlark & Indian Paintbrush	.48	.25	1.25	13,339,000
a	Any single, perf. 11	.50	.30		
b	Pane of 50 (with plate #)	24.00	—	30.00	
c	Pane of 50, perf. 11	25.00	—		
d	Pane of 50, imperf.	—			

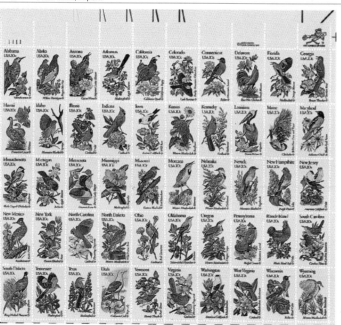

Example of 2002b.

Montana
USA 20c
*Western Meadowlark &
Bitterroot*
1978

Nebraska
USA 20c
*Western Meadowlark &
Goldenrod*
1979

Nevada
USA 20c
*Mountain Bluebird &
Sagebrush*
1980

New Hampshire
USA 20c
*Purple Finch &
Lilac*
1981

New Jersey
USA 20c
*American Goldfinch &
Violet*
1982

New Mexico
USA 20c
*Roadrunner &
Yucca Flower*
1983

New York
USA 20c
*Eastern Bluebird &
Rose*
1984

North Carolina
USA 20c
*Cardinal &
Flowering Dogwood*
1985

North Dakota
USA 20c
*Western Meadowlark &
Wild Prairie Rose*
1986

Ohio
USA 20c
*Cardinal &
Red Carnation*
1987

Oklahoma
USA 20c
*Scissor-tailed Flycatcher &
Mistletoe*
1988

Oregon
USA 20c
*Western Meadowlark &
Oregon Grape*
1989

Pennsylvania
USA 20c
*Ruffed Grouse &
Mountain Laurel*
1990

Rhode Island
USA 20c
*Rhode Island Red &
Violet*
1991

South Carolina
USA 20c
Carolina Wren & Carolina Jessamine
1992

South Dakota
USA 20c
*Ring-Necked Pheasant &
Pasqueflower*
1993

Tennessee
USA 20c
Mockingbird & Iris
1994

Texas
USA 20c
*Mockingbird &
Bluebonnet*
1995

Utah
USA 20c
*California Gull &
Sego Lily*
1996

Vermont
USA 20c
*Hermit Thrush &
Red Clover*
1997

Virginia
USA 20c
*Cardinal &
Flowering Dogwood*
1998

Washington
USA 20c
*American Goldfinch &
Rhododendron*
1999

West Virginia
USA 20c
*Cardinal &
Rhododendron Maximum*
2000

Wisconsin
USA 20c
*Robin &
Wood Violet*
2001

Wyoming
USA 20c
*Western Meadowlark &
Indian Paintbrush*
2002

2003

2004

2005

2006

2007

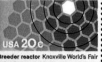

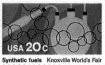

2010

2012

2008

2009

2009a

2011

2013

2014

2015

2016

2019

2020

2017

2018

2021

2022

2022a

	Issues of 1982, Perf. 11	Un	U	PB/PNC/LP	#	FDC	Q
2003	20¢ USA/The Netherlands, Apr. 20	.38	.15	3.50	(6)	1.00	109,245,000
a	Imperf. pair	325.00					
2004	20¢ Library of Congress, Apr. 21	.38	.15	1.60	(4)	1.00	112,535,000
	Coil Stamp, Perf. 10 Vertically						
2005	20¢ Consumer Education, Apr. 27	.75	.15	35.00	(3)	1.00	
a	Imperf. pair	100.00		400.00	(2)		

Value for plate no. coil strip of 3 stamps is for most common plate nos. Other plate nos. and strips of 5 stamps may have higher values.

	Knoxville World's Fair Issue, Apr. 29, Perf. 11						
2006	20¢ Solar Energy	.40	.15			1.00	31,160,000
2007	20¢ Synthetic Fuels	.40	.15			1.00	31,160,000
2008	20¢ Breeder Reactor	.40	.15			1.00	31,160,000
2009	20¢ Fossil Fuels	.40	.15			1.00	31,160,000
a	Block of 4, #2006-09	1.75	1.00	1.75	(4)	2.50	
2010	20¢ Horatio Alger, Apr. 30	.38	.15	1.60	(4)	1.00	107,605,000
2011	20¢ Aging Together, May 21	.38	.15	1.60	(4)	1.00	173,160,000
	Performing Arts Issue, The Barrymores, June 8						
2012	20¢ Portraits of John, Ethel and Lionel Barrymore	.38	.15	1.60	(4)	1.00	107,285,000
2013	20¢ Dr. Mary Walker, June 10	.38	.15	1.60	(4)	1.00	109,040,000
2014	20¢ International Peace Garden, June 30	.38	.15	1.60	(4)	1.00	183,270,000
a	Black and green omitted	200.00					
2015	20¢ America's Libraries, July 13	.38	.15	1.60	(4)	1.00	169,495,000
a	Vertical pair, imperf. horizontally	300.00					
	Black Heritage Issue, Jackie Robinson, Aug. 2, Perf. 10.5 x 11						
2016	20¢ Jackie Robinson Portrait and Robinson Stealing Home Plate	1.00	.15	5.25	(4)	2.00	164,235,000
	Perf. 11						
2017	20¢ Touro Synagogue, Aug. 22	.38	.15	11.50	(20)	1.00	110,130,000
a	Imperf. pair	1,250.00					
2018	20¢ Wolf Trap Farm Park, Sept. 1	.38	.15	1.60	(4)	1.00	110,995,000
	American Architecture Issue, Sept. 30						
2019	20¢ Fallingwater, by Frank Lloyd Wright	.38	.15			1.00	41,335,000
2020	20¢ Illinois Institute of Technology, by Ludwig Mies van der Rohe	.38	.15			1.00	41,335,000
2021	20¢ Gropius House, by Walter Gropius	.38	.15			1.00	41,335,000
2022	20¢ Dulles Airport by Eero Saarinen	.38	.15			1.00	41,335,000
a	Block of 4, #2019-22	1.60	1.00	2.25	(4)	2.50	

	Issues of 1982, Perf. 11	Un	U	PB	#	FDC	Q
2023	20¢ St. Francis of Assisi, Oct. 7	.38	.15	1.60	(4)	1.00	174,180,000
2024	20¢ Ponce de Leon, Oct. 12	.38	.15	3.25	(6)	1.00	110,261,000
a	Imperf. pair	600.00					
	Christmas Issue						
2025	13¢ Puppy and Kitten, Nov. 3	.26	.15	1.25	(4)	1.00	234,010,000
a	Imperf. pair	650.00					
2026	20¢ Madonna and Child, by Tiepolo, Oct. 28	.38	.15	11.00	(20)	1.00	703,295,000
a	Imperf. pair	150.00					
b	Horizontal pair, imperf. vertically	—					
c	Vertical pair, imperf. horizontally	—					
	Seasons Greetings Issue, Oct. 28						
2027	20¢ Children Sledding	.50	.15			1.00	197,220,000
2028	20¢ Children Building a Snowman	.50	.15			1.00	197,220,000
2029	20¢ Children Skating	.50	.15			1.00	197,220,000
2030	20¢ Children Trimming a Tree	.50	.15			1.00	197,220,000
a	Block of 4, #2027-30	2.00	1.00	2.50	(4)	2.50	
b	As "a," imperf.	3,000.00					
c	As "a," imperf. horizontally	—					
	Issues of 1983						
2031	20¢ Science & Industry, Jan. 19	.38	.15	1.60	(4)	1.00	118,555,000
a	Black omitted	1,400.00					
	Balloons Issue, March 31						
2032	20¢ Intrepid, 1861	.38	.15			1.00	56,557,000
2033	20¢ Hot Air Ballooning (wording lower right)	.38	.15			1.00	56,557,000
2034	20¢ Hot Air Ballooning (wording upper left)	.38	.15			1.00	56,557,000
2035	20¢ Explorer II, 1935	.38	.15			1.00	56,557,000
a	Block of 4, #2032-35	1.65	1.00	1.75	(4)	2.50	
b	As "a," imperf.	—					
2036	20¢ U.S./Sweden Treaty, Mar. 24	.38	.15	1.60	(4)	1.00	118,225,000
2037	20¢ Civilian Conservation Corps, Apr. 5	.38	.15	1.60	(4)	1.00	114,290,000
a	Imperf. pair	2,500.00					
2038	20¢ Joseph Priestley, Apr. 13	.38	.15	1.60	(4)	1.00	165,000,000
2039	20¢ Voluntarism, Apr. 20	.40	.15	3.00	(6)	1.00	120,430,000
a	Imperf. pair	800.00					
2040	20¢ Concord—German Immigration, Apr. 29	.38	.15	1.60	(4)	1.00	117,025,000

The stamp listings contain a number of "a," "b," "c," etc. additions which include recognized varieties and errors. These listings are as complete as space permits.

2023

2024

2025

2027   **2028**

2026

2029   **2030**   **2030a**

2033

2031

2032   **2034**   **2035**   **2035a**

2036   **2037**

Joseph Priestley
USA 20c

2039

2040

2038

2041

2042

2043

2044

2045

2046

2047

2048   2049

2050   2051   2051a

2052

2055   2056

2053

2057   2058   2058a

	Issues of 1983, Perf. 11	Un	U	PB	#	FDC	Q
2041	20¢ Brooklyn Bridge, May 17	.38	.15	1.60	(4)	1.00	181,700,000
2042	20¢ Tennessee Valley Authority, May 18	.40	.15	11.50	(20)	1.00	114,250,000
2043	20¢ Physical Fitness, May 14	.38	.15	3.00	(6)	1.00	111,775,000
	Black Heritage Issue, Scott Joplin, June 9						
2044	20¢ Scott Joplin Portrait and Joplin Playing the Piano	.40	.15	1.70	(4)	1.00	115,200,000
a	Imperf. pair	500.00					
2045	20¢ Medal of Honor, June 7	.40	.15	1.75	(4)	1.00	108,820,000
a	Red omitted	250.00					
	American Sports Issue, Babe Ruth, July 6, Perf. 10.5 x 11						
2046	20¢ Babe Ruth Hitting a Home Run	1.00	.15	5.75	(4)	2.50	184,950,000
	Literary Arts Issue, Nathaniel Hawthorne, July 8, Perf. 11						
2047	20¢ Nathaniel Hawthorne, by Cephus Giovanni Thompson	.40	.15	1.70	(4)	1.00	110,925,000
	Olympic Summer Games Issue, July 28 (See also #2082-85, C101-12)						
2048	13¢ Discus Thrower	.35	.15			1.00	98,856,000
2049	13¢ High Jumper	.35	.15			1.00	98,856,000
2050	13¢ Archer	.35	.15			1.00	98,856,000
2051	13¢ Boxers	.35	.15			1.00	98,856,000
a	Block of 4, #2048-51	1.50	1.00	1.40	(4)	2.50	
	American Bicentennial Issue, Treaty of Paris, Sept. 2						
2052	20¢ Signing of Treaty of Paris (John Adams, Benjamin Franklin and John Jay observing David Hartley), by Benjamin West	.38	.15	1.60	(4)	1.00	104,340,000
2053	20¢ Civil Service, Sept. 9	.40	.15	3.00	(6)	1.00	114,725,000
2054	20¢ Metropolitan Opera, Sept. 14	.38	.15	1.65	(4)	1.00	112,525,000
	American Inventors Issue, Sept. 21						
2055	20¢ Charles Steinmetz and Curve on Graph	.45	.15			1.00	48,263,750
2056	20¢ Edwin Armstrong and Frequency Modulator	.45	.15			1.00	48,263,750
2057	20¢ Nikola Tesla and Induction Motor	.45	.15			1.00	48,263,750
2058	20¢ Philo T. Farnsworth and First Television Camera	.45	.15			1.00	48,263,750
a	Block of 4, #2055-58	1.90	1.00	2.40	(4)	2.50	
b	As "a," black omitted	425.00					

A pioneer of electric power

When Charles Steinmetz (1865-1923) immigrated to the United States in 1889, he brought with him one of the greatest scientific minds in history. Steinmetz's groundbreaking theories on alternating-current systems helped pave the way for the explosive growth of electrical power in the United States.

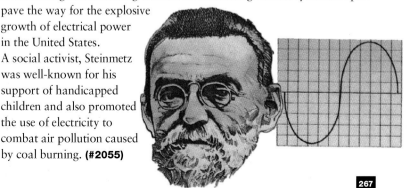

A social activist, Steinmetz was well-known for his support of handicapped children and also promoted the use of electricity to combat air pollution caused by coal burning. **(#2055)**

	Issues of 1983, Perf. 11	Un	U	PB	#	FDC	Q
	Streetcars Issue, Oct. 8						
2059	20¢ First American Streetcar	.40	.15			1.00	51,931,250
2060	20¢ Early Electric Streetcar	.40	.15			1.00	51,931,250
2061	20¢ "Bobtail" Horsecar	.40	.15			1.00	51,931,250
2062	20¢ St. Charles Streetcar	.40	.15			1.00	51,931,250
a	Block of 4, #2059-62	1.70	1.00	2.00	(4)	2.50	
b	As "a," black omitted	475.00					
c	As "a," black omitted on #2059, 2061	—					
	Christmas Issue, Oct. 28						
2063	20¢ Niccolini-Cowper Madonna, by Raphael	.38	.15	1.65	(4)	1.00	715,975,000
2064	20¢ Santa Claus	.38	.15	3.00	(6)	1.00	848,525,000
a	Imperf. pair	175.00					
2065	20¢ Martin Luther, Nov. 11	.38	.15	1.60	(4)	1.50	165,000,000
	Issues of 1984						
2066	20¢ 25th Anniversary of Alaska Statehood, Jan. 3	.38	.15	1.65	(4)	1.00	120,000,000
	Winter Olympic Games Issue, Jan. 6, Perf. 10.5 x 11						
2067	20¢ Ice Dancing	.42	.15			1.00	79,918,750
2068	20¢ Alpine Skiing	.42	.15			1.00	79,918,750
2069	20¢ Nordic Skiing	.42	.15			1.00	79,918,750
2070	20¢ Hockey	.42	.15				79,918,750
a	Block of 4, #2067-70	1.70	1.00	2.25	(4)	2.50	
	Perf. 11						
2071	20¢ Federal Deposit Insurance Corporation, Jan. 12	.38	.15	1.60	(4)	1.00	103,975,000

What carried the first commuters in history?

In 1832, private entrepreneurs in New York City began operating a new type of vehicle called a streetcar. Running on rails to provide a smoother ride, these streetcars were pulled by horses. In 1888, Frank J. Sprague demonstrated a streetcar powered by electricity supplied from an overhead power line, calling it a trolley. By 1915 there were over 45,000 miles of streetcar lines based on Sprague's design, but increasing competition by the automobile industry led to the demise of most trolley lines by the mid-20th century. **(#2059)**

Interesting Fact: Tennessee Williams' Pulitzer Prize-winning play *A Streetcar Named Desire* takes its name from a real New Orleans streetcar line, which has a French-inspired pronunciation of day-zeer-ay. See stamp #2062, and the new Tennessee Williams stamp in the 1995 New Issues section in the front of this book.

2059   2060

2061   2062   2062a

2064

2063   2065

2067   2068

2066   2071

2069   2070   2070a

2072

2073

2074

2075

2076   2077

2080

2081

2078   2079   2079a

2082   2083

2086

2087

2084   2085   2085a

	Issues of 1984, Perf. 11 x 10.5	Un	U	PB	#	FDC	Q
2072	20¢ Love, Jan. 31	.40	.15	11.50	(20)	1.00	554,675,000
a	Horizontal pair, imperf. vertically	175.00					
	Black Heritage Issue, Carter G. Woodson, Feb. 1, Perf. 11						
2073	20¢ Carter G. Woodson Holding History Book	.40	.15	1.75	(4)	1.00	120,000,000
a	Horizontal pair, imperf. vertically	1,500					
2074	20¢ Soil and Water Conservation, Feb. 6	.38	.15	1.60	(4)	1.00	106,975,000
2075	20¢ 50th Anniversary of Credit Union Act, Feb. 10	.38	.15	1.60	(4)	1.00	107,325,000
	Orchids Issue, Mar. 5						
2076	20¢ Wild Pink	.42	.15			1.00	76,728,000
2077	20¢ Yellow Lady's-Slipper	.42	.15			1.00	76,728,000
2078	20¢ Spreading Pogonia	.42	.15			1.00	76,728,000
2079	20¢ Pacific Calypso	.42	.15			1.00	76,728,000
a	Block of 4, #2076-79	1.80	1.00	2.00	(4)	2.50	
2080	20¢ 25th Anniversary of Hawaii Statehood, Mar. 12	.40	.15	1.70	(4)	1.00	120,000,000
2081	20¢ National Archives, Apr. 16	.40	.15	1.70	(4)	1.00	108,000,000
	Olympic Summer Games Issue, May 4 (See also #2048-52, C101-12)						
2082	20¢ Diving	.60	.15			1.00	78,337,500
2083	20¢ Long Jump	.60	.15			1.00	78,337,500
2084	20¢ Wrestling	.60	.15			1.00	78,337,500
2085	20¢ Kayak	.60	.15			1.00	78,337,500
a	Block of 4, #2082-85	2.40	1.00	3.25	(4)	2.50	
2086	20¢ Louisiana World Exposition, May 11	.38	.15	1.60	(4)	1.00	130,320,000
2087	20¢ Health Research, May 17	.40	.15	1.70	(4)	1.00	120,000,000

A state that's for the birds

Called the Pelican State for the once-numerous brown pelicans that populated its coast, Louisiana is still home to a wide variety of birds. Three of the largest egret colonies in the U.S. are located in Louisiana. Louisiana is also home to one of the nation's largest blue-heron colonies. **(#2086)**

Interesting Fact: John Grisham's bestselling novel *The Pelican Brief* is set in Louisiana and draws its title in part from the state's nickname.

Issues of 1984, Perf. 11	Un	U	PB	#	FDC	Q
Performing Arts Issue, Douglas Fairbanks, May 23						
2088 20¢ Douglas Fairbanks Portrait and Fairbanks in Swashbuckling Pirate Role	.38	.15	12.00	(20)	1.00	117,050,000
American Sports Issue, Jim Thorpe, May 24						
2089 20¢ Jim Thorpe on Football Field	.40	.15	1.85	(4)	1.50	115,725,000
Performing Arts Issue, John McCormack, June 6						
2090 20¢ John McCormack Portrait and McCormack in Tenor Role	.40	.15	1.70	(4)	1.00	116,600,000
2091 20¢ 25th Anniversary of St. Lawrence Seaway, June 26	.40	.15	1.70	(4)	1.00	120,000,000
2092 20¢ Migratory Bird Hunting and Preservation Act, July 2	.50	.15	2.50	(4)	1.00	123,575,000
a Horizontal pair, imperf. vertically	400.00					
2093 20¢ Roanoke Voyages, July 13	.38	.15	1.60	(4)	1.00	120,000,000
Pair with full horizontal gutter between	—					
Literary Arts Issue, Herman Melville, Aug. 1						
2094 20¢ Herman Melville	.38	.15	1.60	(4)	1.00	117,125,000
2095 20¢ Horace Moses, Aug. 6	.45	.15	3.50	(6)	1.00	117,225,000
2096 20¢ Smokey the Bear, Aug. 13	.38	.15	1.75	(4)	1.00	95,525,000
a Horizontal pair, imperf. between	300.00					
b Vertical pair, imperf. between	250.00					
c Block of 4, imperf. between vertically and horizontally	4,500.00					
American Sports Issue, Roberto Clemente, Aug. 17						
2097 20¢ Roberto Clemente Wearing Pittsburgh Pirates Cap, Puerto Rican Flag in Background	1.00	.15	6.75	(4)	2.00	119,125,000
a Horizontal pair, imperf. vertically	1,800.00					
American Dogs Issue, Sept. 7						
2098 20¢ Beagle and Boston Terrier	.40	.15			1.00	54,065,000
2099 20¢ Chesapeake Bay Retriever and Cocker Spaniel	.40	.15			1.00	54,065,000
2100 20¢ Alaskan Malamute and Collie	.40	.15			1.00	54,065,000
2101 20¢ Black and Tan Coonhound and American Foxhound	.40	.15			1.00	54,065,000
a Block of 4, #2098-2101	1.75	1.00	2.00	(4)	2.50	

Sailing from the Atlantic to Minnesota without touching land

Opened in 1959, the St. Lawrence Seaway allows vessels to travel between the Atlantic Ocean and Lake Ontario via a 27-foot deep channel. The Seaway, along with channels built among the other four Great Lakes, forms the St. Lawrence & Great Lakes Waterway, which extends for 2,342 miles. **(#2091)**

Interesting Fact: The greatest drop between the Great Lakes (167 feet) occurs between Lakes Erie and Ontario at Niagara Falls. See stamps #297 and 568.

2088   **2089**   **2090**

2091   **2092**

2093

2094   **2095**   **2096**   **2097**

2098   **2099**

2102

2103

2104

2105

2106

2107

2108

2109

2110

2111

2114

2115b

2116

	Issues of 1984, Perf. 11	Un	U	PB/PNC	#	FDC	Q
2102	20¢ Crime Prevention, Sept. 26	.38	.15	1.70	(4)	1.00	120,000,000
2103	20¢ Hispanic Americans, Oct. 31	.38	.15	1.60	(4)	1.00	108,140,000
a	Vertical pair, imperf. horizontally	1,750.00					
2104	20¢ Family Unity, Oct. 1	.40	.15	12.00	(20)	1.00	117,625,000
a	Horizontal pair, imperf. vertically	550.00					
2105	20¢ Eleanor Roosevelt, Oct. 11	.38	.15	1.60	(4)	1.00	112,896,000
2106	20¢ A Nation of Readers, Oct. 16	.38	.15	1.60	(4)	1.00	116,500,000
	Christmas Issue, Oct. 30						
2107	20¢ Madonna and Child, by Fra Filippo Lippi	.40	.15	1.70	(4)	1.00	751,300,000
2108	20¢ Santa Claus	.40	.15	1.70	(4)	1.00	786,225,000
a	Horizontal pair, imperf. vertically	950.00					
	Perf. 10.5						
2109	20¢ Vietnam Veterans' Memorial, Nov. 10	.40	.15	1.75	(4)	1.00	105,300,000
	Issues of 1985, Perf. 11 **Performing Arts Issue, Jerome Kern, Jan. 23**						
2110	22¢ Jerome Kern Portrait and Kern Studying Sheet Music	.40	.15	1.75	(4)	1.00	124,500,000
2111	(22¢)"D" Stamp, Feb. 1	.60	.15	4.50	(6)	1.00	
a	Imperf. pair	50.00					
b	Vertical pair, imperf. horizontally	1,350.00					
	Coil Stamp, Perf. 10 Vertically						
2112	(22¢)"D" green Eagle (2111), Feb. 1	.60	.15	6.00	(3)	1.00	
a	Imperf. pair	50.00					
	Booklet Stamp, Perf. 11						
2113	(22¢)"D" green Eagle (2111), single from booklet	.80	.15			1.00	
a	Booklet pane of 10, Feb. 1	8.00				7.50	
b	As "a," imperf. between horizontally	—					
	Issues of 1985-87, Flag Over Capitol Issue						
2114	22¢ Flag Over Capitol, Mar. 29, 1985	.40	.15	1.80	(4)	1.00	
	Pair with full horizontal gutter between	—					
	Coil Stamp, Perf. 10 Vertically						
2115	22¢ Flag Over Capitol (2114), Mar. 29, 1985	.40	.15	4.00	(3)	1.00	
a	Imperf. pair	10.00					
b	Inscribed "T" at bottom, May 23, 1987	.48	.15	4.00	(3)	1.00	
c	Black field of stars	—	—				
	#2115b issued for test on prephosphored paper. Paper is whiter and colors are brighter than on #2115.						
	Booklet Stamp, Perf. 10 Horizontally						
2116	22¢ Flag over Capitol, single from booklet	.48	.15			1.00	
a	Booklet pane of 5, Mar. 29, 1985	2.50	—			3.50	
	#2116 issued only in booklets. All stamps are imperf. at both sides or imperf. at both sides and bottom.						

	Issues of 1985, Perf. 10 vertically	Un	U	PNC	#	FDC
	Seashells Booklet Issue, Apr. 4					
2117	22¢ Frilled Dogwinkle	.40	.15			1.00
2118	22¢ Reticulated Helmet	.40	.15			1.00
2119	22¢ New England Neptune	.40	.15			1.00
2120	22¢ Calico Scallop	.40	.15			1.00
2121	22¢ Lightning Whelk	.40	.15			1.00
a	Booklet pane of 10	4.00	—			7.50
b	As "a," violet omitted	850.00				
c	As "a," imperf. between vertically	600.00				
e	Strip of 5, #2117-21	2.00	—			
	Express Mail Booklet Issue, Apr. 29					
2122	$10.75 Eagle and Moon, booklet single	17.00	7.00			40.00
a	Booklet pane of 3	52.50	—			95.00
	#2122 issued only in booklets. All stamps are imperf. at top and bottom or at top, bottom and one side.					
	Issues of 1985-89, Coil Stamps, Transportation Issue (See also #1897-1908, 2225-31, 2252-66, 2451-68)					
2123	3.4¢ School Bus 1920s, June 8, 1985	.15	.15	1.00	(3)	1.00
a	Untagged (Bureau precanceled)	.15	.15	5.50	(3)	1.00
2124	4.9¢ Buckboard 1880s, June 21, 1985	.15	.15	1.10	(3)	1.00
a	Untagged (Bureau precanceled)	.16	.16	1.65	(3)	
2125	5.5¢ Star Route Truck 1910s, Nov. 1, 1986	.15	.15	1.75	(3)	1.00
a	Untagged (Bureau precanceled)	.15	.15	1.90	(3)	1.00
2126	6¢ Tricycle 1880s, May 6, 1985	.15	.15	1.40	(3)	1.00
a	Untagged (Bureau precanceled)	.15	.15	2.00	(3)	
b	As "a," imperf. pair	200.00				
2127	7.1¢ Tractor 1920s, Feb. 6, 1987	.15	.15	2.50	(3)	1.00
a	Untagged (Bureau precanceled "Nonprofit org.")	.15	.15	2.75	(3)	5.00
a	Untagged (Bureau precanceled "Nonprofit 5-Digit ZIP + 4"), May 26, 1989	.15	.15	2.50	(3)	1.00
2128	8.3¢ Ambulance 1860s, June 21, 1985	.18	.15	1.50	(3)	1.00
a	Untagged (Bureau precanceled)	.18	.18	1.75	(3)	
2129	8.5¢ Tow Truck 1920s, Jan. 24, 1987	.16	.15	2.75	(3)	1.00
a	Untagged (Bureau precanceled)	.16	.16	2.75	(3)	
2130	10.1¢ Oil Wagon 1890s, Apr. 18, 1985	.22	.15	2.50	(3)	1.00
a	Untagged (Bureau precanceled, black)	.22	.22	2.75	(3)	1.00
a	Untagged (Bureau precanceled, red)	.22	.22	2.50	(3)	1.00
b	As "a," black precancel, imperf. pair	100.00				
b	As "a," red precancel, imperf. pair	15.00				
2131	11¢ Stutz Bearcat 1933, June 11, 1985	.22	.15	1.65	(3)	1.00
2132	12¢ Stanley Steamer 1909, Apr. 2, 1985	.24	.15	2.25	(3)	1.00
a	Untagged (Bureau precanceled)	.24	.24	2.50	(3)	
b	As "a," type II	.24	.24	17.00	(3)	
	Type II has "Stanley Steamer 1909" 1/2mm shorter (171/2mm) than #2132 (18mm).					
2133	12.5¢ Pushcart 1880s, Apr. 18, 1985	.25	.15	2.75	(3)	1.25
a	Untagged (Bureau precanceled)	.25	.25	3.50	(3)	
b	As "a," imperf. pair	50.00				
2134	14¢ Iceboat 1880s, Mar. 23, 1985	.28	.15	2.25	(3)	1.25
a	Imperf. pair	100.00				
2135	17¢ Dog Sled 1920s, Aug. 20, 1986	.30	.15	3.00	(3)	1.25
a	Imperf. pair	500.00				
2136	25¢ Bread Wagon 1880s, Nov. 22, 1986	.45	.15	4.00	(3)	1.25
a	Imperf. pair	10.00				

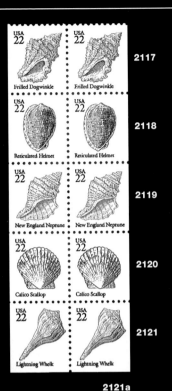

USA 22 Frilled Dogwinkle — USA 22 Frilled Dogwinkle — **2117**

USA 22 Reticulated Helmet — USA 22 Reticulated Helmet — **2118**

USA 22 New England Neptune — USA 22 New England Neptune — **2119**

USA 22 Calico Scallop — USA 22 Calico Scallop — **2120**

USA 22 Lightning Whelk — USA 22 Lightning Whelk — **2121**

2121a

USA $10.75

2122

School Bus 1920s 3.4 USA

2123

Buckboard 1880s USA 4.9

2124

Star Route Truck 5.5 USA 1910s

2125

Tricycle 1880s 6 USA

2126

Tractor 1920s 7.1 USA

2127

Ambulance 1860s 8.3 USA

2128

Tow Truck 1920s 8.5 USA

2129

Oil Wagon 1890s 10.1 USA

2130

Stutz Bearcat 1933 11 USA

2131

Stanley Steamer 1909 USA 12

2132

Pushcart 1880s 12.5 USA

2133

Iceboat 1880s USA 14

2134

Dog Sled 1920s 17 USA

2135

Bread Wagon 1880s 25 USA

2136

2137

2138

2139

2140   **2141**   **2141a**

Winter Special Olympics

2142

2143

2144

2145

2146

2147

2149

2150

2152

2153

	Issues of 1985, Perf. 11	Un	U	PB/PNC	#	FDC	Q
	Black Heritage Issue, Mary McLeod Bethune, Mar. 5						
2137	22¢ Mary McLeod Bethune Portrait	.40	.15	1.75	(4)	1.00	120,000,000
	American Folk Art Issue, Duck Decoys, Mar. 22						
2138	22¢ Broadbill Decoy	.60	.15			1.00	75,000,000
2139	22¢ Mallard Decoy	.60	.15			1.00	75,000,000
2140	22¢ Canvasback Decoy	.60	.15			1.00	75,000,000
2141	22¢ Redhead Decoy	.60	.15			1.00	75,000,000
a	Block of 4, #2138-41	2.50	1.00	3.50	(4)	2.75	
2142	22¢ Winter Special Olympics, Mar. 25	.40	.15	1.70	(4)	1.00	120,580,000
a	Vertical pair, imperf. horizontally	650.00					
2143	22¢ Love, Apr. 17	.40	.15	1.70	(4)	1.00	729,700,000
a	Imperf. pair	1,750.00					
2144	22¢ Rural Electrification Administration, May 11	.45	.15	22.50	(20)	1.00	124,750,000
2145	22¢ AMERIPEX '86, May 25	.40	.15	1.70	(4)	1.00	203,496,000
a	Red, black and blue omitted	200.00					
b	Red and black omitted	1,250.00					
2146	22¢ Abigail Adams, June 14	.40	.15	1.80	(4)	1.00	126,325,000
a	Imperf. pair	275.00					
2147	22¢ Frederic A. Bartholdi, July 18	.40	.15	1.80	(4)	1.00	130,000,000
2148	Not assigned						
	Coil Stamps, Perf. 10 Vertically						
2149	18¢ George Washington, Washington Monument, Nov. 6	.32	.15	3.00	(3)	1.25	
a	Untagged (Bureau precanceled)	.35	.35	3.25	(3)		
b	Imperf. pair	950.00					
c	As "a," imperf. pair	750.00		4.50	(3)		
2150	21.1¢ Sealed Envelopes, Oct. 22	.40	.15	3.25	(3)	1.25	
a	Untagged (Bureau precanceled)	.38	.38	3.75	(3)		
2151	Not assigned						
	Perf. 11						
2152	22¢ Korean War Veterans, July 26	.40	.15	1.90	(4)	1.00	119,975,000
2153	22¢ Social Security Act, 50th Anniversary Aug. 14	.40	.15	1.90	(4)	1.00	120,000,000

Who fought in the Korean War?

Partitioned after World War II, Soviet troops occupied the northern half and American troops were stationed in the southern half of Korea. On June 25, 1950, the country became a battleground when troops from North Korea invaded South Korea. One of the bloodiest wars in history, it was the first war in which the United Nations played a military role.

By the time a cease fire was signed in 1953, over three million civilians and soldiers on both sides were killed or wounded. **(#2152)**

	Issues of 1985, Perf. 11	Un	U	PB	#	FDC	Q
2154	22¢ World War I Veterans, Aug. 26	.40	.15	2.00	(4)	1.00	119,975,000
	American Horses Issue, Sept. 25						
2155	22¢ Quarter Horse	.85	.15			1.00	36,985,000
2156	22¢ Morgan	.85	.15			1.00	36,985,000
2157	22¢ Saddlebred	.85	.15			1.00	36,985,000
2158	22¢ Appaloosa	.85	.15			1.00	36,985,000
a	Block of 4, #2155-58	4.00	1.00	4.75	(4)	2.50	
2159	22¢ Public Education, Oct. 1	.42	.15	2.00	(4)	1.00	120,000,000
	International Youth Year Issue, Oct. 7						
2160	22¢ YMCA Youth Camping	.48	.15			1.00	32,500,000
2161	22¢ Boy Scouts	.48	.15			1.00	32,500,000
2162	22¢ Big Brothers/Big Sisters	.48	.15			1.00	32,500,000
2163	22¢ Camp Fire	.48	.15			1.00	32,500,000
a	Block of 4, #2160-63	2.00	1.00	2.75	(4)	1.25	
2164	22¢ Help End Hunger, Oct. 15	.42	.15	1.90	(4)	1.00	120,000,000
	Christmas Issue, Oct. 30						
2165	22¢ Genoa Madonna, by Luca Della Robbia	.40	.15	1.70	(4)	1.00	759,200,000
a	Imperf. pair	100.00					
2166	22¢ Poinsettia Plants	.40	.15	1.70	(4)	1.00	757,600,000
a	Imperf. pair	130.00					

Education for the common good

The state-supported public schools movement began in the 1820s with the establishment of the common (elementary) school. In 1837, Massachusetts established a state board of education and appointed Horace Mann, lawyer and politician (1796-1859), as its secretary (see #869). One of Mann's many reforms was establishing the first teacher-training schools in

the United States. By the end of the 19th century the common-school system was firmly established across the country. **(#2159)**

Interesting Fact: The first "basic textbook" for education was *The New England Primer.* Used from 1690 until the beginning of the 19th century, its purpose was to teach both religion and reading.

2154

2155   **2156**

2157   **2158**   **2158a**

2160   **2161**

2159

2162   **2163**   **2163a**

Help End Hunger USA22

2164

2165

2166

2167

2168

2169

2170

2171

2172

2173

2176

2177

2178

2179

2179B

2180

2182

2183

2184

2184A

2184B

2185

2186

2188

2190

2191

2192

2193

2194

2194A

2195

2196

	Issues of 1986, Perf. 11	Un	U	PB	#	FDC	Q
2167	22¢ Arkansas Statehood, Jan. 3	.40	.15	1.90	(4)	1.00	130,000,000
a	Vertical pair, imperf. horizontally	—					
	Issues of 1986-91, Great Americans Issue (See also #1844-69)						
2168	1¢ Margaret Mitchell, June 30, 1986	.15	.15	.25	(4)	1.00	
2169	2¢ Mary Lyon, Feb. 28, 1987	.15	.15	.25	(4)	1.00	
2170	3¢ Paul Dudley White, MD, Sept. 15, 1986	.15	.15	.30	(4)	1.00	
2171	4¢ Father Flanagan, July 14, 1986	.15	.15	.35	(4)	1.00	
2172	5¢ Hugo L. Black, Feb. 27, 1986	.15	.15	.40	(4)	1.00	
2173	5¢ Luis Munoz Marin, Feb. 18, 1990	.15	.15	.50	(4)	1.25	
2174-75	Not assigned						
2176	10¢ Red Cloud, Aug. 15, 1987	.18	.15	.85	(4)	1.00	
a	Overall tagging, 1990	.30	.15				
2177	14¢ Julia Ward Howe, Feb. 12, 1987	.25	.15	1.10	(4)	1.00	
2178	15¢ Buffalo Bill Cody, June 6, 1988	.28	.15	1.20	(4)	1.25	
a	Overall tagging, 1990	—	—				
2179	17¢ Belva Ann Lockwood, June 18, 1986	.30	.15	1.45	(4)	1.00	
	Perf. 11 x 11.8						
2179B	20¢ Virginia Apgar, Oct. 24, 1994	.40	.15				
	Perf. 11						
2180	21¢ Chester Carlson, Oct. 21, 1988	.38	.15	1.75	(4)	1.25	
2181	Not assigned						
2182	23¢ Mary Cassatt, Nov. 4, 1988	.42	.15	1.90	(4)	1.25	
2183	25¢ Jack London, Jan. 11, 1986	.45	.15	2.00	(4)	1.25	
a	Booklet pane of 10, May 3, 1988	4.50	—			6.00	
b	Overall tagging, 1990	—	—				
2184	28¢ Sitting Bull, Sept. 28, 1989	.50	.15	2.50	(4)	1.00	
2184A	29¢ Earl Warren, Mar. 9	.50	.15	2.90	(4)		
2184B	29¢ Thomas Jefferson, 1993	.50	.15	2.50	(4)	1.25	
2185	35¢ Dennis Chavez, Apr. 3, 1991	.65	.15	3.25	(4)		
2186	40¢ Claire Lee Chennault, Sept. 6, 1990	.70	.15	3.25	(4)	1.00	
2187	Not assigned						
2188	45¢ Harvey Cushing, MD, June 17, 1988	.80	.15	3.50	(4)	1.00	
a	Overall tagging, 1990	—	—				
2189	Not assigned						
2190	52¢ Hubert H. Humphrey, June 3, 1991	.90	.15	4.00	(4)	1.25	
2191	56¢ John Harvard, Sept. 3, 1986	.90	.15	4.00	(4)	1.25	
2192	65¢ H.H. 'Hap' Arnold, Nov. 5, 1988	1.20	.18	5.00	(4)	1.50	
2193	75¢ Wendell Willkie	1.30	.20	5.50	(4)		
2194	$1 Bernard Revel, Sept. 23, 1986	2.50	.50	9.50	(4)	2.00	
2194A	$1 Johns Hopkins, June 7, 1989	1.75	.50	7.25	(4)	3.00	
b	Overall tagging, 1990	—	—				
2195	$2 William Jennings Bryan, Mar. 19, 1986	3.25	.50	13.00	(4)	5.00	
2196	$5 Bret Harte, Aug. 25, 1987	7.50	1.00	28.00	(4)	15.00	
	Booklet Stamp, Perf. 10						
2197	25¢ Jack London (2183), single from booklet	.45	.15			1.25	
a	Booklet pane of 6, May 3, 1988	2.75				4.00	

	Issues of 1986, Perf. 10 Vertically	Un	U	PB	#	FDC	Q
	United States—Sweden Stamp Collecting Booklet Issue, Jan. 23						
2198	22¢ Handstamped Cover	.45	.15			1.00	16,999,200
2199	22¢ Boy Examining Stamp Collection	.45	.15			1.00	16,999,200
2200	22¢ #836 Under Magnifying Glass	.45	.15			1.00	16,999,200
2201	22¢ 1986 Presidents Miniature Sheet	.45	.15			1.00	16,999,200
a	Booklet pane of 4, #2198-2201	2.00	—			4.00	16,999,200
b	As "a," black omitted on #2198, 2201	50.00					
c	As "a," blue omitted on #2198-2200	2,500.00					
d	As "a," buff omitted	—					
	#2198-2201 issued only in booklets. All stamps are imperf. at top and bottom or imperf. at top, bottom and right side.						
	Perf. 11						
2202	22¢ Love, Jan. 30	.40	.15	1.70	(4)	1.00	948,860,000
	Black Heritage Issue, Sojourner Truth, Feb. 4						
2203	22¢ Sojourner Truth Portrait and Truth Lecturing	.40	.15	1.75	(4)	1.00	130,000,000
2204	22¢ Republic of Texas, 150th Anniversary, Mar. 2	.42	.15	1.75	(4)	1.00	136,500,000
a	Horizontal pair, imperf. vertically	1,250.00					
b	Dark red omitted	2,750.00					
	Fish Booklet Issue, Mar. 21, Perf. 10 Horizontally						
2205	22¢ Muskellunge	.50	.15			1.00	43,998,000
2206	22¢ Atlantic Cod	.50	.15			1.00	43,998,000
2207	22¢ Largemouth Bass	.50	.15			1.00	43,998,000
2208	22¢ Bluefin Tuna	.50	.15			1.00	43,998,000
2209	22¢ Catfish	.50	.15			1.00	43,998,000
a	Booklet pane of 5, #2205-09	3.25	—			2.50	43,998,000
	#2205-09 issued only in booklets. All stamps are imperf. at sides or imperf. at sides and bottom.						
	Perf. 11						
2210	22¢ Public Hospitals, Apr. 11	.40	.15	1.75	(4)	1.00	130,000,000
a	Vertical pair, imperf. horizontally	300.00					
b	Horizontal pair, imperf. vertically	1,350.00					
	Performing Arts Issue, Duke Ellington, Apr. 29						
2211	22¢ Duke Ellington Portrait and Piano Keys	.40	.15	1.90	(4)	1.00	130,000,000
a	Vertical pair, imperf. horizontally	1,000.00					
2212-15	Not assigned						

Minimum value listed for a stamp is 15 cents; for a First Day Cover (FDC), $1.00. This minimum represents a fair-market price for having a dealer locate and provide a single stamp or cover from his or her stock. Dealers may charge less per stamp or cover for a group of such stamps or covers, or less for a single stamp or cover.

2198   2199   2200   2201   2201a

2202   2203   2204

2205

2206

2207

2208

2209

2210

2211

2209a

George Washington 1789-1797   John Adams 1797-1801   Thomas Jefferson 1801-1809   James Madison 1809-1817   James Monroe 1817-1825

2216a   **2216b**   **2216c**   **2216d**   **2216e**

John Quincy Adams 1825-1829   Andrew Jackson 1829-1837   Martin Van Buren 1837-1841   William Henry Harrison 1841-1841

2216f   **2216g**   **2216h**   **2216i**

John Tyler 1841-1845   James K. Polk 1845-1849   Zachary Taylor 1849-1850   Millard Fillmore 1850-1851   Franklin Pierce 1853-1857

2217a   **2217b**   **2217c**   **2217d**   **2217e**

James Buchanan 1857-1861   Abraham Lincoln 1861-1865   Andrew Johnson 1865-1869   Ulysses S. Grant 1869-1877

2217f   **2217g**   **2217h**   **2217i**

Issues of 1986, Perf. 11	Un	U	FDC	Q
AMERIPEX '86 Issue, Presidents Miniature Sheets, May 22				
2216 Sheet of 9	3.50		4.00	5,825,050
a 22¢ George Washington	.38	.20	1.00	
b 22¢ John Adams	.38	.20	1.00	
c 22¢ Thomas Jefferson	.38	.20	1.00	
d 22¢ James Madison	.38	.20	1.00	
e 22¢ James Monroe	.38	.20	1.00	
f 22¢ John Quincy Adams	.38	.20	1.00	
g 22¢ Andrew Jackson	.38	.20	1.00	
h 22¢ Martin Van Buren	.38	.20	1.00	
i 22¢ William H. Harrison	.38	.20	1.00	
j Blue omitted	3,500.00			
k Black inscription omitted	2,000.00			
l Imperf.	10,500.00			
2217 Sheet of 9	3.50		4.00	5,825,050
a 22¢ John Tyler	.38	.20	1.00	
b 22¢ James Polk	.38	.20	1.00	
c 22¢ Zachary Taylor	.38	.20	1.00	
d 22¢ Millard Fillmore	.38	.20	1.00	
e 22¢ Franklin Pierce	.38	.20	1.00	
f 22¢ James Buchanan	.38	.20	1.00	
g 22¢ Abraham Lincoln	.38	.20	1.00	
h 22¢ Andrew Johnson	.38	.20	1.00	
i 22¢ Ulysses S. Grant	.38	.20	1.00	

#2216

#2217

	Issues of 1986, Perf. 11	Un	U	FDC	Q
	AMERIPEX '86 Issue (continued), Presidents Miniature Sheets, May 22				
2218	Sheet of 9	3.50		4.00	5,825,050
a	22¢ Rutherford B. Hayes	.38	.20	1.00	
b	22¢ James A. Garfield	.38	.20	1.00	
c	22¢ Chester A. Arthur	.38	.20	1.00	
d	22¢ Grover Cleveland	.38	.20	1.00	
e	22¢ Benjamin Harrison	.38	.20	1.00	
f	22¢ William McKinley	.38	.20	1.00	
g	22¢ Theodore Roosevelt	.38	.20	1.00	
h	22¢ William H. Taft	.38	.20	1.00	
i	22¢ Woodrow Wilson	.38	.20	1.00	
j	Brown omitted	—			
k	Black inscription omitted	3,000.00			
2219	Sheet of 9	3.50		4.00	5,825,050
a	22¢ Warren G. Harding	.38	.20	1.00	
b	22¢ Calvin Coolidge	.38	.20	1.00	
c	22¢ Herbert Hoover	.38	.20	1.00	
d	22¢ Franklin D. Roosevelt	.38	.20	1.00	
e	22¢ White House	.38	.20	1.00	
f	22¢ Harry S. Truman	.38	.20	1.00	
g	22¢ Dwight D. Eisenhower	.38	.20	1.00	
h	22¢ John F. Kennedy	.38	.20	1.00	
i	22¢ Lyndon B. Johnson	.38	.20	1.00	

#2218

#2219

USA 22 — Rutherford B. Hayes 1877-1881

USA 22 — James A. Garfield 1881-1881

USA 22 — Chester A. Arthur 1881-1885

USA 22 — Grover Cleveland 1885-89, 1893-97

USA 22 — Benjamin Harrison 1889-1893

2218a   **2218b**   **2218c**   **2218d**   **2218e**

USA 22 — William McKinley 1897-1901

USA 22 — Theodore Roosevelt 1901-1909

USA 22 — William H. Taft 1909-1913

USA 22 — Woodrow Wilson 1913-1921

2218f   **2218g**   **2218h**   **2218i**

USA 22 — Warren G. Harding 1921-1924

USA 22 — Calvin Coolidge 1923-1929

USA 22 — Herbert C. Hoover 1929-1933

USA 22 — Franklin D. Roosevelt 1933-1945

USA 22

2219a   **2219b**   **2219c**   **2219d**   **2219e**

USA 22 — Harry S. Truman 1945-1953

USA 22 — Dwight D. Eisenhower 1953-1961

USA 22 — John F. Kennedy 1961-1963

USA 22 — Lyndon B. Johnson 1963-1969

2219f   **2219g**   **2219h**   **2219i**

2220   2221

2222   2223   2223a

2224

2225

2226

2235   2236

2237   2238   2238a

2239

2240   2241

2242   2243   2243a

2244

2245

2246

2247

2248

2249

2250

2251

	Issues of 1986, Perf. 11	Un	U	PB/PNC	#	FDC	Q
	Arctic Explorers Issue, May 28						
2220	22¢ Elisha Kent Kane	.50	.15			1.00	32,500,000
2221	22¢ Adolphus W. Greely	.50	.15			1.00	32,500,000
2222	22¢ Vilhjalmur Stefansson	.50	.15			1.00	32,500,000
2223	22¢ Robert E. Peary, Matthew Henson	.50	.15			1.00	32,500,000
a	Block of 4, #2220-23	2.25	1.00	3.00	(4)	2.50	
b	As "a," black omitted	9,500.00					
2224	22¢ Statue of Liberty, July 4	.40	.15	2.00	(4)	1.00	220,725,000
	Issues of 1986-87, Reengraved Transportation Issue, Coil Stamps, Perf. 10 Vertically						
	(See also #1897-1908, 2123-36, 2252-66, 2452-53A, 2457, 2464, 2468)						
2225	1¢ Omnibus, Nov. 26, 1986	.15	.15	.65	(3)	1.00	
2226	2¢ Locomotive, Mar. 6, 1987	.15	.15	.75	(3)	1.00	
2227, 2229-30, 2232-34 Not assigned							
2228	4¢ Stagecoach (1898A), Aug. 1986	.15	.15	1.40	(3)		
2231	8.3¢ Ambulance (2128) (Bureau precanceled), Aug. 29, 1986	.16	.16	3.75	(3)		
	On #2228, "Stagecoach 1890s" is 17mm long; on #1898A, it is 19¹/₂mm long. On #2231, "Ambulance 1860s" is 18mm long; on #2128, it is 18¹/₂mm long.						
	American Folk Art Issue, Navajo Blankets, Sept. 4, Perf. 11						
2235	22¢ Navajo Art, four "+" marks horizontally through middle	.40	.15			1.00	60,131,250
2236	22¢ Navajo Art, vertical diamond pattern	.40	.15			1.00	60,131,250
2237	22¢ Navajo Art, horizontal diamond pattern	.40	.15			1.00	60,131,250
2238	22¢ Navajo Art, jagged line horizontally through middle	.40	.15			1.00	60,131,250
a	Block of 4, #2235-38	1.65	1.00	2.25	(4)	2.50	
b	As "a," black omitted	350.00					
	Literary Arts Issue, T.S. Eliot, Sept. 26						
2239	22¢ T.S. Eliot Portrait	.40	.15	1.90	(4)	1.00	131,700,000
	American Folk Art Issue, Wood-Carved Figurines, Oct. 1						
2240	22¢ Highlander Figure	.42	.15			1.00	60,000,000
2241	22¢ Ship Figurehead	.42	.15			1.00	60,000,000
2242	22¢ Nautical Figure	.42	.15			1.00	60,000,000
2243	22¢ Cigar Store Figure	.42	.15			1.00	60,000,000
a	Block of 4, #2240-43	1.75	1.00	2.25	(4)	2.50	
b	As "a," imperf. vertically	1,500.00					
	Christmas Issue, Oct. 24						
2244	22¢ Madonna and Child, by Perugino	.40	.15	1.90	(4)	1.00	690,100,000
2245	22¢ Village Scene	.40	.15	1.90	(4)	1.00	882,150,000
	Issues of 1987						
2246	22¢ Michigan Statehood, Jan. 26	.40	.15	1.90	(4)	1.00	167,430,000
	Pair with full vertical gutter between	—					
2247	22¢ Pan American Games, Jan. 29	.40	.15	1.90	(4)	1.00	166,555,000
a	Silver omitted	1,500.00					
	Perf. 11.5 x 11						
2248	22¢ Love, Jan. 30	.40	.15	1.90	(4)	1.00	842,360,000
	Black Heritage Issue, Jean Baptiste Point Du Sable, Feb. 20, Perf. 11						
2249	22¢ Portrait of Du Sable and Chicago Settlement	.40	.15	1.90	(4)	1.00	142,905,000
	Performing Arts Issue, Enrico Caruso, Feb. 27						
2250	22¢ Caruso as the Duke of Mantua in *Rigoletti*	.40	.15	1.90	(4)	1.00	130,000,000
2251	22¢ Girl Scouts, Mar. 12	.40	.15	1.90	(4)	1.00	149,980,000

	Issues of 1987-88, Perf. 10 Vertically	Un	U	PNC	#	FDC	Q
	Coil Stamps, Transportation Issue (See also #1897-1908, 2123-36, 2225-31, 2451-68)						
2252	3¢ Conestoga Wagon 1800s, Feb. 29, 1988	.15	.15	.85	(3)	1.25	
2253	5¢ Milk Wagon 1900s, Sept. 25, 1987	.15	.15	1.10	(3)	1.25	
2254	5.3¢ Elevator 1900s, Bureau precanceled, Sept. 16, 1988	.15	.15	1.25	(3)	1.25	
2255	7.6¢ Carreta 1770s, Bureau precanceled, Aug. 30, 1988	.15	.15	2.50	(3)	1.25	
2256	8.4¢ Wheel Chair 1920s, Bureau precanceled, Aug. 12, 1988	.15	.15	2.50	(3)	1.25	
a	Imperf. pair	750.00					
2257	10¢ Canal Boat 1880s, Apr. 11, 1987	.18	.15	1.50	(3)	1.00	
2258	13¢ Patrol Wagon 1880s, Bureau precanceled, Oct. 29, 1988	.22	.22	2.75	(3)	1.25	
2259	13.2¢ Coal Car 1870s, Bureau precanceled, July 19, 1988	.22	.22	3.00	(3)	1.25	
a	Imperf. pair	100.00					
2260	15¢ Tugboat 1900s, July 12, 1988	.24	.15	3.00	(3)	1.25	
2261	16.7¢ Popcorn Wagon 1902, Bureau precanceled, July 7, 1988	.28	.28	3.75	(3)	1.25	
a	Imperf. pair	150.00					
2262	17.5¢ Racing Car 1911, Sept. 25, 1987	.30	.15	3.75	(3)	1.00	
a	Untagged (Bureau precanceled)	.30	.30	3.75	(3)	1.00	
b	Imperf. pair	1,750.00					
2263	20¢ Cable Car 1880s, Oct. 28, 1988	.35	.15	3.75	(3)	1.25	
a	Imperf. pair	75.00					
2264	20.5¢ Fire Engine 1920s, Bureau precanceled, Sept. 28, 1988	.38	.38	3.75	(3)	1.25	
2265	21¢ Railroad Mail Car 1920s, Bureau precanceled, Aug. 16, 1988	.38	.38	3.75	(3)	1.25	
a	Imperf. pair	65.00					
2266	24.1¢ Tandem Bicycle 1890s, Bureau precanceled, Oct. 26, 1988	.42	.42	4.50	(3)	1.25	
	Issues of 1987 (continued), Special Occasions Booklet Issue, Apr. 20, Perf. 10						
2267	22¢ Congratulations!	.55	.15			1.00	1,222,140,000
2268	22¢ Get Well!	.55	.15			1.00	611,070,000
2269	22¢ Thank you!	.55	.15			1.00	611,070,000
2270	22¢ Love You, Dad!	.55	.15			1.00	611,070,000
2271	22¢ Best Wishes!	.55	.15			1.00	611,070,000
2272	22¢ Happy Birthday!	.55	.15			1.00	1,222,140,000
2273	22¢ Love You, Mother!	.55	.15			1.00	611,070,000
2274	22¢ Keep In Touch!	.55	.15			1.00	611,070,000
a	Booklet pane of 10, #2268-71, 2273-74 and 2 each of #2267, 2272	6.75	—			4.00	611,070,000

#2267-74 issued only in booklets. All stamps are imperf. at one or two sides or imperf. at sides and bottom.

Conestoga Wagon 1800s
3 USA
2252

Milk Wagon 1900s
5 USA
2253

Elevator 1900s
5.3 USA
Nonprofit Carrier Route Sort
2254

Carreta 1770s
7.6 USA
Nonprofit
2255

Wheel Chair 1920s
8.4 USA
Nonprofit
2256

Canal Boat 1880s
10 USA
2257

Patrol Wagon 1880s
USA 13
Presorted First-Class
2258

Coal Car 1870s
13.2 USA
Bulk Rate
2259

Tugboat 1900s
USA 15
2260

Popcorn Wagon 16.7 USA 1902
Bulk Rate
2261

Racing Car 1911
USA 17.5
2262

USA 20
Cable Car 1880s
2263

Fire Engine 1900s
20.5 USA
ZIP+4 Presort
2264

Railroad Mail Car 1920s
Presorted First-Class
21 USA
2265

Tandem Bicycle 1890s
24.1 USA
ZIP+4
2266

2267

Congratulations! 22 USA

2268

Get Well! USA 22

2269

Thank You! USA 22

2270

Love You, Dad! USA 22

2271

Best Wishes! USA 22

2272

Happy Birthday! USA 22

2273

Love You, Mother! USA 22

2274

Keep In Touch! USA 22

Happy Birthday! USA 22

Congratulations! USA 22

2274a

2275

2276

2277

2278

2279

2280

2281

2282a

2283

2283b

2285b

2284   **2285**

	Issues of 1987, Perf. 11	Un	U	PB/PNC	#	FDC	Q
2275	22¢ United Way, Apr. 28	.40	.15	1.90	(4)	1.00	156,995,000
2276	22¢ Flag with Fireworks, May 9	.40	.15	1.90	(4)	1.00	
a	Booklet pane of 20, Nov. 30	8.50	—			18.00	
	Issues of 1988-89 (All issued in 1988 except #2280 on prephosphored paper)						
2277	(25¢) "E" Stamp, Mar. 22	.45	.15	2.00	(4)	1.00	
2278	25¢ Flag with Clouds, May 6	.40	.15	1.90	(4)	1.00	
	Pair with full vertical gutter between	—					
	Coil Stamps, Perf. 10 Vertically						
2279	(25¢) "E" Earth, Mar. 22	.45	.15	3.00	(3)	1.00	
a	Imperf. pair	100.00					
2280	25¢ Flag over Yosemite, May 20	.45	.15	4.25	(3)	1.00	
	Prephosphored paper, Feb. 14, 1989	.45	.15	4.25	(3)		
a	Imperf. pair	15.00					
b	Black trees	100.00	—				
2281	25¢ Honeybee, Sept. 2	.45	.15	3.25	(3)	1.00	
a	Imperf. pair	45.00					
b	Black omitted	60.00					
d	Pair, imperf. between	900.00					
	Booklet Stamp, Perf. 10						
2282	(25¢) "E" Earth (#2277), single from booklet	.50	.15			1.00	
a	Booklet pane of 10, Mar. 22	6.50	—			6.00	
	Pheasant Booklet Issue, Perf. 11						
2283	25¢ Pheasant, single from booklet	.50	.15			1.25	
a	Booklet pane of 10, Apr. 29	6.00	—			6.00	
b	Single, red removed from sky	5.00	.15				
c	As "b," booklet pane of 10	65.00	—				
d	As "a," imperf. horizontally between	—					
	#2283 issued only in booklets. All stamps have one or two imperf. edges. Imperf. and part perf. pairs and panes exist from printer's waste.						
	Owl and Grosbeak Booklet Issue, Perf. 10						
2284	25¢ Grosbeak, single from booklet	.45	.15			1.25	
2285	25¢ Owl, single from booklet	.45	.15			1.25	
b	Booklet pane of 10, 5 each of #2284, 2285, May 28	4.50	—			6.00	
	#2284 and 2285 issued only in booklets. All stamps are imperf. at one side or imperf. at one side and bottom.						
2285A	25¢ Flag with Clouds (#2278), single from booklet	.45	.15			1.25	
c	Booklet pane of 6, July 5	2.75	—			4.00	

Stays up late to hunt

Owls are nocturnal birds of prey subsisting primarily on small rodents, amphibians, insects and birds. With eyes directed forward and specially adapted to seeing in partial darkness, a sense of hearing far more acute than human ears and wings bearing soft plumage that makes them almost silent in flight, owls are the undisputed rulers of the night sky. **(Illustrated: booklet cover for #2285b)**

	Issues of 1987, Perf. 11	Un	U	FDC	Q
	American Wildlife Issue, June 13				
2286	22¢ Barn Swallow	.85	.15	1.00	12,952,500
2287	22¢ Monarch Butterfly	.85	.15	1.00	12,952,500
2288	22¢ Bighorn Sheep	.85	.15	1.00	12,952,500
2289	22¢ Broad-tailed Hummingbird	.85	.15	1.00	12,952,500
2290	22¢ Cottontail	.85	.15	1.00	12,952,500
2291	22¢ Osprey	.85	.15	1.00	12,952,500
2292	22¢ Mountain Lion	.85	.15	1.00	12,952,500
2293	22¢ Luna Moth	.85	.15	1.00	12,952,500
2294	22¢ Mule Deer	.85	.15	1.00	12,952,500
2295	22¢ Gray Squirrel	.85	.15	1.00	12,952,500
2296	22¢ Armadillo	.85	.15	1.00	12,952,500
2297	22¢ Eastern Chipmunk	.85	.15	1.00	12,952,500
2298	22¢ Moose	.85	.15	1.00	12,952,500
2299	22¢ Black Bear	.85	.15	1.00	12,952,500
2300	22¢ Tiger Swallowtail	.85	.15	1.00	12,952,500
2301	22¢ Bobwhite	.85	.15	1.00	12,952,500
2302	22¢ Ringtail	.85	.15	1.00	12,952,500
2303	22¢ Red-winged Blackbird	.85	.15	1.00	12,952,500
2304	22¢ American Lobster	.85	.15	1.00	12,952,500
2305	22¢ Black-tailed Jack Rabbit	.85	.15	1.00	12,952,500
2306	22¢ Scarlet Tanager	.85	.15	1.00	12,952,500
2307	22¢ Woodchuck	.85	.15	1.00	12,952,500
2308	22¢ Roseate Spoonbill	.85	.15	1.00	12,952,500
2309	22¢ Bald Eagle	.85	.15	1.00	12,952,500
2310	22¢ Alaskan Brown Bear	.85	.15	1.00	12,952,500

This national symbol almost disappeared

The American bald eagle (Haliaetus leucocephalus) is brown with a white head, neck and tail plumage. A born hunter, with a beak nearly as long as its head, a wingspan of almost eight feet, talons that can crush bone, and keen eyesight, the bald eagle was nearly driven to extinction by hunters and pollution. Protected by strict conservation laws, bald eagles are making a comeback. **(#2309)**

Interesting Fact:
Instead of the bald eagle, Benjamin Franklin wanted to make the wild turkey the national bird. He admired its intelligence and adaptability.

2286 2287 2288 2289 2290

2291 2292 2293 2294 2295

2296 2297 2298 2299 2300

2301 2302 2303 2304 2305

2306 2307 2308 2309 2310

22 USA Iiwi	22 USA Badger	22 USA Pronghorn	22 USA River Otter	22 USA Ladybug
2311	**2312**	**2313**	**2314**	**2315**

22 USA Beaver	22 USA White-tailed Deer	22 USA Blue Jay	22 USA Pika	22 USA Bison
2316	**2317**	**2318**	**2319**	**2320**

22 USA Snowy Egret	22 USA Gray Wolf	22 USA Mountain Goat	22 USA Deer Mouse	22 USA Black-tailed Prairie Dog
2321	**2322**	**2323**	**2324**	**2325**

22 USA Box Turtle	22 USA Wolverine	22 USA American Elk	22 USA California Sea Lion	22 USA Mockingbird
2326	**2327**	**2328**	**2329**	**2330**

22 USA Raccoon	22 USA Bobcat	22 USA Black-footed Ferret	22 USA Canada Goose	22 USA Red Fox
2331	**2332**	**2333**	**2334**	**2335**

	Issues of 1987, Perf. 11	Un	U	PB	#	FDC	Q
	American Wildlife Issue (continued), June 13						
2311	22¢ Iiwi	.85	.15			1.00	12,952,500
2312	22¢ Badger	.85	.15			1.00	12,952,500
2313	22¢ Pronghorn	.85	.15			1.00	12,952,500
2314	22¢ River Otter	.85	.15			1.00	12,952,500
2315	22¢ Ladybug	.85	.15			1.00	12,952,500
2316	22¢ Beaver	.85	.15			1.00	12,952,500
2317	22¢ White-tailed Deer	.85	.15			1.00	12,952,500
2318	22¢ Blue Jay	.85	.15			1.00	12,952,500
2319	22¢ Pika	.85	.15			1.00	12,952,500
2320	22¢ Bison	.85	.15			1.00	12,952,500
2321	22¢ Snowy Egret	.85	.15			1.00	12,952,500
2322	22¢ Gray Wolf	.85	.15			1.00	12,952,500
2323	22¢ Mountain Goat	.85	.15			1.00	12,952,500
2324	22¢ Deer Mouse	.85	.15			1.00	12,952,500
2325	22¢ Black-tailed Prairie Dog	.85	.15			1.00	12,952,500
2326	22¢ Box Turtle	.85	.15			1.00	12,952,500
2327	22¢ Wolverine	.85	.15			1.00	12,952,500
2328	22¢ American Elk	.85	.15			1.00	12,952,500
2329	22¢ California Sea Lion	.85	.15			1.00	12,952,500
2330	22¢ Mockingbird	.85	.15			1.00	12,952,500
2331	22¢ Raccoon	.85	.15			1.00	12,952,500
2332	22¢ Bobcat	.85	.15			1.00	12,952,500
2333	22¢ Black-footed Ferret	.85	.15			1.00	12,952,500
2334	22¢ Canada Goose	.85	.15			1.00	12,952,500
2335	22¢ Red Fox	.85	.15			1.00	12,952,500
a	Pane of 50, #2286-2335	47.50				30.00	
	Any single, red omitted	—					

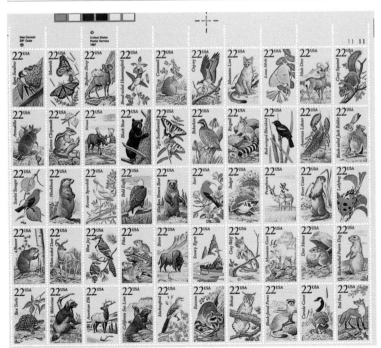

Example of 2335a.

	Issues of 1987-90, Perf. 11	Un	U	PB	#	FDC	Q
	Constitution Bicentennial Issue, Ratification of the Constitution						
2336	22¢ Delaware, July 4, 1987	.40	.15	1.90	(4)	1.00	168,000,000
2337	22¢ Pennsylvania, Aug. 26, 1987	.42	.15	1.90	(4)	1.00	186,575,000
2338	22¢ New Jersey, Sept. 11, 1987	.42	.15	1.90	(4)	1.00	184,325,000
a	Black omitted	5,250.00					
2339	22¢ Georgia, Jan. 6, 1988	.40	.15	1.90	(4)	1.00	168,845,000
2340	22¢ Connecticut, Jan. 9, 1988	.40	.15	1.90	(4)	1.00	155,170,000
2341	22¢ Massachusetts, Feb. 6, 1988	.40	.15	1.90	(4)	1.00	102,100,000
2342	22¢ Maryland, Feb. 15, 1988	.40	.15	1.90	(4)	1.00	103,325,000
2343	25¢ South Carolina, May 23, 1988	.45	.15	2.00	(4)	1.25	162,045,000
2344	25¢ New Hampshire, June 21, 1988	.45	.15	2.00	(4)	1.25	153,295,000
2345	25¢ Virginia, June 25, 1988	.45	.15	2.00	(4)	1.25	160,245,000
2346	25¢ New York, July 26, 1988	.45	.15	2.00	(4)	1.25	183,290,000
2347	25¢ North Carolina, Aug. 22, 1989	.45	.15	2.00	(4)	1.25	
2348	25¢ Rhode Island, May 29, 1990	.45	.15	2.00	(4)	1.25	164,130,000
2349	22¢ Friendship with Morocco, July 18	.40	.15	1.70	(4)	1.00	157,475,000
a	Black omitted	350.00					
	Issues of 1987, Literary Arts Issue, William Faulkner, Aug. 3						
2350	22¢ Portrait of Faulkner	.40	.15	1.70	(4)	1.00	156,225,000
	American Folk Art Issue, Lacemaking, Aug. 14						
2351	22¢ Squash Blossoms	.42	.15			1.00	40,995,000
2352	22¢ Floral Piece	.42	.15			1.00	40,995,000
2353	22¢ Floral Piece	.42	.15			1.00	40,995,000
2354	22¢ Dogwood Blossoms	.42	.15			1.00	40,995,000
a	Block of 4, #2351-54	1.75	1.00	2.25	(4)	2.75	
b	As "a," white omitted	1,100.00					

This state is definitely old-line

Named for Queen Henrietta Maria, Maryland received the nickname Old Line State after its courageous troops of the line during the Revolutionary War. Settled first by Algonquian Indians, Maryland was subsequently occupied by British colonists and ruled by the second Lord Baltimore, Cecilius Calvert. Maryland joined the Union as the seventh state on April 28, 1788. Maryland lies next to Chesapeake Bay, a vital fishing region and the site of important harbor cities, including Baltimore and Annapolis. **(#2342)**

Interesting Fact: The United States Naval Academy is located in Annapolis, Maryland. See stamp #794, as well as the new 1995 issue in the front of the book.

Dec 7, 1787 USA
Delaware 22

2336

22 USA
Dec 12, 1787
Pennsylvania

2337

Dec 18, 1787 USA
New Jersey 22

2338

22 USA
January 2, 1788
Georgia

2339

22 USA
January 9, 1788
Connecticut

2340

22 USA
Feb 6, 1788
Massachusetts

2341

April 28, 1788 USA
Maryland 22

2342

25 USA
May 23, 1788
South Carolina

2343

25 USA
June 21, 1788
New Hampshire

2344

June 25, 1788 USA
Virginia 25

2345

July 26, 1788 USA
New York 25

2346

25 USA
November 21, 1789
North Carolina

2347

25 USA
May 29, 1790
Rhode Island

2348

Friendship with Morocco 1787-1987

USA 22

2349

William Faulkner
USA 22

2350

2351

2352

Lacemaking USA 22 · Lacemaking USA 22

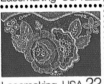

Lacemaking USA 22 · Lacemaking USA 22

2353   **2354**   **2354a**

The Bicentennial of the Constitution of the United States of America
1787-1987 USA 22 — 2355

We the people of the United States, in order to form a more perfect Union...
Preamble, U.S. Constitution USA 22 — 2356

Establish justice, insure domestic tranquility, provide for the common defense, promote the general welfare...
Preamble, U.S. Constitution USA 22 — 2357

And secure the blessings of liberty to ourselves and our posterity...
Preamble, U.S. Constitution USA 22 — 2358

Do ordain and establish this Constitution for the United States of America.
Preamble, U.S. Constitution USA 22 — 2359

2359a

2360

2361

Stourbridge Lion 1829 USA 22 — 2362

Best Friend of Charleston 1830 USA 22 — 2363

John Bull 1831 USA 22 — 2364

Brother Jonathan 1832 USA 22 — 2365

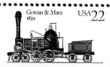

Gowan & Marx 1839 USA 22 — 2366

2366a

2367

2368

Issues of 1987, Perf. 10 Horizontally	Un	U	PB	#	FDC	Q
Constitution Bicentennial Issue, Drafting of the Constitution Booklet Issue, Aug. 28						
2355	22¢ "The Bicentennial..."	.50	.15			1.00	121,944,000
2356	22¢ "We the people..."	.50	.15			1.00	121,944,000
2357	22¢ "Establish justice..."	.50	.15			1.00	121,944,000
2358	22¢ "And secure..."	.50	.15			1.00	121,944,000
2359	22¢ "Do ordain..."	.50	.15			1.00	121,944,000
a	Booklet pane of 5, #2355-59	2.75	—			3.00	121,944,000
#2355-59 issued only in booklets. All stamps are imperf. at sides or imperf. at sides and bottom.						
Signing of the Constitution, Sept. 17, Perf. 11						
2360	22¢ Constitution and Signer's Hand Holding Quill Pen, Sept. 17	.40	.15	1.70	(4)	1.00	168,995,000
2361	22¢ Certified Public Accountants, Sept. 21	1.90	.15	8.75	(4)	2.00	163,145,000
a	Black omitted	700.00					
Locomotives Booklet Issue, Oct. 1, Perf. 10 Horizontally						
2362	22¢ Stourbridge Lion, 1829	.55	.15			1.00	142,501,200
2363	22¢ Best Friend of Charleston, 1830	.55	.15			1.00	142,501,200
2364	22¢ John Bull, 1831	.55	.15			1.00	142,501,200
2365	22¢ Brother Jonathan, 1832	.55	.15			1.00	142,501,200
2366	22¢ Gowan & Marx, 1839	.55	.15			1.00	142,501,200
a	Booklet pane of 5, #2362-66	2.75	—			3.00	142,501,200
b	As "a," black omitted on #2366	—					
#2362-66 issued only in booklets. All stamps are imperf. at sides or imperf. at sides and bottom.						
Christmas Issue, Oct. 23, Perf. 11						
2367	22¢ Madonna and Child, by Moroni	.40	.15	1.70	(4)	1.00	528,790,000
2368	22¢ Christmas Ornaments	.40	.15	1.70	(4)	1.00	978,340,000
	Pair with full vertical gutter between	—					

	Issues of 1988, Perf. 11	Un	U	PB	#	FDC	Q
	Winter Olympic Games Issue, Jan. 10						
2369	22¢ Skier and Olympic Rings	.40	.15	1.70	(4)	1.00	158,870,000
2370	22¢ Australia Bicentennial, Jan. 10	.40	.15	1.70	(4)	1.00	145,560,000
	Black Heritage Issue, James Weldon Johnson, Feb. 2						
2371	22¢ Portrait of Johnson and Music from "Lift Ev'ry Voice and Sing"	.40	.15	1.70	(4)	1.00	97,300,000
	American Cats Issue, Feb. 5						
2372	22¢ Siamese and Exotic Shorthair	.42	.15			1.00	39,639,000
2373	22¢ Abyssinian and Himalayan	.42	.15			1.00	39,639,000
2374	22¢ Maine Coon and Burmese	.42	.15			1.00	39,639,000
2375	22¢ American Shorthair and Persian	.42	.15			1.00	39,639,000
a	Block of 4, #2372-75	1.90	1.00	2.25	(4)	3.50	
	American Sports Issue, Knute Rockne, Mar. 9						
2376	22¢ Rockne Holding Football on Field	.40	.15	2.00	(4)	1.50	97,300,000
	Francis Ouimet, June 13						
2377	25¢ Portrait of Ouimet and Ouimet Hitting Fairway Shot	.45	.15	2.00	(4)	1.50	153,045,000
2378	25¢ Love, July 4	.45	.15	1.90	(4)	1.25	841,240,000
2379	45¢ Love, Aug. 8	.65	.20	3.00	(4)	1.25	179,553,550
	Summer Olympic Games Issue, Aug. 19						
2380	25¢ Gymnast on Rings	.45	.15	1.90	(4)	1.25	157,215,000

One cat for every four Americans

Over 60 million cats are kept as pets in the U.S. Breeds of domestic cats are usually divided into "short-haired" and "long-haired" breeds. The American Shorthair, developed from breeds brought to America by European colonists, is the best known. The Siamese, which was considered royal property in Thailand, is the most popular short-haired cat. The Persian is the most popular long-haired breed. Himalayan is a cross between the Persian and the Siamese and was developed in Britain and America in the 1930s. The largest domestic cat is the Maine Coon cat. This breed probably developed in New England from the mating of American shorthairs and Turkish angoras. **(#2372-75)**

2369

2370

2371

2372   2373

2374   2375   2375a

2376

2377

2378

2379

2381

2382

2383

2384

2385

2385a

2390

2391

2392

2393 2393a

2386

2387

2388

2389 2389a

	Issues of 1988, Perf. 10 Horizontally	Un	U	PB	#	FDC	Q
	Classic Cars Booklet Issue, Aug. 25						
2381	25¢ 1928 Locomobile	.50	.15			1.25	127,047,600
2382	25¢ 1929 Pierce-Arrow	.50	.15			1.25	127,047,600
2383	25¢ 1931 Cord	.50	.15			1.25	127,047,600
2384	25¢ 1932 Packard	.50	.15			1.25	127,047,600
2385	25¢ 1935 Duesenberg	.50	.15			1.25	127,047,600
a	Booklet pane of 5, #2381-85	3.50	—			3.00	127,047,600
	#2381-85 issued only in booklets. All stamps are imperf. at sides or imperf. at sides and bottom.						
	Antarctic Explorers Issue, Sept. 14, Perf. 11						
2386	25¢ Nathaniel Palmer	.55	.15			1.25	40,535,625
2387	25¢ Lt. Charles Wilkes	.55	.15			1.25	40,535,625
2388	25¢ Richard E. Byrd	.55	.15			1.25	40,535,625
2389	25¢ Lincoln Ellsworth	.55	.15			1.25	40,535,625
a	Block of 4, #2386-89	2.50	1.00	2.50	(4)	3.00	
b	As "a," black omitted	1,500.00					
c	As "a," imperf. horizontally	3,000.00					
	American Folk Art Issue, Carousel Animals, Oct. 1						
2390	25¢ Deer	.60	.15			1.50	76,253,750
2391	25¢ Horse	.60	.15			1.50	76,253,750
2392	25¢ Camel	.60	.15			1.50	76,253,750
2393	25¢ Goat	.60	.15			1.50	76,253,750
a	Block of 4, #2390-93	2.50	1.00	2.75	(4)	3.50	

This ride trained knights

Carousels originated in the late 17th century as training devices for jousting. The rider sat on a wooden horse on a contraption that resembled a merry-go-round and tried to strike a hanging ring with his lance as the device was pulled around in a circle. The earliest American carousel can be traced back to 1799. **(#2391)**

See the New Issues section (beginning on page 20) for the new, colorful Carousel Horses stamps.

	Issues of 1988, Perf. 11	Un	U	PB	#	FDC	Q
2394	$8.75 Express Mail, Oct. 4	13.50	8.00	55.00	(4)	25.00	
	Special Occasions Booklet Issue, Oct. 22						
2395	25¢ Happy Birthday	.45	.15			1.25	120,000,000
2396	25¢ Best Wishes	.45	.15			1.25	120,000,000
a	Booklet pane of 6, 3 #2395 and 3 #2396 with gutter between	3.00	—				
2397	25¢ Thinking of You	.45	.15			1.25	120,000,000
2398	25¢ Love You	.45	.15			1.25	120,000,000
a	Booklet pane of 6, 3 #2397 and 3 #2398 with gutter between	3.00	—				
b	As "a," imperf. horizontally	—					
	#2395-98a issued only in booklets. All stamps are imperf. on one side or on one side and top or bottom.						
	Christmas Issue, Oct. 20, Perf. 11						
2399	25¢ Madonna and Child, by Botticelli	.45	.15	1.90	(4)	1.25	843,835,000
a	Gold omitted	30.00					
2400	25¢ One-Horse Open Sleigh and Village Scene	.45	.15	1.90	(4)	1.25	1,037,610,000
	Pair with full vertical gutter between	—					

What is "Express Mail"?

The definition of "express" has changed over time, from the royal couriers of ancient Persia to the fleet of jet aircraft carrying today's U.S. Postal Service Express Mail.

In the United States, the recognized father of express is William Harnden, who in 1839 carried messages from Boston to New York via train or boat. From those beginnings evolved an industry that delivered packages via stagecoach, steamboat, wagon train, pony and, in the Southwest, camels. Today's air express industry was started after World War II by former pilots, and has evolved into a multibillion-dollar industry. **(#2394)**

2394

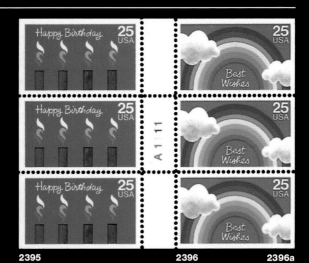

2395   2396   2396a

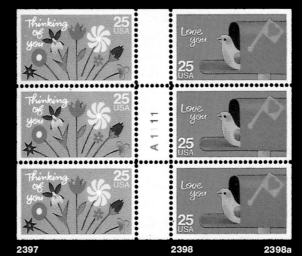

2397   2398   2398a

2399

2400

2401

2402

2403

2404

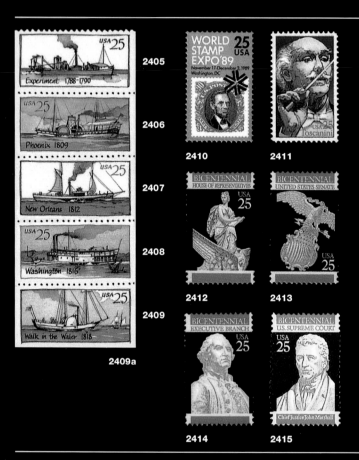

2405

2406

2407

2408

2409

2409a

2410

2411

2412

2413

2414

2415

2416

2417

2418

	Issues of 1989, Perf. 11	Un	U	PB	#	FDC	Q
2401	25¢ Montana Statehood, Jan. 15	.45	.15	1.90	(4)	1.25	165,495,000
	Black Heritage Issue, A. Philip Randolph, Feb. 3						
2402	25¢ Portrait of Randolph, Pullman Porters and Railroad Cars	.45	.15	1.90	(4)	1.25	151,675,000
2403	25¢ North Dakota Statehood, Feb. 21	.45	.15	1.90	(4)	1.25	163,000,000
2404	25¢ Washington Statehood, Feb. 22	.45	.15	1.90	(4)	1.25	264,625,000
	Steamboats Booklet Issue, Mar. 3, Perf. 10 Horizontally						
2405	25¢ Experiment 1788-90	.45	.15			1.25	159,154,200
2406	25¢ Phoenix 1809	.45	.15			1.25	159,154,200
2407	25¢ New Orleans 1812	.45	.15			1.25	159,154,200
2408	25¢ Washington 1816	.45	.15			1.25	159,154,200
2409	25¢ Walk in the Water 1818	.45	.15			1.25	159,154,200
a	Booklet pane of 5, #2405-09	2.25	—			4.00	159,154,200
	#2405-09 issued only in booklets. All stamps are imperf. at sides or imperf. at sides and bottom.						
	Perf. 11						
2410	25¢ World Stamp Expo '89, Mar. 16	.45	.15	1.90	(4)	1.25	163,984,000
	Performing Arts Issue, Arturo Toscanini, Mar. 25						
2411	25¢ Portrait of Toscanini Conducting with Baton	.45	.15	1.90	(4)	1.25	152,250,000
	Issues of 1989-90, Constitution Bicentennial Issue						
2412	25¢ U.S. House of Representatives, Apr. 4, 1989	.45	.15	1.90	(4)	1.25	138,760,000
2413	25¢ U.S. Senate, Apr. 6, 1989	.45	.15	1.90	(4)	1.25	137,985,000
2414	25¢ Executive Branch, George Washington, Apr. 16, 1989	.45	.15	1.90	(4)	1.25	138,580,000
2415	25¢ Supreme Court, Chief Justice John Marshall, Feb. 2, 1990	.45	.15	1.90	(4)	1.25	150,545,000
	Issues of 1989 (continued)						
2416	25¢ South Dakota Statehood, May 3	.45	.15	1.90	(4)	1.25	164,680,000
	American Sports Issue, Lou Gehrig, June 10						
2417	25¢ Portrait of Gehrig, Gehrig Swinging Bat	.48	.15	2.50	(4)	2.50	262,755,000
	Literary Arts Issue, Ernest Hemingway, July 17						
2418	25¢ Portrait of Hemingway, African Landscape in Background	.45	.15	1.90	(4)	1.25	191,755,000

1989

	Issues of 1989	Un	U	PB	#	FDC	Q
	Perf. 11 x 11.5, Priority Mail Issue, July 20						
2419	$2.40 Moon Landing	4.00	2.00	17.00	(4)	7.00	
a	Black omitted	3,000.00					
b	Imperf. pair	1,000.00					
	Perf. 11						
2420	25¢ Letter Carriers, Aug. 30	.45	.15	1.90	(4)	1.25	188,400,000
	Constitution Bicentennial Issue, Drafting of the Bill of Rights, Sept. 25						
2421	25¢ Stylized U.S. Flag, Eagle With Quill Pen in Mouth	.45	.15	1.90	(4)	1.25	191,860,000
a	Black omitted	275.00					
	Prehistoric Animals Issue, Oct. 1						
2422	25¢ Tyrannosaurus	.45	.15			1.25	101,747,000
2423	25¢ Pteranodon	.45	.15			1.25	101,747,000
2424	25¢ Stegosaurus	.45	.15			1.25	101,747,000
2425	25¢ Brontosaurus	.45	.15			1.25	101,747,000
a	Block of 4, #2422-25	2.00	1.00	2.25	(4)	3.00	
b	As "a," black omitted	1,100.00					
	America/PUAS Issue, Oct. 12 (See also #C121)						
2426	25¢ Southwest Carved Figure (A.D. 1150-1350), Emblem of the Postal Union of the Americas	.45	.15	2.00	(4)	1.25	137,410,000
	Christmas Issue, Oct. 19, Perf. 11.5						
2427	25¢ Madonna and Child, by Caracci	.45	.15	1.90	(4)	1.25	913,335,000
a	Booklet pane of 10	4.50	—			6.00	
	Perf. 11						
2428	25¢ Sleigh Full of Presents	.45	.15	1.90	(4)	1.25	900,000,000
a	Vertical pair, imperf. horizontally	2,000.00					
	Booklet Stamp Issue, Perf. 11.5						
2429	25¢ Single from booklet pane (#2428)	.45	.15				399,243,000
a	Booklet pane of 10	4.50	—			6.00	39,924,300
b	As "a," imperf. horiz. between	—					
c	As "a," red omitted	—					
	In #2429, runners on sleigh are twice as thick as in #2428; bow on package at rear of sleigh is same color as package; board running underneath sleigh is pink.						
2430	Not assigned						
	Self-Adhesive, Die-Cut						
2431	25¢ Eagle and Shield, Nov. 10	.50	.20			1.00	75,441,000
a	Booklet pane of 18	9.00					
b	Vertical pair, no die-cutting between	850.00					
2432	Not assigned						

2419

2420

2421

2422   **2423**

2426

2424   **2425**   **2425a**

2427

2428

2431

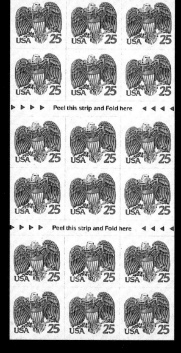

2431a

2431 (coil)

WORLD STAMP EXPO'89

The classic 1869 U.S. Abraham Lincoln stamp is reborn in these four larger versions commemorating World Stamp Expo'89, held in Washington, D.C. during the 20th Universal Postal Congress of the UPU. These stamps show the issued colors and three of the trial proof color combinations.

2433

2434   **2435**

2436   **2437**   **2437a**

20th Universal Postal Congress

A review of historical methods of delivering the mail in the United States is the theme of these four stamps issued in commemoration of the convening of the 20th Universal Postal Congress in Washington, D.C. from November 13 through December 15, 1989. The United States, as host nation to the Congress for the first time in ninety-two years, welcomed more than 1,000 delegates from most of the member nations of the Universal Postal Union to the major international event.

2438

2439

2440

2442

2443

	Issues of 1989	Un	U	PB	#	FDC	Q
	World Stamp Expo '89 Issue Souvenir Sheet, Nov. 17, Imperf.						
2433	Reproduction of #122, 90¢ Lincoln, and three essays of #122	12.00	9.00			7.00	2,227,600
a-d	Single stamp from sheet	2.00	1.75				
	20th UPU Congress Issues, Classic Mail Transportation, Nov. 19, Perf. 11 (See also #C122-25)						
2434	25¢ Stagecoach	.45	.15			1.25	40,956,000
2435	25¢ Paddlewheel Steamer	.45	.15			1.25	40,956,000
2436	25¢ Biplane	.45	.15			1.25	40,956,000
2437	25¢ Depot-Hack Type Automobile	.45	.15			1.25	40,956,000
a	Block of 4, #2434-37	2.00	2.00	2.75	(4)	3.00	
b	As "a," dark blue omitted	1,000.00					
	Souvenir Sheet, Nov. 27, Imperf. (See also #C126)						
2438	Designs of #2434-37	4.00	1.75			2.00	2,047,200
a-d	Single stamp from sheet	.60	.25				
	Issues of 1990, Perf. 11						
2439	25¢ Idaho Statehood, Jan. 6	.45	.15	2.00	(4)	1.25	173,000,000
	Perf. 12.5 x 13						
2440	25¢ Love, January 18	.45	.15	2.00	(4)	1.25	886,220,000
a	Imperf. pair	850.00					
	Booklet Stamp, Perf. 11.5						
2441	25¢ Love, single from booklet	.45	.15			1.25	995,178,000
a	Booklet pane of 10, Jan. 18	4.50	—			6.00	
b	As "a," bright pink omitted	2,250.00					
	Black Heritage Issue, Ida B. Wells, Feb. 1, Perf. 11						
2442	25¢ Portrait of Ida B. Wells, Marchers in Background	.45	.15	2.00	(4)	1.25	153,125,000
	Beach Umbrella Booklet Issue, Perf. 11.5 x 11						
2443	15¢ Beach Umbrella, single from booklet	.28	.15			1.25	
a	Booklet pane of 10, Feb. 3	2.80	—			4.25	
b	As "a," blue omitted	1,500.00					

#2443 issued only in booklets. All stamps are imperf. at one side or imperf. at one side and bottom.

	Issues of 1990, Perf. 11	Un	U	PB	#	FDC	Q
2444	25¢ Wyoming Statehood, Feb. 23	.45	.15	2.00	(4)	1.25	169,495,000
	Classic Films Issue, Mar. 23						
2445	25¢ The Wizard of Oz	.70	.15			1.25	44,202,000
2446	25¢ Gone With the Wind	.70	.15			1.25	44,202,000
2447	25¢ Beau Geste	.70	.15			1.25	44,202,000
2448	25¢ Stagecoach	.70	.15			1.25	44,202,000
a	Block of 4, #2445-48	3.25	1.00	3.50	(4)	3.00	
	Literary Arts Issue, Marianne Moore, Apr. 18						
2449	25¢ Portrait of Marianne Moore	.45	.15	2.00	(4)	1.25	150,000,000
2450	Not assigned						
	Issues of 1990-92, Transportation Issue, Coil Stamps, Perf. 10 Vertically						
2451	4¢ Steam Carriage 1866, Jan. 25, 1991	.15	.15	1.25	(3)	1.25	
a	Imperf. pair	675.00					
2452	5¢ Circus Wagon 1900s, intaglio printing, Aug. 31	.15	.15	1.10	(3)	1.25	
2452B	5¢ Circus Wagon (2452), gravure printing	.15	.15	1.10	(3)		
2453	5¢ Canoe 1800s, precanceled, intaglio printing, May 25, 1991	.15	.15	1.50	(3)	1.25	
2454	5¢ Canoe 1800s, precanceled, gravure printing, Oct. 22, 1991	.15	.15	1.50	(3)	1.25	
2455-56	Not assigned						
2457	10¢ Tractor Trailer, Bureau precanceled, intaglio printing, May 25, 1991	.18	.18	2.00	(3)	1.25	
	Issue of 1994, Transportation Issue, Coil Stamps, Perf. 10 Vertically						
2458	10¢ Tractor Trailer, Bureau precanceled, gravure printing, May 25, 1994	.20	.20				
2459-63	Not assigned						
	Issues of 1990-92, Transportation Issue, Coil Stamps, Perf. 10 Vertically						
2464	23¢ Lunch Wagon 1890s, Apr. 12, 1991	.42	.15	3.75	(3)	1.25	
a	Imperf. pair	175.00					
2465-67	Not assigned						
2468	$1 Seaplane 1914, Apr. 20	1.75	.50	6.50	(3)	2.00	
2469	Not assigned						
	Issues of 1990 (continued), Lighthouses Booklet Issue, Apr. 26, Perf. 10 Vertically						
2470	25¢ Admiralty Head, WA	.45	.15			1.25	146,721,600
2471	25¢ Cape Hatteras, NC	.45	.15			1.25	146,721,600
2472	25¢ West Quoddy Head, ME	.45	.15			1.25	146,721,600
2473	25¢ American Shoals, FL	.45	.15			1.25	146,721,600
2474	25¢ Sandy Hook, NJ	.45	.15			1.25	146,721,600
a	Booklet pane of 5, #2470-74	2.50	—			4.00	146,721,600
b	As "a," white (USA 25) omitted	75.00					
	Self-Adhesive Issue, Die-Cut						
2475	25¢ Flag, single from pane	.50	.25			1.25	36,168,000
a	Pane of 12, May 18	6.00					3,140,000

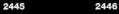

2444

2445

2446

2449

2447

2448   **2448a**

2451

2452

2453

2454

2457

2464

2468

2470

2471

2472

2473

2474

2474a

2476

2478

2479

2480

2481

2482

2487

2489

2491

2493

2494

2495

2496

2497

2498

2499

2500

2500a

2501

2502

2503

2504

2505

2505a

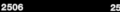

2506

2507

2507a

	Issues of 1990-1993	Un	U	PB	#	FDC	Q
	Wildlife Issue, Perf. 11						
2476	$2 Bobcat, June 1	3.00	1.25	13.50	(4)	5.00	
2477	Not assigned						
	Issues of 1993 (Self-Adhesive)						
2478	29¢ Red Squirrel	.50	.15				
2479	29¢ Rose	.50	.15				
2480	29¢ Pine cone	.50	.15				
	Issues of 1991-92						
2481	1¢ American Kestrel, June 22	.15	.15	.15	(4)	1.25	
2482	3¢ Eastern Bluebird, June 22	.15	.15	.30	(4)	1.25	
2483-86	Not assigned						
	Perf. 11.5 x 11						
2487	19¢ Fawn, Mar. 11	.35	.15	1.90	(4)	1.25	
2488	Not assigned						
2489	30¢ Cardinal, June 22	.50	.15	2.25	(4)	1.25	
2490	Not assigned						
2491	45¢ Pumpkinseed Sunfish, Dec. 2, 1992	.78	.15	3.90	(4)		
a	Black omitted	500.00	—				
2492	Not assigned						
	Wood Duck Booklet Issue, April 12, Perf. 10						
2493	29¢ Black and multicolored	.50	.15			1.25	
a	Booklet pane of 10	5.00				7.25	
	Perf. 11						
2494	29¢ Red and multicolored	.50	.15			1.25	
a	Booklet pane of 10	5.00				7.25	
2495	29¢ African Violet	.50	.15				
a	Booklet pane of 10	5.00					
	#2493-95a issued only in bklts. All stamps are imperf. top or bottom, or top or bottom and right edge.						
	Issues of 1990 (continued), Olympians Issue, July 6, Perf. 11						
2496	25¢ Jesse Owens	.45	.15			1.25	35,717,500
2497	25¢ Ray Ewry	.45	.15			1.25	35,717,500
2498	25¢ Hazel Wightman	.45	.15			1.25	35,717,500
2499	25¢ Eddie Eagan	.45	.15			1.25	35,717,500
2500	25¢ Helene Madison	.45	.15			1.25	35,717,500
a	Strip of 5, #2496-2500	2.50	—	5.00	(10)	3.00	7,143,500
	Indian Headdresses Booklet Issue, Aug. 17						
2501	25¢ Assiniboine Headdress	.45	.15			1.25	123,825,600
2502	25¢ Cheyenne Headdress	.45	.15			1.25	123,825,600
2503	25¢ Comanche Headdress	.45	.15			1.25	123,825,600
2504	25¢ Flathead Headdress	.45	.15			1.25	123,825,600
2505	25¢ Shoshone Headdress	.45	.15			1.25	123,825,600
a	Booklet pane of 10, 2 each of #2501-05	4.75	—			6.00	61,912,800
b	As "a," black omitted	—					
	#2501-05 issued only in booklets. All stamps imperf. top or bottom, or top or bottom and right edge.						
	Micronesia/Marshall Islands Issue, Sept. 28						
2506	25¢ Canoe and Flag of the Federated States of Micronesia	.45	.15			1.25	76,250,000
a	Black omitted	—					
2507	25¢ Stick Chart, Canoe and Flag of the Marshall Islands	.45	.15			1.25	76,250,000
a	Pair, #2506-07	1.00	.16	2.25	(4)	2.00	61,000,000

	Issues of 1990, Perf. 11	Un	U	PB	#	FDC	Q
	Creatures of the Sea Issue, Oct. 1						
2508	25¢ Killer Whales	.45	.15			1.25	69,566,000
2509	25¢ Northern Sea Lions	.45	.15			1.25	69,566,000
2510	25¢ Sea Otter	.45	.15			1.25	69,566,000
2511	25¢ Common Dolphin	.45	.15			1.25	69,566,000
a	Block of 4, #2508-11	2.00	—	2.25	(4)	3.00	69,566,000
b	As "a," black omitted	1,000.00					
	America/PUAS Issue, Oct. 12 (See also #C127)						
2512	25¢ Grand Canyon	.45	.15	2.00	(4)	1.25	150,760,000
2513	25¢ Dwight D. Eisenhower	.45	.15	2.00	(4)	1.25	142,692,000
a	Imperf. pair	2,000.00					
	Christmas Issue, Oct. 18, Perf. 11.5						
2514	25¢ Madonna and Child, by Antonello	.45	.15	2.00	(4)	1.25	499,995,000
a	Booklet pane of 10	4.50				6.00	22,892,400
	Perf. 11						
2515	25¢ Christmas Tree	.45	.15	2.00	(4)	1.25	599,400,000
	Booklet Stamp, Perf. 11.5 x 11 on two or three sides						
2516	Single (2515) from booklet pane	.45	.15			1.25	
a	Booklet pane of 10	4.50	—			6.00	32,030,400
	Issues of 1991, Perf. 13						
2517	(29¢) "F" Stamp, Jan. 22	.50	.15	2.50	(4)	1.25	
	Coil Stamp, Perf. 10 Vertically						
2518	(29¢) "F" Tulip (2517), Jan. 22	.50	.15	4.00	(3)	1.25	
	Booklet Stamps, Perf. 11 on two or three sides						
2519	(29¢) "F", single from booklet	.50	.15			1.25	
a	Booklet pane of 10, Jan. 22	5.50				7.25	
2520	(29¢) "F", single from booklet	.50	.15			1.25	
a	Booklet pane of 10, Jan. 22	6.25				7.25	
	#2519 has bull's-eye perforations that measure approximately 11.2. #2520 has less-pronounced black lines in the leaf, which is a much brighter green than on #2519.						
	Perf. 11						
2521	(4¢) Makeup Rate, Jan. 22	.15	.15	.40	(4)	1.25	
	Self-Adhesive, Die-Cut, Imperf.						
2522	(29¢) F Flag, single from pane	.50	.25			1.25	
a	Pane of 12	6.00				8.25	
	Coil Stamps, Perf. 10 Vertically						
2523	29¢ Flag Over Mt. Rushmore, intaglio printing, Mar. 29	.50	.15	4.75	(3)	1.25	
b	Imperf. pair	20.00					
2523A	29¢ Flag Over Mt. Rushmore, gravure printing, July 4	.50	.15	4.50	(3)	1.25	
	Perf. 11						
2524	29¢ Tulip, Apr. 5	.50	.15	2.25	(4)	1.25	
a	Perf. 13	.50	.15				
	Coil Stamps, Roulette 10 Vertically						
2525	29¢ Tulip, Aug. 16	.50	.15	4.50	(3)	1.25	
	Perf. 10 Vertically						
2526	29¢ Tulip, Mar. 3	.50	.15	4.75	(3)		
	Booklet Stamp, Perf. 11 on two or three sides						
2527	29¢ Tulip (2524), single from bklt.	.50	.15			1.25	
a	Booklet pane of 10, Apr. 5	5.00				7.25	
b	As "a," vertically imperf. between —						

2508   **2509**

2510   **2511**   **2511a**

2512

2513

2514

2515

2517

2519

2520

2521

2522

2523

2523A

2524

2525

2526

1991

2528

2529

2529C

2530

2531

2531A

2532

2533

2534

2535

2537

2538

2539

2540

2541

2542

2543

2545

2546

2547

2548

2549

2549a

	Issues of 1991, Perf. 10	Un	U	PB	#	FDC	Q
	Flag With Olympic Rings Booklet Issue, Apr. 21						
2528	29¢ U.S. Flag, Olympic Rings, single from booklet	.50	.15			1.25	
a	Booklet pane of 10	5.00				7.25	
	Perf. 10 Vertically						
2529	19¢ Fishing Boat, Aug. 8	.35	.15	3.50	(3)	1.25	
a	New printing, Type II, 1993	.35	.15	3.75	(3)		
b	As "a," untagged	1.00	.42	9.50	(3)		
2529C	19¢ Fishing Boat, June 25, 1994, perf. 9.8	.50	.15	3.50	(3)	1.25	
	Type II stamps have finer dot pattern, smoother edges along type. #2529C has only one loop of rope tying up boat.						
	Ballooning Booklet Issue, May 17, Perf. 10						
2530	19¢ Overhead View of Balloon, single from booklet	.35	.15			1.25	
a	Booklet pane of 10	3.50				4.75	
	#2530 was issued only in booklets. All stamps are imperf. on one side or on one side and bottom.						
	Perf. 11						
2531	29¢ Flags on Parade, May 30	.50	.15	2.25	(4)	1.25	
	Self-Adhesive, Die-Cut, Imperf.						
2531A	29¢ Liberty Torch, single stamp from pane	.58	.25			1.25	
a	Pane of 18, June 25	10.50				12.00	
	Perf. 11						
2532	50¢ Founding of Switzerland, Feb. 22	1.00	.25	5.00	(4)	2.00	100,000,000
2533	29¢ Vermont Statehood, Mar. 1	.50	.15	2.50	(4)	1.25	181,,000
2534	29¢ Savings Bonds, Apr. 30	.50	.15	2.50	(4)	1.25	150,560,000
	Perf. 12.5 x 13						
2535	29¢ Love, May 9	.50	.15	2.50	(4)	1.25	631,330,000
	Booklet Stamp, Perf. 11 on two or three sides						
2536	29¢ (2535), single from booklet	.50	.15			1.25	
a	Booklet pane of 10, May 9	5.00				7.25	
	Perf. 11						
2537	52¢ Love, May 9	.90	.20	4.50	(4)	2.00	200,000,000
	Literary Arts Issue, William Saroyan, May 22						
2538	29¢ Portrait of Saroyan	.50	.15	2.50	(4)	1.25	161,498,000
2539	$1 USPS Logo/Olympic Rings, Sept. 29	1.75	.50	7.75	(4)	1.25	
2540	$2.90 Priority Mail, July 7	5.00	2.50	25.00	(4)	6.00	
2541	$9.95 Domestic Express Mail, June 16	15.00	7.50	85.00	(4)	20.00	
2542	$14 International Express Mail, Aug. 31	22.50	10.00	110.00	(4)	28.00	
2543	$2.90 Space Vehicle, 1993	5.00	—	25.00	(4)		
	Fishing Flies Booklet Issue, May 31, Perf. 11 Horizontally						
2545	29¢ Royal Wulff	.50	.15			1.25	148,983,600
2546	29¢ Jock Scott	.50	.15			1.25	148,983,600
2547	29¢ Apte Tarpon Fly	.50	.15			1.25	148,983,600
2548	29¢ Lefty's Deceiver	.50	.15			1.25	148,983,600
2549	29¢ Muddler Minnow	.50	.15			1.25	148,983,600
a	Booklet pane of 5, #2545-49	2.50	—			4.50	148,983,600
	#2545-49 were issued only in booklets. All stamps are imperf. at sides or imperf. at sides and bottom.						

	Issues of 1991, Perf. 11	Un	U	PB	#	FDC	Q
	Performing Arts Issue, Cole Porter, June 8, Perf. 11						
2550	29¢ Portrait of Porter at Piano, Sheet Music	.50	.15	2.50	(4)	1.25	149,848,000
a	Vertical pair, imperf. horizontally	600.00					
2551	29¢ Operations Desert Shield/ Desert Storm, July 2	.50	.15	2.50	(4)	1.25	200,003,000
	Booklet Stamp, Perf. 11 on one or two sides						
2552	29¢ Operations Desert Shield/ Desert Storm (2551), July 2, single from booklet	.50	.15			1.25	200,000,000
a	Booklet pane of 5	2.50	—	4.50			40,000,000
	Summer Olympic Games Issue, July 12						
2553	29¢ Pole Vaulter	.50	.15			1.25	34,005,120
2554	29¢ Discus Thrower	.50	.15			1.25	34,005,120
2555	29¢ Women Sprinters	.50	.15			1.25	34,005,120
2556	29¢ Javelin Thrower	.50	.15			1.25	34,005,120
2557	29¢ Women Hurdlers	.50	.15			1.25	34,005,120
a	Strip of 5, #2553-57	2.50		5.50	(10)	3.25	34,005,120
2558	29¢ Numismatics, Aug. 13	.50	.15	2.50	(4)	1.25	150,310,000
	World War II Miniature Sheet, Sept. 3						
2559	Sheet of 10 and central label	5.25	—			6.00	15,218,000
a	29¢ Burma Road	.52	.29			1.25	15,218,000
b	29¢ America's First Peacetime Draft	.52	.29			1.25	15,218,000
c	29¢ Lend-Lease Act	.52	.29			1.25	15,218,000
d	29¢ Atlantic Charter	.52	.29			1.25	15,218,000
e	29¢ Arsenal of Democracy	.52	.29			1.25	15,218,000
f	29¢ Destroyer *Reuben James*	.52	.29			1.25	15,218,000
g	29¢ Civil Defense	.52	.29			1.25	15,218,000
h	29¢ Liberty Ship	.52	.29			1.25	15,218,000
i	29¢ Pearl Harbor	.52	.29			1.25	15,218,000
j	29¢ U.S. Declaration of War	.52	.29			1.25	15,218,000
2560	29¢ Basketball, Aug. 28	.50	.15	2.50	(4)	1.25	149,810,000
2561	29¢ District of Columbia, Sept. 7	.50	.15	2.50	(4)	1.25	149,260,000
	Comedians Booklet Issue, Aug. 29, Perf. 11 on two or three sides						
2562	29¢ Stan Laurel and Oliver Hardy	.50	.15			1.25	139,995,600
2563	29¢ Edgar Bergen and Dummy Charlie McCarthy	.50	.15			1.25	139,995,600
2564	29¢ Jack Benny	.50	.15			1.25	139,995,600
2565	29¢ Fanny Brice	.50	.15			1.25	139,995,600
2566	29¢ Bud Abbott and Lou Costello	.50	.15			1.25	139,995,600
a	Booklet pane of 10, 2 each of #2562-66	5.50	—			7.25	69,997,800
b	As "a," scarlet and bright violet omitted	750.00					
	#2562-66 issued only in booklets. All stamps are imperf. at top or bottom, or at top or bottom and right side.						
	Black Heritage Issue, Jan Matzeliger, Sept. 15, Perf. 11						
2567	29¢ Portrait of Matzeliger and Shoe-Lasting Machine Diagram	.50	.15	2.50	(4)	1.25	148,973,000

2550

2551

2553

2554

2555

2556

2557 2557a

a   b   c   d   e

1941: A World at War

f   g   h   i   j   2559

2562   2563   2564   2565   2566

2558

2560

2561

2567

2568 **2569** **2570** **2571** **2572**

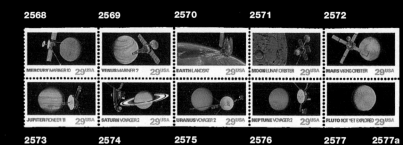

2573 **2574** **2575** **2576** **2577** **2577a**

2578

2579 **2580** **2581** **2581A**

2582 **2583** **2584** **2585**

2590 **2592**

2593 **2594** **2595** **2596** **2597**

	Issues of 1991, Perf. 11	Un	U	PB	#	FDC	Q
	Space Exploration Booklet Issue, Oct. 1						
2568	29¢ Mercury, Mariner 10	.50	.15			1.25	33,394,800
2569	29¢ Venus, Mariner 2	.50	.15			1.25	33,394,800
2570	29¢ Earth, Landsat	.50	.15			1.25	33,394,800
2571	29¢ Moon, Lunar Orbiter	.50	.15			1.25	33,394,800
2572	29¢ Mars, Viking Orbiter	.50	.15			1.25	33,394,800
2573	29¢ Jupiter, Pioneer 11	.50	.15			1.25	33,394,800
2574	29¢ Saturn, Voyager 2	.50	.15			1.25	33,394,800
2575	29¢ Uranus, Voyager 2	.50	.15			1.25	33,394,800
2576	29¢ Neptune, Voyager 2	.50	.15			1.25	33,394,800
2577	29¢ Pluto	.50	.15			1.25	33,394,800
a	Booklet pane of 10, #2568-77	5.50	—			7.25	33,394,800
	#2568-77 issued only in booklets. All stamps are imperf. at top or bottom, or at top or bottom and right side.						
	Christmas Issue, Oct. 17, Perf. 11						
2578	29¢ Madonna and Child, by Romano	.50	.15	2.50	(4)	1.25	401,000,000
a	Booklet pane of 10	5.80					30,000,000
2579	29¢ Santa Claus Sliding Down Chimney	.50	.15	2.50	(4)	1.25	900,000,000
	Booklet Stamps						
2580	29¢ Santa Claus Type I, single from booklet	.50	.15			1.25	
2581	29¢ Santa Claus Type II, single from booklet	.50	.15			1.25	
a	Pair, #2580, 2581	1.00	.25			3.50	28,000,000
	The extreme left brick in top row of chimney is missing from Type II, #2581.						
2582	29¢ Santa Claus Checking List, single from booklet	.50	.15			1.25	
a	Booklet pane of 4	2.00	—			3.50	28,000,000
2583	29¢ Santa Claus Leaving Present Under Tree, single from booklet	.50	.15			1.25	
a	Booklet pane of 4	2.00	—			3.50	28,000,000
2584	29¢ Santa Claus Going Up Chimney, single from booklet	.50	.15			1.25	
a	Booklet pane of 4	2.00	—			3.50	28,000,000
2585	29¢ Santa Claus Flying Away in Sleigh, single from booklet	.50	.15			1.25	
a	Booklet pane of 4	2.00	—			3.50	28,000,000
	#2582-85 issued only in booklets. All stamps are imperf. at top or bottom, or at top or bottom and right side.						
	Issues of 1994, Perf. 11.5						
2590	$1 Victory at Saratoga, May 5	2.00	.50	10.00	(4)	2.00	
2592	$5 Washington and Jackson, Aug. 19	10.00	—	50.00	(4)	7.50	
	Issue of 1992						
2593	29¢ Pledge of Allegiance	.50	.15			1.25	
a	Booklet of 10	5.00	—				
	Issue of 1993						
2594	29¢ Pledge of Allegiance	.50	.15				
a	Booklet of 10	5.00	—				
	Issues of 1992, Self-Adhesive Booklet and Coil Stamps, Sept. 25						
2595	29¢ Eagle and Shield (brown lettering)	.50	.25			1.25	
a	Pane of 17 + label	9.50					
2596	29¢ Eagle and Shield (green lettering)	.50	.25			1.25	
a	Pane of 17 + label	9.50					
2597	29¢ Eagle and Shield (red lettering)	.50	.25			1.25	
a	Pane of 17 + label	9.50					

	Issues of 1992 (continued), Perf. 10	Un	U	PB	#	FDC	Q
2598	29¢ Eagle, Self-Adhesive, Feb. 4	.50	.15				
2599	29¢ Statue of Liberty, June 24	.50	.15				
	Issues of 1991, Perf. 11						
2602	10¢ Eagle and Shield (inscribed "Bulk Rate USA"), Dec. 13	.20	.20	3.25	(3)		
2603	10¢ Eagle and Shield (inscribed "USA Bulk Rate")	.40	.40				
2604	10¢ Eagle and Shield (metallic, inscribed "USA Bulk Rate")	.40	.40				
2605	23¢ Flag, Presorted First-Class	.40	.40	4.50	(3)		
	Issues of 1992						
2606	23¢ USA, July 21	.40	.40	3.75	(3)		
2607	23¢ USA (Bureau) (In #2607, "23" is 7mm long)	.40	.15	3.75	(3)		
2608	23¢ USA (violet)	.40	.40	3.75	(3)		
2609	29¢ Flag Over White House, April 23	.50	.15	5.00	(3)	1.25	
	Winter Olympic Games Issue						
2611	29¢ Hockey	.50	.15			1.25	32,000,000
2612	29¢ Figure Skating	.50	.15			1.25	32,000,000
2613	29¢ Speed Skating	.50	.15			1.25	32,000,000
2614	29¢ Skiing	.50	.15			1.25	32,000,000
2615	29¢ Bobsledding	.50	.15			1.25	32,000,000
a	Strip of 5, #2611-15	2.50	—	5.50	(10)		
2616	29¢ World Columbian Stamp Expo, Jan. 24	.50	.15	2.50	(4)	1.25	148,665,000
	Black Heritage Issue						
2617	29¢ W.E.B. DuBois, Jan. 31	.50	.15	2.50	(4)	1.25	149,990,000
2618	29¢ Love, Feb. 6	.50	.15	2.50	(4)	1.25	835,000,000
2619	29¢ Olympic Baseball, April 3	.50	.15	2.50	(4)	1.25	160,000,000
	First Voyage of Christopher Columbus Issue, April 24						
2620	29¢ Seeking Queen Isabella's Support	.50	.15			1.25	40,005,000
2621	29¢ Crossing The Atlantic	.50	.15			1.25	40,005,000
2622	29¢ Approaching Land	.50	.15			1.25	40,005,000
2623	29¢ Coming Ashore	.50	.15			1.25	40,005,000
a	Block of 4, #2620-23	2.00	1.00	2.50	(4)	3.00	

W.E.B. DuBois

William Edward Burghardt DuBois (1868-1963) was an African-American civil rights leader and intellectual. DuBois earned a Ph.D. from Harvard and taught history and economics at Atlanta University. He co-founded the National Negro Committee in 1909, which later became the National Association for the Advancement of Colored People (NAACP). DuBois was editor of the NAACP magazine *Crisis* until 1932. A first-rate scholar and eloquent speaker, DuBois promoted worldwide black liberation and pan-Africanism. **(#2617)**

2598　　**2599**　　**2602**　　**2603**　　**2604**

2605　　**2606**　　**2607**　　**2608**　　**2609**

2611　　**2612**　　**2613**　　**2614**　　**2615**　　**2615a**

2616　　**2617**

2618

2619

2620　　　　**2621**

2622　　**2623**　　**2623a**

2624

2625

2626

2627

2628

2629

	Issues of 1992, Perf. 10.5	Un	U	FDC	Q
	The Voyages of Columbus Souvenir Sheets, May 22				
2624	First Sighting of Land, sheet of 3	1.60	—	2.10	2,000,000
a	1¢ deep blue	.15	.15	1.25	
b	4¢ ultramarine	.15	.15	1.25	
c	$1 salmon	1.50	1.00	2.00	
2625	Claiming a New World, sheet of 3	6.25	—	8.10	2,000,000
a	2¢ brown violet	.15	.15	1.25	
b	3¢ green	.15	.15	1.25	
c	$4 crimson lake	6.00	4.00	8.00	
2626	Seeking Royal Support, sheet of 3	1.25	—	1.70	2,000,000
a	5¢ chocolate	.15	.15	1.25	
b	30¢ orange brown	.45	.30	1.25	
c	50¢ slate blue	.75	.50	1.50	
2627	Royal Favor Restored, sheet of 3	4.75	—	6.25	2,000,000
a	6¢ purple	.15	.15	1.25	
b	8¢ magenta	.15	.15	1.25	
c	$3 yellow green	4.50	3.00	6.00	
2628	Reporting Discoveries, sheet of 3	3.50	—	4.50	2,000,000
a	10¢ black brown	.15	.15	1.25	
b	15¢ dark green	.22	.15	1.25	
c	$2 brown red	3.00	2.00	4.00	
2629	$5 Christopher Columbus, sheet of 1	7.75	—	10.00	2,000,000

Three errors that led to the New World

When Christopher Columbus left the small port town of Palos on August 3, 1492, he sailed west under three assumptions: the exactness of Marco Polo's location of Japan as 1500 miles east of China, the accuracy of Ptolemy's estimations of the earth's circumference and the size of the Eurasian land mass. These figures should have placed Japan 3000 miles west of Portugal. Of course, both Marco Polo and Ptolemy were wrong and Columbus ended up half a world away from his destination of the Far East, landing in San Salvador on October 12, 1492. **(#2625)**

Interesting Fact: Martin Alonzo Pinzon commanded the *Pinta* and his younger brother Vincente Vanez Pinzon commanded the *Nina*.

	Issues of 1992, Perf. 11	Un	U	PB	#	FDC	Q
2630	29¢ New York Stock Exchange Bicentennial, May 17	.50	.15	2.50	(4)	1.25	148,000,000
	Space Adventures Issue, May 29						
2631	29¢ Cosmonaut, US Space Shuttle	.50	.15			1.25	37,315,000
2632	29¢ Astronaut, Russian Space Station	.50	.15			1.25	37,315,000
2633	29¢ Sputnik, Vostok, Apollo Command and Lunar Modules	.50	.15			1.25	37,315,000
2634	29¢ Soyuz, Mercury and Gemini Spacecraft	.50	.15			1.25	37,315,000
a	Block of 4, #2631-34	2.00	1.00	2.50	(4)	3.00	
2635	29¢ Alaska Highway, 50th Anniversary, May 30	.50	.15	2.50	(4)	1.25	146,610,000
a	Black (engr.) omitted	700.00					
2636	29¢ Kentucky Statehood Bicentennial, June 11	.50	.15	2.50	(4)	1.25	160,000,000
	Summer Olympic Games Issue, June 1						
2637	29¢ Soccer	.50	.15			1.25	32,000,000
2638	29¢ Gymnastics	.50	.15			1.25	32,000,000
2639	29¢ Volleyball	.50	.15			1.25	32,000,000
2640	29¢ Boxing	.50	.15			1.25	32,000,000
2641	29¢ Swimming	.50	.15			1.25	32,000,000
a	Strip of 5, #2637-41	2.50	—	5.50	(10)	4.00	
	Hummingbirds Issue, June 15						
2642	29¢ Ruby-Throated	.50	.15			1.25	87,728,000
2643	29¢ Broad-Billed	.50	.15			1.25	87,728,000
2644	29¢ Costa's	.50	.15			1.25	87,728,000
2645	29¢ Rufous	.50	.15			1.25	87,728,000
2646	29¢ Calliope	.50	.15			1.25	87,728,000
a	Booklet pane of 5, #2642-46	2.50	—			4.00	

How did the U.S. switch partners in space?

The first seeds of U.S.-Russian cooperation in space was the Apollo-Soyuz Test Project. On July 17, 1975, a U.S. Apollo spacecraft docked in orbit with a Soviet Soyuz spacecraft, and crew members conducted two days of joint scientific experiments. When the joint missions of the 1990s were first discussed, the Soviet Union was America's partner; by the time these stamps had been released, however, that partner had become the single country of Russia, due to the fall of communism and the breakup of the Soviet Union. (#2631-34)

2630

2631   **2632**

2633   **2634**   **2634a**

2635

2636

2637   **2638**   **2639**   **2640**   **2641**   **2641a**

2647	2648	2649	2650	2651

Indian Paintbrush — Fragrant Water Lily — Meadow Beauty — Jack-in-the-Pulpit — California Poppy

2652	2653	2654	2655	2656

Large-flowered Trillium — Tickseed — Shooting Star — Stream Violet — Bluets

2657	2658	2659	2660	2661

Herb Robert — Marsh Marigold — Sweet White Violet — Claret Cup Cactus — White Mountain Avens

2662	2663	2664	2665	2666

Sessile Bellwort — Blue Flag — Harlequin Lupine — Twinflower — Common Sunflower

2667	2668	2669	2670	2671

Sego Lily — Virginia Bluebells — Ohi's Lehua — Rosebud Orchid — Showy Evening Primrose

	Issues of 1992, Perf. 11	Un	U	FDC	Q
	Wildflowers Issue, July 24				
2647	29¢ Indian Paintbrush	.50	.15	1.25	11,000,000
2648	29¢ Fragrant Water Lily	.50	.15	1.25	11,000,000
2649	29¢ Meadow Beauty	.50	.15	1.25	11,000,000
2650	29¢ Jack-in-the-Pulpit	.50	.15	1.25	11,000,000
2651	29¢ California Poppy	.50	.15	1.25	11,000,000
2652	29¢ Large-Flowered Trillium	.50	.15	1.25	11,000,000
2653	29¢ Tickseed	.50	.15	1.25	11,000,000
2654	29¢ Shooting Star	.50	.15	1.25	11,000,000
2655	29¢ Stream Violet	.50	.15	1.25	11,000,000
2656	29¢ Bluets	.50	.15	1.25	11,000,000
2657	29¢ Herb Robert	.50	.15	1.25	11,000,000
2658	29¢ Marsh Marigold	.50	.15	1.25	11,000,000
2659	29¢ Sweet White Violet	.50	.15	1.25	11,000,000
2660	29¢ Claret Cup Cactus	.50	.15	1.25	11,000,000
2661	29¢ White Mountain Avens	.50	.15	1.25	11,000,000
2662	29¢ Sessile Bellwort	.50	.15	1.25	11,000,000
2663	29¢ Blue Flag	.50	.15	1.25	11,000,000
2664	29¢ Harlequin Lupine	.50	.15	1.25	11,000,000
2665	29¢ Twinflower	.50	.15	1.25	11,000,000
2666	29¢ Common Sunflower	.50	.15	1.25	11,000,000
2667	29¢ Sego Lily	.50	.15	1.25	11,000,000
2668	29¢ Virginia Bluebells	.50	.15	1.25	11,000,000
2669	29¢ Ohi'a Lehua	.50	.15	1.25	11,000,000
2670	29¢ Rosebud Orchid	.50	.15	1.25	11,000,000
2671	29¢ Showy Evening Primrose	.50	.15	1.25	11,000,000

The Blue Beard-less iris

The Blue Flag iris (*I. Cristata*) is a hybrid iris that is small, crested and beardless. Beardless and crested are characteristics of the flower's three sepals, which enclose the bud, surrounding and protecting the petals before the flower blossoms. **(#2663)**

Interesting Fact: The genus of the Blue Flag was named after Iris, the personification of the rainbow in Greek mythology.

	Issues of 1992, Perf. 11	Un	U	PB	#	FDC	Q
	Wildflowers Issue (continued)						
2672	29¢ Fringed Gentian	.50	.15			1.25	11,000,000
2673	29¢ Yellow Lady's Slipper	.50	.15			1.25	11,000,000
2674	29¢ Passionflower	.50	.15			1.25	11,000,000
2675	29¢ Bunchberry	.50	.15			1.25	11,000,000
2676	29¢ Pasqueflower	.50	.15			1.25	11,000,000
2677	29¢ Round-Lobed Hepatica	.50	.15			1.25	11,000,000
2678	29¢ Wild Columbine	.50	.15			1.25	11,000,000
2679	29¢ Fireweed	.50	.15			1.25	11,000,000
2680	29¢ Indian Pond Lily	.50	.15			1.25	11,000,000
2681	29¢ Turk's Cap Lily	.50	.15			1.25	11,000,000
2682	29¢ Dutchman's Breeches	.50	.15			1.25	11,000,000
2683	29¢ Trumpet Honeysuckle	.50	.15			1.25	11,000,000
2684	29¢ Jacob's Ladder	.50	.15			1.25	11,000,000
2685	29¢ Plains Prickly Pear	.50	.15			1.25	11,000,000
2686	29¢ Moss Campion	.50	.15			1.25	11,000,000
2687	29¢ Bearberry	.50	.15			1.25	11,000,000
2688	29¢ Mexican Hat	.50	.15			1.25	11,000,000
2689	29¢ Harebell	.50	.15			1.25	11,000,000
2690	29¢ Desert Five Spot	.50	.15			1.25	11,000,000
2691	29¢ Smooth Solomon's Seal	.50	.15			1.25	11,000,000
2692	29¢ Red Maids	.50	.15			1.25	11,000,000
2693	29¢ Yellow Skunk Cabbage	.50	.15			1.25	11,000,000
2694	29¢ Rue Anemone	.50	.15			1.25	11,000,000
2695	29¢ Standing Cypress	.50	.15			1.25	11,000,000
2696	29¢ Wild Flax	.50	.15			1.25	11,000,000
a	Pane of 50, #2647-96	25.00	—			32.50	11,000,000

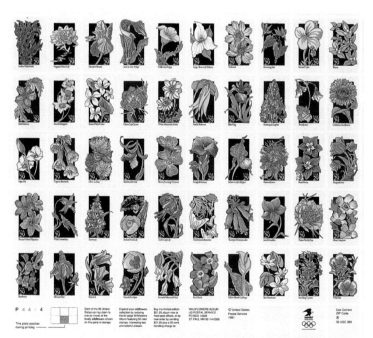

Example of #2696a.

Fringed Gentian — 2672
Yellow Lady's Slipper — 2673
Passionflower — 2674
Bunchberry — 2675
Pasqueflower — 2676

Round-lobed Hepatica — 2677
Wild Columbine — 2678
Fireweed — 2679
Indian Pond Lily — 2680
Turk's Cap Lily — 2681

Dutchman's Breeches — 2682
Trumpet Honeysuckle — 2683
Jacob's Ladder — 2684
Plains Prickly Pear — 2685
Moss Campion — 2686

Bearberry — 2687
Mexican Hat — 2688
Harebell — 2689
Desert Five Spot — 2690
Smooth Solomon's Seal — 2691

Red Maids — 2692
Yellow Skunk Cabbage — 2693
Rue Anemone — 2694
Standing Cypress — 2695
Wild Flax — 2696

a — 29 USA — *B-25s take off to raid Tokyo April 18, 1942*

b — 29 USA — *Food and other commodities rationed, 1942*

c — 29 USA — *U.S. wins Battle of the Coral Sea May 1942*

d — 29 USA — *Corregidor falls to Japanese May 6, 1942*

e — 29 USA — *Japan invades Aleutian Islands June 1942*

1942: Into the Battle

29 USA — *Allies decipher secret enemy codes, 1942*

29 USA — *Yorktown lost, U.S. wins at Midway, 1942*

29 USA — *Millions of women join war effort, 1942*

29 USA — *Marines land on Guadalcanal Aug. 7, 1942*

29 USA — *Allies land in North Africa November 1942*

f   g   h   i   j   2697

29 USA — Dorothy Parker — American Writer 1893–1967

2698

Theodore von Kármán — Aerospace Scientist — USA 29

2699

2700   2701

Minerals USA 29 — Azurite

Minerals USA 29 — Copper

Minerals USA 29 — Variscite

Minerals USA 29 — Wulfenite

2702   2703   2703a

Explorer of California 1542 — 29 USA — Juan Rodríguez CABRILLO

2704

	Issues of 1992, Perf. 11	Un	U	PB	#	FDC	Q
	World War II Issue Miniature Sheet, Aug. 17						
2697	Sheet of 10 and central label	5.25	2.90				12,000,000
a	29¢ B-25s Take Off to Raid Tokyo	.52	.29			1.25	12,000,000
b	29¢ Food and Other Commodities Rationed	.52	.29			1.25	12,000,000
c	29¢ U.S. Wins Battle of the Coral Sea	.52	.29			1.25	12,000,000
d	29¢ Corregidor Falls to Japanese	.52	.29			1.25	12,000,000
e	29¢ Japan Invades Aleutian Islands	.52	.29			1.25	12,000,000
f	29¢ Allies Decipher Secret Enemy Codes	.52	.29			1.25	12,000,000
g	29¢ *Yorktown* Lost	.52	.29			1.25	12,000,000
h	29¢ Millions of Women Join War Effort	.52	.29			1.25	12,000,000
i	29¢ Marines Land on Guadalcanal	.52	.29			1.25	12,000,000
j	29¢ Allies Land in North Africa	.52	.29			1.25	12,000,000
2698	29¢ Dorothy Parker, Aug. 22	.50	.15	2.50	(4)	1.25	105,000,000
2699	29¢ Dr. Theodore von Karman, Aug. 31	.50	.15	2.50	(4)	1.25	142,500,000
	Minerals Issue, Sept. 17						
2700	29¢ Azurite	.50	.15			1.25	36,831,000
2701	29¢ Copper	.50	.15			1.25	36,831,000
2702	29¢ Variscite	.50	.15			1.25	36,831,000
2703	29¢ Wulfenite	.50	.15			1.25	36,831,000
a	Block of 4, #2700-03	2.00	1.10	2.50	(4)	3.00	
2704	29¢ Juan Rodriguez Cabrillo, Sept. 28	.50	.15	2.50	(4)	1.25	85,000,000

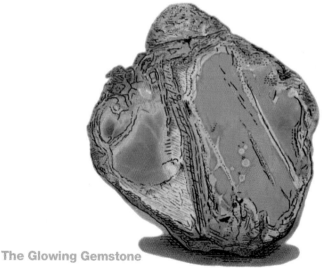

The Glowing Gemstone

Valued as a semiprecious gemstone, variscite is cut *en cabochon* (with a round, convex, polished surface) for use in jewelry designed and carved into bowls and other decorative objects. Usually green, variscite forms as glassy nodules, veins or crusts in near-surface rock deposits. Because it is a phosphate mineral, it appears to give off an eerie, beautiful glow. **(#2702)**

Interesting Fact: The largest deposit of variscite in the United States is found in Fairfield, Utah.

	Issues of 1992, Perf. 11	Un	U	PB	#	FDC	Q
	Wild Animals Issue, Oct. 1, Horizontal						
2705	29¢ Giraffe	.50	.15			1.25	80,000,000
2706	29¢ Giant Panda	.50	.15			1.25	80,000,000
2707	29¢ Flamingo	.50	.15			1.25	80,000,000
2708	29¢ King Penguins	.50	.15			1.25	80,000,000
2709	29¢ White Bengal Tiger	.50	.15			1.25	80,000,000
a	Booklet pane of 5, #2705-09	2.50	—			4.00	
	Christmas Issue, Oct. 22, Perf. 11.5 x 11						
2710	29¢ Madonna and Child by Giovanni Bellini	.50	.15	2.50	(4)	1.25	300,000,000
a	Booklet pane of 10	5.00					349,254,000
2711	29¢ Horse and Rider	.50	.15			1.25	125,000,000
2712	29¢ Toy Train	.50	.15			1.25	125,000,000
2713	29¢ Toy Steamer	.50	.15			1.25	125,000,000
2714	29¢ Toy Ship	.50	.15			1.25	125,000,000
a	Block of 4, #2711-14	2.00		2.50	(4)	3.00	
	Perf. 11						
2715	29¢ Horse and Rider	.50	.15			1.25	102,137,500
2716	29¢ Toy Train	.50	.15			1.25	102,137,500
2717	29¢ Toy Steamer	.50	.15			1.25	102,137,500
2718	29¢ Toy Ship	.50	.15			1.25	102,137,500
a	Booklet pane of 4, #2715-18	2.00	—			3.00	
2719	29¢ Toy Train (self-adhesive)	.58	.15			1.25	21,600,000
a	Booklet pane of 18	10.50					
2720	29¢ Happy New Year	.50	.15	2.50	(4)		

A toy train graces this self-adhesive sheet of 18 greeting stamps designed for use in Automated Teller Machines (ATMs). The sheet must be the same size and thickness as U.S. currency in order to be vended by ATMs. **(#2719a)**

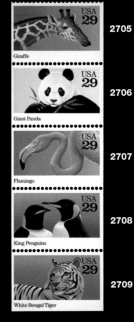

2705
2706
2707
2708
2709

2709a

Giraffe
Giant Panda
Flamingo
King Penguins
White Bengal Tiger

CHRISTMAS

Bellini c.1480 National Gallery

2710

2711   2712

GREETINGS   GREETINGS

GREETINGS   GREETINGS

2713   2714   2714a

2715   2716

GREETINGS   GREETINGS

GREETINGS   GREETINGS

2717   2718   2718a

GREETINGS

2719

HAPPY NEW YEAR!

2720

2721

2722

2723

2724   2725   2726   2727   2728

2729   2730

 2731

 2732

 2733

2734

 2735

 2736

 2737

 2731

2737a   2737b

	Issues of 1993, Perf. 11	Un	U	PB	#	FDC	Q
	American Music Series						
2721	29¢ Elvis Presley	.50	.15	2.50	(4)	1.25	517,000,000
	Perf. 10						
2722	29¢ Oklahoma!	.50	.15	2.50	(4)	1.25	150,000,000
2723	29¢ Hank Williams	.50	.15	2.50	(4)	1.25	152,000,000
	Rock & Roll/Rhythm & Blues Issue						
2724	29¢ Elvis Presley	.50	.15			1.25	14,285,715
2725	29¢ Bill Haley	.50	.15			1.25	14,285,715
2726	29¢ Clyde McPhatter	.50	.15			1.25	14,285,715
2727	29¢ Ritchie Valens	.50	.15			1.25	14,285,715
2728	29¢ Otis Redding	.50	.15			1.25	14,285,715
2729	29¢ Buddy Holly	.50	.15			1.25	14,285,715
2730	29¢ Dinah Washington	.50	.15			1.25	14,285,715
a	Vertical strip of 7, #2724-30	3.50	—	17.50	(35)	5.00	
	Perf. 11 Horizontal						
2731	29¢ Elvis Presley	.50	.15			1.25	98,841,000
2732	29¢ Bill Haley (2725)	.50	.15			1.25	32,947,000
2733	29¢ Clyde McPhatter (2726)	.50	.15			1.25	32,947,000
2734	29¢ Ritchie Valens (2727)	.50	.15			1.25	32,947,000
2735	29¢ Otis Redding	.50	.15			1.25	65,894,000
2736	29¢ Buddy Holly	.50	.15			1.25	65,894,000
2737	29¢ Dinah Washington	.50	.15			1.25	65,894,000
a	Booklet pane, 2 #2731, 1 each #2732-37	4.00	—			5.25	
b	Booklet pane of 4, #2731, 2735-37	2.00	—			2.75	
2738-40 Not assigned							

Music that took the world by storm

Rock-and-roll is the hybrid of other American musical forms: blues, rhythm and blues, gospel, and country and western. Although black musicians established this genre, they were excluded from most radio play.

In 1955, Bill Haley and the Comets' "Rock Around the Clock" popularized rock-and-roll, but Elvis Presley is best known to have made rock-and-roll the dominant form of popular music. **(Full pane illustrated contains 5 strips of #2730a.)**

For more stamps of American musicians, see the Jazz stamps in the New Issues section.

	Issues of 1993, Perf. 11	Un	U	PB	#	FDC	Q
	Space Fantasy Issue, Jan. 25, Perf. 11 Vertical on 1 or 2 sides						
2741	29¢ multicolored	.50	.15			1.25	140,000,000
2742	29¢ multicolored	.50	.15			1.25	140,000,000
2743	29¢ multicolored	.50	.15			1.25	140,000,000
2744	29¢ multicolored	.50	.15			1.25	140,000,000
2745	29¢ multicolored	.50	.15			1.25	140,000,000
a	Booklet pane of 5, #2741-45	2.50				3.25	
2746	29¢ Percy Lavon Julian	.50	.15	2.50	(4)	1.25	105,000,000
2747	29¢ Oregon Trail	.50	.15	2.50	(4)	1.25	110,000,000
2748	29¢ World University Games	.50	.15	2.50	(4)	1.25	110,000,000
2749	29¢ Grace Kelly	.50	.15	2.50	(4)	1.25	172,870,000
	Circus Issue, Apr. 6						
2750	29¢ Clown	.50	.15			1.25	65,625,000
2751	29¢ Ringmaster	.50	.15			1.25	65,625,000
2752	29¢ Trapeze Artist	.50	.15			1.25	65,625,000
2753	29¢ Elephant	.50	.15			1.25	65,625,000
a	Block of 4 #2750-53	2.00	1.10	3.50	(6)	2.75	
2754	29¢ Cherokee Strip	.50	.15	2.50	(4)	1.25	110,000,000
2755	29¢ Dean Acheson	.50	.15	2.50	(4)	1.25	115,870,000
b	As "a," black omitted	—					
	Sporting Horses Issue, May 1, Perf. 11 x 11.5						
2756	29¢ Steeplechase	.50	.15			1.25	40,000,000
2757	29¢ Thoroughbred Racing	.50	.15			1.25	40,000,000
2758	29¢ Harness Racing	.50	.15			1.25	40,000,000
2759	29¢ Polo	.50	.15			1.25	40,000,000
a	Block of 4, #2756-59	2.00	1.10	2.50	(4)	2.75	

Example of #2753a. This is the arrangement of the images as originally designed and intended. Collectors and the general public couldn resist the urge to "joir the spotlight to create the arrangement many prefer, as shown on the opposite page.

2741   **2742**   **2743**   **2744**   **2745**   **2745a**

2747

2748

2746

2749

2750   **2751**

2754

2755

2752   **2753**   **2753a**

2756   **2757**

2758   **2759**   **2759a**

1993

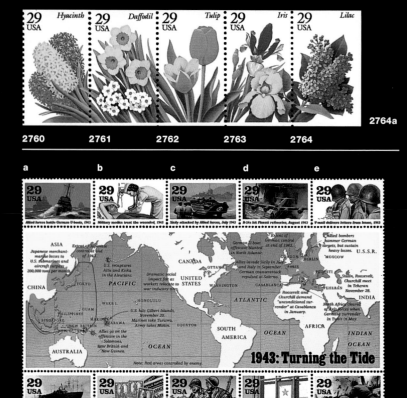

| 29 USA Hyacinth | 29 USA Daffodil | 29 USA Tulip | 29 USA Iris | 29 USA Lilac |

2764a

2760   2761   2762   2763   2764

a   b   c   d   e

1943: Turning the Tide

f   g   h   i   j   2765

2766

2767

2768

2769

2770

2770a

Issues of 1993, Perf. 11	Un	U	PB	#	FDC	Q
Garden Flowers Issue, May 15, Perf. 11 Vertical						
2760 29¢ Hyacinth	.50	.15			1.25	199,784,500
2761 29¢ Daffodil	.50	.15			1.25	199,784,500
2762 29¢ Tulip	.50	.15			1.25	199,784,500
2763 29¢ Iris	.50	.15			1.25	199,784,500
2764 29¢ Lilac	.50	.15			1.25	199,784,500
a Booklet pane of 5, #2760-64	2.50	—			3.25	
b As "a," black omitted	475.00					
c As "a," imperf.	3,000.00					
World War II Issue Miniature Sheet, May 31, Perf. 11						
2765 Sheet of 10 and central label	5.80	3.00			6.50	
a 29¢ Allied Forces Battle German U-boats	.58	.30			1.25	12,000,000
b 29¢ Military Medics Treat the Wounded	.58	.30			1.25	12,000,000
c 29¢ Sicily Attacked by Allied Forces	.58	.30			1.25	12,000,000
d 29¢ B-24s Hit Ploesti Refineries	.58	.30			1.25	12,000,000
e 29¢ V-Mail Delivers Letters from Home	.58	.30			1.25	12,000,000
f 29¢ Italy Invaded by Allies	.58	.30			1.25	12,000,000
g 29¢ Bonds and Stamps Help War Effort	.58	.30			1.25	12,000,000
h 29¢ "Willie and Joe" Keep Spirits High	.58	.30			1.25	12,000,000
i 29¢ Gold Stars Mark World War II Losses	.58	.30			1.25	12,000,000
j 29¢ Marines Assault Tarawa	.58	.30			1.25	12,000,000
2766 29¢ Joe Louis	.50	.15	2.50	(4)	1.25	160,000,000
American Music Series, July 14						
2767 29¢ Show Boat	.50	.15			1.25	128,735,000
2768 29¢ Porgy & Bess	.50	.15			1.25	128,735,000
2769 29¢ Oklahoma!	.50	.15			1.25	128,735,000
2770 29¢ My Fair Lady	.50	.15			1.25	128,735,000
a Booklet pane of 4, #2767-70	2.00				3.25	

What was the first modern musical?

Considered the first "modern" musical, *Oklahoma!* debuted on Broadway in 1943. With music by Richard Rogers, lyrics by Oscar Hammerstein II and choreography by Agnes DeMille, the show combined music, story and dance in a fully integrated format. Among the songs made famous by the show are "Oklahoma," and "Oh, What a Beautiful Morning." **(#2769)**

Note that the same design was produced in a sheet version, #2722.

	Issues of 1993, Perf. 10	Un	U	PB	#	FDC	Q
	Country & Western, American Music Series						
2771	29¢ Hank Williams (2775)	.50	.15			1.25	25,000,000
2772	29¢ Patsy Cline (2777)	.50	.15			1.25	25,000,000
2773	29¢ The Carter Family (2776)	.50	.15			1.25	25,000,000
2774	29¢ Bob Willis (2778)	.50	.15			1.25	25,000,000
a	Block or horiz. strip of 4, #2771-74	2.00	1.10	2.50	(4)	2.75	
	Booklet Stamps, Perf. 11 Horizontal						
2775	29¢ Hank Williams	.50	.15			1.25	170,000,000
2776	29¢ The Carter Family	.50	.15			1.25	170,000,000
2777	29¢ Patsy Cline	.50	.15			1.25	170,000,000
2778	29¢ Bob Willis	.50	.15			1.25	170,000,000
a	Booklet pane of 4, #2775-78	2.00	—			2.75	
	National Postal Museum Issue, July 30, Perf. 11						
2779	Independence Hall, Benjamin Franklin, Printing Press, Colonial Post Rider	.50	.15			1.25	37,500,000
2780	Pony Express Rider, Civil War Soldier, Concord Stagecoach	.50	.15			1.25	37,500,000
2781	Biplane, Charles Lindbergh, Railway Mail Car, 1931 Model A Ford Mail Truck	.50	.15			1.25	37,500,000
2782	California Gold Rush Miner's Letter, Barcode and Circular Date Stamp	.50	.15			1.25	37,500,000
a	Block or strip of 4, #2779-82	2.00	1.10	2.50	(4)	2.75	
	American Sign Language Issue, Sept. 20, Perf. 11.5						
2783	29¢ Recognizing Deafness	.50	.15			1.25	41,840,000
2784	29¢ American Sign Language	.50	.15			1.25	41,840,000
a	Pair, #2783-84	1.00	.20	2.50	(4)	2.00	
	Classic Books Issues, Oct. 23						
2785	29¢ *Rebecca of Sunnybrook Farm*	.50	.15			1.25	37,550,000
2786	29¢ *Little House on the Prairie*	.50	.15			1.25	37,550,000
2787	29¢ *The Adventures of Huckleberry Finn*	.50	.15			1.25	37,550,000
2788	29¢ *Little Women*	.50	.15			1.25	37,550,000
a	Block or horiz. strip of 4, #2785-88	2.00	1.10	2.50	(4)	2.75	

He put country music on the map

The seminal figure in modern country and western music, Alabama-born singer and guitarist Hank Williams (1923-1953) made his radio debut at age 13. In 1947 Williams became an international celebrity. Among his most famous songs are "Cold, Cold Heart," "Your Cheatin' Heart,"

"Hey, Good Lookin'," "Jambalaya" and "I'm So Lonesome I Could Cry." **(#2771)**

Note that the same design was produced in a sheet version, #2723.

Interesting Fact: Hank Williams recorded many songs under the pseudonym "Luke and the Drifting Cowboys."

2771 2772

2773 2774 2774a

2775

2776

2777

2778

2778a

2779 2780

2781 2782 2782a

2783 2784 2784a

2785 2786

2787 2788 2788a

2789

2790

2791 **2792**

2793 **2794**

2795 **2796**

2797 **2798**

2799 **2800**

2801 **2802** **2802a**

2803

2804

2805

2806

2806a

	Issues of 1993, Perf. 10	Un	U	PB	#	FDC	Q
	Christmas Issue, Oct. 21						
2789	29¢ Madonna and Child	.50	.15	2.50	(4)	1.25	500,000,000
	Booklet Stamps, Perf. 11.5 x 11 on 2 or 3 sides						
2790	29¢ Madonna and Child (2789)	.50	.15			1.25	500,000,000
a	Booklet pane of 4	2.00	—			2.00	
	Perf. 11.5						
2791	29¢ Jack-in-the-Box	.50	.15			1.25	250,000,000
2792	29¢ Red-Nosed Reindeer	.50	.15			1.25	250,000,000
2793	29¢ Snowman	.50	.15			1.25	250,000,000
2794	29¢ Toy Soldier	.50	.15			1.25	250,000,000
a	Block or strip of 4, #2791-94	2.00	1.10	2.50	(4)	2.75	
	Booklet Stamps, Perf 11 x 10 on 2 or 3 sides						
2795	29¢ Toy Soldier (2794)	.50	.15			1.25	200,000,000
2796	29¢ Snowman (2793)	.50	.15			1.25	200,000,000
2797	29¢ Red-Nosed Reindeer (2792)	.50	.15			1.25	200,000,000
2798	29¢ Jack-in-the-Box (2791)	.50	.15			1.25	200,000,000
a	Booklet pane, 3 each #2795-96, 2 each #2797-98	5.00	—			6.50	
b	Booklet pane, 3 each #2797-98, 2 each #2795-96	5.00	—			6.50	
	Self-adhesive						
2799	29¢ Snowman	.50	.15			1.25	120,000,000
2800	29¢ Toy Soldier	.50	.15			1.25	120,000,000
2801	29¢ Jack-in-the-Box	.50	.15			1.25	120,000,000
2802	29¢ Red-Nosed Reindeer	.50	.15			1.25	120,000,000
a	Booklet pane, 3 each #2799-802	6.00					
2803	29¢ Snowman	.50	.15			1.25	18,000,000
a	Booklet pane of 18	9.00					
	Perf. 11						
2804	29¢ Northern Mariana Islands	.50	.15	2.50	(4)	1.25	88,300,000
2805	29¢ Columbus Landing in Puerto Rico	.50	.15	2.50	(4)	1.25	105,000,000
2806	29¢ AIDS Awareness	.50	.15	2.50	(4)	1.25	100,000,000
a	Booklet version	.50	.15			1.25	250,000,000
b	Booklet pane of 5	2.50	—			3.25	

Examples
of #2794a (marginal
block of 10 with plate numbers, at left on top); 2802a (self-adhesive pane
of 12, at left on bottom); self-adhesive coil strip of 4 (top right); and 2798a
and 2798b, booklet and booklet panes (bottom right).

	Issues of 1994	Un	U	PB	#	FDC	Q
	Winter Olympic Games Issue, January 6, Perf. 11.2						
2807	29¢ Slalom	.50	.15			1.25	35,800,000
2808	29¢ Luge	.50	.15			1.25	35,800,000
2809	29¢ Ice Dancing	.50	.15			1.25	35,800,000
2810	29¢ Cross-Country Skiing	.50	.15			1.25	35,800,000
2811	29¢ Ice Hockey	.50	.15			1.25	35,800,000
a	Strip of 5, #2807-11	2.50	—	5.50	(10)	3.00	35,800,000
	Perf. 11.2						
2812	29¢ Edward R. Murrow, Jan. 21	.50	.15	2.50	(4)	1.25	150,500,000
2813	29¢ Love Sunrise, Jan. 27	.50	.15	5.00	(5)	1.25	357,949,584
a	Booklet of 18 (self-adhesive)	9.00					
	Perf. 10.9 x 11.1						
2814	29¢ Love Stamp, Feb. 14	.50	.15			1.25	830,000,000
a	Booklet pane of 10	5.00	—			6.50	
	Perf. 11.1						
2814C	29¢ Love Stamp, June 11	.50	.15	2.50	(4)	1.25	300,000,000
	Perf. 11.2						
2815	52¢ Love Birds, Feb. 14	1.00	.20	5.00	(4)	1.35	174,800,000
2816	29¢ Dr. Allison Davis, Feb. 1	.50	.15	2.50	(4)	1.25	155,500,000
2817	29¢ Chinese New Year, Feb. 5	.50	.15	2.50	(4)	1.25	105,000,000
	Perf. 11.5 x 11.2						
2818	29¢ Buffalo Soldiers, Apr. 22	.50	.15	2.50	(4)	1.25	185,500,000
	Stars of the Silent Screen Issue, April 22, Perf. 11.2						
2819	29¢ Rudolph Valentino	.50	.15			1.25	18,600,000
2820	29¢ Clara Bow	.50	.15			1.25	18,600,000
2821	29¢ Charlie Chaplin	.50	.15			1.25	18,600,000
2822	29¢ Lon Chaney	.50	.15			1.25	18,600,000
2823	29¢ John Gilbert	.50	.15			1.25	18,600,000
2824	29¢ Zasu Pitts	.50	.15			1.25	18,600,000
2825	29¢ Harold Lloyd	.50	.15			1.25	18,600,000
2826	29¢ Keystone Cops	.50	.15			1.25	18,600,000
2827	29¢ Theda Bara	.50	.15			1.25	18,600,000
2828	29¢ Buster Keaton	.50	.15			1.25	18,600,000
a	Block of 10 #2819-2828	5.00	—	5.50	(10)	6.50	18,600,000
b	As "a" black (litho.) omitted	—					
c	As "a" black (litho.) and red & brt. vio (engr.) omitted	—					

Customers could purchase this full pane, which contained 2 "minature sheets" of 20, each containing 2 blocks of #2828a.

2807   **2808**   **2809**   **2810**   **2811   2811a**

2812

2813

2814

2814C

2815

2816

2817

29 USA Buffalo Soldiers

2818

2819   **2820**   **2821**   **2822**   **2823**

2824   **2825**   **2826**   **2827**   **2828**

2828a

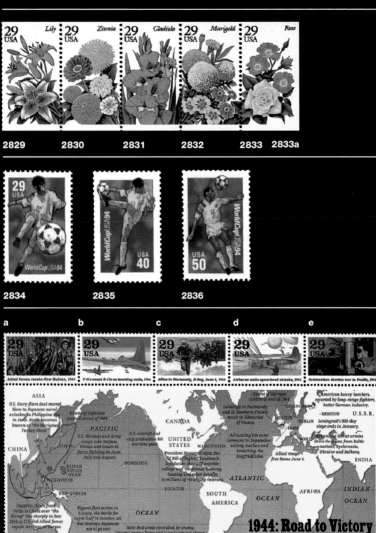

2829   2830   2831   2832   2833   2833a

2834   2835   2836

a   b   c   d   e

f   g   h   i   j   2838

	Issues of 1994	Un	U	PB	#	FDC	Q
	Garden Flowers Booklet Issue, April 28, Perf. 10.9 Vert.						
2829	29¢ Lily	.50	.15			1.25	166,000,000
2830	29¢ Zinnia	.50	.15			1.25	166,000,000
2831	29¢ Gladiola	.50	.15			1.25	166,000,000
2832	29¢ Marigold	.50	.15			1.25	166,000,000
2833	29¢ Rose	.50	.15			1.25	166,000,000
a	Booklet Pane of 5 #2829-2833	2.50	—			3.25	166,000,000
	1994 World Cup Soccer Championships Issue, May 26, Perf. 11.1						
2834	29¢ Soccer Player	.50	.15	2.50	(4)	1.25	201,000,000
2835	40¢ Soccer Player	.80	.18	4.00	(4)	1.25	300,000,000
2836	50¢ Soccer Player	1.00	.20	5.00	(4)	1.35	269,370,000
2837	Souvenir Sheet of 3, #2834-2836	2.50	—			2.50	60,000,000
a	29¢ Soccer Player						
b	40¢ Soccer Player						
c	50¢ Soccer Player						
	World War II Issue Miniature Sheet, June 6, Perf. 10.9						
2838	Sheet of 10 and central label	5.80	3.00	11.60	(20)	6.50	12,060,000
a	29¢ Allies Retake New Guinea	.58	.30			1.25	12,060,000
b	29¢ Bombing Raids	.58	.30			1.25	12,060,000
c	29¢ Allies in Normandy, D-Day	.58	.30			1.25	12,060,000
d	29¢ Airborne Units	.58	.30			1.25	12,060,000
e	29¢ Submarines Shorten War	.58	.30			1.25	12,060,000
f	29¢ Allies Free Rome, Paris	.58	.30			1.25	12,060,000
g	29¢ Troops Clear Siapan Bunkers	.58	.30			1.25	12,060,000
h	29¢ Red Ball Express	.58	.30			1.25	12,060,000
i	29¢ Battle for Leyte Gulf	.58	.30			1.25	12,060,000
j	29¢ Battle of the Bulge	.58	.30			1.25	12,060,000

Example of #2837.

	Issues of 1994	Un	U	PB	#	FDC	Q
	Norman Rockwell Issue, July 1, Perf. 10.9 x 11.1						
2839	29¢ Norman Rockwell	.50	.15	2.50	(4)	1.25	209,000,000
2840	Four Freedoms souvenir sheet	4.00	—			3.25	20,000,000
a	50¢ Freedom from Want	1.00	.65			1.35	20,000,000
b	50¢ Freedom from Fear	1.00	.65			1.35	20,000,000
c	50¢ Freedom of Speech	1.00	.65			1.35	20,000,000
d	50¢ Freedom of Worship	1.00	.65			1.35	20,000,000
	First Moon Landing Issue, Perf. 11.2 x 11.1, July 20						
2841	29¢ sheet of 12	7.50	—			6.50	12,958,000
a	Single stamp	.60	.60			1.25	155,496,000
	Perf. 10.7 x 11.1						
2842	$9.95 Moon Landing	17.50	7.50	85.00	(4)	15.00	100,500,000
	Locomotives Issue, July 28, Perf. 11 Horiz.						
2843	29¢ Hudson's General	.50	.15			1.25	159,200,000
2844	29¢ McQueen's Jupiter	.50	.15			1.25	159,200,000
2845	29¢ Eddy's No. 242	.50	.15			1.25	159,200,000
2846	29¢ Ely's No. 10	.50	.15			1.25	159,200,000
2847	29¢ Buchanan's No. 999	.50	.15			1.25	159,200,000
a	Booklet pane of 5 #2843-2847	2.50	—			3.25	159,200,000
2848	29¢ George Meany, Aug. 16	.50	.15	2.50	(4)	1.25	150,500,000
	Popular Singers Issue, Sept. 1, Perf. 10.1 x 10.2						
2849	29¢ Al Jolson	.50	.15				35,436,000
2850	29¢ Bing Crosby	.50	.15				35,436,000
2851	29¢ Ethel Waters	.50	.15				35,436,000
2852	29¢ Nat "King" Cole	.50	.15				35,436,000
2853	29¢ Ethel Merman	.50	.15				35,436,000
a	Vert. strip of 5, #2849-2861	2.50	—				

One more giant step for mankind

On July 20, 1969, Neil Armstrong stepped onto the moon and said, "That's one small step for (a) man, one giant leap for mankind." Twenty-five years later, the achievement is celebrated by Paul and Chris Calle. The Calles teamed up to design a 29¢ commemorative stamp and a $9.95 stamp for Express Mail in tribute to the Apollo XI flight.

(#2841)

2839

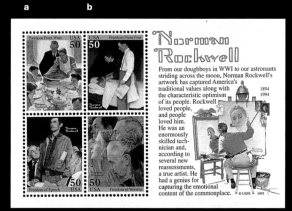

a   b

Freedom From Want · USA 50

Freedom From Fear · 50

Freedom of Speech · 50 USA

USA 50 · Freedom of Worship

Norman Rockwell

From our doughboys in WWI to our astronauts striding across the moon, Norman Rockwell's artwork has captured America's traditional values along with the characteristic optimism of its people. Rockwell loved people, and people loved him. He was an enormously skilled technician and, according to several new reassessments, a true artist. He had a genius for capturing the emotional content of the commonplace.

1894 1894

© USPS 1993

c   d   **2840**

First Moon Landing, 1969

2841a

$9.95 USA

25th Anniversary First Moon Landing, 1969

2842

HUDSON'S GENERAL 1855, 1870 · USA 29

2843

McQUEEN'S JUPITER 1869 · USA 29

2844

EDDY'S Nº 242 1874 · USA 29

2845

ELY'S Nº 10 1881 · USA 29

2846

BUCHANAN'S Nº 999 1893 · USA 29

2847

2847a

George Meany

Labor Leader · USA 29

2848

29 · AL JOLSON · USA

2849

29 · BING CROSBY · USA

2850

29 · ETHEL WATERS · USA

2851

29 · NAT 'KING' COLE · USA

2852

29 · ETHEL MERMAN · USA

2853

2853a

2854   2855   2856   2857   2858

2859   2860   2861

2862

2863   2864

2865   2866   2866a

2867   2868

2870g

a   b   c   d   e   2869
f   g   h   i   j
k   l   m   n   o
p   q   r   s   t

	Issues of 1994	Un	U	PB	#	FDC	Q
	Jazz and Blues Singers Issue, Sept. 17, Perf. 11 x 10.8						
2854	29¢ Bessie Smith	.50	.15				24,986,000
2855	29¢ Muddy Waters	.50	.15				24,986,000
2856	29¢ Billie Holiday	.50	.15				24,986,000
2857	29¢ Robert Johnson	.50	.15				19,988,800
2858	29¢ Jimmy Rushing	.50	.15				19,988,800
2859	29¢ "Ma" Rainey	.50	.15				19,988,800
2860	29¢ Mildred Bailey	.50	.15				19,988,800
2861	29¢ Howlin' Wolf	.50	.15				19,988,800
a	Block of 9, #2854-2861 + 1 additional stamp	4.50	—				
	Literary Arts Issue, Sept. 10, Perf. 11						
2862	29¢ James Thurber	.50	.15				150,750,000
	Wonders of the Sea Issue, Oct. 3, Perf. 11 x 10.9						
2863	29¢ Diver, Motorboat	.50	.15				56,475,000
2864	29¢ Diver, Ship	.50	.15				56,475,000
2865	29¢ Diver, Ship's Wheel	.50	.15				56,475,000
2866	29¢ Diver, Coral	.50	.15				56,475,000
a	Block of 4, #2963-2966	2.00	1.10				56,475,000
b	As "a" imperf.	—					
	Cranes Issue, Oct. 9, Perf. 10.8 x 11						
2867	29¢ Black-Necked Crane	.50	.15				77,748,000
2868	29¢ Whooping Crane	.50	.15				77,748,000
a	Pair, #2867-2868	1.00	.20				77,748,000
b	Black and magenta (engr.) omitted	—					
	Legends of the West Issue, Oct. 18, Perf. 10.1 x 10						
2869	Sheet of 20	12.00	—				20,000,000
a	29¢ Home on the Range	.60	.15				20,000,000
b	29¢ Buffalo Bill Cody	.60	.15				20,000,000
c	29¢ Jim Bridger	.60	.15				20,000,000
d	29¢ Annie Oakley	.60	.15				20,000,000
e	29¢ Native American Culture	.60	.15				20,000,000
f	29¢ Chief Joseph	.60	.15				20,000,000
g	29¢ Bill Pickett	.60	.15				20,000,000
h	29¢ Bat Masterson	.60	.15				20,000,000
i	29¢ John C. Fremont	.60	.15				20,000,000
j	29¢ Wyatt Earp	.60	.15				20,000,000
k	29¢ Nellie Cashman	.60	.15				20,000,000
l	29¢ Charles Goodnight	.60	.15				20,000,000
m	29¢ Geronimo	.60	.15				20,000,000
n	29¢ Kit Carson	.60	.15				20,000,000
o	29¢ Wild Bill Hickok	.60	.15				20,000,000
p	29¢ Western Wildlife	.60	.15				20,000,000
q	29¢ Jim Beckwourth	.60	.15				20,000,000
r	29¢ Bill Tilghman	.60	.15				20,000,000
s	29¢ Sacagawea	.60	.15				20,000,000
t	29¢ Overland Mail	.60	.15				20,000,000
2870	29¢ Sheet of 20 (recalled)	—	—				150,186

	Issues of 1994	Un	U	PB	#	FDC	Q
	Christmas Issue, Oct. 20, Perf. 11.1						
2871	29¢ Madonna and Child	.50	.15				
a	Perf. 9.8 x 10.8	.50	.15				
b	As "a," booklet pane of 10	5.00	—				50,000,000
c	As "a," Imperf.	—					
2872	29¢ Stocking	.50	.15				602,500,000
a	Booklet pane of 20	10.00	—				30,125,000
	Self-Adhesive						
2873	29¢ Santa Claus	.50	.15				239,997,600
a	Booklet pane of 12	6.00					19,999,800
2874	29¢ Cardinal in Snow	.50	.15				36,072,000
a	Booklet pane of 18	9.00					2,004,000
	Bureau of Engraving and Printing Issue, Nov. 3, Perf.11						
2875	$2.00 Sheet of 4	15.00	—				5,000,000
a	Single stamp	3.00	1.25				20,000,000
	Chinese New Year Issue, Dec. 30, Perf. 11.2 x 11.1						
2876	29¢ Year of the boar	.50	.15				80,000,000
	Untagged, Dec. 13, Perf. 11 x 10.8						
2877	(4¢) Dove Make-Up Rate	.15	.15				
	Perf. 10.8 x 10.9						
2878	(4¢) Dove Make-Up Rate	.15	.15				
	Tagged, Perf. 11.2 x 11.1						
2879	(20¢) Old Glory Postcard Rate	.40	.15				
	Perf. 11 x 10.9						
2880	(20¢) Old Glory Postcard Rate	.40	.15				
	Perf. 11.2 x 11.1						
2881	(32¢) "G" Old Glory	.60	.15		°		
a	Booklet pane of 10	6.00	—				
	Perf. 11 x 10.9						
2882	(32¢) "G" Old Glory	.60	.15				
	Booklet Stamps, Perf. 10 x 9.9 on 2 or 3 sides						
2883	(32¢) "G" Old Glory	.60	.15				
a	Booklet pane of 10	6.00	—				
	Perf. 10.9						
2884	(32¢) "G" Old Glory	.60	.15				
a	Booklet pane of 10	6.00	—				
	Perf. 11 x 10.9						
2885	(32¢) "G" Old Glory	.60	.15				
a	Booklet pane of 10	6.00	—				
	Self Adhesive, Die Cut						
2886	(32¢) "G" Old Glory	.60	.15				
a	Booklet pane of 18	11.00					
2887	(32¢) "G" Old Glory	.60	.15				
a	Booklet pane of 18	11.00					
	Coil Stamps, Perf. 9.8 Vert.						
2888	(25¢) Old Glory First-Class Presort	.50	.15				
2889	(32¢) Black "G"	.60	.15				
2890	(32¢) Blue "G"	.60	.15				
2891	(32¢) Red "G"	.60	.15				
	Rouletted						
2892	(32¢) Red "G"	.60	.15				

2871

2873

2875

2872

2874

2876

2877

2878

2879

2880

2881

2882

2883

2884

2885

2886

2887

2888

2889

2890

2891

2892

2893

For details and illustrations of the new 1995 issues, see pages 20-43.

The Thrill of Favorite Topics on Stamps

- Comprehensive stamp collections devoted to special subjects
- Interesting, informative text in colorfully illustrated books
- Includes protective stamp mounts

There's a Topical Collection Just For You

Whether it's the pure visual appeal of some of America's best stamp designs, the psychological appeal of subjects that evoke fond memories or stir emotions, or the educational appeal of interesting background material on intriguing topics, Topical Stamp Collections contain something for everyone.

Legends of the West

This specially commissioned edition holds two full panes of the 1994 Legends of the West stamps, 80 pages of fascinating background information on each of the 20 stamp designs, and facts about the Old West. ($24.95)

The Civil War

Including two full panes of the 1995 Civil War stamps, this informative hardbound book provides the background behind each of the 20 stamp designs. This beautiful 96-page book is filled with carefully researched details and dozens of historical photographs and illustrations. ($29.95)

World War II

Now complete, this set of five WWII hardbound albums covers each of the five years, 1941-45, in which the United States played a major role. Each volume includes two of the miniature sheets of 10 stamps for that year; the five-volume set includes a handsome slipcase at no extra charge. ($79.95)

To Obtain Topical Collections

Some Topical Stamp Collections are available at local post offices and Philatelic Centers. You can also fill out the postage-paid request card in this book or call toll-free:

1-800-STAMP24

Airmail and Special Delivery Stamps

1918-1938

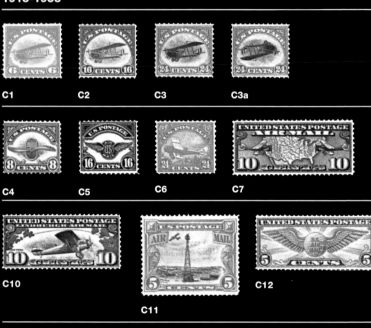

C1   C2   C3   C3a

C4   C5   C6   C7

C10   C11   C12

C13   C14

C15   C18

C20   C21   C23

	Issues of 1918, Perf. 11	Un	U	PB	#	FDC	Q
	For prepayment of postage on all mailable matter sent by airmail. All unwatermarked.						
C1	6¢ Curtiss Jenny, Dec. 10	55.00	25.00	650.00	(6)	17,500.00	3,395,900
	Double transfer	80.00	40.00				
C2	16¢ Curtiss Jenny, July 11	80.00	27.50	1,150.00	(6)	22,500.00	3,793,900
C3	24¢ Curtiss Jenny, May 13	75.00	32.50	360.00	(4)	27,500.00	2,134,900
a	Center Inverted	135,000.00		1,100,000.00	(4)		100
	Issues of 1923						
C4	8¢ Airplane Radiator and Wooden Propeller, Aug. 15	20.00	12.00	250.00	(6)	400.00	6,414,600
C5	16¢ Air Service Emblem, Aug. 17	75.00	25.00	1,900.00	(6)	600.00	5,309,300
C6	24¢ De Havilland Biplane, Aug. 21	75.00	22.50	2,250.00	(6)	750.00	5,285,800
	Issues of 1926-27						
C7	10¢ Map of U.S. and Two Mail Planes, Feb. 13, 1926	2.25	.25	40.00	(6)	55.00	42,092,800
	Double transfer	5.00	1.00				
C8	15¢ olive brown (C7), Sept. 18, 1926	2.75	1.90	45.00	(6)	75.00	15,597,300
C9	20¢ yellow green (C7), Jan. 25, 1927	7.00	1.65	95.00	(6)	100.00	17,616,350
	Issue of 1927-28						
C10	10¢ Lindbergh's "Spirit of St. Louis," June 18, 1927	6.00	1.75	140.00	(6)	20.00	20,379,200
a	Booklet pane of 3, May 26, 1928	75.00	50.00			825.00	
	Issue of 1928						
C11	5¢ Beacon on Rocky Mountains, July 25	4.50	.40	175.00	(8)		106,887,700
a	Recut frame line at left	6.00	1.00				
	Issues of 1930						
C12	5¢ Winged Globe, Feb. 10	8.00	.25	160.00	(6)	11.50	97,641,200
a	Horizontal pair, imperf. between	4,500.00					
	Graf Zeppelin Issue, Apr. 19						
C13	65¢ Zeppelin over Atlantic Ocean	260.00	150.00	2,000.00	(6)	1,700.00	93,500
C14	$1.30 Zeppelin Between Continents	500.00	350.00	5,000.00	(6)	1,200.00	72,400
C15	$2.60 Zeppelin Passing Globe	800.00	500.00	7,750.00	(6)	1,450.00	61,300
	Issues of 1931-32, Perf. 10.5 x 11						
C16	5¢ violet (C12), Aug. 19, 1931	4.75	.35	75.00	(4)	175.00	57,340,050
C17	8¢ olive bister (C12), Sept. 26, 1932	1.90	.20	30.00	(4)	15.00	76,648,800
	Issue of 1933, Century of Progress Issue, Oct. 2, Perf. 11						
C18	50¢ Zeppelin, Federal Building at Chicago Exposition and Hangar at Friedrichshafen	80.00	65.00	650.00	(6)	225.00	324,050
	Beginning with #C19, unused values are for never-hinged stamps.						
	Issue of 1934, Perf. 10.5 x 11						
C19	6¢ dull orange (C12), June 30	2.25	.15	25.00	(4)	175.00	302,205,100
	Issues of 1935-37, Trans-Pacific Issue, Perf. 11						
C20	25¢ "China Clipper" over the Pacific, Nov. 22, 1935	1.10	.75	25.00	(6)	20.00	10,205,400
C21	20¢ "China Clipper" over the Pacific, Feb. 15, 1937	8.00	1.40	110.00	(6)	20.00	12,794,600
C22	50¢ carmine (C21), Feb. 15, 1937	7.50	4.00	110.00	(6)	20.00	9,285,300
	Issue of 1938						
C23	6¢ Eagle Holding Shield, Olive Branch and Arrows, May 14	.40	.15	8.00	(4)	15.00	349,946,500
a	Vertical pair, imperf. horizontally	375.00					
b	Horizontal pair, imperf. vertically	10,000.00					
	6¢ ultramarine and carmine	150.00					

	Issue of 1939, Perf. 11	Un	U	PB/LP	#	FDC	Q
	Trans Atlantic Issue, May 16						
C24	30¢ Winged Globe	8.00	1.00	165.00	(6)	45.00	19,768,150
	Issues of 1941-44, Perf. 11 x 10.5						
C25	6¢ Twin-Motor Transport, June 25, 1941	.15	.15	.70	(4)	2.25	4,476,527,700
a	Booklet pane of 3, Mar. 18, 1943	3.50	*1.00*			25.00	
	Singles of #C25a are imperf. at sides or imperf. at sides and bottom.						
b	Horizontal pair, imperf. between	1,500.00					
C26	8¢ olive green (C25), Mar. 21, 1944	.16	.15	1.25	(4)	3.75	1,744,878,650
C27	10¢ violet (C25), Aug. 15, 1941	1.10	.20	8.50	(4)	8.00	67,117,400
C28	15¢ brn. carmine (C25), Aug. 19, 1941	2.25	.35	12.00	(4)	10.00	78,434,800
C29	20¢ bright green (C25), Aug. 27, 1941	1.75	.30	11.00	(4)	12.50	42,359,850
C30	30¢ blue (C25), Sept. 25, 1941	2.00	.30	12.00	(4)	20.00	59,880,850
C31	50¢ orange (C25), Oct. 29, 1941	9.50	2.75	75.00	(4)	40.00	11,160,600
	Issue of 1946						
C32	5¢ DC-4 Skymaster, Sept. 25	.15	.15	.45	(4)	2.00	864,753,100
	Issues of 1947, Perf. 10.5 x 11						
C33	5¢ DC-4 Skymaster, Mar. 26	.15	.15	.45	(4)	2.00	971,903,700
	Perf. 11 x 10.5						
C34	10¢ Pan American Union Building, Washington, D.C. and Martin 2-0-2, Aug. 30	.25	.15	1.10	(4)	2.00	207,976,550
C35	15¢ Statue of Liberty, N.Y. Skyline and Lockheed Constellation, Aug. 20	.35	.15	1.25	(4)	2.00	756,186,350
a	Horizontal pair, imperf. between	1,750.00					
b	Dry printing	.55	.15	2.50	(4)		
C36	25¢ San Francisco-Oakland Bay Bridge and Boeing Stratocruiser, July 30	.85	.15	3.50	(4)	2.75	132,956,100
	Issues of 1948, Coil Stamp, Perf. 10 Horizontally						
C37	5¢ carmine (C33), Jan. 15	.80	.75	8.50	(2)	2.00	33,244,500
	Perf. 11 x 10.5						
C38	5¢ New York City, July 31	.15	.15	3.75	(4)	1.75	38,449,100
	Issues of 1949, Perf. 10.5 x 11						
C39	6¢ carmine (C33), Jan. 18	.15	.15	.50	(4)	1.50	5,070,095,200
a	Booklet pane of 6, Nov. 18	9.50	*4.00*			9.00	
b	Dry printing	.50	.15	2.25	(4)		
c	As "a," dry printing	15.00	—				
	Perf. 11 x 10.5						
C40	6¢ Alexandria, Virginia, May 11	.15	.15	.60	(4)	1.25	75,085,000
	Coil Stamp, Perf. 10 Horizontally						
C41	6¢ carmine (C33), Aug. 25	2.75	.15	12.00	(2)	1.25	260,307,500
	Universal Postal Union Issue, Perf. 11 x 10.5						
C42	10¢ Post Office Dept. Bldg., Nov. 18	.20	.18	1.40	(4)	1.75	21,061,300
C43	15¢ Globe and Doves Carrying Messages, Oct. 7	.30	.25	1.25	(4)	2.25	36,613,100
C44	25¢ Boeing Stratocruiser and Globe, Nov. 30	.50	.40	5.75	(4)	3.00	16,217,100
C45	6¢ Wright Brothers, Dec. 17	.15	.15	.65	(4)	3.50	80,405,000
	Issue of 1952						
C46	80¢ Diamond Head, Honolulu, Hawaii, Mar. 26	5.50	1.00	27.50	(4)	17.50	18,876,800
	Issue of 1953						
C47	6¢ Powered Flight, May 29	.15	.15	.55	(4)	1.50	78,415,000
	Issue of 1954						
C48	4¢ Eagle in Flight, Sept. 3	.15	.15	1.50	(4)	1.00	50,484,000

C24

C25

C32

C33

C34

C35

C36

C38

C40

C42

C43

C44

C45

C46

C47

C48

C49

C51

C53

C54

C55

C56

C57

C58

C59

C61

C62

C63

C64

C66

C67

C68

C69

	Issue of 1957, Perf. 11 x 10.5	Un	U	PB/LP	#	FDC	Q
C49	6¢ Air Force, Aug. 1	.15	.15	.75	(4)	1.75	63,185,000
	Issues of 1958						
C50	5¢ rose red (C48), July 31	.15	.15	1.50	(4)	1.00	72,480,000
	Perf. 10.5 x 11						
C51	7¢ Jet Airliner, July 31	.15	.15	.60	(4)	1.00	1,326,960,000
a	Booklet pane of 6	11.00	6.00			9.50	221,190,000
	Coil Stamp, Perf. 10 Horizontally						
C52	7¢ blue (C51), July 31	2.25	.15	14.00	(2)	1.00	157,035,000
	Issues of 1959, Perf. 11 x 10.5						
C53	7¢ Alaska Statehood, Jan. 3	.15	.15	.75	(4)	1.00	90,055,200
	Perf. 11						
C54	7¢ Balloon Jupiter, Aug. 17	.15	.15	.75	(4)	1.10	79,290,000
	Perf. 11 x 10.5						
C55	7¢ Hawaii Statehood, Aug. 21	.15	.15	.75	(4)	1.00	84,815,000
	Perf. 11						
C56	10¢ Pan American Games, Aug. 27	.24	.24	1.40	(4)	1.00	38,770,000
	Issues of 1959-60						
C57	10¢ Liberty Bell, June 10, 1960	1.25	.70	6.00	(4)	1.25	39,960,000
C58	15¢ Statue of Liberty, Nov. 20, 1959	.35	.15	1.50	(4)	1.25	98,160,000
C59	25¢ Abraham Lincoln, Apr. 22, 1960	.45	.15	1.90	(4)	1.75	
a	Tagged, Dec. 29, 1966	.45	.30			15.00	
	Issues of 1960, Perf. 10.5 x 11						
C60	7¢ carmine (C61), Aug. 12	.15	.15	.60	(4)	1.00	1,289,460,000
	Pair with full horizontal gutter between	—					
a	Booklet pane of 6, Aug. 19	15.00	7.00			9.50	
	Coil Stamp, Perf. 10 Horizontally						
C61	7¢ Jet Airliner, Oct. 22	4.00	.25	32.50	(2)	1.00	87,140,000
	Issues of 1961-67, Perf. 11						
C62	13¢ Liberty Bell, June 28, 1961	.40	.15	1.65	(4)	1.00	
a	Tagged, Feb. 15, 1967	.75	.50			10.00	
C63	15¢ Statue of Liberty, Jan. 13, 1961	.30	.15	1.25	(4)	1.00	
a	Tagged, Jan. 11, 1967	.32	.20			15.00	
b	As "a," hor. pair, imperf. vertically	15,000.00					
	#C63 has a gutter between the two parts of the design; #C58 does not.						
	Issues of 1962-65, Perf. 10.5 x 11						
C64	8¢ Jetliner over Capitol, Dec. 5, 1962	.15	.15	.65	(4)	1.00	
a	Tagged, Aug. 1, 1963	.15	.15			2.00	
b	Bklt. pane of 5 + label, Dec. 5, 1962	6.75	2.50			2.00	
c	As "b," tagged, 1964	1.65	.50				
	Coil Stamp, Perf. 10 Horizontally						
C65	8¢ carmine (C64), Dec. 5, 1962	.40	.15	3.75	(2)	1.00	
a	Tagged, Jan. 14, 1965	.35	.15			—	
	Issue of 1963, Perf. 11						
C66	15¢ Montgomery Blair, May 3	.60	.55	2.75	(4)	1.10	42,245,000
	Issues of 1963-67, Perf. 11 x 10.5						
C67	6¢ Bald Eagle, July 12, 1963	.15	.15	1.80	(4)	1.00	
a	Tagged, Feb. 15, 1967	3.00	1.50			15.00	
	1963 continued, Perf. 11						
C68	8¢ Amelia Earhart, July 24	.20	.15	1.00	(4)	1.75	63,890,000
	Issue of 1964						
C69	8¢ Robert H. Goddard, Oct. 5	.40	.15	1.75	(4)	1.75	62,255,000

	Issues of 1967, Perf. 11	Un	U	PB/LP	#	FDC	Q
C70	8¢ Alaska Purchase, Mar. 30	.24	.15	1.40	(4)	1.00	55,710,000
C71	20¢ "Columbia Jays," by Audubon, Apr. 26 (See also #1241)	.80	.15	3.50	(4)	2.00	165,430,000
	Issues of 1968, Unwmk., Perf. 11 x 10.5						
C72	10¢ 50-Star Runway, Jan. 5	.18	.15	.90	(4)	1.00	
b	Booklet pane of 8	2.00	.75			3.50	
c	Booklet pane of 5 + label, Jan. 6	3.75	.75			125.00	
	Coil Stamp, Perf. 10 Vertically						
C73	10¢ carmine (C72), Jan. 5	.30	.15	1.70	(2)	1.00	
a	Imperf. pair	600.00		900.00	(2)		
	Perf. 11						
C74	10¢ U.S. Air Mail Service, May 15	.25	.15	2.00	(4)	1.50	
a	Red (tail stripe) omitted		—				
C75	20¢ USA and Jet, Nov. 22	.35	.15	1.75	(4)	1.10	
	Issue of 1969						
C76	10¢ Moon Landing, Sept. 9	.20	.15	.95	(4)	4.50	152,364,800
a	Rose red omitted	500.00	—				
	Issues of 1971-73, Perf. 10.5 x 11						
C77	9¢ Delta Wing Plane, May 15, 1971	.18	.15	.80	(4)	1.00	
	Perf. 11 x 10.5						
C78	11¢ Silhouette of Jet, May 7, 1971	.18	.15	.90	(4)	1.00	
a	Booklet pane of 4 + 2 labels	1.10	.75			1.75	
C79	13¢ Winged Airmail Envelope, Nov. 16, 1973	.22	.15	1.05	(4)	1.00	
a	Booklet pane of 5 + label, Dec. 27, 1973	1.25	.75			1.75	
b	Untagged (Bureau precanceled)		.28				
	Perf. 11						
C80	17¢ Statue of Liberty, July 13, 1971	.32	.15	1.50	(4)	1.00	
C81	21¢ USA and Jet, May 21, 1971	.35	.15	1.65	(4)	1.00	
	Coil Stamps, Perf. 10 Vertically						
C82	11¢ carmine (C78), May 7, 1971	.25	.15	.80	(2)	1.00	
a	Imperf. pair	250.00		225.00	(2)		
C83	13¢ carmine (C79), Dec. 27, 1973	.26	.15	1.00	(2)	1.00	
a	Imperf. pair	80.00		110.00	(2)		
	Issues of 1972, National Parks Centennial Issue, May 3, Perf. 11 (See also #1448-54)						
C84	11¢ Kii Statue and Temple at City of Refuge Historical National Park, Honaunau, Hawaii	.20	.15	.90	(4)	1.00	78,210,000
a	Blue and green omitted	1,110.00					
	Olympic Games Issue, Aug. 17, Perf. 11 x 10.5 (See also #1460-62)						
C85	11¢ Skiers and Olympic Rings	.18	.15	2.25	(10)	1.00	96,240,000
	Issues of 1973, Progress in Electronics Issue, July 10, Perf. 11 (See also #1500-02)						
C86	11¢ DeForest Audions	.22	.15	.95	(4)	1.00	58,705,000
a	Vermilion and green omitted	1,400.00					
	Issues of 1974						
C87	18¢ Statue of Liberty, Jan. 11	.35	.25	1.65	(4)	1.00	
C88	26¢ Mount Rushmore National Memorial, Jan. 2	.48	.15	2.00	(4)	1.25	
	Issues of 1976						
C89	25¢ Plane and Globes, Jan. 2	.45	.15	2.10	(4)	1.25	
C90	31¢ Plane, Globes and Flag, Jan. 2	.52	.15	2.30	(4)	1.25	

C70   **C71**   **C72**   **C74**

C75

C76

C77

C78   **C79**   **C80**   **C81**

C84   **C85**   **C86**

C87   **C88**

C89   **C90**

371

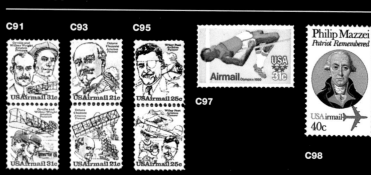

C91 C93 C95

C97

C98

C92 C92a C94 C94a C96 C96a

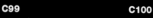

C99 C100

C101 C102

C105 C106

C107 C108 C108a

C103 C104 C104a

C109 C110

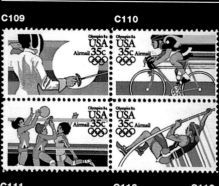

C111 C112 C112a

	Issues of 1978, Perf. 11	Un	U	PB	#	FDC	Q
	Aviation Pioneers Issue, Wright Brothers, Sept. 23 (See also #C93-96)						
C91	31¢ Orville and Wilbur Wright, Flyer A	.60	.30			3.00	157,445,000
C92	31¢ Wright Brothers, Flyer A and Shed	.60	.30			3.00	157,445,000
a	Vert. pair, #C91-92	1.20	.85	2.75	(4)	4.00	
b	As "a," ultramarine and black omitted	800.00					
c	As "a," black omitted	—					
d	As "a," black, yellow, magenta, blue and brown omitted	2,250.00					
	Issues of 1979, Aviation Pioneers Issue, Octave Chanute, Mar. 29						
C93	21¢ Chanute and Biplane Hang-Glider	.70	.32			3.00	29,012,500
C94	21¢ Biplane Hang-Glider and Chanute	.70	.32			3.00	29,012,500
a	Attached pair, #C93-94	1.40	.95	3.50	(4)	4.00	
b	As "a," ultramarine and black omitted	4,500.00					
	Aviation Pioneers Issue, Wiley Post, Nov. 20 (See also #C99-100)						
C95	25¢ Wiley Post and "Winnie Mae"	1.10	.35			3.00	32,005,000
C96	25¢ NR-105-W, Post in Pressurized Suit and Portrait	1.10	.35			3.00	32,005,000
a	Attached pair, #C95-96	2.25	.95	9.50	(4)	4.00	
	Olympic Summer Games Issue, Nov. 1 (See also #1790-94)						
C97	31¢ High Jumper	.65	.30	9.50	(12)	1.25	47,200,000
	Issues of 1980-82						
C98	40¢ Philip Mazzei, Oct. 13, 1980	.60	.15	8.75	(12)	1.35	80,935,000
a	Perf. 10.5 x 11, 1982	3.00	—				
b	Imperf. pair	3,500.00					
	Issues of 1980, Aviation Pioneers Issues, Blanche Stuart Scott, Dec. 30						
C99	28¢ Portrait of Scott and Biplane	.55	.15	6.75	(12)	1.25	20,190,000
	Glenn Curtiss, Dec. 30 (See also #C113-14)						
C100	35¢ Portrait of Curtiss and "Pusher" Biplane	.60	.15	8.00	(12)	1.25	22,945,000
	Issues of 1983, Olympic Summer Games Issue, June 17 (See also #2048-51, 2082-85)						
C101	28¢ Gymnast	.60	.28			1.25	42,893,750
C102	28¢ Hurdler	.60	.28			1.25	42,893,750
C103	28¢ Basketball Player	.60	.28			1.25	42,893,750
C104	28¢ Soccer Player	.60	.28			1.25	42,893,750
a	Block of 4, #C101-04	2.50	1.75	3.50	(4)	3.75	
	Olympic Summer Games Issue, Apr. 8 (See also #2048-51 and 2082-85)						
C105	40¢ Shotputter	.90	.40			1.35	66,573,750
C106	40¢ Gymnast	.90	.40			1.35	66,573,750
C107	40¢ Swimmer	.90	.40			1.35	66,573,750
C108	40¢ Weightlifter	.90	.40			1.35	66,573,750
a	Block of 4, #C105-08	3.60	2.00	4.00	(4)	5.00	
b	As "a," imperf.	1,350.00					
d	As "a," perf. 11 x 10½	4.25	—				
	Olympic Summer Games Issue, Nov. 4 (See also #2048-51 and 2082-85)						
C109	35¢ Fencer	.90	.35			1.25	42,587,500
C110	35¢ Bicyclist	.90	.35			1.25	42,587,500
C111	35¢ Volleyball Players	.90	.35			1.25	42,587,500
C112	35¢ Pole Vaulter	.90	.35			1.25	42,587,500
a	Block of 4, #C109-12	3.60	1.85	6.00	(4)	4.50	

	Issues of 1985, Perf. 11	Un	U	PB	#	FDC	Q
	Aviation Pioneers Issues, Alfred Verville, Feb. 13						
C113	33¢ Portrait of Verville and Airplane Diagram	.60	.20	3.00	(4)	1.25	168,125,000
a	Imperf. pair	800.00					
	Lawrence and Elmer Sperry, Feb. 13 (See also #C118-19)						
C114	39¢ Portrait of Sperrys and Seaplane	.70	.20	3.25	(4)	1.35	167,825,000
a	Imperf. pair	1,250.00					
C115	44¢ Transpacific Airmail, Feb. 15	.80	.20	3.75	(4)	1.35	209,025,000
a	Imperf. pair	800.00					
C116	44¢ Junipero Serra, Aug. 22	.80	.20	6.50	(4)	1.35	164,350,000
a	Imperf. pair	1,500.00					
	Issues of 1988						
C117	44¢ New Sweden, Mar. 29	1.00	.20	5.50	(4)	1.35	136,900,000
	Aviation Pioneers Issues, Langley and Sikorsky (See also #C128-29)						
C118	45¢ Samuel P. Langley, May 14	.80	.20	3.75	(4)	1.40	406,475,000
C119	36¢ Igor Sikorsky, June 23	.65	.20	3.10	(4)	1.25	179,004,000
	Issues of 1989, Perf. 11.5 x 11						
C120	45¢ French Revolution, July 14	.80	.22	4.25	(4)	1.40	38,922,000
	America/PUAS Issue, Oct. 12, Perf. 11 (See also #2426)						
C121	45¢ Southeast Carved Wood Figure, Key Marco Cat (A.D. 700-1450), Emblem of the Postal Union of the Americas and Spain	.80	.22	3.75	(4)	1.40	39,325,000
	20th UPU Congress Issue, Future Mail Transportation, Nov. 28 (See also #2434-38)						
C122	45¢ Hypersonic Airliner	.90	.30			1.40	26,590,000
C123	45¢ Air-Cushion Vehicle	.90	.30			1.40	26,590,000
C124	45¢ Surface Rover	.90	.30			1.40	26,590,000
C125	45¢ Shuttle	.90	.30			1.40	26,590,000
a	Block of 4, #C122-25	3.60	2.25	4.50	(4)	5.00	
b	As "a," light blue omitted	1,000.00					

How Big is the Space Shuttle?

The first space shuttle, *Columbia*, was launched April 12, 1981. Since that time, more than 50 missions have been flown. The space shuttle is made up of three main components: the orbiter, the external tank and two solid rocket boosters. Weighing 2,250 tons and standing 184.2 feet tall, once in orbit the shuttle reaches speeds up to 25 times the speed of sound.
(#C125)

C113

C114

C115

C116

C117

C118

C119

C120

C121

C122   C123

C124   C125   C125a

20th Universal Postal Congress

A glimpse at several potential mail delivery methods of the future is the theme of these four stamps issued by the U.S. in commemoration of the convening of the 20th Universal Postal Congress in Washington, D.C. from November 13 through December 14, 1989. The United States, as host nation to the Congress for the first time in ninety-two years, welcomed more than 1,000 delegates from most of the member nations of the Universal Postal Union to the major international event.

©USPS 1989

C126

C127

C128

C129

C130

C131

CE1

CE2

E1

E3

E4

	Issues of 1989, Imperf.	Un	U	PB	#	FDC	Q
	20th UPU Congress Issue Souvenir Sheet, Nov. 24						
C126	Designs of #C122-25	4.25	3.25			3.00	2,182,400
a-d	Single stamp from sheet	.90	.50				
	Issue of 1990, America/PUAS Issue, Oct. 12, Perf. 11 (See also #2512)						
C127	45¢ Tropical Coast	.80	.20	4.00	(4)	1.40	39,350,000
	Issues of 1991, Aviation Pioneers Issues, Harriet Quimby, Apr. 27						
C128	50¢ Portrait of Quimby and Early Plane	.90	.24	4.50	(4)	2.00	
C128b	50¢ Portrait of Quimby (C128)	.90	.24	4.50	(4)		
	William T. Piper, May 17						
C129	40¢ Portrait of Piper and Piper Cub Airplane	.80	.22	4.00	(4)	1.75	
C130	50¢ Antarctic Treaty, June 21	.90	.24	4.50	(4)	2.00	113,000,000
	America/PUAS Issue, Oct. 12						
C131	50¢ Eskimo and Bering Land Bridge	.90	.24	4.75	(4)	2.00	15,260,000
C132	40¢ Portrait of Piper	.80	.22	4.00	(4)		
	Airmail Special Delivery Stamps						
	Issues of 1934						
CE1	16¢ Great Seal of the United States, Aug. 30	.55	.65			25.00	
	For imperforate variety see #771.						
	Issue of 1936						
CE2	16¢ red and blue, Feb. 10	.30	.20	6.50	(4)	17.50	
a	Horizontal pair, imperf. vertically	4,000.00					
	Special Delivery Stamps						
	Issue of 1885, Oct. 1, Perf. 12, Unwmkd.						
E1	10¢ Messenger Running	200.00	30.00	10,000.00	(8)	8,000.00	
	Issue of 1888, Sept. 6						
E2	10¢ blue Messenger Running (E3)	185.00	9.00	10,000.00	(8)		
	Issue of 1893, Jan. 24						
E3	10¢ Messenger Running	120.00	15.00	6,000.00	(8)		
	Issue of 1894, Oct. 10, Line under "Ten Cents"						
E4	10¢ Messenger Running	500.00	15.00	12,000.00	(6)		

The William T. Piper stamp was first issued May 17, 1991 (#C129, at left). The blue sky is plainly visible all the way across the top of the stamp, above Piper's head. When reissued in 1993 (#C132, right), the image cropping had been adjusted, and Piper's hair touches the top edge of the design.

	Issue of 1895	Un	U	PB	#	FDC
	Aug. 16, Perf. 12, Wmkd. (191)					
E5	10¢ blue Messenger Running (E4)	100.00	2.00	*4,000.00*	(6)	
	Double transfer	—	15.00			
	Line of color through "POSTAL DELIVERY"	130.00	9.00			
	Dots in curved frame above messenger	115.00	6.00			
	Issue of 1902, Dec. 9					
E6	10¢ Messenger on Bicycle	65.00	2.50	*2,500.00*	(6)	
	Damaged transfer under "N" of "CENTS"	85.00	3.00			
	Issue of 1908, Dec. 12					
E7	10¢ Mercury Helmet and Olive Branch	40.00	25.00	850.00	(6)	
	Issue of 1911, Jan., Wmkd. (190)					
E8	10¢ ultramarine Messenger on Bicycle (E6)	65.00	3.50	*2,250.00*	(6)	
	Top frame line missing	72.50	3.50			
	Issue of 1914, Sept., Perf. 10					
E9	10¢ ultramarine Messenger on Bicycle (E6)	115.00	4.00	*4,250.00*	(6)	
	Issue of 1916, Oct. 19, Unwmkd.					
E10	10¢ ultramarine Messenger on Bicycle (E6)	210.00	20.00	5,550.00	(6)	
	Issue of 1917, May 2, Perf. 11					
E11	10¢ ultramarine Messenger on Bicycle (E6)	10.00	.25	850.00	(6)	
c	Blue	30.00	.60			
d	Perf. 10 at left	—				
	Issue of 1922, July 12					
E12	10¢ Postman and Motorcycle	20.00	.15	275.00	(6)	400.00
a	10¢ deep ultramarine	27.50	.20			
	Double transfer	35.00	1.00			
	Issues of 1925					
E13	15¢ Postman and Motorcycle, Apr. 11	16.00	.50	150.00	(6)	225.00
E14	20¢ Post Office Truck, Apr. 25	1.65	.85	25.00	(6)	90.00
	Issue of 1927, Nov. 29, Perf. 11 x 10.5					
E15	10¢ gray violet Postman and Motorcycle (E12)	.60	.15	4.00	(4)	90.00
c	Horizontal pair, imperf. between	275.00				
	Cracked plate	35.00				
	Issue of 1931, Aug. 13					
E16	15¢ or. Postman and Motorcycle (E13)	.70	.15	3.75	(4)	125.00
	Beginning with #E17, unused values are for never-hinged stamps.					
	Issues of 1944, Oct. 30					
E17	13¢ Postman and Motorcycle	.60	.15	3.00	(4)	12.00
E18	17¢ Postman and Motorcycle	2.75	1.75	22.50	(4)	12.00
	Issue of 1951, Nov. 30					
E19	20¢ black Post Office Truck (E14)	1.25	.15	5.50	(4)	5.00
	Issues of 1954-57					
E20	20¢ Delivery of Letter, Oct. 13, 1954	.40	.15	2.00	(4)	3.00
E21	30¢ Delivery of Letter, Sept. 3, 1957	.50	.15	2.40	(4)	2.25
	Issues of 1969-71, Perf. 11					
E22	45¢ Arrows, Nov. 21, 1969	1.25	.15	5.50	(4)	3.50
E23	60¢ Arrows, May 10, 1971	1.10	.15	4.75	(4)	3.50

E6

E7

E12

E13

E14

E18

E20

E21

E22

E23

Registration, Certified Mail and Postage Due Stamps

1879-1959

F1

FA1

J2   J19   J25

J33

J69   J78

J88   J98

J101

	Issue of 1911	Un	U	PB	#	FDC	Q
	Perf. 12, Wmkd. (190)						
	Registration Stamp						
	Issued for the prepayment of registry; not usable for postage. Sale discontinued May 28, 1913.						
F1	10¢ Bald Eagle, Dec. 11	60.00	4.00	*1,350.00*	(6)	*8,000.00*	
	Certified Mail Stamp						
	For use on First-Class mail for which no indemnity value was claimed, but for which proof of mailing and proof of delivery were available at less cost than registered mail.						
	Issue of 1955, Perf. 10.5 x 11						
FA1	15¢ Letter Carrier, June 6	.40	.25	4.00	(4)	3.25	54,460,300
	Postage Due Stamps						
	For affixing by a postal clerk to any mail to denote amount to be collected from addressee because of insufficient prepayment of postage.						
	Issues of 1879, Printed by American Bank Note Co., Design of #J2, Perf. 12, Unwmkd.						
J1	1¢ brown	30.00	5.00				
J2	2¢ Figure of Value	200.00	4.00				
J3	3¢ brown	25.00	2.50				
J4	5¢ brown	325.00	30.00				
J5	10¢ brown, Sept. 19	350.00	15.00				
a	Imperf. pair	*1,600.00*					
J6	30¢ brown, Sept. 19	175.00	35.00				
J7	50¢ brown, Sept. 19	225.00	40.00				
	Special Printing, Soft, Porous Paper						
J8	1¢ deep brown	*6,250.00*					
J9	2¢ deep brown	*4,250.00*					
J10	3¢ deep brown	*3,900.00*					
J11	5¢ deep brown	*3,250.00*					
J12	10¢ deep brown	*2,250.00*					
J13	30¢ deep brown	*2,250.00*					
J14	50¢ deep brown	*2,400.00*					
	Issues of 1884, Design of #J19						
J15	1¢ red brown	30.00	2.50				
J16	2¢ red brown	40.00	2.50				
J17	3¢ red brown	525.00	100.00				
J18	5¢ red brown	250.00	15.00				
J19	10¢ Figure of Value	250.00	12.50				
J20	30¢ red brown	110.00	30.00				
J21	50¢ red brown	1,000.00	125.00				
	Issues of 1891, Design of #J25						
J22	1¢ bright claret	14.00	.50				
J23	2¢ bright claret	15.00	.45				
J24	3¢ bright claret	32.50	5.00				
J25	5¢ Figure of Value	40.00	5.00				
J26	10¢ bright claret	75.00	11.00				
J27	30¢ bright claret	250.00	90.00				
J28	50¢ bright claret	275.00	90.00				
	Issues of 1894, Printed by the Bureau of Engraving and Printing, Design of #J33, Perf. 12						
J29	1¢ vermilion	800.00	200.00	5,250.00	(6)		
J30	2¢ vermilion	325.00	60.00	2,400.00	(6)		
	Design of #J33, Unwmkd., Perf. 12						
J31	1¢ deep claret, Aug. 14, 1894	22.50	3.00	375.00	(6)		
J32	2¢ deep claret, July 20, 1894	22.50	1.75	325.00	(6)		
J33	3¢ Figure of Value, Apr. 27, 1895	90.00	20.00	850.00	(6)		

	Issues of 1894-95	Un	U	PB	#
J34	5¢ deep claret, Apr. 27, 1895	140.00	22.50	950.00	(6)
J35	10¢ deep claret, Sept. 24, 1894	140.00	17.50	950.00	(6)
J36	30¢ deep claret, Apr. 27, 1895	250.00	60.00		
b	30¢ pale rose	210.00	55.00	2,100.00	(6)
J37	50¢ deep claret, Apr. 27, 1895	550.00	150.00		
a	50¢ pale rose	500.00	135.00	5,000.00	(6)
	Issues of 1895-97, Design of #J33, Wmkd. (191)				
J38	1¢ deep claret, Aug. 29, 1895	5.00	.30	190.00	(6)
J39	2¢ deep claret, Sept. 14, 1895	5.00	.20	190.00	(6)
J40	3¢ deep claret, Oct. 30, 1895	35.00	1.00	425.00	(6)
J41	5¢ deep claret, Oct. 15, 1895	37.50	1.00	450.00	(6)
J42	10¢ deep claret, Sept. 14, 1895	40.00	2.00	550.00	(6)
J43	30¢ deep claret, Aug. 21, 1897	350.00	32.50	3,750.00	(6)
J44	50¢ deep claret, Mar. 17, 1896	210.00	25.00	2,250.00	(6)
	Issues of 1910-12, Design of #J33, Wmkd. (190)				
J45	1¢ deep claret, Aug. 30, 1910	20.00	2.00		
a	1¢ rose carmine	17.50	1.75	400.00	(6)
J46	2¢ deep claret, Nov. 25, 1910	20.00	.30		
a	2¢ rose carmine	17.50	.30	350.00	(6)
J47	3¢ deep claret, Aug. 31, 1910	375.00	20.00	3,850.00	(6)
J48	5¢ deep claret, Aug. 31, 1910	60.00	3.50		
a	5¢ rose carmine	—	—	600.00	(6)
J49	10¢ deep claret, Aug. 31, 1910	75.00	7.50	1,150.00	(6)
J50	50¢ deep claret, Sept. 23, 1912	625.00	75.00	7,500.00	(6)
	Issues of 1914, Design of #J33, Perf. 10				
J52	1¢ carmine lake	40.00	7.50		
J53	2¢ carmine lake	32.50	.20		
J54	3¢ carmine lake	500.00	25.00		
J55	5¢ carmine lake	25.00	1.50		
	5¢ deep claret	—	—		
J56	10¢ carmine lake	40.00	1.00		
J57	30¢ carmine lake	145.00	12.00	2,100.00	(6)
J58	50¢ carmine lake	*6,500.00*	400.00	*50,000.00*	(6)
	Issues of 1916, Design of #J33, Unwmkd.				
J59	1¢ rose	1,250.00	200.00	8,750.00	(6)
	Experimental Bureau precancel, New Orleans		*125.00*		
J60	2¢ rose	95.00	12.50	800.00	(6)
	Issues of 1917-25, Design of #J33, Perf. 11				
J61	1¢ carmine rose	1.75	.15		
J62	2¢ carmine rose	1.50	.15		
J63	3¢ carmine rose	8.50	.15		
J64	5¢ carmine	8.50	.15		
J65	10¢ carmine rose	12.50	.20		
	Double transfer	—	—		
J66	30¢ carmine rose	65.00	.40		
J67	50¢ carmine rose	80.00	.15		
J68	1/2¢ dull red, Apr. 13, 1925	.70	.15	11.00	(6)

	Issue of 1930-31	Un	U	PB	#
	Design of #J69, Perf. 11				
J69	¹/₂¢ Figure of Value	3.75	1.00	35.00	(6)
J70	1¢ carmine	2.60	.15	27.50	(6)
J71	2¢ carmine	3.25	.15	40.00	(6)
J72	3¢ carmine	16.00	1.00	250.00	(6)
J73	5¢ carmine	15.00	1.50	225.00	(6)
J74	10¢ carmine	32.50	.50	425.00	(6)
J75	30¢ carmine	90.00	1.00	1,000.00	(6)
J76	50¢ carmine	110.00	.30	1,250.00	(6)
	Design of #J78				
J77	$1 carmine	27.50	.15		
a	$1 scarlet	22.50	.15	275.00	(6)
J78	$5 "FIVE" on $	35.00	.15		
a	$5 scarlet	30.00	.15		
b	As "a," wet printing	27.50	.15	375.00	(6)
	Issues of 1931-56, Design of #J69, Perf. 11 x 10.5				
J79	¹/₂¢ dull carmine	.75	.15		
J80	1¢ dull carmine	.15	.15		
J81	2¢ dull carmine	.15	.15		
J82	3¢ dull carmine	.25	.15		
b	Scarlet, wet printing	.25	.15		
J83	5¢ dull carmine	.35	.15		
J84	10¢ dull carmine	1.10	.15		
b	Scarlet, wet printing	1.25	.15		
J85	30¢ dull carmine	8.00	.15		
J86	50¢ dull carmine	9.50	.15		
	Design of J78, Perf. 10.5 x 11				
J87	$1 scarlet	35.00	.20	250.00	(4)
	Beginning with #J88, unused values are for never-hinged stamps.				
	Issues of 1959, June 19, Designs of #J88, J98 and J101, Perf. 11 x 10.5				
J88	¹/₂¢ Figure of Value	1.25	.85	165.00	(4)
J89	1¢ carmine rose	.15	.15	.35	(4)
a	"1 CENT" omitted	300.00			
b	Pair, one without "1 CENT"	450.00			
J90	2¢ carmine rose	.15	.15	.45	(4)
J91	3¢ carmine rose	.15	.15	.50	(4)
J92	4¢ carmine rose	.15	.15	.60	(4)
J93	5¢ carmine rose	.15	.15	.65	(4)
J94	6¢ carmine rose	.15	.15	.70	(4)
a	Pair, one without "6 CENTS"	800.00			
J95	7¢ carmine rose	.15	.15	.80	(4)
J96	8¢ carmine rose	.16	.15	.90	(4)
J97	10¢ carmine rose	.20	.15	1.00	(4)
J98	30¢ Figure of Value	.55	.15	2.75	(4)
J99	50¢ carmine rose	.90	.15	4.50	(4)
	Design of #J101				
J100	$1 carmine rose	1.50	.15	7.50	(4)
J101	$5 Outline Figure of Value	8.00	.15	40.00	(4)
	Issues of 1978-85, Designs of #J98				
J102	11¢ carmine rose, Jan. 2, 1978	.25	.15	2.00	(4)
J103	13¢ carmine rose, Jan. 2, 1978	.25	.15	2.00	(4)
J104	17¢ carmine rose, June 10, 1985	.40	.15	25.00	(4)

Official and Penalty Mail Stamps

1873-1991

O3   O7   O11   O14   O16

O18   O25   O34   O37   O44

O47   O52

O57   O74   O76   O87   O91

O121   O124   O125   O126

O127   O129A   O139   O140   O143

Issues of 1873	Un	U

Thin, Hard Paper, Perf. 12, Unwmkd

Official Stamps

The franking privilege having been abolished as of July 1, 1873, these stamps were provided for each of the departments of government for the prepayment on official matter. These stamps were supplanted on May 1, 1879, by penalty envelopes and on July 5, 1884, were declared obsolete.

Department of Agriculture Issue: Yellow

		Un	U
O1	1¢ Franklin	90.00	75.00
	Ribbed paper	100.00	65.00
O2	2¢ Jackson	70.00	27.50
O3	3¢ Washington	65.00	5.00
	Double transfer	—	—
O4	6¢ Lincoln	75.00	20.00
O5	10¢ Jefferson	150.00	90.00
	10¢ golden yellow	155.00	72.50
	10¢ olive yellow	165.00	75.00
O6	12¢ Clay	200.00	105.00
	12¢ golden yellow	225.00	100.00
O7	15¢ Webster	150.00	95.00
	15¢ olive yellow	160.00	85.00
O8	24¢ Scott	175.00	85.00
	24¢ golden yellow	190.00	85.00
O9	30¢ Hamilton	225.00	130.00
	30¢ olive yellow	250.00	125.00

Executive Dept. Issue: Carmine

		Un	U
O10	1¢ Franklin	350.00	190.00
O11	2¢ Jackson	225.00	110.00
	Double transfer	—	—
O12	3¢ Washington	275.00	100.00
O13	6¢ Lincoln	400.00	275.00
O14	10¢ Jefferson	375.00	225.00

Dept. of the Interior Issue: Vermilion

		Un	U
O15	1¢ Franklin	20.00	5.00
	Ribbed paper	25.00	4.50
O16	2¢ Jackson	17.50	3.00
O17	3¢ Washington	27.50	3.00
O18	6¢ Lincoln	20.00	3.00
O19	10¢ Jefferson	19.00	5.00
O20	12¢ Clay	30.00	4.00
O21	15¢ Webster	50.00	9.00
	Double transfer of left side	100.00	17.50
O22	24¢ Scott	37.50	7.50
O23	30¢ Hamilton	50.00	7.50
O24	90¢ Perry	110.00	20.00

Dept. of Justice Issue: Purple

		Un	U
O25	1¢ Franklin	60.00	45.00
O26	2¢ Jackson	95.00	42.50
O27	3¢ Washington	95.00	9.00
O28	6¢ Lincoln	90.00	15.00

Issues of 1873, Perf. 12	Un	U

Dept. of Justice Issue (continued): Purple

		Un	U
O29	10¢ Jefferson	100.00	32.50
	Double transfer	—	—
O30	12¢ Clay	75.00	20.00
O31	15¢ Webster	165.00	70.00
O32	24¢ Scott	450.00	160.00
O33	30¢ Hamilton	400.00	100.00
	Double transfer at top	425.00	85.00
O34	90¢ Perry	600.00	225.00

Navy Dept. Issue: Ultramarine

		Un	U
O35	1¢ Franklin	45.00	15.00
a	1¢ dull blue	52.50	17.50
O36	2¢ Jackson	32.50	9.00
a	2¢ dull blue	42.50	9.00
	2¢ gray blue	35.00	11.00
O37	3¢ Washington	37.50	5.00
a	3¢ dull blue	42.50	7.00
O38	6¢ Lincoln	32.50	7.50
a	6¢ dull blue	42.50	7.50
	Vertical line through "N" of "NAVY"	65.00	10.00
O39	7¢ Stanton	225.00	80.00
a	7¢ dull blue	250.00	80.00
O40	10¢ Jefferson	45.00	17.50
a	10¢ dull blue	50.00	17.50
	Cracked plate	*125.00*	—
O41	12¢ Clay	57.50	12.50
	Double transfer of left side	110.00	30.00
O42	15¢ Webster	95.00	25.00
O43	24¢ Scott	95.00	32.50
a	24¢ dull blue	110.00	—
O44	30¢ Hamilton	85.00	15.00
O45	90¢ Perry	425.00	90.00
a	Double impression		*3,750.00*

Post Office Dept. Issue: Black

		Un	U
O47	1¢ Figure of Value	7.25	3.00
O48	2¢ Figure of Value	7.00	2.50
a	Double impression	300.00	
O49	3¢ Figure of Value	2.50	.55
	Cracked plate	—	—
O50	6¢ Figure of Value	8.00	1.40
	Vertical ribbed paper	—	7.50
O51	10¢ Figure of Value	40.00	17.50
O52	12¢ Figure of Value	22.50	5.00
O53	15¢ Figure of Value	25.00	7.50
a	Imperf. pair	*600.00*	
	Double transfer	—	—
O54	24¢ Figure of Value	32.50	9.00
O55	30¢ Figure of Value	32.50	7.50
O56	90¢ Figure of Value	47.50	7.50

	Issues of 1873, Perf. 12	Un	U
	Dept. of State Issue: Green		
O57	1¢ Franklin	60.00	22.50
O58	2¢ Jackson	125.00	30.00
O59	3¢ Washington	50.00	11.00
	Double paper	—	—
O60	6¢ Lincoln	47.50	11.00
O61	7¢ Stanton	90.00	22.50
	Ribbed paper	110.00	21.00
O62	10¢ Jefferson	75.00	15.00
	Short transfer	100.00	27.50
O63	12¢ Clay	110.00	45.00
O64	15¢ Webster	125.00	32.50
O65	24¢ Scott	250.00	75.00
O66	30¢ Hamilton	250.00	60.00
O67	90¢ Perry	500.00	150.00
O68	$2 Seward	550.00	425.00
O69	$5 Seward	4,500.00	2,000.00
O70	$10 Seward	3,000.00	1,500.00
O71	$20 Seward	2,250.00	850.00
	Treasury Dept. Issue: Brown		
O72	1¢ Franklin	22.50	2.25
	Double transfer	30.00	3.50
O73	2¢ Jackson	25.00	2.25
	Double transfer	—	5.00
	Cracked plate	40.00	—
O74	3¢ Washington	16.00	.90
	Shaded circle outside right frame line	—	—
O75	6¢ Lincoln	22.50	2.00
	Worn plate	24.00	2.50
O76	7¢ Stanton	57.50	12.50
O77	10¢ Jefferson	57.50	4.00
O78	12¢ Clay	57.50	3.00
O79	15¢ Webster	50.00	4.00
O80	24¢ Scott	250.00	32.50
O81	30¢ Hamilton	82.50	5.00
	Short transfer top right	—	—
O82	90¢ Perry	87.50	5.00
	War Dept. Issue: Rose		
O83	1¢ Franklin	82.50	4.00
O84	2¢ Jackson	75.00	5.00
	Ribbed paper	67.50	7.50
O85	3¢ Washington	72.50	1.25
O86	6¢ Lincoln	250.00	3.00
O87	7¢ Stanton	75.00	45.00
O88	10¢ Jefferson	22.50	5.00

	Issues of 1873, Perf. 12	Un	U
	War Dept. Issue (continued): Rose		
O89	12¢ Clay	75.00	3.00
	Ribbed paper	90.00	3.50
O90	15¢ Webster	20.00	3.50
	Ribbed paper	25.00	4.50
O91	24¢ Scott	20.00	3.50
O92	30¢ Hamilton	22.50	3.00
O93	90¢ Perry	50.00	15.00
	Issues of 1879, Soft, Porous Paper **Dept. of Agriculture: Yellow**		
O94	1¢ Franklin, issued without gum	1,600.00	
O95	3¢ Washington	175.00	40.00
	Dept. of the Interior Issue: Vermilion		
O96	1¢ Franklin	120.00	95.00
O97	2¢ Jackson	2.50	1.00
O98	3¢ Washington	2.00	.60
O99	6¢ Lincoln	3.00	2.50
O100	10¢ Jefferson	37.50	30.00
O101	12¢ Clay	70.00	45.00
O102	15¢ Webster	160.00	75.00
	Double transfer	200.00	—
O103	24¢ Scott	2,100.00	
O104-05	Not assigned		
	Dept. of Justice Issue: Bluish Purple		
O106	3¢ Washington	50.00	30.00
O107	6¢ Lincoln	110.00	95.00
	Post Office Dept. Issue: Black		
O108	3¢ Figure of Value	7.50	2.50
	Treasury Dept. Issue: Brown		
O109	3¢ Washington	27.50	3.00
O110	6¢ Lincoln	50.00	17.50
O111	10¢ Jefferson	70.00	20.00
O112	30¢ Hamilton	800.00	140.00
O113	90¢ Perry	825.00	140.00
	War Dept. Issue: Rose Red		
O114	1¢ Franklin	2.00	1.50
O115	2¢ Jackson	3.00	1.50
O116	3¢ Washington	3.00	.75
a	Imperf. pair	900.00	
b	Double impression	750.00	
	Double transfer	6.00	4.00
O117	6¢ Lincoln	2.50	.80
O118	10¢ Jefferson	20.00	17.50
O119	12¢ Clay	15.00	5.00
O120	30¢ Hamilton	47.50	40.00

Issues of 1910-11	Un	U
Perf. 12		

Official Postal Savings Mail

These stamps were used to prepay postage on official correspondence of the Postal Savings Division of the Post Office Department. Discontinued Sept. 23, 1914.

O121	2¢ Postal Savings	9.00	1.10
	Double transfer	12.50	2.00
O122	50¢ dark green	110.00	25.00
O123	$1 ultramarine	100.00	7.00
	Wmkd. (190)		
O124	1¢ dark violet	5.50	1.00
O125	2¢ Postal Savings (O121)	30.00	3.50
O126	10¢ carmine	10.00	1.00

Penalty Mail Stamps

Stamps for use by government departments were reinstituted in 1983. Now known as Penalty Mail stamps, they help provide a better accounting of actual mail costs for official departments and agencies, etc.

Beginning with #O127, unused values are for never-hinged stamps.

Issues of 1983-91, Unwmkd., Perf. 11 x 10.5		
O127	1¢, Jan. 12, 1983	.15	.15
O128	4¢, Jan. 12, 1983	.15	.25
O129	13¢, Jan. 12, 1983	.26	.75
O129A	14¢, May 15, 1985	.28	.50
O130	17¢, Jan. 12, 1983	.34	.40

Issues of 1983-91	Un	U
Perf 11 x 10.5		
O131, O134, O137, O142 Not assigned		
O132	$1, Jan. 12, 1983	1.75	1.00
O133	$5, Jan. 12, 1983	9.00	5.00
Coil Stamps, Perf. 10 Vertically		
O135	20¢, Jan. 12, 1983	2.00	2.00
a	Imperf. pair	2,000.00	
O136	22¢, May 15, 1985	.60	2.00
Perf. 11		
O138	"D" postcard rate (14¢) Feb. 4, 1985	3.50	5.00
Coil Stamps, Perf. 10 Vertically		
O138A	15¢, June 11, 1988	.30	.50
O138B	20¢, May 19, 1988	.40	.30
O139	"D" (22¢), Feb. 4, 1985	4.50	3.00
O140	"E" (25¢), Mar. 22, 1988	.50	2.00
O141	25¢, June 11, 1988	.50	.50
Perf. 11		
O143	1¢, July 5, 1989	.15	.15
Perf. 10		
O144	"F" (29¢), Jan. 22, 1991	.58	.35
O145	29¢, May 24, 1991	.58	.25
Perf. 11		
O146	4¢, Apr. 6, 1991	.15	.30
O147	19¢, May 24, 1991	.38	.50
O148	23¢, May 24, 1991	.46	.30

Variable Rate Coil Stamps

Date of Issue: August 20, 1992
Printing: Intaglio

Date of Issue: February 19, 1994
Printing: Gravure

These are coil postage stamps printed without denominations. The denomination is imprinted by the dispensing equipment called a Postage and Mailing Center (PMC). Denominations can be set between 1¢ and $99.99. In 1993, the minimum denomination was adjusted to 19¢ (the postcard rate at the time).

1912-1955

Q1   Q2   Q3

Q4   Q5   Q6

Q7   Q8   Q9

Q10   Q11   Q12

QE1   QE2   QE3

	Issues of 1913	Un	U	PB	#	FDC
	Wmkd. (190), Perf. 12					
	Parcel Post Stamps					
	Issued for the prepayment of postage on parcel post packages only. Beginning July 1, 1913 these stamps were valid for all postal purposes.					
Q1	1¢ Post Office Clerk, July 1, 1913	2.50	.85	30.00	(4)	*1,500.00*
	Double transfer	5.00	3.00			
Q2	2¢ City Carrier, July 1, 1913	3.00	.60	35.00	(4)	*1,500.00*
	2¢ lake	—				
	Double transfer	—	—			
Q3	3¢ Railway Postal Clerk, Apr. 5, 1913	6.50	4.50	65.00	(4)	*3,000.00*
	Retouched at lower right corner	15.00	12.50			
	Double transfer	15.00	12.50			
Q4	4¢ Rural Carrier, July 1, 1913	17.50	1.90	250.00	(4)	*3,000.00*
	Double transfer	—	—			
Q5	5¢ Mail Train, July 1, 1913	15.00	1.25	250.00	(4)	*3,000.00*
	Double transfer	25.00	5.00			
Q6	10¢ Steamship and Mail Tender	25.00	1.75	300.00	(4)	
	Double transfer	—	—			
Q7	15¢ Automobile Service, July 1, 1913	40.00	7.75	500.00	(4)	
Q8	20¢ Aeroplane Carrying Mail	80.00	15.00	1,050.00	(4)	
Q9	25¢ Manufacturing	37.50	4.00	2,500.00	(6)	
Q10	50¢ Dairying, Mar. 15, 1913	150.00	27.50	1,500.00	(4)	
Q11	75¢ Harvesting	45.00	22.50	3,000.00	(6)	
Q12	$1 Fruit Growing, Jan. 3, 1913	240.00	17.00	*20,000.00*	(6)	
	Special Handling Stamps					
	Issued for use on parcel post packages to secure the same expeditious handling accorded first class mail matter.					
	Issues of 1925, 1928-29, 1955, Unwmkd., Perf. 11,					
QE1	10¢ Special Handling, 1955	1.00	.80	15.00	(6)	
a	Wet printing, June 25, 1928	2.50	.80			45.00
QE2	15¢ Special Handling, 1955	1.10	.70	27.50	(6)	
a	Wet printing, June 25, 1928	2.50	.70			45.00
QE3	20¢ Special Handling, 1955	1.75	1.00	30.00	(6)	
a	Wet printing, June 25, 1928	3.00	1.00			45.00
QE4	25¢ Special Handling, 1929	15.00	5.50	240.00	(6)	
a	25¢ deep grn., Apr. 11, 1925	25.00	4.50	325.00	(6)	225.00
	"A" and "T" of "STATES" joined at top	37.50	20.00			
	"T" and "A" of "POSTAGE" joined at top	37.50	37.50			
	Parcel Post Postage Due Stamps					
	Issued for affixing by a postal clerk to any parcel post package to denote the amount to be collected from the addressee because of insufficient prepayment of postage. Beginning July 1, 1913 these stamps were valid for use as regular postage due stamps.					
	Issues of 1913, Wmkd. (190), Perf. 12					
JQ1	1¢ Figure of Value, Nov. 27	6.00	2.75	550.00	(6)	
JQ2	2¢ dark green, Dec. 9	50.00	13.00	4,000.00	(6)	
JQ3	5¢ dark green, Nov. 27	8.00	3.50	675.00	(6)	
JQ4	10¢ dark green, Dec. 12	110.00	30.00	*10,000.00*	(6)	
JQ5	25¢ Figure of Value, Dec. 16	55.00	3.25	4,500.00	(6)	

Migratory Bird Hunting & Conservation

1934-1969

RW1

RW3

RW10

RW13

RW15

RW16

RW23

RW26

	Issues of 1934-69	Un	U	PB	#	Q
	Department of Agriculture Duck Stamps					
RW1	1934, $1 Mallards Alighting	475.00	90.00	6,000.00	(6)	635,001
a	Imperf. pair	—				
b	Vert. pair, imperf. horiz.	—				
RW2	1935, $1 Canvasbacks	425.00	110.00	7,000.00	(6)	448,204
RW3	1936, $1 Canada Geese	225.00	55.00	2,500.00	(6)	603,623
RW4	1937, $1 Scaup Ducks	190.00	35.00	1,750.00	(6)	783,039
RW5	1938, $1 Pintail Drake and Hen Alighting	190.00	35.00	1,800.00	(6)	1,002,715
	Department of the Interior Duck Stamps					
RW6	1939, $1 Green-winged Teal	125.00	25.00	1,250.00	(6)	1,111,561
RW7	1940, $1 Black Mallards	125.00	25.00	1,250.00	(6)	1,260,810
RW8	1941, $1 Ruddy Ducks	125.00	25.00	1,000.00	(6)	1,439,967
RW9	1942, $1 Baldpates	125.00	25.00	1,050.00	(6)	1,383,629
RW10	1943, $1 Wood Ducks	55.00	20.00	425.00	(6)	1,169,352
RW11	1944, $1 White-fronted Geese	50.00	20.00	400.00	(6)	1,487,029
RW12	1945, $1 Shoveller Ducks	37.50	15.00	300.00	(6)	1,725,505
RW13	1946, $1 Redhead Ducks	32.50	10.00	260.00	(6)	2,016,841
RW14	1947, $1 Snow Geese	32.50	10.00	260.00	(6)	1,722,677
RW15	1948, $1 Buffleheads in Flight	35.00	10.00	250.00	(6)	2,127,603
RW16	1949, $2 Goldeneye Ducks	45.00	8.00	250.00	(6)	1,954,734
RW17	1950, $2 Trumpeter Swans	47.50	8.00	325.00	(6)	1,903,644
RW18	1951, $2 Gadwall Ducks	47.50	5.00	325.00	(6)	2,167,767
RW19	1952, $2 Harlequin Ducks	50.00	5.00	325.00	(6)	2,296,628
RW20	1953, $2 Blue-winged Teal	50.00	5.00	350.00	(6)	2,268,446
RW21	1954, $2 Ring-necked Ducks	50.00	5.00	325.00	(6)	2,184,550
RW22	1955, $2 Blue Geese	50.00	5.00	325.00	(6)	2,369,940
RW23	1956, $2 American Merganser	50.00	5.00	325.00	(6)	2,332,014
RW24	1957, $2 American Eider	50.00	5.00	340.00	(6)	2,355,190
RW25	1958, $2 Canada Geese	50.00	5.00	325.00	(6)	2,176,425
RW26	1959, $3 Labrador Retriever Carrying Mallard Drake	80.00	5.00	300.00	(4)	1,626,115
RW27	1960, $3 Redhead Ducks	65.00	5.00	285.00	(4)	1,725,634
RW28	1961, $3 Mallard Hen and Ducklings	70.00	5.00	285.00	(4)	1,344,236
RW29	1962, $3 Pintail Drakes	80.00	6.00	350.00	(4)	1,147,212
RW30	1963, $3 Pair of Brant Landing	80.00	6.00	350.00	(4)	1,448,191
RW31	1964, $3 Hawaiian Nene Geese	80.00	6.00	1,750.00	(6)	1,573,155
RW32	1965, $3 Three Canvasback Drakes	75.00	6.00	325.00	(4)	1,558,197
RW33	1966, $3 Whistling Swans	75.00	6.00	300.00	(4)	1,805,341
RW34	1967, $3 Old Squaw Ducks	75.00	6.00	300.00	(4)	1,934,697
RW35	1968, $3 Hooded Mergansers	55.00	6.00	225.00	(4)	1,837,139
RW36	1969, $3 White-winged Scoters	55.00	5.00	225.00	(4)	2,072,108

Migratory Bird Hunting and Conservation Stamps (popularly known as "Duck Stamps") are sold as hunting permits. While they are sold through many post offices, they are not usable for postage.

	Issues of 1970-1994	Un	U	PB	#	Q
	Department of the Interior Duck Stamps (continued)					
RW37	1970, $3 Ross's Geese	50.00	5.00	225.00	(4)	2,420,244
RW38	1971, $3 Three Cinnamon Teal	35.00	5.00	125.00	(4)	2,441,664
RW39	1972, $5 Emperor Geese	20.00	5.00	85.00	(4)	2,179,628
RW40	1973, $5 Steller's Eiders	17.00	5.00	85.00	(4)	2,113,594
RW41	1974, $5 Wood Ducks	16.00	5.00	75.00	(4)	2,190,268
RW42	1975, $5 Canvasbacks Decoy, 3 Flying Canvasbacks	12.50	5.00	50.00	(4)	2,218,589
RW43	1976, $5 Canada Geese	10.00	5.00	50.00	(4)	2,248,394
RW44	1977, $5 Pair of Ross's Geese	11.00	5.00	55.00	(4)	2,180,625
RW45	1978, $5 Hooded Merganser Drake	10.00	5.00	52.50	(4)	2,196,758
RW46	1979, $7.50 Green-winged Teal	12.00	5.00	55.00	(4)	2,209,572
RW47	1980, $7.50 Mallards	12.00	5.00	55.00	(4)	2,103,021
RW48	1981, $7.50 Ruddy Ducks	12.00	5.00	55.00	(4)	1,907,114
RW49	1982, $7.50 Canvasbacks	12.00	5.00	55.00	(4)	1,926,253
RW50	1983, $7.50 Pintails	12.00	5.00	55.00	(4)	1,867,998
RW51	1984, $7.50 Widgeons	12.00	5.00	55.00	(4)	1,913,509
RW52	1985, $7.50 Cinnamon Teal	12.00	5.00	55.00	(4)	1,780,760
RW53	1986, $7.50 Fulvous Whistling Duck	10.00	5.00	55.00	(4)	1,794,448
a	Black omitted	3,250.00				
RW54	1987, $10 Redheads	14.00	7.50	60.00	(4)	1,663,112
RW55	1988, $10 Snow Goose	14.00	7.50	65.00	(4)	1,394,923
RW56	1989, $12.50 Lesser Scaup	17.50	7.50	80.00	(4)	
RW57	1990, $12.50 Black Bellied Whistling Duck	17.50	7.50	85.00	(4)	
RW58	1991, $15 King Eiders	20.00	7.50	100.00	(4)	
RW59	1992, $15 Spectacled Eider	20.00	7.50	100.00	(4)	
RW60	1993, $15 Canvasbacks	20.00	7.50	100.00	(4)	
RW61	1994, $15 Red-breasted Merganser	20.00	—			

RW26-34

RW37-53

RW57

RW58-present

Gum side (back) of duck stamps.

RW38

RW39

RW46

RW49

RW54

RW57

RW58

RW59

RW60

RW61

Stamped Envelopes

1853-1886

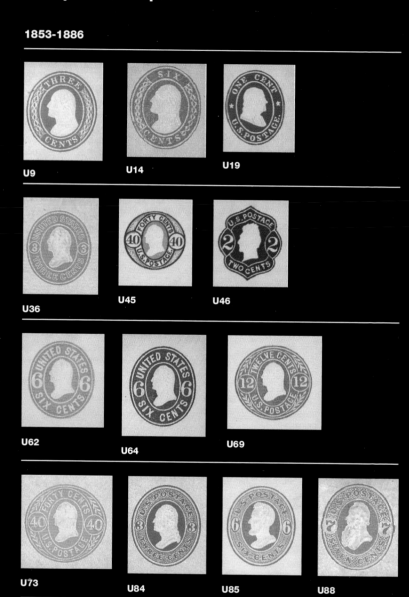

U9

U14

U19

U36

U45

U46

U62

U64

U69

U73

U84

U85

U88

U97

U103

U113

Issues of 1853-64		Un	U

Represented below is only a partial listing of stamped envelopes. At least one example is listed for most die types; most die types exist on several colors of envelope paper. Values are for cut squares; prices for entire envelopes are higher. Color in italic is the color of the envelope paper; when no color is specified, envelope paper is white. "W" with catalog number indicates wrapper instead of envelope.

		Un	U
U1	3¢ red Washington (top label 13mm wide), *buff*	200.00	20.00
U4	3¢ red Washington(top label 15mm wide) *buff*	225.00	20.00
U5	3¢ red (label has octagonal ends)	4,000.00	375.00
U7	3¢ red (label 20mm wide)	600.00	85.00
U9	3¢ red (label 14½mm)	20.00	2.75
U12	6¢ red Washington, *buff*	100.00	55.00
U14	6¢ green Washington, *buff*	185.00	80.00
U15	10¢ green Washington (label 15½mm wide)	150.00	70.00
U17	10¢ green (label 20mm)	200.00	100.00
a	10¢ pale green	175.00	100.00
U19	1¢ blue Franklin (period after "POSTAGE"), *buff*	27.50	12.50
U23	1¢ blue (bust touches inner frame line), *orange*	450.00	350.00
U24	1¢ blue (no period after "POSTAGE"), *buff*	200.00	90.00
U27	3¢ red, no label, *buff*	17.50	12.50
U28	3¢ + 1¢ (U12 and U9)	325.00	225.00
U30	6¢ red Wash., no label	2,250.00	1,250.00
U33	10¢ green, no label, *buff*	1,100.00	250.00
U34	3¢ pink Washington (outline lettering)	17.50	5.00
U36	3¢ pink, *blue* (letter sheet)	70.00	50.00
U39	6¢ pink Washington, *buff*	60.00	55.00
U40	10¢ yellow green Wash.	30.00	30.00
U42	12¢ red, brn. Wash., *buff*	170.00	150.00
U44	24¢ Washington, *buff*	180.00	140.00
U45	40¢ blk., red Wash., *buff*	275.00	275.00
U46	2¢ black Jackson ("U.S. POSTAGE" downstroke, tail of "2" unite near point)	32.50	15.00
U49	2¢ black ("POSTAGE" downstroke and tail of "2" touch but do not merge), *orange*	1,050.00	
U50	2¢ blk. Jack. ("U.S. POST." stamp 24-25mm wide), *buff*	9.00	8.50

Issues of 1863-86		Un	U
W51	2¢ blk. Jack. ("U.S. POST." stamp 24-25mm wide), *buff*	160.00	150.00
U54	2¢ blk. Jack. ("U.S. POST." stp. 25½-26½mm), *buff*	11.00	9.00
W55	2¢ blk. Jack. ("U.S. POST." stp. 25½-26½mm), *buff*	75.00	50.00
U58	3¢ pink Washington (solid lettering)	6.50	1.50
U60	3¢ brown Washington	40.00	20.00
U62	6¢ pink Washington	60.00	25.00
U64	6¢ purple Washington	42.50	20.00
U66	9¢ lemon Washington, *buff*	350.00	200.00
U67	9¢ orange Washington, *buff*	90.00	72.50
U68	12¢ brn. Wash., *buff*	350.00	195.00
U69	12¢ red brown Wash., *buff*	85.00	50.00
U70	18¢ red Washington, *buff*	85.00	80.00
U71	24¢ bl. Washington, *buff*	90.00	72.50
U72	30¢ green Washington, *buff*	60.00	50.00
U73	40¢ rose Washington, *buff*	80.00	*200.00*
U75	1¢ blue Franklin (bust points to end of "N" of "ONE"), *amber*	27.50	22.50
U78	2¢ brown Jackson (bust narrow at back; small, thick numerals)	35.00	12.50
U84	3¢ grn. Washington ("ponytail" projects below bust), *cream*	7.50	3.00
U85	6¢ dark red Lincoln (neck very long at back)	16.00	12.50
a	6¢ vermilion	12.50	12.50
U88	7¢ verm. Stanton (figures 7 normal), *amber*	42.50	*165.00*
U89	10¢ olive blk. Jefferson	425.00	375.00
U92	10¢ brown Jefferson, *amber*	65.00	45.00
U93	12¢ plum Clay (chin prominent)	105.00	70.00
U97	15¢ red orange Webster (has side whiskers), *amber*	135.00	165.00
U99	24¢ purple Scott (locks of hair project, top of head)	110.00	100.00
U103	30¢ black Hamilton (back of bust very narrow), *amber*	175.00	200.00
U105	90¢ carmine Perry (front of bust very narrow, pointed)	130.00	185.00
U113	1¢ lt. blue Frank. (lower part of bust points to end of "E" in "ONE")	1.25	.75
a	1¢ dark blue	7.00	5.00

Issues of 1874-86		Un	U
U114	1¢ lt. blue (lower part of bust points to end of "E" in "Postage"), *amber*	3.75	3.00
U122	2¢ brown Jackson (bust narrow at back; numerals thin)	90.00	35.00
U128	2¢ brown Jackson (numerals in long ovals)	40.00	27.50
U132	2¢ brown, die 3 (left numeral touches oval)	55.00	20.00
U134	2¢ brown Jackson (similar to U128-31 but "O" of "TWO" has center netted instead of plain)	550.00	110.00
U139	2¢ brown (bust broad; numerals short, thick)	40.00	30.00
U142	2¢ verm. Jackson (U139)	5.50	2.25
U149	2¢ verm. Jackson (similar to U139-48 but circles around ovals much heavier)	45.00	25.00
W155	2¢ verm. Jackson (like U149 but middle stroke of "N" as thin as verticals), *manila*	17.50	8.00
U156	2¢ verm. Jackson (bottom of bust cut almost semi-circularly)	550.00	100.00
U159	3¢ grn. Wash. (thin letters, long numerals)	20.00	5.00
U163	3¢ grn. Wash. (thick letters, "ponytail" does not project below bust)	1.00	.25
U169	3¢ grn. (top of head egg-shaped; "ponytail" knot projects as point), *amber*	200.00	90.00
U172	5¢ Taylor, die 1 (numerals have thick, curved tops)	9.00	7.00
U177	5¢ blue, die 2 (numerals have long, thin tops)	6.50	5.25
U183	6¢ red Lincoln (neck short at back), *cream*	15.00	9.00
U186	7¢ verm. Stanton (figures turned up at ends), *amber*	90.00	52.50
U187	10¢ brown Jefferson (very large head)	27.50	15.00
U190	10¢ choc. Jeff. (knot of "ponytail" stands out) *amb.*	6.50	5.50
U195	12¢ plum Clay (chin receding)	160.00	72.50
U198	15¢ orange Webster (no side whiskers)	37.50	27.50
U201	24¢ purple Scott (hair does not project)	140.00	100.00
U204	30¢ blk. Hamilton (back of bust rather broad)	60.00	25.00
U212	90¢ carm. Perry (front of bust broad, sloping), *amber*	140.00	185.00
U218	3¢ red Post Rider, Train (1 line under "POSTAGE")	50.00	22.50
U225	5¢ brown Garfield, *blue*	45.00	32.50

Issues of 1883-93		Un	U
U228	2¢ red Washington, *amber*	4.25	1.75
U234	2¢ red, four wavy lines in oval (wavy lines fine, clear), *fawn*	4.50	2.50
U236	2¢ red (wavy lines thick, blurred)	6.00	3.00
U240	2¢ red Washington (3½ links over left "2")	55.00	30.00
U244	2¢ red Wash. (2 links below right "2"), *amber*	125.00	60.00
U249	2¢ red Washington (round "O" in "TWO"), *fawn*	575.00	325.00
U250	4¢ green Jackson, die 1 (left numeral 2¾mm wide)	3.00	2.50
U256	4¢ green, die 2 (left numeral 3¼mm wide)	4.00	4.00
U259	4¢, die 2, *amber manila*	7.75	5.00
U262	2¢ brn. Wash. (U234), *blue*	11.50	8.00
U267	2¢ brn. Wash. (U236)	12.00	5.00
U270	2¢ brown Washington (2 links below right "2")	80.00	32.50
U274	2¢ brown Wash. (round "O" in "TWO"), *amber*	175.00	65.00
U277	2¢ brn. Washington (extremity of bust below "ponytail" forms point)	.35	.15
U288	2¢ brn. Wash. (extremity of bust is rounded)	150.00	30.00
U294	1¢ blue Franklin, no wavy lines	.50	.20
U302	1¢ dark blue, *manila*	19.00	8.00
U307	2¢ grn. Washington ("G" of "POSTAGE" has no bar), *oriental buff*	65.00	25.00
U314	2¢ green ("G" has bar, ear indicated by 1 heavy line), *blue*	.50	.20
U320	2¢ green (like U314 but ear indicated by 2 curved lines), *oriental buff*	155.00	37.50
U327	4¢ carmine Jackson, *blue*	4.00	3.50
U331	5¢ blue Grant (space between beard and collar), *amber*	3.75	1.75
U335	5¢ blue (collar touches beard), *amber*	9.00	5.00
U340	30¢ red brown Hamilton (U204), *manila*	40.00	40.00
U344	90¢ pur. Perry (U212), *oriental buff*	70.00	75.00
U348	1¢ Columbus and Liberty	2.00	1.00
U351	10¢ slate brown	30.00	25.00

U142   W155   U159

U172   U190   U204

U218   U250   U294

U314   U348   U351

U358

U368

U374

U377

U379

U386

U390

U393

U398

U400

U406

U416

Issues of 1899-1906	Un	U
U355	1¢ grn. Frank. (U294), *bl.*	9.00	6.00
U358	2¢ carm. Washington (bust points to first notch of inner oval)	2.50	1.50
U362	2¢ carmine (bust points to middle of second notch of inner oval, "ponytail")	.25	.20
U368	2¢ carm. (same as U362 but hair flowing; no ribbon "ponytail"), *amber*	7.50	6.25
U371	4¢ brown Lincoln (bust pointed, undraped)	15.00	10.00
U374	4¢ brown (head larger; inner oval has no notches)	9.00	7.00
U377	5¢ blue Grant (like U331, U335 but smaller)	8.75	8.50
U379	1¢ green Franklin, horizontal oval	.45	.15
U386	2¢ carm. Wash. (1 short, 2 long vertical lines at right of "CENTS"), *amber*	1.50	.20
U390	4¢ chocolate Grant	18.00	11.00
U393	5¢ blue Lincoln	16.00	9.50
U398	2¢ carm. Washington, recut die (lines at end of "TWO CENTS" all short), *blue*	3.00	.90
U400	1¢ grn. Frank., oval, die 1 (wide "D" in "UNITED")	.25	.15
U401a	1¢ grn. Frank., die 2 (narrow "D"), *amber*	.85	.70
U402b	1¢, grn. die 3 (wide "S" in "STATES"), *oriental buff*	6.00	1.50
U403c	1¢, die 4 (sharp angle at back of bust, "N," "E" of "ONE" are parallel), *blue*	3.50	1.25
U406	2¢ brn. red Wash., die 1 (oval "O" in "TWO" and "C" in "CENTS")	.70	.15
U407a	2¢, die 2 (like die 1, but hair recut in 2 distinct locks, top of head), *amb.*	100.00	45.00
U408b	2¢ die 3 (round "O" in "TWO" and "C" in "CENTS," coarse letters), *or. buff*	6.00	2.50
U411c	2¢ carmine, die 4 (like die 3 but lettering, hair lines fine, clear)	.35	.16
U412d	2¢ carmine Wash., die 5 (all S's wide), *amber*	.55	.35
U413e	2¢ carm., die 6 (like die 1 but front of bust narrow), *oriental buff*	.50	.35
U414f	2¢ carm., die 7 (like die 6 but upper corner of front of bust cut away), *blue*	12.50	7.50
U414g	2¢ carm., die 8 (like die 7 but lower stroke of "S" in "CENTS" straight line; hair as in die 2), *blue*	12.50	7.50

Issues of 1907-32	Un	U
U416	4¢ blk. Wash., die 2 ("F" is 1³⁄₄mm from left "4")	3.50	2.25
a	4¢, die 1 ("F" is 1mm from left "4")	4.25	3.00
U420	1¢ grn. Frank., round, die 1 ("UNITED" nearer inner circle than outer circle)	.15	.15
U421a	1¢, die 2 (large "U"; "NT" closely spaced), *amber*	3.00	175.00
U423a	1¢ grn. die 3 (knob of hair at back of neck; large "NT" widely spaced), *blue*	.75	.45
b	1¢, die 4 ("UNITED" nearer outer circle than inner)	1.25	.65
c	1¢, die 5 (narrow, oval "C")	.65	.35
U429	2¢ carmine Washington, die 1 (letters broad, numerals vertical, "E" closer than "N" to inner circle)	.15	.15
a	2¢, die 2 (like die 1 but "U" far from left circle), *amber*	9.00	6.00
b	2¢, die 3 (like die 2 but inner circles very thin)	30.00	25.00
U430b	2¢, die 4 (like die 1 but "C" very close to left circle), *amber*	20.00	10.00
c	2¢, die 5 (small head, 8³⁄₄mm from tip of nose to back of neck; "TS" of "CENTS" close at bottom)	1.10	.35
U431d	2¢, die 6 (like die 6 but "TS" of "CENTS" far apart at bottom; left numeral slopes right), *oriental buff*	3.00	2.00
e	2¢, die 7 (large head, both numerals slope right, T's have short top strokes)	2.75	1.75
U432h	2¢, die 8 (like die 7 but all T's have long top strokes), *blue*	.60	.25
i	2¢, die 9 (narrow, oval "C")	.90	.30

Issues of 1916-62	Un	U
U436	3¢ dk. violet Washington, die 1 (as 2¢)	.50	.16
U440	4¢ black Washington	1.00	.60
U447	2¢ on 3¢ dark violet, rose surcharge	6.00	5.50
U458	Same as U447, black surcharge, bars 2mm apart	.45	.35
U468	Same as U458, bars 1½mm apart	.60	.45
U481	1½¢ brown Washington, die 1 (as U429)	.15	.15
W485	1½¢ brown, *manila*	.75	.15
U490	1½¢ on 1¢ grn. Franklin, black surcharge	3.75	3.50
U499	1½¢ on 1¢, *manila*	10.00	6.00
U510	1½¢ on 1¢ grn., outline numeral in surcharge	1.75	1.25
U522	2¢ carmine Liberty Bell	1.00	.50
a	2¢, center bar of "E" of "Postage" same length as top bar	6.00	4.00
U523	1¢ ol. grn. Mount Vernon	1.10	1.00
U524	1½¢ choc. Mount Vernon	2.00	1.50
U525	2¢ carmine Mount Vernon	.40	.16
a	2¢, die 2 "S" of "POSTAGE" raised	70.00	16.00
U526	3¢ violet Mount Vernon	2.00	.35
U527	4¢ black Mount Vernon	18.00	15.00
U528	5¢ dark blue Mount Vernon	4.00	3.25
U529	6¢ orange Washington	5.00	2.75
U530	6¢ orange Wash., *amber*	10.00	7.50
U531	6¢ or. Washington, *blue*	10.00	8.50
U532	1¢ green Franklin	5.00	1.75
U533	2¢ carmine Wash. (oval)	.70	.25
U534	3¢ dk. violet Washington, die 4 (short N in UNITED, thin crossbar in A of STATES)	.40	.16
U535	1½¢ brown Washington	4.50	3.50
U536	4¢ red violet Franklin	.75	.16
U537	2¢ + 2¢ Wash. (U429)	3.00	1.50
U538	2¢ + 2¢ Washington (U533)	.75	.20
U539	3¢ + 1¢ purple, die 1 (4½mm tall, thick "3")	14.00	10.00
U540	3¢ + 1¢ purple, die 3 (4mm tall, thin "3")	.50	.15
a	Die 2 (4½mm tall, thin "3" in medium circle), entire	1,000.00	—
U541	1¼¢ turquoise Franklin	.70	.50
a	Die 2 ("4" 3½mm high), precanceled		2.00
U542	2½¢ dull blue Washington	.80	.50
U543	4¢ brn. Pony Express Rider	.60	.30
U544	5¢ dark blue Lincoln	.80	.20
c	With albino impression of 4¢ (U536)	50.00	—

Issues of 1962-78	Un	U
U545	4¢ + 1¢, type 1 (U536)	1.30	.50
U546	5¢ New York World's Fair	.60	.40
U547	1¼¢ brown Liberty Bell		.15
U548	1⁴⁄₁₀¢ brown Liberty Bell		.15
U548a	16⁶⁄₁₀¢ orange Liberty Bell		.15
U549	4¢ blue Old Ironsides	.75	.15
U550	5¢ purple Eagle	.75	.15
a	Tagged	1.00	.15
U551	6¢ green Statue of Liberty	.70	.15
U552	4¢ + 2¢ brt. bl. (U549)	3.75	2.00
U553	5¢ + 1¢ brt. pur. (U550)	3.50	2.25
U554	6¢ lt. blue Herman Melville	.50	.15
U555	6¢ Youth Conference	.75	.15
U556	1⁷⁄₁₀¢ lilac Liberty Bell		.15
U557	8¢ ultramarine Eagle	.40	.15
U561	6¢ + (2¢) lt. grn.	1.00	.30
U562	6¢ + (2¢) lt. blue	2.00	1.50
U563	8¢ rose red Bowling	.50	.15
U564	8¢ Aging Conference	.50	.15
U565	8¢ Transpo '72	.50	.15
U566	8¢ + 2¢ brt. ultra.	.40	.15
U567	10¢ emerald Liberty Bell	.40	.15
U568	1⁸⁄₁₀¢ Volunteer Yourself		.15
U569	10¢ Tennis Centenary	.30	.16
U571	10¢ Compass Rose	.30	.15
a	Brown "10¢/USA" omitted, entire	125.00	
U572	13¢ Quilt Pattern	.35	.15
U573	13¢ Sheaf of Wheat	.35	.15
U574	13¢ Mortar and Pestle	.35	.15
U575	13¢ Tools	.35	.15
U576	13¢ Liberty Tree	.30	.15
U577	2¢ red Nonprofit		.15
U578	2.1¢ yel. green Nonprofit		.15
U579	2.7¢ green Nonprofit		.15
U580	15¢ orange Eagle, A	.35	.15
U581	15¢ red Uncle Sam	.35	.15
U582	13¢ emerald Centennial	.35	.15
U583	13¢ Golf	.45	.20
U584	13¢ Energy Conservation	.40	.15
d	Blk, red omitted, ent.	300.00	
U585	13¢ Energy Development	.40	.15
U586	15¢ on 16¢ blue USA	.35	.15
U587	15¢ Auto Racing	.35	.15
a	Black omitted, entire	125.00	

U447

U468

W485

U522

U523

U524

U530

U531

U541

U542

U543

U569

U576

U581

U587

401

U601

U609

U610

U611

U614

U616

U617

U631

Issues of 1978-92		Un	U
U588	15¢ on 13¢ (U576)	.35	.15
U589	3.1¢ ultramarine nonprofit		.15
U590	3.5¢ purple Violins		.15
U591	5.9¢ Auth Nonprofit Org		.15
U592	18¢ violet Eagle, B	.45	.18
U593	18¢ dark blue Star	.45	.18
U594	20¢ brown Eagle, C	.45	.15
U595	15¢ Veterinary Medicine	.35	.15
U596	15¢ Summer Oly. Games	.60	.15
a	Red, grn. omitted, ent.	225.00	
U597	15¢ Highwheeler Bicycle	.40	.15
a	Blue "15¢ USA" omitted, entire	100.00	
U598	15¢ America's Cup	.40	.15
U599	Brown 15¢ Honeybee	.35	.15
a	Brown "15¢ USA" omitted, entire	125.00	
U600	18¢ Blind Veterans	.45	.18
U601	20¢ Capitol Dome	.45	.15
U602	20¢ Great Seal of U.S.	.45	.15
U603	20¢ Purple Heart	.45	.15
U604	5.2¢ Auth Nonprofit Org		.15
U605	20¢ Paralyzed Veterans	.45	.15
U606	20¢ Small Business	.50	.15
U607	22¢ Eagle, D	.55	.15

Issues of 1978-92		Un	U
U608	22¢ Bison	.55	.15
U609	6¢ USS Constitution		.15
U610	8.5¢ Mayflower		.15
U611	25¢ Stars	.60	.15
U612	8.4¢ USF Constellation		.15
U613	25¢ Snowflake	.50	.25
U614	25¢ USA, Stars (Philatelic Mail)	.50	.25
U615	25¢ Stars (lined paper)	.50	.25
U616	25¢ Love	.50	.25
U617	25¢ Space hologram	.60	.28
U618	25¢ Football hologram	.50	.25
U619	29¢ Star	.58	.29
U620	11.1¢ Birds		.20
U621	29¢ Love	.58	.29
U622	29¢ Magazine Industry	.58	.29
U623	29¢ Star and Bars	.58	.29
U624	29¢ Country Geese	.58	.58
U625	29¢ Space Shuttle	.58	.29
U626	29¢ Western Americana	.58	.29
U627	29¢ Protect the Environment	.58	.29
U628	19.8¢ Bulk Rate precanceled		.38
U629	29¢ Disabled Americans	.58	.29
U630	29¢ Kitten	.60	.30
U631	29¢ Football	.60	.30

Who's the father of American football?

Played under a variety of rules and formats since the early 19th century, football as we know it today took shape under the influence of Walter Camp, who coached the Yale University team in the late 1800s.

Camp led an intercollegiate rules committee that standardized players per team from 15 to 11, cut the size of the field and instituted the scrimmage and system of downs. Within ten years, President Theodore Roosevelt called upon Yale, Harvard and Princeton to place additional reforms to make the game safer. This committee expanded to over 60 schools, which evolved into the National Collegiate Athletic Association. **(#U631)**

Stand Out in a Crowd

- Let the pros address your envelopes
- The convenient and economical way to get high-quality and distinctive personalized envelopes

Save Time and Money

With personalized stamped envelopes from your US Postal Service, addressing correspondence couldn't be easier. No more typing your return address or affixing postage. That's time saved. And each envelope costs only a few cents more than the stamp —

that's money saved.

To make it even easier, your order will be delivered directly to your home or office.

Personal and Professional

These envelopes are ideal for business or personal use. The brightly colored stamps demand attention and the

unique, professional appearance of the return address denotes credibility. You can even designate two lines to boldly call out your title, business or service.

Impress your friends, family and business associates. Make a statement with the Postal Service's personalized stamped envelopes.

For Information

For more information or an order form call our new toll-free number:

1-800-STAMP24

PERSONALIZED STAMPED ENVELOPES
"MAKE AN IMPRESSION"
BOX 419208
KANSAS CITY, MO 64141-6208

USA
BULK
RATE

Nonprofit
USA

LD ENVELOPES

1-6208

PERSONALIZED STAMPED ENVELOPES
"MAKE AN IMPRESSION"
BOX 419208
KANSAS CITY, MO 64141-6208

USA 32

PERSONALIZED STAMPED ENVELOPES
"MAKE AN IMPRESSION"
BOX 419208
KANSAS CITY, MO 64141-6208

32
USA

PERSONALIZED STAMPED ENVELOPES
"MAKE AN IMPRESSION"
BOX 419208
KANSAS CITY, MO 64141-6208

Airmail Envelopes and Aerogrammes

1929-1973

UC1 UC3 UC7

UC14

UC8

UC21 UC25

UC26 UC30

Issues of 1929-46		Un	U
UC1	5¢ blue Airplane, die 1 (vertical rudder is not semicircular)	3.50	2.00
	1933 wmk., entire	700.00	700.00
	1937 wmk., entire	—	2000.00
	Bicolored border omitted, entire	600.00	
UC2	5¢ blue, die 2 (vertical rudder is semicircular)	11.00	5.00
	1929 wmk., entire	—	1,500.00
	1933 wmk., entire	600.00	
UC3	6¢ orange Airplane, die 2a ("6" is 6½mm wide)	1.45	.40
a	With #U436a added impression	*3,000.00*	
UC4	6¢ orange, die 2b ("6" is 6mm wide)	2.75	2.00
UC5	6¢ orange, die 2c ("6" is 5½mm wide)	.75	.30
UC6	6¢ orange, die 3 (vertical rudder leans forward)	1.00	.35
a	6¢ orange, *blue*, entire	*3,500.00*	*2,400.00*
UC7	8¢ olive green Airplane	13.00	3.50
UC8	6¢ on 2¢ carm. Washington (U429)	1.25	.65
a	6¢ on 1¢ green (U420)	*1,750.00*	
c	6¢ on 3¢ purple (U437a)	*3,000.00*	
UC9	6¢ on 2¢ Wash. (U525)	75.00	40.00
UC10	5¢ on 6¢ orange (UC3)	2.75	1.50
a	Double surcharge	60.00	
Issues of 1946-58			
UC11	5¢ on 6¢ orange (UC4)	9.00	5.50
UC13	5¢ on 6¢ orange (UC6)	.80	.60
a	Double surcharge	60.00	
UC14	5¢ carm. DC-4, die 1 (end of wing on right is smooth curve)	.75	.20
UC16	10¢ red, DC-4 2-line back inscription, entire, *pale blue*	7.50	6.00
a	"Air Letter" on face, 4-line back inscription	16.00	14.00
	Die-cutting reversed	275.00	
b	10¢ chocolate	400.00	
c	"Air Letter" and "Aerogramme" on face	45.00	12.50
d	3-line back inscription	8.00	8.00

Issues of 1946-58		Un	U
UC17	5¢ Postage Centenary	.40	.25
UC18	6¢ carm. Airplane (UC14), type I (6's lean right)	.35	.15
a	Type II (6's upright)	.75	.25
UC20	6¢ on 5¢ (UC15)	.80	.50
a	6¢ on 6¢ carmine, entire	*1,500.00*	
b	Double surcharge	*250.00*	
UC21	6¢ on 5¢ (UC14)	26.00	17.50
UC22	6¢ on 5¢ (UC14)	3.50	2.50
a	Double surcharge	75.00	
UC23	6¢ on 5¢ (UC17)	1,400.00	
UC25	6¢ red Eagle	.75	.50
UC26	7¢ blue (UC14)	.65	.50
Issues of 1958-73			
UC27	6¢ + 1¢ orange (UC3)	225.00	225.00
UC28	6¢ + 1¢ orange (UC4)	65.00	75.00
UC29	6¢ + 1¢ orange (UC5)	37.50	50.00
UC30	6¢ + 1¢ (UC5)	1.00	.50
UC32	10¢ Jet Airliner, back inscription in 2 lines	6.00	5.00
a	Type 1, entire	10.00	5.00
UC33	7¢ blue Jet Silhouette	.60	.25
UC34	7¢ carmine (UC33)	.60	.25
UC35	11¢ Jet, Globe, entire	2.75	1.50
a	Red omitted	875.00	
a	Die-cutting reversed	35.00	
UC36	8¢ red Jet Airliner	.55	.15
UC37	8¢ red Jet in Triangle	.35	.15
a	Tagged	1.25	.30
UC39	13¢ John Kennedy, entire	3.00	1.50
a	Red omitted	*500.00*	
UC40	10¢ Jet in Triangle	.50	.15
UC41	8¢ + 2¢ (UC37)	.65	.15
UC42	13¢ Human Rights, entire	7.50	4.00
	Die-cutting reversed	75.00	
UC43	11¢ Jet in Circle	.50	.15
UC44	15¢ gray, red, white and blue Birds in Flight	1.50	1.10
UC45	10¢ + (1¢) (UC40)	1.50	.20
UC46	15¢ red, white, bl.	.75	.40

Issues of 1973-91		Un	U
UC47	13¢ red Bird in Flight	.30	.15
UC48	18¢ USA, entire	.90	.30
UC50	22¢ red and bl. USA, entire	.90	.40
UC51	22¢ blue USA, entire	.70	.25
	Die-cutting reversed	25.00	
UC52	22¢ Summer Olympic Games	1.50	.22
UC53	30¢ blue, red, brn. Tour the United States, entire	.65	.30
a	Red "30" omitted	75.00	
UC54	30¢ *yellow, magenta, blue* and *black* (UC53), entire	.65	.30
	Die-cutting reversed	20.00	
UC55	30¢ Made in USA, entire	.65	.30
UC56	30¢ World Communications Year, entire	.65	.30
	Die-cutting reversed	27.50	
UC57	30¢ Olympic Games, entire	.65	.30
UC58	36¢ Landsat, entire	.72	.36
UC59	36¢ Tourism Week, entire	.72	.36
UC60	36¢ Mark Twain/ Halley's Comet, entire	.72	.36
UC61	39¢ Envelope	.78	.40
UC62	39¢ Montgomery Blair	.78	.40
UC63	45¢ Eagle, entire, *blue*	.90	.45
a	White paper	.90	.45

Issues of 1873-75		Un	U
Official Envelopes			
Post Office Department			
Numeral 9¹/₂mm high			
UO1	2¢ black, *lemon*	12.50	6.00
Numeral 10¹/₂mm high			
UO5	2¢ black, *lemon*	5.00	4.00
UO9	3¢ black, *amber*	40.00	35.00
Postal Service			
UO16	blue, *amber*	35.00	22.50
War Department			
UO20	3¢ dk. red Washington	50.00	35.00
UO26	12¢ dark red Clay	100.00	42.00
UO39	10¢ vermilion Jefferson	200.00	
UO48	2¢ red Jackson, *amber*	25.00	12.50
UO55	3¢ red Washington, *fawn*	4.00	2.50
Issues of 1983-91 (Enteres), Penalty Mail Envelopes			
UO73	20¢ blue Great Seal	1.00	*30.00*
UO74	22¢ (seal embossed)	.65	*5.00*
UO75	22¢ (seal typographed)	.60	*20.00*
UO76	"E" (25¢) Great Seal	.65	*20.00*
UO77	25¢ black, blue Great Seal (seal embossed)	.65	*5.00*
UO78	25¢ (seal typographed)	.65	*25.00*
UO79	45¢ (stars illegible)	1.25	*40.00*
UO80	65¢ (stars illegible)	1.50	*50.00*
UO81	45¢ (stars clear)	1.25	*40.00*
UO82	65¢ (stars clear)	1.50	*50.00*
UO83	"F" (29¢) Great Seal	1.00	*20.00*
UO84	29¢ black, blue, entire	.70	*1.00*

Montgomery Blair, U.S. Postmaster General 1861-64

Free city delivery
Railway mail service
Money order system

USA 39

AEROGRAMME · VIA AIRMAIL · PAR AVION

2 Second fold

The Paris Conference of 1863, initiated by Postmaster General Blair, led, in 1874, to the founding of the Universal Postal Union.

Do not use tape or stickers to seal · No enclosures permitted
◄— 1 Fold first at notches ►——►

Additional message area:

What is an Aerogramme?

Airmail service was explored and tested as early as 1911. In 1939, service routes between North America and Europe became operational. The aerogramme originated in Great Britain during World War II as an inexpensive, lightweight air-letter service for correspondence with troops stationed overseas. In 1952, the Universal Postal Union christened the service as the aerogramme. **(#UC62)**

UC53

UC52

UC59

UC57

UC63

UO16

UO20

JX5 **UX6** **UX11** **UX14**

JX16 **UX18** **UX25** **UX27**

JX28 **UX37** **UX43**

UX45 **UX46** **UX48**

JX44

JX50

Issues of 1873-1918		Un	U

Represented below is only a partial listing of postal cards. Values are for entire cards. Color in italic is color of card. Cards preprinted with written address or message usually sell for much less.

		Un	U
UX1	1¢ brown Liberty, wmkd. (90 x 60mm)	300.00	15.00
UX3	1¢ brown Liberty, wmkd. (53 x 36mm)	60.00	2.25
UX4	1¢ blk. Liberty, wmkd USPOD in monogram	1,750.00	300.00
UX5	1¢ blk. Liberty, unwmkd.	50.00	.40
UX6	2¢ blue Liberty, *buff*	20.00	17.50
a	2¢ dark blue, *buff*	25.00	19.00
UX7	1¢ (UX5), inscribed "Nothing But The Address"	50.00	.35
a	23 teeth below "One Cent"	500.00	30.00
b	Printed on both sides	*575.00*	*400.00*
UX8	1¢ brown Jefferson, large "one-cent" wreath	35.00	1.25
c	1¢ chocolate	60.00	6.00
UX9	1¢ blk. Jefferson, *buff*	10.00	.55
a	1¢ blk., *dark buff*	16.50	1.25
UX10	1¢ black Grant	25.00	1.40
UX11	1¢ blue Grant	10.00	2.50
UX12	1¢ black Jefferson, wreath smaller than UX14	27.50	.40
UX13	2¢ blue Liberty, *cream*	125.00	75.00
UX14	1¢ Jefferson	22.50	.40
UX15	1¢ black John Adams	30.00	15.00
UX16	2¢ black Liberty	9.00	9.00
UX17	1¢ black McKinley	4,000.00	2,250.00
UX18	1¢ black McKinley, facing left	9.00	.30
UX19	1¢ black McKinley, triangles in top corners	27.50	.50
UX20	1¢ (UX19), correspondence space at left	40.00	5.00
UX21	1¢ blue McKinley, shaded background	90.00	6.50
a	1¢ bronze blue, *bluish*	165.00	12.50
UX22	1¢ blue McKinley, white background	12.50	.25
UX23	1¢ red Lincoln, solid background	6.00	5.50
UX24	1¢ red McKinley	8.00	.25
UX25	2¢ red Grant	1.25	8.50
UX26	1¢ green Lincoln, solid background	7.00	6.00
UX27	1¢ Jefferson, *buff*	.25	.25
a	1¢ green, *cream*	3.50	.60
UX27C	1¢ green Jefferson, *gray*, die I	*2,000.00*	150.00
UX28	1¢ green Lincoln, *cream*	.60	.30
a	1¢ green, *buff*	1.50	.60
UX29	2¢ red Jefferson, *buff*	35.00	2.00
a	2¢ lake, *cream*	45.00	2.50
c	2¢ vermilion, *buff*	275.00	60.00

Issues of 1917-68		Un	U
UX30	2¢ red Jefferson, *cream*	19.00	1.50
	Surcharged in one line by canceling machine.		
UX31	1¢ on 2¢ red Jefferson	*3,500.00*	*3,500.00*
	Surcharged in two lines by canceling machine.		
UX32	1¢ on 2¢ red Jeff., *buff*	40.00	12.50
a	1¢ on 2¢ vermilion	*95.00*	60.00
b	Double surcharge	—	*82.50*
UX33	1¢ on 2¢ red Jefferson, *cream*	7.50	1.75
a	Inverted surcharge	55.00	
b	Double surcharge	55.00	35.00
d	Triple surcharge	350.00	
	Surcharged in two lines by press printing.		
UX34	1¢ on 2¢ red (UX29)	500.00	45.00
UX35	1¢ on 2¢ red Jefferson, *cream*	200.00	30.00
UX36	1¢ on 2¢ red (UX25)		28,500.00
UX37	3¢ red McKinley, *buff*	3.75	*9.00*
UX38	2¢ carmine rose Franklin	.35	.25
a	Double impression	200.00	
	Surcharged by canceling machine in light green.		
UX39	2¢ on 1¢ grn. Jefferson, *buff*	.50	.35
b	Double surcharge	17.50	20.00
UX40	2¢ on 1¢ green (UX28)	.65	.45
	Surcharged typographically in dark green.		
UX41	2¢ on 1¢ green Jefferson, *buff*	3.50	1.50
a	Invrtd surchge lower left	75.00	125.00
UX42	2¢ on 1¢ green (UX29)	5.00	2.00
a	Surcharged on back	80.00	
UX43	2¢ carmine Lincoln	.25	*1.00*
UX44	2¢ FIPEX	.25	*1.00*
b	Dk. vio. blue omitted	450.00	225.00
UX45	4¢ Statue of Liberty	1.50	*40.00*
UX46	3¢ purple Statue of Liberty	.40	.20
a	"N GOD WE TRUST"	12.00	25.00
UX47	2¢ + 1¢ carmine rose Franklin	160.00	250.00
UX48	4¢ red violet Lincoln	.25	.20
UX49	7¢ World Vacationland	3.00	*35.00*
UX50	4¢ U.S. Customs	.40	*1.00*
a	Blue omitted	450.00	
UX51	4¢ Social Security	.40	*1.00*
b	Blue omitted	*700.00*	
UX52	4¢ blue & red Coast Guard	.30	*1.00*
UX53	4¢ Bureau of the Census	.30	*1.00*
UX54	8¢ blue & red (UX49)	3.00	*35.00*
UX55	5¢ emerald Lincoln	.30	*.50*
UX56	5¢ Women Marines	.35	*1.00*

1970-1990

Issues of 1970-83		Un	U
UX57	5¢ Weather Services	.30	1.00
a	Yellow, black omitted	700.00	
b	Blue omitted	650.00	
c	Black omitted	600.00	
UX58	6¢ brown Paul Revere	.30	1.00
a	Double impression	300.00	
UX59	10¢ blue & red (UX49)	3.00	35.00
UX60	6¢ America's Hospitals	.30	1.00
a	Blue, yellow omitted	700.00	
UX61	6¢ USF *Constellation*	.60	3.00
a	Address side blank	300.00	
UX62	6¢ black Monument Valley	.35	3.00
UX63	6¢ Gloucester, MA	.35	3.00
UX64	6¢ blue John Hanson	.25	1.00
UX65	6¢ magenta Liberty	.25	1.00
UX66	8¢ orange Samuel Adams	.25	1.00
UX67	12¢ Visit USA/ Ship's Figurehead	.35	30.00
UX68	7¢ Charles Thomson	.30	5.00
UX69	9¢ John Witherspoon	.25	1.00
UX70	9¢ blue Caesar Rodney	.25	1.00
UX71	9¢ Federal Court House	.25	1.00
UX72	9¢ green Nathan Hale	.25	1.00
UX73	10¢ Cincinnati Music Hall	.30	1.00
UX74	10¢ John Hancock	.30	1.00
UX75	10¢ John Hancock	.30	.15
UX76	14¢ Coast Guard Eagle	.40	15.00
UX77	10¢ Molly Pitcher	.30	1.00
UX78	10¢ George Rogers Clark	.30	1.00
UX79	10¢ Casimir Pulaski	.30	1.00
UX80	10¢ Olympic Sprinter	.50	1.00
UX81	10¢ Iolani Palace	.30	1.00
UX82	14¢ Olympic Games	.50	10.00
UX83	10¢ Salt Lake Temple	.25	1.00
UX84	10¢ Landing of Rochambeau	.25	1.00
UX85	10¢ Battle of Kings Mtn.	.25	1.00
UX86	19¢ Drake's Golden Hinde	.55	10.00
UX87	10¢ Battle of Cowpens	.25	2.50
UX88	12¢ violet Eagle, nondenominated	.30	.50
UX89	12¢ lt. bl. Isaiah Thomas	.30	.50
UX90	12¢ Nathanael Greene	.30	1.00
UX91	12¢ Lewis and Clark	.30	3.00
UX92	13¢ buff Robert Morris	.30	.50
UX93	13¢ buff Robert Morris	.30	.50
UX94	13¢ "Swamp Fox" Francis Marion	.30	.75
UX95	13¢ LaSalle Claims Louisiana	.30	.75
UX96	13¢ Academy of Music	.30	.75
UX97	13¢ Old Post Office, St. Louis, Missouri	.30	.75
UX100	13¢ Olympic Yachting	.30	.75

Issues of 1984-90		Un	U
UX101	13¢ *Ark* and *Dove,* Maryland	.30	.75
UX102	13¢ Olympic Torch	.30	.75
UX103	13¢ Frederic Baraga	.30	.75
UX104	13¢ Dominguez Adobe	.30	.75
UX105	14¢ Charles Carroll	.30	.50
UX106	14¢ green Charles Carroll	.30	.15
UX107	25¢ Clipper *Flying Cloud*	.70	5.00
UX108	14¢ brt. grn. George Wythe	.30	.50
UX109	14¢ Settlement of Connecticut	.30	.75
UX110	14¢ Stamp Collecting	.30	.75
UX111	14¢ Francis Vigo	.30	.75
UX112	14¢ Settling of Rhode Island	.30	.75
UX113	14¢ Wisconsin Territory	.30	.75
UX114	14¢ National Guard	.30	.75
UX115	14¢ Self-Scouring Plow	.30	.50
UX116	14¢ Constitutional Convention	.30	.50
UX117	14¢ Stars and Stripes	.30	.50
UX118	14¢ Take Pride in America	.30	.50
UX119	14¢ Timberline Lodge	.30	.50
UX120	15¢ Bison and Prairie	.30	.25
UX121	15¢ Blair House	.30	.30
UX122	28¢ *Yorkshire*	.60	3.00
UX123	15¢ Iowa Territory	.30	.50
UX124	15¢ Ohio, Northwest Terr.	.30	.50
UX125	15¢ Hearst Castle	.30	.50
UX126	15¢ The Federalist Papers	.30	.50
UX127	15¢ Hawk and Desert	.30	.50
UX128	15¢ Healy Hall	.30	.50
UX129	15¢ Blue Heron and Marsh	.30	.50
UX130	15¢ Settling of Oklahoma	.30	.50
UX131	21¢ Geese and Mountains	.42	3.00
UX132	15¢ Seagull and Seashore	.30	.50
UX133	15¢ Deer and Waterfall	.30	.50
UX134	15¢ Hull House, Chicago	.30	.50
UX135	15¢ Ind. Hall, Philadelphia	.30	.50
UX136	15¢ Inner Harbor, Baltimore	.30	.50
UX137	15¢ Bridge, New York	.30	.50
UX138	15¢ Capitol, Washington	.30	.50
	#UX139-42 issued in sheets of 4 plus 2 inscribed labels, rouletted 9½ on 2 or 3 sides.		
UX139	15¢ (UX135)	.30	.90
UX140	15¢ The White House	.30	.90
UX141	15¢ (UX137)	.30	.90
UX142	15¢ (UX138)	.30	.90
a	Sheet of 4, #UX139-42	1.20	
UX143	15¢ The White House	1.00	1.00
UX144	15¢ Jefferson Memorial	1.00	1.00
UX145	15¢ Papermaking	.30	.30
UX146	15¢ World Literacy Year	.30	.30

Casimir Pulaski, Savannah, 1779

UX79

Historic Preservation

UX70

UX81

UX83

"Swamp Fox" Francis Marion, 1782

UX94

Settling of Connecticut, 1636

UX109

Settling of Rhode Island, 1636

UX112

Wisconsin Territory, 1836

UX113

Self-scouring steel plow, 1837

UX115

Constitutional Convention, 1787

UX116

Take Pride in America 14 USA

UX118

Historic Preservation USA 14

UX119

America the Beautiful USA 21

UX131

UX143

UX144

UX143 (picture side)

UX144 (picture side)

UX174

UX175

UX176

UX177

UY12

UXC1

UXC2

UXC4

UXC5

UXC6

UXC7

UXC8

UXC9

UXC10

Issues of 1990-93	Un	U
UX147 15¢ George Caleb Bingham	1.00	*1.00*
UX148 15¢ Isaac Royall House	.30	*.50*
UX150 15¢ Stanford University	.30	*.50*
UX151 15¢ Constitution Hall	1.00	*1.00*
UX152 15¢ Chgo. Orchestra Hall	.30	*.50*
UX153 19¢ Flag	.38	.38
UX154 19¢ Carnegie Hall	.38	.38
UX155 19¢ Old Red, UT-Galveston	.38	.38
UX156 19¢ Bill of Rights	.38	.38
UX157 19¢ Notre Dame	.38	.38
UX158 30¢ Niagara Falls	.60	.60
UX159 19¢ The Old Mill	.38	.38
UX160 19¢ Wadsworth Atheneum	.38	.38
UX161 19¢ Cobb Hall	.38	.38
UX162 19¢ Waller Hall	.38	.38
UX163 19¢ America's Cup	1.00	1.00
UX164 19¢ Columbia River Gorge	.38	.38
UX165 19¢ Ellis Island	.38	.38
UX166 19¢ National Cathedral	.38	.38
UX167 19¢ Wren Building	.38	.38
UX168 19¢ Holocaust Memorial	1.00	1.00
UX169 19¢ Fort Recovery	.38	.38
UX170 19¢ Playmakers Theatre	.38	.38
UX171 19¢ O'Kane Hall	.38	.38
UX172 19¢ Beecher Hall	.38	.38
UX173 19¢ Massachusetts Hall	.38	.38
UX174 19¢ Lincoln's Home	.38	.38
UX175 19¢ Wittenberg University	.38	.38
UX176 19¢ Canyon de Chelly	.38	.38
UX177 19¢ St. Louis Union Station	.38	.38

Issues of 1892-1988	Un	U
Paid Reply Postal Cards		
Prices are: Un=unsevered, U=severed card.		
UY1 1¢ + 1¢ black Grant	35.00	7.50
UY6 1¢ + 1¢ green G. and M. Washington, double frame line around instructions	140.00	22.50
UY7 1¢ + 1¢ green G. and M. Washington, single frame line	1.00	.50
UY12 3¢ + 3¢ red McKinley	9.00	25.00
UY18 4¢ + 4¢ Lincoln	2.50	2.50
UY23 6¢ + 6¢ John Adams	.75	2.00
UY31 "A" (12¢ + 12¢) Eagle	.75	2.00
UY39 15¢ + 15¢ Bison and Prairie	.75	*1.00*
UY40 19¢ + 19¢ Flag	.76	*1.00*
Issues of 1949-91, Airmail Postal Cards		
UXC1 4¢ orange Eagle	.45	*.75*
UXC2 5¢ red Eagle (C48)	1.50	.75
UXC3 5¢ UXC2 redrawn—"Air Mail-Postal Card" omitted	6.00	2.00
UXC4 6¢ red Eagle	.45	*.75*
UXC5 11¢ Visit The USA	.50	*12.50*
UXC6 6¢ Virgin Islands	.40	*6.00*
a Red, yellow omitted	1,700.00	
UXC7 6¢ Boy Scout World Jamboree	.40	*6.00*
UXC8 13¢ blue & red (UXC5)	1.25	*8.00*
UXC9 8¢ Stylized Eagle	.60	*2.00*
UXC10 9¢ red & blue (UXC5)	.50	*1.00*

America's oldest apartment complex

Carved out of red sandstone walls by Pueblo Indians 1,000 years ago, the apartment houses of Canyon de Chelly (pronounced "de-SHAY") are among the oldest dwellings in North America.

The Canyon de Chelly National Monument is located in the northeast corner of Arizona near Chinle, and is the site of more than 60 major ruins. Many dwellings are inaccessible; however, visitors can view the ancient homes from the canyon's bottom or the 16-mile road that hugs the rim of the canyon. **(#UX176)**

Issues of 1990-93	Un	U
UXC11 15¢ Travel Service	1.50	12.50
UXC12 9¢ black Grand Canyon	.50	8.00
UXC13 15¢ black Niagara Falls	.65	15.00
UXC14 11¢ Stylized Eagle	.70	2.00
UXC15 18¢ Eagle Weather Vane	.85	7.00
UXC16 21¢ Angel Weather Vane	.80	7.50
UXC17 21¢ Curtiss Jenny	.75	6.00
UXC18 21¢ Olympic Gymnast	.95	10.00
UXC19 28¢ First Transpacific Flight	.90	4.00
UXC20 28¢ Gliders	.90	3.00
UXC21 28¢ Olympic Speed Skater	.90	2.00
UXC22 33¢ China Clipper	.90	2.00
UXC23 33¢ AMERIPEX '86	.65	2.00
UXC24 36¢ DC-3	.70	1.00
UXC25 40¢ Yankee Clipper	.80	1.00

Issues of 1913-91, Official Mail Postal Cards		Un	U
UZ1	1¢ black Numeral	325.00	150.00
UZ2	13¢ blue Great Seal	.50	35.00
UZ3	14¢ blue Great Seal	.50	35.00
UZ4	15¢ blue Great Seal	.50	30.00
UZ5	19¢ blue Great Seal	.38	5.00

©USPS 1991

This is the last airmail postal card issued by the U.S. Postal Service. International cards and letters all go by air now, so there will no longer be any distinction between air and surface cards and letters. The word "airmail" will not appear on current or future stamps and postal cards. **(#UXC25)**

UXC11

UXC12

UXC13

UXC19

UXC20

UXC23

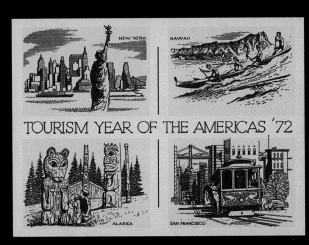

Back of UXC12

Collect Every First Day Issue

- Features every stamp issued each year
- Complete with First Day cancellation and informative text
- A convenient, affordable way to collect

The U.S. Postal Service's Souvenir Pages Subscription Program is your ticket to all the year's stamp issues. It's a great way to collect and learn about the stamps and stamp subjects honored during the year.

Fun and Attractive

A Souvenir Page is issued for every stamp—all definitives and commemoratives, peel and stick stamps, coil stamps and booklet panes. Each Souvenir Page includes the featured stamp(s), postmarked with a First Day of Issue cancellation, mounted on an 8″ x 10½″ page. Information on relevant philatelic specifications and a lively narrative about the history of the stamp's subject are included.

Affordable Collectibles

Souvenir Pages are printed in a limited quantity each year. The cost of a Souvenir Page currently is approximately $1.50 per page. (In the rare event that the face value of the stamp[s] affixed exceeds $1.50, the price will be the face value.)

Money-back Guarantee

If you are ever dissatisfied, return your Souvenir Pages within 30 days for a full refund. For more information and an order form, fill out the request card in this book, or call toll-free:

1-800-STAMP24

Souvenir Pages

With First Day Cancellations

The Postal Service offers Souvenir Pages for new stamps. The series began with a page for the Yellowstone Park Centennial stamp issued March 1, 1972. The Pages feature one or more stamps tied by the first day cancel, along with technical data and information on the subject of the issue. More than just collectors' items, Souvenir Pages make wonderful show and conversation pieces. Souvenir Pages are issued in limited editions. Number in parentheses ( ) indicates number of stamps on page if there are more than one.

1972

72-0	Family Planning	450.00
72-1	Yellowstone Park	100.00
72-1a	Yellowstone Park with DC cancel	500.00
72-2	2¢ Cape Hatteras	100.00
72-3	14¢ Fiorello LaGuardia	110.00
72-4	11¢ City of Refuge Park	110.00
72-5	6¢ Wolf Trap Farm Park	37.50
72-6	Colonial Craftsmen (4)	20.00
72-7	15¢ Mount McKinley	30.00
72-8	6¢-11¢ Olympic Games (4)	20.00
72-8E	Olympic Games with broken red circle on 6¢ stamp	1,000.00
72-9	PTA	9.50
72-10	Wildlife Conservation (4)	10.00
72-11	Mail Order	7.75
72-12	Osteopathic Medicine	7.50
72-13	Tom Sawyer	7.50
72-14	7¢ Benjamin Franklin	9.25
72-15	Christmas (2)	10.00
72-16	Pharmacy	7.50
72-17	Stamp Collecting	7.50

1973

73-1	$1 Eugene O'Neill	15.00
73-1E	$1 Eugene O'Neill picture perf. error	750.00
73-2	Love	10.00
73-3	Pamphleteer	6.00
73-4	George Gershwin	7.75
73-5	Broadside	8.00
73-6	Copernicus	6.50
73-7	Postal Employees	8.75
73-8	Harry S. Truman	6.25
73-9	Post Rider	8.00
73-10	21¢ Amadeo Giannnini	6.25
73-11	Boston Tea Party (4)	8.25
73-12	6¢-15¢ Electronics (4)	7.25
73-13	Robinson Jeffers	4.75
73-14	Lyndon B. Johnson	5.25
73-15	Henry O. Tanner	5.25
73-16	Willa Cather	4.25
73-17	Colonial Drummer	5.75
73-18	Angus Cattle	4.25
73-19	Christmas (2)	7.00
73-20	13¢ Winged Envelope airmail	3.50
73-21	10¢ Crossed Flags	3.50
73-22	10¢ Jefferson Memorial	3.50
73-23	13¢ Winged Envelope airmail coil (2)	3.50

1974

74-1	26¢ Mount Rushmore airmail	5.75
74-2	ZIP Code	4.75
74-2E	ZIP Code with date error 4/4/74	500.00
74-3	18¢ Statue of Liberty airmail	7.50
74-4	18¢ Elizabeth Blackwell	3.25
74-5	VFW	3.25
74-6	Robert Frost	3.50
74-7	Expo '74	3.25
74-8	Horse Racing	3.50
74-9	Skylab	6.75
74-10	UPU (8)	6.50
74-11	Mineral Heritage (4)	6.75
74-12	Fort Harrod	3.25
74-13	Continental Congress (4)	5.00
74-14	Chautauqua	2.75
74-15	Kansas Wheat	2.75
74-16	Energy Conservation	2.75
74-17	6.3¢ Liberty Bell coil (2)	4.00
74-18	Sleepy Hollow	3.50
74-19	Retarded Children	3.25
74-20	Christmas (3)	6.25

1975

75-1	Benjamin West	3.25
75-2	Pioneer/Jupiter	6.25
75-3	Collective Bargaining	3.50
75-4	8¢ Sybil Ludington	3.25
75-5	Salem Poor	3.25
75-6	Haym Salomon	3.25
75-7	18¢ Peter Francisco	3.25
75-8	Mariner 10	6.00
75-9	Lexington & Concord	3.50
75-10	Paul Dunbar	4.25
75-11	D.W. Griffith	3.50
75-12	Bunker Hill	3.50
75-13	Military Uniforms (4)	6.50
75-14	Apollo Soyuz (2)	6.50
75-15	International Women's Year	3.25
75-16	Postal Service Bicentennial (4)	5.25
75-17	World Peace Through Law	3.25
75-18	Banking & Commerce (2)	3.25
75-19	Christmas (2)	4.25
75-20	3¢ Francis Parkman	4.00
75-21	11¢ Freedom of the Press	2.50
75-22	24¢ Old North Church	2.75
75-23	Flag over Independence Hall (2)	3.00
75-24	9¢ Freedom to Assemble (2)	3.00
75-25	Liberty Bell coil (2)	4.00
75-26	Eagle & Shield	2.50

1976

76-1	Spirit of '76 (3)	4.25
76-1E	Spirit of '76 with cancellation error Jan. 2, 1976 (3)	1,000.00
76-2	25¢ and 31¢ Plane and Globes airmails (2)	4.00
76-3	Interphil '76	2.75
76-4	State Flags, DE to VA (10)	8.75
76-5	State Flags, NY to MS (10)	8.75
76-6	State Flags, IL to WI (10)	8.75
76-7	State Flags, CA to SD (10)	8.75

Issue Date: July 16, 1976
First Day City: Lake Placid, New York
Designer: Donald Moss
Modeler: Esther Porter
Press: Gravure
Colors: Blue, red, yellow, green, dark yellow, black
Image area: .84 x 1.34 inches (each stamp) or 21.3 x 34.036 millimeters
Plate Numbers: 6
Stamps to Pane: 50
Salvage: "Mail Early in the Day" "Use ZIP Code" and "Mr. ZIP"

1976 Olympics Commemorative Stamps

Each stamp in the colorful Olympics block of four 13-cent stamps features an Olympic event. Diving and ice skating are represented by female figures, cross-country skiing and running by male figures. The stamps do not portray real athletes.

These commemoratives evidence U.S. interest in the 1976 Olympic Games and call attention to the Winter Olympic Games scheduled in Lake Placid in 1980.

Orders should be addressed to "Olympics Stamps, Postmaster, Lake Placid, NY 12946." The cost is 13 cents per stamp to be affixed to the self-addressed envelopes which must accompany orders. Do not send cash. Remittance should be by money order, cashier's check, certified check or, when the amount is less than $26.00, by personal check. Postage stamps are unacceptable as payment.

Each envelope should be marked lightly in pencil in the upper right corner showing which stamps are desired. The return address should be written well to the left. A filler of postal card thickness helps assure clear cancellations and prevents damage to envelopes. Orders must be postmarked no later than July 16, 1976.

78-11	Early Cancer Detection	2.50
78-12	"A" (15¢) sheet and coil (2)	4.50
78-13	Jimmie Rodgers	4.75
78-14	CAPEX '78 (8)	7.50
78-15	Oliver Wendell Holmes coil	2.75
78-16	Photography	2.50
78-17	Fort McHenry Flag sheet and coil (2)	4.00
78-18	George M. Cohan	2.50
78-19	Rose booklet single	2.75
78-20	8.4¢ Piano coil (2)	3.25
78-21	Viking Missions	4.25
78-22	28¢ Remote Outpost	3.00
78-23	American Owls (4)	3.50
78-24	31¢ Wright Brothers airmails (2)	3.50
78-25	American Trees (4)	3.50
78-26	Christmas, Madonna	2.50
78-27	Christmas, Hobby Horse	2.50
78-28	$2 Kerosene Lamp	7.50

1979

79-1	Robert F. Kennedy	2.50
79-2	Martin Luther King, Jr.	5.00
79-3	International Year of the Child	2.50
79-4	John Steinbeck	2.50
79-5	Albert Einstein	2.75
79-6	21¢ Octave Chanute airmails (2)	3.50
79-7	Pennsylvania Toleware (4)	2.75
79-8	American Architecture (4)	3.25
79-9	Endangered Flora (4)	3.50
79-10	Seeing Eye Dogs	2.50
79-11	$1 Lamp & Candle	7.25
79-12	Special Olympics	2.75
79-13	$5 Lantern	20.00
79-14	30¢ Schoolhouse	4.75
79-15	10¢ Summer Olympics (2)	4.25
79-16	50¢ Whale Oil Lamp	5.00
79-17	John Paul Jones	3.25
79-18	Summer Olympics (4)	5.50
79-19	Christmas, Madonna	3.25
79-20	Christmas, Santa Claus	3.25
79-21	3.1¢ Guitar coil (2)	5.75
79-22	31¢ Summer Olympics airmail	6.25
79-23	Will Rogers	2.75
79-24	Vietnam Veterans	2.75
79-25	25¢ Wiley Post airmails (2)	4.25

1980

80-1	W.C. Fields	3.00
80-2	Winter Olympics (4)	6.50
80-3	Windmills booklet pane (10)	6.00
80-4	Benjamin Banneker	5.00

80-5	Letter Writing (6)	3.50
80-6	1¢ Ability to Write (2)	3.00
80-7	Frances Perkins	2.25
80-8	Dolley Madison	4.00
80-9	Emily Bissell	2.25
80-10	3.5¢ Violins coil (2)	4.00
80-11	Helen Keller/ Anne Sullivan	3.00
80-12	Veterans Administration	2.25
80-13	General Bernardo de Galvez	2.25
80-14	Coral Reefs (4)	2.75
80-15	Organized Labor	4.00
80-16	Edith Wharton	3.75
80-17	Education	2.75
80-18	Indian Masks (4)	3.00
80-19	American Architecture (4)	3.00
80-20	40¢ Philip Mazzei airmail	3.25
80-21	Christmas, Madonna	3.25
80-22	Christmas, Antique Toys	4.00
80-23	Sequoyah	2.25
80-24	28¢ Blanche Scott airmail	2.25
80-25	35¢ Glenn Curtiss airmail	2.25

1981

81-1	Everett Dirksen	2.25
81-2	Whitney M. Young	4.00
81-3	"B" (18¢) sheet and coil (3)	3.00
81-4	"B" (18¢) booklet pane (8)	3.00
81-5	12¢ Freedom of Conscience sheet and coil (3)	4.00
81-6	Flowers block (4)	2.50
81-7	Flag and Anthem sheet and coil (3)	4.00
81-8	Flag and Anthem booklet pane (8 - 6 - 8¢ and 18¢)	3.00
81-9	American Red Cross	2.25
81-10	George Mason	2.25
81-11	Savings & Loans	2.25
81-12	Wildlife booklet pane (10)	2.75
81-13	Surrey coil (2)	4.00
81-14	Space Achievement (8)	7.50
81-15	17¢ Rachel Carson (2)	2.25
81-16	35¢ Charles Drew, MD	3.25
81-17	Professional Management	2.25
81-18	17¢ Electric Auto coil (2)	4.50
81-19	Wildlife Habitat (4)	2.75
81-20	International Year of the Disabled	2.25
81-21	Edna St. Vincent Millay	2.25
81-22	Alcoholism	3.00
81-23	American Architecture (4)	3.25
81-24	Babe Zaharias	3.00
81-25	Bobby Jones	3.00
81-26	Frederic Remington	2.50
81-27	"C" (20¢) sheet and coil (3)	4.25

81-28	"C" (18¢) booklet pane (10)	4.25
81-29	18¢ and 20¢ Hoban (2)	2.50
81-30	Yorktown/ Virginia Capes (2)	3.00
81-31	Christmas, Madonna	3.00
81-32	Christmas, Bear on Sleigh	3.00
81-33	John Hanson	2.25
81-34	Fire Pumper coil (2)	7.00
81-35	Desert Plants (4)	2.75
81-36	9.3¢ Mail Wagon coil (3)	6.00
81-37	Flag over Supreme Court sheet and coil (3)	6.00
81-38	Flag over Supreme Court booklet pane (6)	5.00

1982

82-1	Sheep booklet pane (10)	3.50
82-2	Ralph Bunche	4.25
82-3	13¢ Crazy Horse (2)	2.25
82-4	37¢ Robert Millikan	2.00
82-5	Franklin D. Roosevelt	2.25
82-6	Love	2.25
82-7	5.9¢ Bicycle coil (4)	7.50
82-8	George Washington	3.50
82-9	10.9¢ Hansom Cab coil (2)	6.00
82-10	Birds & Flowers, AL-GE (10)	12.00
82-11	Birds & Flowers, HI-MD (10)	12.00
82-12	Birds & Flowers, MA-NJ (10)	12.00
82-13	Birds & Flowers, NM-SC (10)	12.00
82-14	Birds & Flowers, SD-WY (10)	12.00
82-15	USA/Netherlands	2.25
82-16	Library of Congress	2.25
82-17	Consumer Education coil (2)	3.75
82-18	Knoxville World's Fair (4)	2.50
82-19	Horatio Alger	2.25
82-20	2¢ Locomotive coil (2)	5.25
82-21	Aging Together	2.25
82-22	The Barrymores	3.75
82-23	Mary Walker	2.25
82-24	Peace Garden	2.25
82-25	America's Libraries	2.25
82-26	Jackie Robinson	15.00
82-27	4¢ Stagecoach coil (3)	4.25
82-28	Touro Synagogue	2.25
82-29	Wolf Trap Farm Park	2.25
82-30	American Architecture (4)	2.50
82-31	Francis of Assisi	2.25
82-32	Ponce de Leon	2.25
82-33	13¢ Kitten & Puppy (2)	3.25
82-34	Christmas, Madonna	3.25
82-35	Christmas, Seasons Greetings (4)	4.00

82-36	2¢ Igor Stravinsky (2)	3.25

1983

83-1	1¢, 4¢, 13¢ Penalty Mail (5)	3.25
83-2	1¢ and 17¢ Penalty Mail (4)	3.25
83-3	Penalty Mail coil (2)	3.25
83-4	$1 Penalty Mail	5.00
83-5	$5 Penalty Mail	10.00
83-6	Science & Industry	2.00
83-7	5.2¢ Antique Sleigh coil (4)	5.25
83-8	Sweden/USA Treaty	2.50
83-9	3¢ Handcar coil (3)	4.00
83-10	Balloons (4)	2.75
83-11	Civilian Conservation Corps	2.00
83-12	40¢ Olympics airmails (4)	3.50
83-13	Joseph Priestley	2.00
83-14	Volunteerism	2.00
83-15	Concord/German Immigration	2.00
83-16	Physical Fitness	2.00
83-17	Brooklyn Bridge	2.50
83-18	TVA	2.00
83-19	4¢ Carl Schurz (5)	2.00
83-20	Medal of Honor	3.00
83-21	Scott Joplin	4.00
83-22	Thomas H. Gallaudet	2.00
83-23	28¢ Olympics (4)	4.75
83-24	5¢ Pearl S. Buck (4)	2.00
83-25	Babe Ruth	10.00
83-26	Nathaniel Hawthorne	2.00
83-27	3¢ Henry Clay (7)	2.00
83-28	13¢ Olympics (4)	4.00
83-29	$9.35 Eagle booklet single	140.00
83-30	$9.35 Eagle booklet pane (3)	190.00
83-31	1¢ Omnibus coil (3)	4.00
83-32	Treaty of Paris	2.50
83-33	Civil Service	2.00
83-34	Metropolitan Opera	2.50
83-35	Inventors (4)	3.00
83-36	1¢ Dorothea Dix (3)	2.00
83-37	Streetcars (4)	2.50
83-38	5¢ Motorcycle coil (4)	5.25
83-39	Christmas, Madonna	2.50
83-40	Christmas, Santa Claus	2.50
83-41	35¢ Olympics airmails (4)	3.50
83-42	Martin Luther	2.50
83-43	Flag over Supreme Court booklet pane (10)	4.00

1984

84-1	Alaska Statehood	2.00
84-2	Winter Olympics (4)	3.25
84-3	FDIC	2.00
84-4	Harry S. Truman	2.00
84-5	Love	2.00
84-6	Carter G. Woodson	3.00
84-7	11¢ RR Caboose coil (2)	4.00
84-8	Soil & Water Conservation	2.00
84-9	Credit Union Act	2.00
84-10	40¢ Lillian M. Gilbreth	2.00
84-11	Orchids (4)	3.00
84-12	Hawaii Statehood	2.00
84-13	7.4¢ Baby Buggy coil (3)	4.00
84-14	National Archives	2.00
84-15	20¢ Summer Olympics (4)	4.50
84-16	New Orleans World's Fair	2.00
84-17	Health Research	2.00
84-18	Douglas Fairbanks	2.50
84-19	Jim Thorpe	6.00
84-20	10¢ Richard Russell (2)	2.00
84-21	John McCormack	2.50
84-22	St. Lawrence Seaway	2.00
84-23	Migratory Bird Hunting and Conservation Stamp Act	4.50
84-24	Roanoke Voyages	2.00
84-25	Herman Melville	2.00
84-26	Horace Moses	2.00
84-27	Smokey Bear	5.00
84-28	Roberto Clemente	8.00
84-29	30¢ Frank C. Laubach	2.00
84-30	Dogs (4)	4.00
84-31	Crime Prevention	2.00
84-32	Family Unity	3.75
84-33	Eleanor Roosevelt	3.00
84-34	Nation of Readers	3.00
84-35	Christmas, Madonna	3.00
84-36	Christmas, Santa Claus	3.00
84-37	Hispanic Americans	2.00
84-38	Vietnam Veterans Memorial	3.75

1985

85-1	Jerome Kern	3.25
85-2	7¢ Abraham Baldwin (3)	3.25
85-3	"D" (22¢) sheet and coil (3)	2.50
85-4	"D" (22¢) booklet pane (10)	4.00
85-5	"D" (22¢) Penalty Mail sheet and coil (3)	4.00
85-6	11¢ Alden Partridge (2)	2.00
85-7	33¢ Alfred Verville airmail	2.25
85-8	39¢ Lawrence & Elmer Sperry airmail	2.25
85-9	44¢ Transpacific airmail	2.25
85-10	50¢ Chester Nimitz	2.75
85-11	Mary McLeod Bethune	3.50
85-12	39¢ Grenville Clark	2.00
85-13	14¢ Sinclair Lewis (2)	2.00
85-14	Duck Decoys (4)	3.00
85-15	14¢ Iceboat coil (2)	5.00
85-16	Winter Special Olympics	2.00
85-17	Flag over Capitol sheet and coil (3)	4.00
85-18	Flag over Capitol booklet pane (5)	4.00
85-19	12¢ Stanley Steamer coil (2)	5.00
85-20	Seashells booklet pane (10)	5.00
85-21	Love	3.75
85-22	10.1¢ Oil Wagon coil (3)	4.00
85-23	12.5¢ Pushcart coil (2)	4.00
85-24	John J. Audubon	2.50
85-25	$10.75 Eagle booklet single	42.50
85-26	$10.75 Eagle booklet pane (3)	100.00
85-27	6¢ Tricycle coil (4)	4.00
85-28	Rural Electrification Administration	2.00
85-29	14¢ and 22¢ Penalty Mail sheet	
	and coil (4)	3.75
85-30	AMERIPEX '86	2.00
85-31	9¢ Sylvanus Thayer (3)	3.00
85-32	3.4¢ School Bus coil (7)	5.00
85-33	11¢ Stutz Bearcat coil (2)	4.00
85-34	Abigail Adams	2.00
85-35	4.9¢ Buckboard coil (5)	5.00
85-36	8.3¢ Ambulance coil (3)	4.00
85-37	Frederic Bartholdi	3.75
85-38	8¢ Henry Knox (3)	2.00
85-39	Korean War Veterans	2.75
85-40	Social Security Act	3.00
85-41	44¢ Father Junipero Serra airmail	2.50
85-42	World War I Veterans	2.50
85-43	6¢ Walter Lippman (4)	2.50
85-44	Horses (4)	4.00
85-45	Public Education	2.50
85-46	International Youth Year (4)	3.25
85-47	Help End Hunger	2.50
85-48	21.1¢ Letters coil (2)	3.00
85-49	Christmas, Madonna	2.50
85-50	Christmas, Poinsettias	2.50
85-51	18¢ Washington/ Washington Monument coil (2)	3.50

1986

86-1	Arkansas Statehood	2.25
86-2	25¢ Jack London	2.00
86-3	Stamp Collecting booklet pane (4)	4.75
86-4	Love	2.50
86-5	Sojourner Truth	2.50
86-6	5¢ Hugo L. Black (5)	3.25
86-7	Republic of Texas (2)	2.25
86-8	$2 William Jennings Bryan	4.25
86-9	Fish booklet pane (5)	4.25
86-10	Public Hospitals	1.75
86-11	Duke Ellington	3.00
86-12	Presidents, Washington-Harrison (9)	5.00
86-13	Presidents, Tyler-Grant (9)	5.00
86-14	Presidents, Hayes-Wilson (9)	5.00
86-15	Presidents, Harding-Johnson (9)	5.00
86-16	Polar Explorers (4)	3.50
86-17	17¢ Belva Ann Lockwood (2)	3.00
86-18	1¢ Margaret Mitchell (3)	1.75
86-19	Statue of Liberty	5.00
86-20	4¢ Father Flanagan (3)	1.75
86-21	17¢ Dog Sled coil (2)	3.50
86-22	56¢ John Harvard	2.75
86-23	Navajo Blankets (4)	3.25
86-24	3¢ Paul Dudley White, MD (8)	2.00
86-25	$1 Bernard Revel	2.75
86-26	T.S. Eliot	1.75
86-27	Wood-Carved Figurines (4)	2.75
86-28	Christmas, Madonna	2.00
86-29	Christmas, Village Scene	2.00
86-30	5.5¢ Star Route Truck coil (4)	5.00

Copyright U.S. Postal Service 1985

Issue Date: September 25, 1985

First Day City: Lexington, Kentucky

Designer: Roy Andersen
Sedona, Arizona

Art Director & Typographer:
Howard Paine, Design Coordinator,
Citizens' Stamp Advisory Committee

Modeler: Ronald C. Sharpe

Process: Gravure

Colors: Yellow, magenta, cyan, black and
black tone

Image Area: 1.10 x 1.44 inches or
28.0 x 36.5 millimeters

Plate Numbers: One group

Stamps per Pane: 40

Selvage: ©U.S. Postal Service 1985
Use Correct ZIP Code®
Mr. ZIP® (standing position)

American Horses
Commemorative Stamp

A block of four 22-cent stamps featuring American horses was issued September 25 in Lexington, Kentucky. The dedication ceremony was held in the Parade of Breeds Barn at the Kentucky Horse Park. The ceremony also served as a preliminary event for National Stamp Collecting Month, October 1-31.

Often called "The Showplace of the Bluegrass," the state-operated Kentucky Horse Park features more than 30 different breeds and types of horses, mules and donkeys as well as many unique exhibits. The four breeds depicted on the stamps are represented in the park and were featured in the first day of issue ceremony.

During the late 18th and early 19th century, a rapidly expanding America required horses for transportation, ranching, farming and the U.S. Cavalry. But, with the Industrial Revolution of the late 19th century came a decline in the practical uses for the horse. Instead, their influence was redirected to areas such as sport and pleasure riding.

The stamps, designed by Roy Andersen, were executed in oil using rich, earth tones, feature the Saddlebred (lower left corner), Morgan (upper right corner), Appaloosa (lower right corner) and Quarter horse (upper left corner). Mr. Andersen also designed the popular dogs block of four commemorative stamps issued in 1984.

88-8	Maryland Statehood	3.00
88-9	3¢ Conestoga Wagon coil (8)	3.50
88-10	Knute Rockne	3.50
88-11	"E" (25¢) Earth sheet and coil (3)	3.00
88-12	"E" (25¢) Earth booklet pane (10)	6.00
88-13	"E" (25¢) Penalty Mail coil (2)	3.00
88-14	44¢ New Sweden airmail	3.00
88-15	Pheasant booklet pane (10)	6.00
88-16	Jack London booklet pane (6)	4.00
88-17	Jack London booklet pane (10)	5.75
88-18	Flag with Clouds	2.50
88-19	45¢ Samuel Langley airmail	3.00
88-19A	20¢ Penalty Mail coil (2)	3.00
88-20	Flag over Yosemite coil (2)	3.00
88-21	South Carolina Statehood	3.00
88-22	Owl & Grosbeak booklet pane (10)	5.00
88-23	15¢ Buffalo Bill Cody (2)	3.00
88-24	15¢ and 25¢ Penalty Mail coils (4)	4.00
88-25	Francis Ouimet	3.00
88-26	45¢ Harvey Cushing, MD	2.50
88-27	New Hampshire Statehood	3.00
88-28	36¢ Igor Sikorsky airmail	3.00
88-29	Virginia Statehood	3.00
88-30	10.1¢ Oil Wagon coil, precancel (3)	4.00
88-31	Love	3.00
88-32	Flag with Clouds booklet pane (6)	6.00
88-33	16.7¢ Popcorn Wagon coil (2)	3.00
88-34	15¢ Tugboat coil (2)	3.00
88-35	13.2¢ Coal Car coil (2)	3.00
88-36	New York Statehood	3.00
88-37	45¢ Love	3.00
88-38	8.4¢ Wheel Chair coil (3)	3.00
88-39	21¢ Railroad Mail Car coil (2)	3.00
88-40	Summer Olympics	3.00
88-41	Classic Cars booklet pane (5)	6.00
88-42	7.6¢ Carreta coil (4)	3.00
88-43	Honeybee coil (2)	3.00
88-44	Antarctic Explorers (4)	3.00
88-45	5.3¢ Elevator coil (5)	3.00
88-46	20.5¢ Fire Engine coil (2)	4.00
88-47	Carousel Animals (4)	3.00
88-48	$8.75 Eagle	22.50
88-49	Christmas, Madonna	3.00
88-50	Christmas, Snow Scene	3.00
88-51	21¢ Chester Carlson	2.50
88-52	Special Occasions booklet pane (6), Love You	5.00
88-53	Special Occasions booklet pane (6), Thinking of You	5.00
88-54	24.1¢ Tandem Bicycle coil (2)	3.00
88-55	20¢ Cable Car coil (2)	3.00
88-56	13¢ Patrol Wagon coil (2)	3.00
88-57	23¢ Mary Cassatt	2.50
88-58	65¢ H.H. "Hap" Arnold	2.50

1989

89-1	Montana Statehood	3.00
89-2	A. Philip Randolph	3.50
89-3	Flag over Yosemite coil, prephosphored paper (2)	3.50

89-4	North Dakota Statehood	3.00
89-5	Washington Statehood	3.00
89-6	Steamboats booklet pane (5)	5.00
89-7	World Stamp Expo '89	3.00
89-8	Arturo Toscanini	3.00
89-9	U.S. House of Representatives	3.00
89-10	U.S. Senate	3.00
89-11	Executive Branch	3.00
89-12	South Dakota Statehood	3.00
89-13	7.1¢ Tractor coil, precancel (4)	4.00
89-14	$1 Johns Hopkins	3.50
89-15	Lou Gehrig	7.50
89-16	1¢ Penalty Mail	3.50
89-17	45¢ French Revolution airmail	3.00
89-18	Ernest Hemingway	3.00
89-19	$2.40 Moon Landing	12.50
89-20	North Carolina Statehood	3.00
89-21	Letter Carriers	2.50
89-22	28¢ Sitting Bull	2.50
89-23	Drafting of the Bill of Rights	2.50
89-24	Prehistoric Animals (4)	7.50
89-25	25¢ and 45¢ PUAS-America (2)	3.50
89-26	Christmas, Madonna	7.50
89-27	Christmas, Antique Sleigh	6.50
89-28	Eagle and Shield, self-adhesive	3.50
89-29	$3.60 World Stamp Expo '89 souvenir sheet	9.00
89-30	Classic Mail Transportation (4)	3.50
89-31	$1.80 Future Mail Transportation souvenir sheet	6.00
89-32	45¢ Future Mail Transportation airmails (4)	5.50
89-33	$1 Classic Mail Transportation souvenir sheet	5.00

1990

90-1	Idaho Statehood	3.00
90-2	Love sheet and booklet pane (11)	7.50
90-3	Ida B. Wells	3.00
90-4	U.S. Supreme Court	3.00
90-5	15¢ Beach Umbrella booklet pane (10)	5.00
90-6	5¢ Luis Munoz Marin (5)	3.00
90-7	Wyoming Statehood	3.00
90-8	Classic Films (4)	6.00
90-9	Marianne Moore	3.00
90-10	$1 Seaplane coil (2)	5.00
90-11	Lighthouses booklet pane (5)	6.00
90-12	Plastic Flag stamp	5.00
90-13	Rhode Island Statehood	4.00
90-14	$2 Bobcat	7.50
90-15	Olympians (5)	8.00
90-16	Indian Headdresses booklet pane (10)	9.00
90-17	5¢ Circus Wagon coil (5)	4.00
90-18	40¢ Claire Lee Chennault	4.50
90-19	Federated States of Micronesia/ Marshall Islands (2)	4.00
90-20	Creatures of the Sea (4)	5.00
90-21	25¢ and 45¢ PUAS/America (2)	4.00
90-22	Dwight D. Eisenhower	3.00
90-23	Christmas, Madonna, sheet and booklet pane (11)	7.50

90-24	Christmas,Yule Tree, sheet and booklet pane (11)	7.50

1991

91-1	"F" (29¢) Flower sheet and coil (3)	4.00
91-2	"F" (29¢) Flower booklet panes (20)	12.50
91-3	4¢ Makeup	3.50
91-4	"F" (29¢) ATM booklet single	4.00
91-5	"F" (29¢) Penalty Mail coil (2)	4.00
91-6	4¢ Steam Carriage coil (7)	4.00
91-7	50¢ Switzerland	4.00
91-8	Vermont Statehood	4.00
91-9	19¢ Fawn (2)	4.00
91-10	Flag over Mount Rushmore coil (2)	4.00
91-11	35¢ Dennis Chavez	4.00
91-12	Flower sheet and booklet pane (11)	7.50
91-13	4¢ Penalty Mail (8)	4.00
91-14	Wood Duck booklet panes (20)	12.50
91-15	23¢ Lunch Wagon coil (2)	4.00
91-16	Flag with Olympic Rings booklet pane (10)	7.50
91-17	50¢ Harriet Quimby	4.00
91-18	Savings Bond	4.00
91-19	Love sheet and booklet pane, 52¢ Love (12)	12.50
91-20	19¢ Balloon booklet pane (10)	7.50
91-21	40¢ William Piper airmail	4.00
91-22	William Saroyan	4.00
91-23	Penalty Mail coil and 19¢ and 23¢ sheet (4)	5.00
91-24	5¢ Canoe and 10¢ Tractor-Trailer coils (4)	4.00
91-25	Flags on Parade	4.00
91-26	Fishing Flies booklet pane (5)	7.50
91-27	52¢ Hubert H. Humphrey	4.00
91-28	Cole Porter	4.00
91-29	50¢ Antarctic Treaty airmail	4.00
91-30	1¢ Kestrel, 3¢ Bluebird and 30¢ Cardinal (3)	4.00
91-31	Torch ATM booklet single	4.00
91-32	Desert Shield/ Desert Storm sheet and booklet pane (11)	4.00
91-33	Flag over Mount Rushmore coil, gravure printing (darker, 3)	4.00
91-34	Summer Olympics (5)	8.00
91-35	Flower coil, slit perforations (3)	4.00
91-36	Numismatics	4.00
91-37	Basketball	8.00
91-48	19¢ Fishing Boat coil (3)	4.00
91-49	Comedians booklet pane (10)	8.00
91-50	World War II miniature sheet (10)	8.00
91-51	District of Columbia	4.00
91-52	Jan Matzeliger	4.00
91-53	$1 USPS/ Olympic Logo	7.50
91-54	Space Exploration booklet pane (10)	8.00
91-55	50¢ PUASP/America airmail	4.00
91-56	Christmas, Madonna sheet and booklet pane (11)	8.00
91-57	Christmas, Santa Claus sheet and booklet pane (11)	8.00
91-58	5¢ Canoe coil, gravure printing (red, 6)	4.00

91-59	(10¢) Eagle and Shield, self-adhesive (3)	4.00
91-60	23¢ Flag presort	3.00
91-61	$9.95 Express Mail	25.00
91-62	$2.90 Priority Mail	9.00
91-63	$14.00 Express Mail International	35.00

1992

92-01	Winter Olympic Games (5)	8.00
92-02	World Columbian Stamp Expo '92	4.00
92-03	W.E.B. Du Bois	4.00
92-04	Love	4.00
92-05	75¢ Wendell Willkie	4.00
92-06	29¢ Flower coil, round perforations (2)	4.00
92-07	Earl Warren	4.00
92-08	Olympic Baseball	8.00
92-09	Flag over White House, coil (2)	4.00
92-10	First Voyage of Christopher Columbus (4)	8.00
92-11	New York Stock Exchange	4.00
92-18	Space Adventures (4)	8.00
92-19	Alaska Highway	4.00
92-20	Kentucky Statehood	4.00
92-21	Summer Olympic Games (5)	8.00
92-22	Hummingbirds booklet pane (5)	8.00
92-23	Wildflowers (10)	6.00
92-24	Wildflowers (10)	6.00
92-25	Wildflowers (10)	6.00
92-26	Wildflowers (10)	6.00
92-27	Wildflowers (10)	6.00
92-28	World War II miniature sheet (10)	8.00
92-30	Dorothy Parker	4.00
92-31	Theodore von Karman	4.00
92-33	Minerals (4)	8.00
92-35	Juan Rodriguez Cabrillo	4.00
92-36	Wild Animals booklet pane (5)	8.00
92-38	Christmas Contemporary, sheet and booklet pane (8)	7.50
92-39	Christmas Traditional, sheet and booklet pane (11)	7.50
92-40	Pumpkinseed Sunfish	4.00
92-41	Circus Wagon	5.00
92-42	Happy New Year	6.00

1993

93-01	Elvis	15.00
93-02	Space Fantasy (5)	10.00
93-03	Percy Lavon Julian	5.00
93-04	Oregon Trail	5.00
93-05	World University Games	5.00
93-06	Grace Kelly	5.00
93-07	Oklahoma!	5.00
93-08	Circus	7.50
93-09	Thomas Jefferson	5.00
93-10	Cherokee Strip	5.00
93-11	Dean Acheson	5.00
93-12	Sporting Horses	7.50
93-13	USA Coil	5.00
93-14	Garden Flowers (5)	5.00
93-15	Eagle and Shield, coil	5.00
93-16	World War II (10)	7.50
93-17	Futuristic Space Shuttle	12.50
93-18	Hank Williams, sheet	7.50
93-19	Rock & Roll/Rhythm & Blues, sheet single, booklet pane (8)	12.50
93-20	Joe Louis	5.00
93-21	Red Squirrel	5.00
93-22	Broadway Musicals, booklet pane (4)	7.50
93-23	National Postal Museum, strip (4)	7.50
93-24	Rose	5.00
93-25	American Sign Language, pair	5.00
93-26	Country & Western Music, sheet and booklet pane (4)	7.50

93-27	African Violets, booklet pane (10)	7.50
93-28	Official Mail	5.00
93-29	Contemporary Christmas, booklet pane (10), sheet and self-adhesive stamps	12.00
93-30	Traditional Christmas, sheet, booklet pane (4)	12.00
93-31	Classic Books, (4)	7.50
93-32	Mariana Islands	7.50
93-33	Pine Cone	5.00
93-34	Columbus' Landing in Puerto Rico	7.50
93-35	AIDS Awareness	10.00

1994

94-01	Winter Olympics	10.00
94-02	Edward R. Murrow	7.50
94-03	Love	7.50
94-04	Dr. Allison Davis	7.50
94-05	Eagle	—
94-06	Happy New Year	—
94-07	Love	12.50
94-08	Postage and Mailing Center	—
94-09	Buffalo Soldiers	—
94-10	Stars of the Silent Screen	—
94-11	Garden Flowers	—
94-12	Surrender at Saratoga	—
94-13	Tractor Trailer	—
94-14	World Cup Soccer	—
94-15	World Cup Soccer	—
94-16	World War II	—
94-17	Love	—
94-18	Statue of Liberty	—
94-19	Fishing Boat	—
94-20	Norman Rockwell (4+1)	—
94-21	Moon Landing (1+1)	—
94-22	Locomotives (5)	—
94-23	George Meany	—
94-24	Washington/Jackson	—
94-25	Popular Singers (5)	—
94-26	James Thurber	—
94-27	Jazz Singers/Blues Singers (10)	—
94-28	Wonders of the Sea (4)	—
94-29	Chinese/Joint Issue (2)	7.50
94-30	Holiday Traditional	—
94-31	Holiday Contemporary	—
94-32	Holiday	—
94-33	Virginia Apgar	—
94-34	BEP Centennial	—
94-35	Happy New Year!	—
94-G1	G1 (4)	—
94-G2	G2 (6)	—
94-G3	G3 (5)	—
94-G4	G4 (2)	—

1995

95-01	Love (2)	—
95-02	Florida State	—
95-03	Butte (7)	—
95-04	Automobile (4)	—
95-05	Flag Over Field	—
95-06	Juke Box (2+2)	—
95-07	Tail Fin (2+2)	—
95-08	Circus (7)	—
95-09	Kids Care! (4)	—
95-10	Richard Nixon	—
95-11	Bessie Coleman	—
95-12	Official Mail	—
95-13	Kestrel (2 stamps w/Cardinal)	—
95-14	Love 1 oz. and 2 oz.	—
95-15	Flag Over Porch	—
95-16	Recreational Sports (5)	—
95-17	POW & MIA	—
95-18	Marilyn Monroe	—
95-19	Pink Rose	—
95-20	Ferry Boat (3)	—
95-21	Cog Railway Car (3)	—
95-22	Blue Jay (10)	—
95-23	Texas Statehood	—
95-24	Great Lake Lighthouses (5)	—
95-25	Challenger Shuttle	—
95-26	United Nations	—
95-27	Civil War (front and back)	—
95-28	Two Fruits	—
95-29	Alice Hamilton	—
95-30	Carousel Horses	—
95-31	Endeavor Shuttle	—
95-32	Alice Paul	—

95-33	Women's Suffrage	—
95-34	Louis Armstrong	—
95-35	World War II	—
95-36	Milton Hershey	—
95-37	Jazz Musicians	—
95-38	Fall Garden Flowers (5)	—
95-39	Eddie Rickenbaker (airmail)	—
95-40	Republic of Palau	—
95-41	Holiday Contemporary/Santa	—
95-42	American Comic Strips	—
95-43	Naval Academy	—
95-44	Tennessee Williams	—
95-45	Holiday Contemporary	—
95-46	Holiday Traditional	—
95-47	Holiday Midnight Angel	—
95-48	Ruth Bendict	—
95-49	James K. Polk	—
95-50	Antique Automobiles	—

Note : Numbers and prices may be changed without notice, due to additional USPS stamp issues and/or different information that may become available on older issues.

History on Panels

- Includes block of four or more mint-condition commemorative stamps mounted on 8½" x 11¼" high-quality paper

Valuable, Elegant Keepsakes

Since the American Commemorative Panel series began in 1972, collectors have recognized these keepsakes as significant milestones in philatelic history. These limited-edition panels are available individually and on an advance subscription basis.

Accompanying the acetate-mounted block of four or more mint stamps are intaglio-printed reproductions of historical steel line engravings and informative articles on the stamp subject.

For Subscription Information

For more information, use the postage-paid request card in this book or call toll-free:

1-800-STAMP24

American Commemorative Panels

The Postal Service offers American Commemorative Panels for each new commemorative stamp and special Christmas and Love stamp issued. The series began in 1972 with the Wildlife Commemorative Panel. The panels feature mint stamps complemented by fine reproductions of steel line engravings and the stories behind the commemorated subjects.

1972
1	Wildlife	7.00
2	Mail Order	6.75
3	Osteopathic Medicine	7.00
4	Tom Sawyer	6.75
5	Pharmacy	7.00
6	Christmas, Angels	11.00
7	Christmas, Santa Claus	11.00
7E	Same with error date (1882)	750.00
8	Stamp Collecting	6.75

1973
9	Love	9.50
10	Pamphleteers	7.75
11	George Gershwin	8.25
12	Posting a Broadside	7.75
13	Copernicus	7.75
14	Postal People	7.75
15	Harry S. Truman	9.00
16	Post Rider	9.00
17	Boston Tea Party	27.50
18	Electronics	7.50
19	Robinson Jeffers	7.50
20	Lyndon B. Johnson	9.50
21	Henry O. Tanner	7.50
22	Willa Cather	7.50
23	Drummer	11.00
24	Angus Cattle	7.50
25	Christmas, Madonna	11.00
26	Christmas Tree, Needlepoint	11.00

1974
27	VFW	7.50
28	Robert Frost	7.50
29	Expo '74	9.00
30	Horse Racing	9.00
31	Skylab	10.00
32	Universal Postal Union	9.00
33	Mineral Heritage	9.00
34	First Kentucky Settlement	7.50
35	Continental Congress	9.00
35A	Same with corrected logo	150.00

36	Chautauqua	7.50
37	Kansas Wheat	7.50
38	Energy Conservation	7.50
39	Sleepy Hollow	7.50
40	Retarded Children	7.50
41	Christmas, Currier & Ives	11.00
42	Christmas, Angel Altarpiece	10.50

1975
43	Benjamin West	7.00
44	Pioneer	11.50
45	Collective Bargaining	7.50
46	Contributors to the Cause	7.50
47	Mariner 10	11.50
48	Lexington & Concord	7.75
49	Paul Laurence Dunbar	7.50
50	D.W. Griffith	7.50
51	Bunker Hill	7.75
52	Military Uniforms	8.50
53	Apollo Soyuz	11.50
54	World Peace Through Law	7.50
54A	Same with August 15, 1975 date	150.00
55	Women's Year	7.50
56	Postal Service Bicentennial	9.00
57	Banking and Commerce	8.50
58	Early Christmas, Card	10.50
59	Christmas, Madonna	10.50

1976
60	Spirit of '76	12.50
61	Interphil 76	12.00
62	State Flags	22.50
63	Telephone	9.00
64	Commercial Aviation	13.00
65	Chemistry	10.00
66	Benjamin Franklin	10.50
67	Declaration of Independence	10.50

68	12th Winter Olympics	12.50
69	Clara Maass	10.00
70	Adolph S. Ochs	10.00
70A	Same with charter logo	18.00
71	Christmas, Winter Pastime	13.50
71A	Same with charter logo	21.00
72	Christmas, Nativity	13.50
72A	Same with charter logo	21.00

1977
73	Washington at Princeton	20.00
73A	Same with charter logo	18.00
74	Sound Recording	25.00
74A	Same with charter logo	33.00
75	Pueblo Art	90.00
75A	Same with charter logo	110.00
76	Solo Transatlantic Lindbergh Flight	100.00
77	Colorado Statehood	17.50
78	Butterflies	19.00
79	Lafayette	17.50
80	Skilled Hands	17.50
81	Peace Bridge	17.50
82	Battle of Oriskany	17.50
83	Alta, CA, Civil Settlement	17.50
84	Articles of Confederation	25.00
85	Talking Pictures	17.50
86	Surrender at Saratoga	24.00
87	Energy	17.50
88	Christmas, Valley Forge	20.00
89	Christmas, Mailbox	35.00

1978

90	Carl Sandburg	11.00
91	Captain Cook	17.50
92	Harriet Tubman	11.00
93	Quilts	19.00
94	Dance	14.00
95	French Alliance	14.00
96	Early Cancer Detection	12.00
97	Jimmie Rodgers	15.00
98	Photography	11.00
99	George M. Cohan	19.00
100	Viking Missions	35.00
101	Owls	35.00
102	Trees	32.50
103	Christmas, Madonna	15.00
104	Christmas, Hobby Horse	17.50

1979

105	Robert F. Kennedy	10.50
106	Martin Luther King, Jr.	10.00
107	International Year of the Child	10.00
108	John Steinbeck	10.00
109	Albert Einstein	10.50
110	Pennsylvania Toleware	10.00
111	Architecture	9.50
112	Endangered Flora	10.00
113	Seeing Eye Dogs	10.50
114	Special Olympics	13.00
115	John Paul Jones	12.50
116	15¢ Olympics	15.00
117	Christmas, Madonna	14.00
118	Christmas, Santa Claus	14.00
119	Will Rogers	13.00
120	Vietnam Veterans	12.50
121	10¢, 31¢ Olympics	14.00

1980

122	W.C. Fields	14.00
123	Winter Olympics	9.50
124	Benjamin Banneker	9.50
125	Frances Perkins	9.50
126	Emily Bissell	9.50
127	Helen Keller/ Anne Sullivan	9.50
128	Veterans Administration	9.50
129	General Bernardo de Galvez	9.50
130	Coral Reefs	11.00
131	Organized Labor	9.00
132	Edith Wharton	8.25
133	Education	9.00
134	Indian Masks	12.00
135	Architecture	9.50
136	Christmas, Epiphany Window	13.00
137	Christmas, Toys	13.00

1981

138	Everett Dirksen	9.50
139	Whitney Moore Young	9.50
140	Flowers	11.00
141	Red Cross	10.00
142	Savings & Loans	9.50
143	Space Achievement	13.75
144	Professional Management	9.00
145	Wildlife Habitats	14.00
146	Int'l. Year of Disabled Persons	9.00
147	Edna St. Vincent Millay	8.50
148	Architecture	9.50
149	Babe Zaharias/ Bobby Jones	11.00
150	James Hoban	9.00
151	Frederic Remington	9.50
152	Battle of Yorktown/ Virginia Capes	9.00
153	Christmas, Bear and Sleigh	12.00
154	Christmas, Madonna	12.50
155	John Hanson	8.50
156	U.S. Desert Plants	11.00

1982

157	Roosevelt	13.50
158	Love	14.75
159	George Washington	20.00
160	State Birds & Flowers	27.50
161	U.S./ Netherlands	20.00
162	Library of Congress	22.50
163	Knoxville World's Fair	14.75
164	Horatio Alger	13.00
165	Aging Together	15.50
166	The Barrymores	16.50
167	Dr. Mary Walker	14.00
168	Peace Garden	15.50
169	America's Libraries	16.00
170	Jackie Robinson	25.00
171	Touro Synagogue	14.50
172	Architecture	16.00
173	Wolf Trap Farm Park	14.50
174	Francis of Assisi	16.00
175	Ponce de Leon	16.00
176	Christmas, Madonna	20.00
177	Christmas, Season's Greetings	20.00
178	Kitten & Puppy	22.50

1983

179	Science and Industry	7.00
180	Sweden/ USA Treaty	7.00

181	Balloons	9.50
182	Civilian Conservation Corps	7.00
183	40¢ Olympics	9.00
184	Joseph Priestley	7.50
185	Voluntarism	6.50
186	Concord/German Immigration	6.50
187	Physical Fitness	6.75
188	Brooklyn Bridge	7.50
189	TVA	6.50
190	Medal of Honor	9.00
191	Scott Joplin	10.00
192	28¢ Olympics	9.00
193	Babe Ruth	12.50
194	Nathaniel Hawthorne	7.50
195	13¢ Olympics	10.50
196	Treaty of Paris	8.00
197	Civil Service	8.00
198	Metropolitan Opera	8.00
199	Inventors	8.50
200	Streetcars	10.00
201	Christmas, Madonna	12.00
202	Christmas, Santa Claus	12.00
203	35¢ Olympics	10.50
204	Martin Luther	10.00

1984

205	Alaska Statehood	6.50
206	Winter Olympics	8.00
207	FDIC	6.00
208	Love	6.50
209	Carter G. Woodson	8.00
210	Soil and Water Conservation	6.00
211	Credit Union Act	6.00
212	Orchids	8.00
213	Hawaii Statehood	8.00
214	National Archives	6.50
215	20¢ Olympics	8.00
216	Louisiana World Exposition	7.50
217	Health Research	6.00
218	Douglas Fairbanks	6.00
219	Jim Thorpe	10.00
220	John McCormack	6.00
221	St. Lawrence Seaway	8.00
222	Preserving Wetlands	10.00
223	Roanoke Voyages	6.00
224	Herman Melville	6.00
225	Horace Moses	6.00
226	Smokey Bear	10.00
227	Roberto Clemente	12.00
228	Dogs	8.00
229	Crime Prevention	7.50
230	Family Unity	6.00
231	Christmas, Madonna	8.00
232	Christmas, Santa Claus	8.00

233	Eleanor Roosevelt	7.00
234	Nation of Readers	7.00
235	Hispanic Americans	6.00
236	Vietnam Veterans Memorial	10.50

1985

237	Jerome Kern	8.00
238	Mary McLeod Bethune	8.00
239	Duck Decoys	11.00
240	Winter Special Olympics	8.50
241	Love	7.50
242	Rural Electrification Administration	7.00
243	AMERIPEX '86	9.50
244	Abigail Adams	6.50
245	Frederic Auguste Bartholdi	11.00
246	Korean War Veterans	8.00
247	Social Security Act	7.00
248	World War I Veterans	7.00
249	Horses	10.00
250	Public Education	6.50
251	Youth	8.00
252	Help End Hunger	7.00
253	Christmas, Poinsettias	9.00
254	Christmas, Madonna	11.50

1986

255	Arkansas Statehood	7.50
256	Stamp Collecting Booklet	9.50
257	Love	12.00
258	Sojourner Truth	9.50
259	Republic of Texas	10.00
260	Fish Booklet	9.50
261	Public Hospitals	9.00
262	Duke Ellington	9.50
263	U.S. Presidents' Sheet #1	9.00
264	U.S. Presidents' Sheet #2	9.00
265	U.S. Presidents' Sheet #3	9.00
266	U.S. Presidents' Sheet #4	9.00
267	Polar Explorers	9.50
268	Statue of Liberty	9.50
269	Navajo Blankets	9.50
270	T.S. Eliot	9.00
271	Wood-Carved Figurines	7.50

| 272 | Christmas, Madonna | 7.00 |
| 273 | Christmas, Village Scene | 7.00 |

1987

274	Michigan Statehood	7.00
275	Pan American Games	7.00
276	Love	12.00
277	Jean Baptiste Pointe Du Sable	7.50
278	Enrico Caruso	7.50
279	Girl Scouts	7.50
280	Special Occasions Booklet	7.00
281	United Way	7.00
282	#1 American Wildlife	9.00
283	#2 American Wildlife	9.00
284	#3 American Wildlife	9.00
285	#4 American Wildlife	9.00
286	#5 American Wildlife	9.00
287	Delaware Statehood	7.00
288	Morocco/U.S. Diplomatic Relations	7.00
289	William Faulkner	7.00
290	Lacemaking	7.00
291	Pennsylvania Statehood	7.00
292	Constitution Booklet	7.00
293	New Jersey Statehood	7.00
294	Signing of the Constitution	7.00
295	Certified Public Accountants	8.00
296	Locomotives Booklet	8.00
297	Christmas, Madonna	9.00
298	Christmas, Ornaments	8.00

1988

299	Georgia Statehood	9.00
300	Connecticut Statehood	9.00
301	Winter Olympics	9.00
302	Australia	9.00
303	James Weldon Johnson	9.00
304	Cats	10.00
305	Massachusetts Statehood	9.00
306	Maryland Statehood	9.00
307	Knute Rockne	15.00
308	New Sweden	9.00
309	South Carolina Statehood	9.00

310	Francis Ouimet	9.00
311	New Hampshire Statehood	9.00
312	Virginia Statehood	9.00
313	Love	10.00
314	New York Statehood	9.00
315	Classic Cars Booklet	9.00
316	Summer Olympics	11.00
317	Antarctic Explorers	9.00
318	Carousel Animals	9.00
319	Christmas, Madonna	11.00
320	Christmas, Village Scene	11.00

1989

321	Montana Statehood	10.00
322	A. Philip Randolph	12.50
323	North Dakota Statehood	10.00
324	Washington Statehood	10.00
325	Steamboats Booklet	10.00
326	World Stamp Expo '89	10.00
327	Arturo Toscanini	10.00
328	U.S. House of Representatives	10.00
329	U.S. Senate	10.00
330	Executive Branch	10.00
331	South Dakota Statehood	10.00
332	Lou Gehrig	12.50
333	French Revolution	10.00
334	Ernest Hemingway	9.00
335	North Carolina Statehood	9.00
336	Letter Carriers	9.00
337	Drafting of the Bill of Rights	9.00
338	Prehistoric Animals	10.00
339	25¢ and 45¢ America/PUAS	10.00
340	Christmas, Traditional and Contemporary	12.50
341	Classic Mail Transportation	10.00
342	Future Mail Transportation	10.00

1990

| 343 | Idaho Statehood | 10.00 |

344	Love	10.00
345	Ida B. Wells	11.00
346	U.S. Supreme Court	10.00
347	Wyoming Statehood	10.00
348	Classic Films	10.00
349	Marianne Moore	10.00
350	Lighthouses Booklet	12.50
351	Rhode Island Statehood	10.00
352	Olympians	12.50
353	Indian Headdresses Booklet	12.50
354	Micronesia/ Marshall Islands	12.50
355	Creatures of the Sea	15.00
356	25¢ and 45¢ America/PUAS	12.50
357	Dwight D. Eisenhower	10.00
358	Christmas, Traditional and Contemporary	12.50

1991

359	Switzerland	12.50
360	Vermont Statehood	12.50
361	Savings Bonds	10.00
362	29¢ and 52¢ Love	12.50
363	Saroyan	12.50
364	Fishing Flies Booklet	15.00
365	Cole Porter	12.50
366	Antartic Treaty	12.50
367	Desert Shield/ Desert Storm	20.00
368	Summer Olympics	12.50
369	Numismatics	12.50
370	Basketball	12.50
371	World War II Miniature Sheet	12.50
372	Comedians Booklet	10.00
373	District of Columbia	12.50
374	Jan Matzeliger	10.00
375	Space Exploration Booklet	15.00
376	America/PUASP	12.50
377	Christmas, Traditional and Contemporary	12.50

1992

378	Winter Olympics	12.50
379	World Columbian Stamp Expo '92	12.50
380	W.E.B. Du Bois	12.50
381	Love	12.50
382	Olympic Baseball	15.00
383	First Voyage of Christopher Columbus	20.00

384	Space Adventures	15.00
385	New York Stock Exchange	12.50
386	Alaska Highway	12.50
387	Kentucky Statehood	12.50
388	Summer Olympics	12.50
389	Hummingbirds Booklet	15.00
390	World War II Miniature Sheet	12.50
391	Dorothy Parker	12.50
392	Theodore von Karman	12.50
393	Minerals	12.50
394	Juan Rodriguez Cabrillo	12.50
395	Wild Animals Booklet	15.00
396	Christmas, Traditional and Contemporary	12.50
397	Columbian Souvenir Sheets	25.00
398	Columbian Souvenir Sheets	25.00
399	Columbian Souvenir Sheets	25.00
400	Wildflowers #1	15.00
401	Wildflowers #2	15.00
402	Wildflowers #3	15.00
403	Wildflowers #4	15.00
404	Wildflowers #5	15.00
405	Happy New Year	12.50

1993

406	Elvis	30.00
407	Space Fantasy	17.50
408	Percy Julian	15.00
409	Oregon Trail	15.00
410	World Univ. Games	15.00
411	Grace Kelly	15.00
412	Oklahoma	15.00
413	Circus	15.00
414	Cherokee Strip	15.00
415	Dean Acheson	15.00
416	Sport Horses	15.00
417	Garden Flowers	15.00
418	World War II	15.00
419	Hank Williams	15.00
420	Rock/Roll/R&B	17.50
421	Joe Louis	15.00
422	Broadway Musicals	15.00
423	National Postal Museum	15.00
424	Deaf Communication	15.00
425	Country Western	17.50
426	Youth Classics	15.00
427	Christmas	17.50
428	Mariana Islands	15.00

429	Columbus Landing In Puerto Rico	15.00
430	AIDS Awareness	17.50

1994

431	Winter Olympics	20.00
432	Edward R. Murrow	17.50
433	Love	20.00
434	Dr. Allison Davis	17.50
435	Chinese New Year	17.50
436	Buffalo Soldiers	20.00
437	Silent Screen Stars	25.00
438	Garden Flowers	20.00
439	World Cup Soccer	25.00
440	World War II	20.00
441	Norman Rockwell	—
442	Moon Landing	—
443	Locomotives	—
444	George Meany	—
445	Popular Singers	—
446	James Thurber	—
447	Jazz/Blues	—
448	Wonders of the Sea	—
449	Birds (Cranes)	—
450	Christmas	—
451	Special	—
452	Happy New Year	—

1995

453	Florida	—
454	Bessie Coleman	—
455	Kids Care!	—
456	Richard Nixon	—
457	Love	—
458	Recreational Sports	—
459	POW & MIA	—
460	Marilyn Monroe	—
461	Texas Statehood	—
462	Great Lakes Lighthouses	—
463	United Nations	—
464	Carousel Horses	—
465	Jazz Musicians	—
466	Women's Suffage	—
467	Louis Armstrong	—
468	World War II, 1945	—
469	Fall Garden Flowers	—
470	Republic of Palau	—
471	Holiday Contemporary	—
472	Naval Academy	—
473	Tennessee Williams	—
474	Holiday Traditional	—
475	James K. Polk	—
476	Antique Automobiles	—

*1995 issues subject to change.

Subject Index

The numbers listed next to the stamp description are the Scott numbers, and the numbers in parentheses are the numbers of the pages on which the stamps are listed.

D

Postmasters General of the United States

Appointed by the Continental Congress

1775   Benjamin Franklin, PA
1776   Richard Bache, PA
1782   Ebenezer Hazard, NY

Appointed by the President with the advice and consent of the Senate

1789   Samuel Osgood, MA
1791   Timothy Pickering, PA
1795   Joseph Habersham, GA
1801   Gideon Granger, CT
1814   Return J. Meigs, Jr., OH
1823   John McLean, OH
1829   William T. Barry, KY
1835   Amos Kendall, KY
1840   John M. Niles, CT
1841   Francis Granger, NY
1841   Charles A. Wickliffe, KY
1845   Cave Johnson, TN
1849   Jacob Collamer, VT
1850   Nathan K. Hall, NY
1852   Samuel D. Hubbard, CT
1853   James Campbell, PA
1857   Aaron V. Brown, TN
1859   Joseph Holt, KY
1861   Horatio King, ME
1861   Montgomery Blair, DC
1864   William Dennison, OH
1866   Alexander W. Randall, WI
1869   John A.J. Creswell, MD
1874   James W. Marshall, NJ
1874   Marshall Jewell, CT
1876   James N. Tyner, IN
1877   David McK. Key, TN
1880   Horace Maynard, TN
1881   Thomas L. James, NY
1882   Timothy O. Howe, WI
1883   Walter Q. Gresham, IN
1884   Frank Hatton, IA

1885   William F. Vilas, WI
1888   Don M. Dickinson, MI
1889   John Wanamaker, PA
1893   Wilson S. Bissell, NY
1895   William L. Wilson, WV
1897   James A. Gary, MD
1898   Charles Emory Smith, PA
1902   Henry C. Payne, WI
1904   Robert J. Wynne, PA
1905   George B. Cortelyou, NY
1907   George von L. Meyer, MA
1909   Frank H. Hitchcock, MA
1913   Albert S. Burleson, TX
1921   Will H. Hays, IN
1922   Hubert Work, CO
1923   Harry S. New, IN
1929   Walter F. Brown, OH
1933   James A. Farley, NY
1940   Frank C. Walker, PA
1945   Robert E. Hannegan, MO
1947   Jesse M. Donaldson, IL
1953   Arthur E. Summerfield, MI
1961   J. Edward Day, CA
1963   John A. Gronouski, WI
1965   Lawrence F. O'Brien, MA
1968   W. Marvin Watson, TX
1969   Winton M. Blount, AL

Selected by the Presidentially appointed U.S. Postal Service Board of Governors

1971   Elmer T. Klassen, MA
1975   Benjamin Franklin Bailar, MD
1978   William F. Bolger, CT
1985   Paul N. Carlin, WY
1986   Albert V. Casey, MA
1986   Preston R. Tisch, NY
1988   Anthony M. Frank, CA
1992   Marvin Runyon, TN

Credits and Acknowledgments:

This stamp collecting catalog was produced by Stamp Services, United States Postal Service.

U.S. Postal Service:

Marvin Runyon
  Postmaster General and Chief Executive Officer

Loren E. Smith
  Chief Marketing Officer and Senior Vice President

Azeezaly S. Jaffer
  Manager, Stamp Services

Joseph P. Brockert
  Editor-in-Chief

Peggy Tartal
  Contract Administration

W. Lee Roberts
  Printing Procurement

Printing:

R.R. Donnelley & Sons Company
Crawfordsville Divisions
Crawfordsville, IN 47933
Crawfordsville Book Services Division

Department CSA1	Account Administration
Department CMP	Preliminary
Department CTM	Pressroom
Department CSW	Shipping

Binding:

Stream International Inc.
Crawfordsville, IN 47933
Crawfordsville Division

Department CHT	Gather/Binding

Editorial and Design:

Mobium
Suite 2000
The Merchandise Mart
200 World Trade Center
Chicago, IL 60654-1003

Database Publishing Group	Project Management
	Editorial Services
	Layout and Production Services
Design and Marketing Communications Group	Design Services

Selected stamps for illustrations and advice on content were provided by:

Richard E. Drews
Stamp King
7139 W. Higgins Rd.
Chicago, IL 60656
(312) 775-2100

Photography:

Howard Ash Photography
Morrison Photography

Cover photo courtesy of Archive Photos/Frank Driggs

Page 14 photo courtesy of The Kobal Collection